INTERNATIONAL TRADE POLICY AND THE PACIFIC RIM

This is IEA conference volume no. 120

International Trade Policy and the Pacific Rim

Proceedings of the IEA Conference held in Sydney, Australia

Edited by

John Piggott
School of Economics
University of New South Wales
Sydney, Australia

and

Alan Woodland
Department of Econometrics
University of Sydney
Sydney, Australia

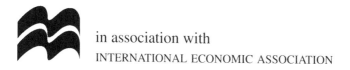

in association with
INTERNATIONAL ECONOMIC ASSOCIATION

First published in Great Britain 1999 by
MACMILLAN PRESS LTD
Houndmills, Basingstoke, Hampshire RG21 6XS and London
Companies and representatives throughout the world

A catalogue record for this book is available from the British Library.

This book is published in the *International Economic Association* series
General Editor: Michael Kaser
Series Standing Order ISBN 0–333–71242–0 (*outside North America only*)

ISBN 0–333–69810–X

First published in the United States of America 1999 by
ST. MARTIN'S PRESS, INC.,
Scholarly and Reference Division,
175 Fifth Avenue, New York, N.Y. 10010

ISBN 0–312–21801–X

Library of Congress Cataloging-in-Publication Data
International trade policy and the Pacific Rim : proceedings of the
IEA conference held in Sydney / edited by John Piggott and Alan
Woodland.
p.   cm.
Includes bibliographical references and index.
ISBN 0–312–21801–X (cloth)
1. Commercial policy—Congresses.   2. International trade–
–Congresses.   3. Pacific Area—Commercial policy—Congresses.
4. Free trade—Pacific Area—Congresses.   5. Asia Pacific Economic
Cooperation (Organization)—Congresses.   I. Piggott, John (John R.)
II. Woodland, A. D.   III. International Economic Association.
HF1410.5.I587   1998
382'.091823—dc21   98–25637
                                                          CIP

This book is printed on paper suitable for recycling and made from fully managed and sustained forest sources.

10   9   8   7   6   5   4   3   2   1
08   07   06   05   04   03   02   01   00   99

Printed and bound in Great Britain by Antony Rowe Ltd, Chippenham, Wiltshire

Contents

PART II TRADE POLICY AND THE 'ISMS'

PART III APEC

The International Economic Association

A non-profit organization with purely scientific aims, the International Economic Association (IEA) was founded in 1950. It is a federation of some sixty national economic associations in all parts of the world. Its basic purpose is the development of economics as an intellectual discipline, recognising a diversity of problems, systems and values in the world, and taking note of methodological diversities.

The IEA has since its creation sought to fulfil that purpose by promoting mutual understanding among economists through the organization of scientific meetings and common research programmes, and by means of publications on problems of fundamental as well as of current importance. Deriving from its long-term concern to assure professional contacts between East and West, and North and South, the IEA pays special attention to issues of economies in systemic transition and in the course of development. During its nearly fifty years of existence, it has organized some hundred round-table conferences for specialists on topics ranging from fundamental theories to methods and tools of analysis and major problems of the present-day world. Participation in round tables is at the invitation of a specialist programme committee, but eleven triennial World Congresses have regularly attracted the participation of individual economists from all over the world.

The Association is governed by a Council, composed of representatives of all member associations, and by a fifteen-member Executive Committee, which is elected by the Council. The Executive Committee (1995–98) at the time of the Sydney Conference was:

President: Professor Jacques Drèze, Belgium
Vice-President: Professor Anne Krueger, USA
Treasurer: Professor Erich Streissler, Austria
Past President: Professor Michael Bruno, Israel (deceased 26 December 1996)

Other Members: Professor Anthony B. Atkinson, UK
                       Professor Vittorio Corbo, Chile
                       Professor Karel Dyba, Czech Republic
                       Professor Jean-Michel Grandmont, France
                       Professor Yujiro Hayami, Japan
                       Professor Seppo Honkapohja, Finland

Professor Valery Makarov, Russia
Professor Luigi Pasinetti, Italy
Professor Hans Werner Sinn, Germany
Professor Rehman Sobhan, Bangladesh
Professor Alan D. Woodland, Australia

Advisers: Professor Kenneth J. Arrow, USA
Academician Oleg T. Bogomolov, Russia
Professor Mustapha Nabli, Tunisia
Professor Amartya Sen, India
Professor Stefano Zamagni, Italy

Secretary-General: Professor Jean-Paul Fitoussi, France

General Editor: Professor Michael Kaser, UK

Sir Austin Robinson was an active Adviser on the publication of IEA conference proceedings from 1954 until his final short illness in 1993.

The Association has also been fortunate in having secured many outstanding economists to serve as President: Gottfried Haberler (1950–3), Howard S. Ellis (1953–6), Erik Lindahl (1956–9), E. A. G. Robinson (1959–62), Ugo Papi (1962–5), Paul A. Samuelson (1965–8), Erik Lundberg (1968–71), Fritz Machlup (1971–4), Edmund Malinvaud (1974–7), Shigeto Tsuru (1977–80), Victor L. Urquidi (1980–3), Kenneth J. Arrow (1983–6), Amartya Sen (1986–9), Anthony B. Atkinson (1989–92) and Michael Bruno (1992–5).

The activities of the Association are mainly funded from the subscriptions of members and grants from a number of organizations, including continuing support from UNESCO, through the International Social Science Council.

Acknowledgements

We would like to thank the many people and organizations involved in the development and execution of the conference, and in the preparation of the proceedings. Without their generous support, the conference, which forms the basis for this book, would not have taken place.

The conference programme was developed by a committee comprising:

Professor Elhanan Helpman, Tel Aviv University, Israel
Professor Motoshige Itoh, University of Tokyo, Japan
Professor John McMillan, University of California at San Diego, USA
Professor John Piggott, University of New South Wales, Australia (Co-Chair)
Professor John Whalley, University of Western Ontario, Canada
Professor Alan Winters, World Bank, USA
Professor Alan Woodland, University of Sydney, Australia (Co-Chair)

Financial support was generously provided by various Australian institutions. We are especially grateful to the following sponsors:

Centre for Economic Policy Analysis, Research School of Social Sciences, Australian National University
Centre for International Economic Studies, University of Adelaide
Department of Foreign Affairs and Trade, Australian government
Economic Society of Australia
Faculty of Commerce and Economics, University of New South Wales
Faculty of Economics, University of Sydney
Reserve Bank of Australia
State and Regional Development, NSW government

Special thanks go to the Reserve Bank of Australia for providing the venue for the conference as well as sponsorship. The Coombs Conference Centre, with its spectacular harbour views, provided a very congenial setting for a productive meeting. Qantas and the National Australia Bank also gave valuable support.

Logistic support for the local organization of the conference was provided by the Department of Econometrics at the University of Sydney, assisted by the School of Economics, University of New South Wales. The organizers are especially appreciative of the enthusiastic and efficient support provided by the Conference Secretariat: Sheilah Whyte provided support over the two years leading up to (and beyond) the conference, ably assisted by Nicole Woodland during the conference itself.

Finally, we wish to thank all the participants at the conference for generating a lively and productive discussion of trade policy issues in the Pacific Rim region. The authors and discussants, in particular, provided the basis for the conference, and the quality of their contributions, as well as their patience in meeting various editorial deadlines, has been much appreciated. Nita Watts, the conference volume editor, participated and gave excellent editorial support to authors, discussants and the editors in preparing the proceedings for publication.

List of Contributors

Professor **James E.** Anderson, Department of Economics, Boston College, Chestnut Hill, MA0216

Professor **Kym Anderson**, Centre for International Economic Studies, School of Economics, University of Adelaide, Australia

Professor **Mohamed Ariff**, Department of Economics and Administration, University of Malaya, Kuala Lumpur, Malaysia

Professor **Kyle Bagwell**, Columbia University and National Bureau of Economic Research

Dr **Sumana Dhar**, The World Bank, Washington DC, USA

Professor **Wilfred J.** Ethier, Department of Economics, University of Pennsylvania, Philadelphia, USA

Professor **Rod Falvey**, Department of Economics, University of Nottingham, UK

Professor **Junichi Goto**, Research Institute for Economics and Business, Kobe University, Japan

Professor **David Greenaway**, Department of Economics, University of Nottingham, UK

Professor **Wen Hai**, China Centre for Economic Research, Beijing University, China

Professor **Richard G. Harris**, Department of Economics, Simon Fraser University, Burnaby, BC, Canada

Professor **Elhanan Helpman**, The Eitan Berglas School of Economics, Tel Aviv University, Israel

Professor **Motoshige Itoh**, Department of Economics, University of Tokyo, Japan

Professor **Ryutaro Komiya**, Aoyama Gakuin University and Research Institute of International Trade and Industry, Tokyo, Japan

Professor **Peter J.** Lloyd, Asian Business Centre, Faculty of Economics and Commerce, University of Melbourne, Australia

Professor **Wolfgang Mayer**, Department of Economics, University of Cincinnati, Ohio, USA

Professor **Barry Naughton**, Graduate School of International Relations and Pacific Studies, University of California, San Diego, USA

Professor **Arvind Panagariya**, Department of Economics, University of Maryland, USA

Dr **Mari Pangestu**, Centre for Strategic and International Studies, Jakarta, Indonesia

Professor **John Piggott**, School of Economics, University of New South Wales, Sydney, Australia

Professor **Martin Richardson**, Department of Economics, University of Otago, Dunedin, New Zealand

Professor **Nicolas Schmitt**, Department of Economics, Simon Fraser University, Burnaby, BC, Canada

Professor **Robert W.** Staiger, University of Wisconsin-Madison, USA, and National Bureau of Economic Research

Dr **Eu Chye Tan**, Department of Economics and Administration, University of Malaya, Kuala Lumpur, Malaysia

Professor **M.** Scott **Taylor**, Department of Economics, University of British Columbia, Vancouver, Canada

Professor **Arja Turunen-Red**, Department of Economics and Finance, University of New Orleans, USA

Dr **Pham Hoang Van**, Department of Economics, Cornell University, Ithaca, USA

Dr **Neil Vousden**, National Centre for Development Studies, Australian National University, Canberra, Australia

Professor **Henry Y. Wan, Jnr**, Department of Economics, Cornell University, Ithaca, USA

Professor **Peter G. Warr**, Research School of Pacific Studies, Australian National University, Canberra, Australia

Professor **L. Alan Winters**, International Economics Department, The World Bank, Washington DC, USA

Professor **Alan Woodland**, Department of Econometrics, University of Sydney, Australia

Mr **Gordon de Brouwer**, Reserve Bank of Australia, Australia

Ms **Michelle Bullock**, Reserve Bank of Australia, Australia

Mr **Michael Carmen**, New South Wales Department of State and Regional Development, Australia

Dr **Bob Conlon**, University of New South Wales, Australia

Mr **Matthew Cumberworth**, University of Sydney, Australia

Professor **Peter Drysdale**, Australian National University, Australia

Ms **Diane Enaharo**, University of New South Wales, Australia

Dr **Chris Findlay**, University of Adelaide, Australia

Dr **Joshua Gans**, University of New South Wales, Australia

Mr **Peter Hartcher**, Australian Financial Review, Australia

Mr **Bob Johnson**, New South Wales Department of State and Regional Development, Australia

Ms **Sally Jones**, Department of Foreign Affairs and Trade, Australia

Professor **Murray Kemp**, University of New South Wales, Australia

Ms **Micheline Lane**, New South Wales, Department of State and Regional Development, Austrilia

Professor **Ross Milbourne**, University of New South Wales, Australia

Ms **Frances Perkins**, Department of Foreign Affairs and Trade, Australia

Dr **Pascalis Raimondos-Moller**, Economic Policy Reserch Unit, Copenhagen Business School, and University of Sydney, Australia

Mr **Geoff Raby**, Department of Foreign Affairs and Trade, Australia

Mr **Mark Rider**, Reserve Bank of Australia, Australia

Professor **Bill Schworm**, University of Sydney, Australia

Dr **Jeff Sheen**, University of Sydney, Australia

Professor **Koji Shimomura**, Kobe University, Japan

Professor **Richard Snape**, Monash University, Australia

Dr **Truong Truong**, University of New South Wales, Australia

Dr **Rod Tyers**, Australian National University, Australia

Dr **Peter Urban**, Department of Foreign Affairs and Trade, Australia

Dr **Don Wright**, University of Sydney, Australia

Dr **Steffen Ziss**, University of Sydney, Australia

Professor **James E. Anderson**, Department of Economics, Boston College, Chestnut Hill, MA0216 USA

List of Abbreviations and Acronyms

AFTA	ASEAN Free Trade Area (followed and absorbed APTA)
APEC	Asia-Pacific Economic Co-operation forum
APTA	ASEAN Preferential Trading Arrangements (see AFTA)
ASEAN	Association of South-East Asian Nations
CAP	Collective Action Plan (in China)
CER/ANZCER	Australia New Zealand Closer Economic Relations Agreement
CES	Constant elasticity of substitution
CGE	Computable general equilibrium
CRS	Constant returns to scale
CUSTA	Canada/USA Trade Agreement
CVD	Countervailing duty
DME	Developed market economy
EA	European Agreements (with EU)
EAEC	East Asian Economic Caucus
EAEG	East Asian Economic Group (later EAEC)
EC	European Community
EEC	European Economic Community
EFTA	European Free Trade Area
EMU	European Monetary Union
EPFTZ	Export-processing free trade zone
EPG	Eminent Persons Group (of APEC)
ETC	Economic and technical co-operation
EU	European Union
FDI	Foreign direct investment
FIE	Foreign-invested enterprise/firm
FTA	Free trade area
FTC	Foreign trade corporation/company
FTZ	Free trade zone
GATS	General Agreement on Trade in Services
GATT	General Agreement on Tariffs and Trade
GDP	Gross domestic product
GNP	Gross national product
GSP	Generalized System of Preferences
IAP	Individual action plan (in China)
IGA	Investment guarantee agreement

IMF	International Monetary Fund
ITA	Investment tax allowance
JV	Joint venture
LDC	Less developed country
LLDC	Least developed country
MCF	Marginal cost of funds
Mercosur	Acronym of Spanish title of Customs Union of Argentina, Brazil, Paraguay and Uruguay, with Chile and Bolivia 'associated'
MFA	Multi-fibre agreement
MFN	Most favoured nation
MIDA	Malaysian Industrial Development Authority
MNC/E	Multi national corporation/enterprise
MOFTEC	Ministry of Foreign Trade and Economic Co-operation (in Japan)
MP	Marginal product
MTN	Multilateral trade negotiations
NAFTA	North American Free Trade Association/Area
NIE	Newly industrialized economy
NTB	Non-tariff barrier
OAA	Osaka Action Agenda
OECD	Organization for Economic Co-operation and Development
PBEC	Pacific Basin Economic Council
PECC	Pacific Economic Co-operation Council
PPF	Production possibility frontier
PRC	People's Republic of China
PTA	Preferential trading area/arrangement
QR	Quantitative restrictions
R&D	Research and development
RMB	Ren Min Bi (Chinese national currency or yuan)
RTA	Regional trading area/arrangement
SAARC	South Asian Agreement on Regional Co-operation
SAPTA	South Asian Preferential Trading Arrangement
SEZ	Special Economic Zone
SOE	State-owned enterprise
TAFTA	Transatlantic Free Trade Area
TILF	Trade and investment liberalization and facilitation
TPRM	Trade Policy Review Mechanism
TRI	Trade restrictiveness index
TRIM	Trade-related investment measure
TRIP	Trade-related intellectual property
TVE	Township and village enterprise (in China)
UR	Uruguay round (of trade negotiations under GATT)
WTO	World Trade Organization
VER	Voluntary export restraint

Introduction

John Piggott
UNIVERSITY OF NEW SOUTH WALES

and

Alan Woodland
UNIVERSITY OF SYDNEY

1 INTRODUCTION

This conference had its genesis in the desire of the International Economic Association (IEA) to mount a round-table conference in Australia. In 1992, the President of the IEA, Professor Tony Atkinson, met with the President of the Economic Society of Australia, John McLeod, encouraging the society to become involved in the project. Four years on, the idea became reality, and this volume is the result.

It was natural, given the global orientation of the IEA and the Asian region's dynamic economic performance in the period since the Second World War, that the conference should be about Asia's economic perform-ance and international trade, the channel through which the region's chang-ing economic characteristics are transmitted to the rest of the world. The international trade policy focus was given additional impetus because of the implications of the recently concluded Uruguay Round of negotiations under the General Agreement on Tariffs and Trade (GATT), the establishment of the World Trade Organization (WTO) and the developing debate about regional trade arrangements.

The facts about the post-war Asian economic experience, while not agreed upon in every detail, are easy enough to recount in broad terms. The World Bank (1993) analyses the high performers of East Asia, and has made a classic of the already popular reference to the performance of the economies in this region as a 'miracle'. The eight economies the bank singles out for special attention include, first of all, Japan; then the four 'tigers' (Hong Kong, the Republic of Korea, Singapore, and Taiwan); and the three newly industrialis-ing economies (or countries) the NIEs or NICs – Indonesia, Malaysia and Thailand. All these countries are grouped together under yet another category – the high performing Asian economies (or HPAEs). According to the Bank:

> Between 1960 and 1985, real income per capita increased more than four times in Japan and the Four Tigers and more than doubled in the South

East Asian NIEs...If growth were randomly distributed, there is roughly one chance in ten thousand that success would have been so regionally concentrated.   (World Bank 1993, p. 2)

The bank also identifies a number of characteristics that set the eight HPAEs apart from other economies (see, for example, World Bank, 1993, p. 27). Among these are 'getting the policy basics right' – in the present context, moderate and controlled import substitution policies should be emphasized – and rapid export growth. The report goes on to assert that one obvious effect of rapid export growth has been a marked increase in the openness of these economies.

Along with this dynamic performance within Asia, there have been major regional trade agreements implemented or developed over recent years. These include, in particular, the North American Free Trade agreement, between the USA, Canada and Mexico, and the evolution of the Asia Pacific Economic Policy (APEC) Forum. These regional agreements have the potential to change the direction of trade policy formation in the Pacific region, representing as they do a departure from the multilateral approach to trade policy embodied in the GATT-sponsored rounds of negotiations.

It was our impression that two specialist groups of trade economists were required to analyze the phenomena outlined above. On the one hand, trade policy specialists saw an obvious connection between economic growth and increased welfare, and trade liberalization. On the other, more rigorous theoretical analysts had opened up anew the question whether freer trade would increase welfare, but had not focused their attention on the linkages between trade and growth. The two groups had also entered the ongoing debate over the relative merits of regional and multilateral trade liberalization.

As a result, we resolved early on to try to bring theorists and more policy-orientated analysts together to discuss what had now, in our minds, become the title of the volume: 'International Trade Policy and the Pacific Rim'. This implied two further requirements: some factual background would have to be introduced into the conference programme; and, if the conference were to be analytically cohesive, theoretical advances would have to be identified which stood a good chance of illuminating their interpretation. Also, in an academic and policy environment very much alive to policy innovation in the wake of the Uruguay Round, it would be important to differentiate the product.

2 CONFERENCE THEMES

This led to the identification of the three conference 'themes': trade and welfare; the application of game theory to the analysis of trade agreements;

and the application of endogenous growth theory to explain trade-growth linkages. In all these areas, theorists had been, and of course continue to be, active. However, we felt that these were areas of particular relevance to the Pacific Rim region and therefore of particular interest to this conference.

At the heart of international trade theory is the relationship between the trade policies of nations and the welfare of their citizens. The demonstration of the gains from free trade for small and large economies has been the intellectual basis for both unilateral and multilateral policies aimed at reducing tariff, quota and other distortions to trade, the latter being institutionalized in the GATT, and now WTO. There have been exceptions to this general rule, of course, exceptions that are based typically upon such things as immovable domestic distortions, externalities, and monopolistic power in world markets (leading to optimal tariffs). The traditional links between trade liberalization and economic welfare have also been challenged by Brander (1981), and Brander and Krugman (1983), who introduce imperfectly competitive behaviour, thus leading to the strategic trade policy literature. The importance of the traditional unilateral and multilateral policy–welfare connection to countries in the Pacific Rim region confirmed this as an essential theme for the conference.

An important off-shoot from the policy welfare literature concerns the static analysis of regional trade arrangements, beginning with Viner (1950) and developed by, among others, Lipsey (1960) and Kemp and Wan (1976), and which continues with, for example, the recent review by Bliss (1994). However, in recent years there has been an increasing acceptance of the view that regional trade agreements are best viewed as outcomes of repeated games. This dynamic time-path analysis, and the questions it raises about whether regional trade agreements act as 'stumbling blocks' or 'building blocks' toward global trade liberalization, was first introduced by Bhagwati (1991). These ideas are extended by Bhagwati and Panagariya (1996), who identify alternative approaches to the latter question.

It is notable, however, that, in spite of the pervasiveness of regional trading arrangements, particularly in Asia (for example, the only APEC member not a signatory to a WTO-recognized agreement is Japan), and the obvious importance of the question for further progress towards free trade, relatively few theoretical papers have attempted to provide a rigorous framework for analysis. Accordingly, the game-theoretic approach to regional agreements seemed a topic of particular interest and importance.

'Endogenous growth' is a term used to cover a number of developments in the literature of the 1980s, which once again drew attention to issues of increasing returns to scale, complementarity and externality in the allocation of resources, and the implications of these phenomena for economic growth. The rapid economic growth experienced by many countries in the Asian region suggests that here may be a fertile testing ground for many of the ideas of endogenous growth theory. Again, however, only a few economists are working on the problem of explicitly linking endogenous growth with trade liberalization. A notable exception is Romer (1994), who used a numerical example to show how the welfare costs of protection could be much greater than the estimates produced with more conventional models when some of the ideas associated with endogenous growth (especially the process of new product innovation) are incorporated. Again, given the importance of these recent developments in growth theory and the focus of attention on the high growth rates in the region, it seemed natural to have the third theme deal with the connections between trade policy, growth and technology transfer.

The conference was organized with the above observations in mind. In what follows, we offer a brief overview of the conference papers.

3 THE PAPERS

Trade and Policy Experience

As indicated above, the Asia-Pacific region has seen some remarkable economic performances over the last two decades and has become a region of intense interest on the part of international businesses and international trade economists. The high growth rates among the 'Asian tigers', the increased openness of many of the region's economies in terms of their trade policies and in terms of the increasing volume of intra- and inter-regional trade, the emergence of China as a more open economy with enormous growth potential, and the evolution of a variety of regional trade arrangements have contributed to this increased interest in the Asia-Pacific region.

To understand properly the possible future paths of growth and trade in the region, and the better to come to grips with the trade policy choices and dynamics that are likely to emerge, it is necessary to examine what the current trade policy situation is and how it came to be where it is. Accordingly, the conference devoted considerable space to an analysis of the recent trade and trade policy experience of the Asia-Pacific region.

The survey paper by David Greenaway was commissioned to provide an overview of the trade policy issues in the region, and hence to provide a foundation for the subsequent papers on more specific topics. As Greenaway observes, it is not possible to provide a comprehensive account of trade and trade policy in so vast and diverse a region as the Asia-Pacific, which covers all the countries bordering the Pacific Ocean, from New Zealand to Malaysia to Japan, to the NAFTA countries, and to Chile.

Greenaway quotes this diversity as a reason for his scepticism about the viability of APEC as a regional free trade area, despite the evidence of the region experiencing the fastest growth of trade in the world and the region being as advanced in its intra-regional trade as the European Community. The questions he raises: whether the Asia-Pacific region is in any sense a 'natural' trading bloc, and why there should be such interest in regional agreements, recurred at various times during the conference. Certainly, the juxtaposition of regional agreements such as the Closer Economic Relations Agreement (CER) between Australia and New Zealand, the Association of South East Asian Nations (ASEAN), the North American Free Trade Area (NAFTA), and now the emergence of APEC alongside unilateral trade policy reforms and a general adherence to the ideals of multilateralism, via the mechanisms of the WTO, provide for interesting speculation about the policy stance of countries of the region.

Greenaway also reviews the Uruguay Round outcomes and argues that there are still many unresolved or 'live' issues to do with the implementation of the decisions taken. He suggests that this process may generate conflicts, and discusses the potential role of regional agreements such as APEC in reconciling them.

Time constraints precluded specific reviews of a large number of countries. Instead, three countries with diverse experiences were chosen for this purpose. Perhaps the most obvious choice was China, a previously closed economy now emerging as a potentially dominant player in the trading region. The second was in fact a pair of countries, Australia and New Zealand, forming what is virtually a 'deep' free trade area implemented through the CER. These countries on the edge of Asia have similar trade policy histories and have become much more open to world trade in the last decade, with their trade being redirected away from Europe and North America and towards Asia. The third country chosen for special study was Malaysia, one of the Asian NIEs. In addition to these three country studies, an empirical study of trade involving a large number of countries was undertaken by Sumana Dhar and Arvind Panagariya to determine the openness of East Asian economies as a group.

In his paper, Barry Naughton considers China's existing trade regimes and future prospects for change. He identifies two separate regimes of trade policy. The first he calls the 'export promotion regime' under which foreign invested enterprises (FIEs) undertake trade with very little in the way of administrative red tape or tariff protection. This accounts for about half the exports and two-thirds of imports. The second, the 'import substitution regime', allows various foreign trade companies to trade under fairly stringent administrative rules and very high tariffs and non-tariff barriers. As argued by Wen Hai, this dual system is a consequence of the Chinese government's desire to have gradual liberalization of trade with tight control and concern for the possible social and welfare consequences of liberalization.

Naughton highlights the challenges facing China as it emerges as a freer trading nation. Perhaps the most important is China's accession to the WTO.

The present dual trading regime contains many features that violate WTO rules, and so China's admission requires important policy changes. Another issue emphasised by Naughton is exchange-rate management. This is likely to become more difficult as the economy opens up and foreign investment flows become even larger. Additionally, a challenge for trade policy-makers in China will be the reduction in what are generally very high tariffs and the replacement of non-tariff barriers by tariff measures.

Peter Lloyd reviews the trade policies of Australia and New Zealand and, in doing so, examines their CER agreement and their role as members of GATT and APEC. These countries are interesting in that, though there are important differences between them, they each had very protective trade policies until the late 1970s, with trade patterns very much focused on Europe, and each subsequently embarked upon a trade liberalization programme. Hence, while protection is still quite high in some sectors, current trade policies are far more open than those of 30 years ago.

Lloyd also reviews the CER agreement between Australia and New Zealand, established in 1983 to replace an earlier agreement, and argues that the integration of the two economies is rivaled only by that obtained by the European Union (EU). And this has been achieved without a secretariat! Also discussed by Peter Lloyd are the mixed roles of both countries in multilateral trade policy initiatives under GATT, such as the formation of the 'Cairns Group' of countries that helped to force the Uruguay Round to deal seriously with agricultural trade policy issues, and the leading role Australia has taken in conceiving and implementing APEC.

Eu Chye Tan and Mohammed Ariff consider the trade and trade policy experience of Malaysia. They focus attention upon the relationship between economic growth and the volume of trade, a relationship suggested by the idea that exports are an 'engine of growth'. Their chapter reviews the post-colonial policies employed by the Malaysian government. While the early import substitution policies of the pre-1970s were judged to be inadequate to meet the needs of industrial development and more liberal trade policies have since been employed, free trade has not been embraced. Thus, while tariff protection has been reduced, trade policy has important foundations in Malaysia's investment promotion policies, focusing on foreign direct investment and on its export-promotion policies. The latter were initiated in the 1970s with the formation of export-processing free trade zones (EPFTZs), and with the formation in 1988 of the Malaysian Industrial Development Authority. Incentives to promote industrialization and exports are therefore very much industry-based.

Within this policy context, Tan and Ariff undertake a time-series econometric analysis of trade measures and GDP to test whether these variables are cointegrated and whether there is one-way causation between them, as would be suggested by the 'engine of growth' hypothesis. They find no substantial evidence of cointegration or causation, and conclude that these data do not provide evidence in favour of the 'trade engine' theory. However, they suggest that their study is not conclusive, citing data deficiencies as one possible reason for their failure to identify a clear causal link.

The final investigation of policy experience in the region was undertaken by Sumana Dhar and Arvind Panagariya. Using a data set comprising time-series observations for a large number of countries on imports, exports and country characteristics, such as GDP and population, Dhar and Panagariya specify a gravity model of imports and exports to measure empirically the openness of several blocks of countries and, more specifically, to test whether East Asian countries are more, or less, open than those in North America and Europe. The test proceeds by grouping countries into regions and including regional dummy variables in their pooled cross-section and time-series sample, thereby enabling estimation of the role played by membership of a region in determining the value of trade relative to GDP. The primary conclusion reached by the authors is that the empirical results do not support the hypothesis that East Asian markets are relatively closed to outsiders. Indeed, they argue that North America is more closed to trade than the countries of East Asia.

Issues in Trade Policy

One of the most important tasks, arguably *the* most important task, facing international trade theorists is to come to grips with the implications and design of international trade policy. Attention is now being devoted increasingly to these questions. In reviewing this literature, it is useful to distinguish between *policy impact* and *policy choice*. Policy impact deals with the consequences of some exogenously-specified policy, such as the imposition of tariffs, or of their reduction or removal by one or more economies. The policy choice literature treats the design of economic policy as endogenous and also models the dynamics of policy choice by governments. In other words, rather than taking the policy choices of governments as a given, this strand of the literature deals with how policy is formed and how it evolves over time.

Policy choice analysis is particularly relevant to the resurgence of interest in preferential trading arrangements. The EU has undergone much recent change, in terms both of membership and of the extent of integration of the markets of member countries. This is an important phenomenon which attracts researchers interested in policy choice. But the field has been given new prominence through the proliferation of preferential trading arrangements such as NAFTA and, in the Asia-Pacific region, ASEAN and APEC. These have become known as regional trading arrangements, and the collection of such arrangements as *regionalism*.

This policy development has raised many questions. Two of them are, first, why is it that regionalism has become so popular in recent years? Is it because many countries have found that the *multilateralism* embedded in the GATT process of regular and ongoing multilateral trade policy negotiations was not delivering the expected outcomes in terms of trade policy reform and of welfare improvements? Or, because of some other process at work? Second, given the advance of regionalism, will the process of multilateral trade policy reform be helped or hindered?

There are arguments on both sides. On the one hand, the theory of 'the second best' argues, as it did effectively in the early days of the theory of free trade areas and customs unions, that reductions of some tariffs will not necessarily lead to welfare improvements. An extension of this argument is that regional agreements will make it more difficult to obtain multilateral reductions in trade distortions. On the other hand, the Kemp–Wan (1976) theorem on customs unions indicated a way for customs unions to be Pareto-improving and suggested a sequence of union formations that would culminate in world free trade, with Pareto improvements at each stage. Under this scheme, each union would eliminate tariffs on internal trade and set its common external tariff such that the union's trade with the rest of the world was exactly equal to its pre-union trade. Internal income transfers ensure that all union members gain, while the rest of the world is unaffected, and hence should not object to the union's formation. This side of the argument is, then, that regional agreements can be (but, unfortunately, will not necessarily be) consistent with continuing multilateral trade policy reform. These policy questions raise theoretical issues: are there models that can explain the evolution of trade policy as its emphasis has shifted from multilateralism to regionalism?

The question of regionalism versus multilateralism provides the backdrop to the papers by Wilfred Ethier and by Kyle Bagwell and Robert Staiger. In his paper, Ethier argues that the current context is quite different from that of the 1950s and 1960s, which saw the first free trade areas, and that these changed circumstances can be used to explain why regionalism is now so popular. He discusses two different models in which regional arrangements between large developed countries and smaller, less-developed countries occur, and concludes that such arrangements are the result of the success of multilateralism, not of its failure.

In the first model, Ethier assumes that the 'effectiveness' of a partnership in getting benefits from trade reform negotiations is a decreasing function of the proportion of intra-partner trade, and he obtains the result that successful multilateral tariff reductions can generate regionalism. His second model divides the world into less-developed and developed countries, and focuses upon foreign direct investment as the driving force for regional agreements between partners from each category of economy. Less developed economies are protective to the extreme of autarky, while developed countries engage in trade exhibiting Nash equilibrium tariffs with other developed countries. Regional agreements between pairs from each category of economy allow the less developed countries to embark upon trade liberalization. Developed countries can undertake foreign direct investment to provide a cheaper source of materials for final goods production. Ethier argues that this form of regionalism is 'the consequence of multilateral success, not failure, and it in turn strengthens rather than undermines the basis for a commitment to the multilateral order'.

Kyle Bagwell and Robert Staiger tackle the question of how the endogenous tariff policy choices of countries are affected by the creation of a preferential trading arrangement between two countries. They analyze a world comprising three countries trading three goods and setting tariffs on their imports in a Nash equilibrium context. Within this framework, they consider a preferential trade agreement (a free trade area and a customs union, in turn) between any two countries and calculate the impact this has on the equilibrium levels of tariffs and welfare under various assumptions about behaviour. Results are mixed, although the flavour of the paper suggests that regional arrangements may on balance help rather than hinder multilateral trade liberalization.

Bagwell and Staiger specify a highly structured model with linear demand and supply functions, and assume that each nation and regional grouping participates in a Nash tariff game. They find that, in the static game, a preferential trading arrangement (PTA) between two nations leads them to reduce their external tariff on trade with the third – a case of what the authors term *tariff complementarity*. The third nation does not change its tariff but obtains welfare benefits from the lower tariff on its exports. Thus, regional agreements may help rather than hinder multilateral trade policy reform. Bagwell and Staiger recognize that an important issue in trade policy agreements is the incentive compatibility or enforcement of the agreement, and so consider a dynamic game framework that allows a partner to an agreement to depart from the agreement if it so wishes. In this extended context it is found that PTAs may hinder or encourage overall trade policy reform, depending on a number of factors, including the degree of time impatience of the partners and the third country. If the latter is rather impatient, the trade agreement is more likely to hinder the tariff reform process.

While it has long been recognized that political considerations are crucial to the understanding of real-world policy choices of governments, it is only in recent times that the role of politics in policy choice and analysis has been investigated systematically. See, for example, the work by Hillman (1993), and Grossman and Helpman (1994). Wolfgang Mayer's paper follows this political economy approach to trade-policy formulation. It provides an innovative view of policy formation, arguing that policy consists of two separate aspects:

legislative enactment of tariff (or other trade) policies in the form of general rules and schedules, and administrative decisions about how the laws are put into practice and the extent to which they are enforced. Mayer models the former as a long-run decision altered only occasionally, while the administrative decisions are made continuously and are sufficiently discretionary to make a real policy difference. Embedded in a model with a political support function, this distinction is shown to be important for the understanding and analysis of policy. Mayer argues that the model helps to explain how governments use the administrative arm of policy, in the form of non-tariff barriers, to deal with a temporary loss of competitiveness in a politically important industry; how uncertainty about future prices drives the desire for both tariff and non-tariff barriers to trade; and how a permanent change in prices might induce governments to revise their tariff laws.

Policy impact analysis has long been part of the international trade literature. Many of the countries in the Asia-Pacific region may be classed unambiguously as small open economies, in the sense that these economies are sufficiently small relative to the rest of the world that they are unable to alter world prices by any unilateral policies available to them. Accordingly, their trade policy choices are suitably viewed from the backdrop of the literature on the analysis of trade policy for small open economies. Two issues arising here have to do with the budgetary implications of tariff reform, and with the countervailing aspects of export promotion and import protection policies.

For the most part, investigations of the consequences of changes in tariffs and quotas in small open economies have assumed that the government has in place a system of tariffs and quotas on its international trade, and contemplates a change in these, with any change in the government's revenue being passed on to, or obtained from, a representative consumer in a lump sum (non-distorting) fashion. The consequence of the assumed existence of lump sum transfers between the government and the consumer is that the welfare consequences of trade policy reform depend totally upon the efficiency of the reform itself. Various policies have been shown to be welfare-improving under such conditions. Proportional reductions in tariffs yield welfare improvements by reducing the wedge between domestic and world prices, thereby creating efficiency gains. In addition, the so-called 'concertina' policy reform whereby the largest *ad valorem* tariff rate is reduced, or the smallest one raised, is also guaranteed to increase welfare, provided that goods are sufficiently substitutable for each other. These results, and many others, are established under various assumptions. Relaxation of these assumptions may lead to weaker results, but the essential message tends to remain intact.

However, if lump-sum transfers are not feasible, redistribution of the efficiency gains from trade policy reforms needs to rely upon changes in commodity (consumption) taxes or by changes in government production of public goods and services if the budget balance is to be preserved. For small countries contemplating trade policy reform in the form of tariff reductions, the question whether public production is to be cut or the short-fall in revenue is to be raised by domestic commodity taxes becomes an important issue.

In this context, the paper by James Anderson addresses the question whether certain trade policy reforms will be welfare-improving for a small open economy that has a single consumer and a government that does not have the luxury of lump-sum transfers. Anderson considers two different policy scenarios. In the first, the government reduces its tariffs on imports, keeps domestic taxes unchanged, and adjusts the government's production of the public good to preserve the budget balance. Whether the tariff policy results in a welfare gain for the consumer hinges on whether the public good is 'over-supplied' relative to the optimum. In the second scenario, the pro-duction of the public good is unchanged and the tariff reform is accompanied by a proportional change in domestic taxes in order to preserve the budget balance. The welfare implications now depend on complicated substitutability conditions, and thus a policy of proportionally reducing tariffs and replacing them by proportionately higher domestic taxes may or may not be a good thing. Anderson also links the trade reform and tax reform literature, which have gone in somewhat different directions.

Another trade policy issue relates to the famous Lerner symmetry theorem, which establishes that a uniform import duty on all imports is equivalent to a uniform tax on all exports. One implication of this is that the imposition of both sets of taxes would bring the economy back to the free trade equilibrium in a competitive framework. This suggests that a combination of export promotion and import protection policies might approximate a free-trade policy. Many countries employ such a combination of policies.

Richard Harris and Nicolas Schmitt employ two structured models of import protection and export promotion to investigate some of the interrela-tionships that arise when both policies are applied. In the first model they consider an open economy that has a protected import-competing sector controlled by a limit-pricing monopolist. Protection of the import-competing sector causes the monopolist to raise its price and reduce output, thus releasing resources and allowing an *expansion* of the export sector. Moreover, export enhancement policies have no effect upon the equilibrium and there-fore do not neutralize the effects of import protection. Their second model allows the use of discretionary export enhancement policies to maximize an approximation to the true welfare function, leading to enhancement policies that are independent of the tariff on imports. Thus the analysis of these two models shows that export enhancement and import protection policies do not always work in opposite directions, and that their combined use does not necessarily approximate the free-trade equilibrium.

APEC

APEC received much attention throughout the conference, not only in the symposium devoted to it, but also in the overview and summary conference papers. In this volume, we have included a short institutional introduction to APEC, together with the symposium papers.

The APEC forum was seen by many conference participants as an important regional trade liberalization initiative in an era which Ethier describes as embracing the 'new regionalism'. This is especially the case since the USA, under the Clinton Administration, effectively changed the focus of APEC from a consultative mechanism to one promoting trade liberalization within the Pacific region. This led directly to the 'Bogor Declaration', in which APEC members agreed to establish free trade in developed countries by the year 2010, and in developing countries by 2020.

But it was also seen as being distinct from the many regional trade arrangements which have developed between groups of GATT signatories since the establishment of that agreement. The essential difference lay in APEC's approach. As Mari Pangestu's paper emphasizes, members of APEC did not want to make the forum a negotiating body. Instead, the leaders of member countries view it as a means of getting to know one another, and working together towards mutually beneficial trade liberalization, without a formal legal document specifying members' obligations and sanctions. She suggests that this lends a peculiarly 'Asian' flavour to the forum – progress through consensus rather than 'Western negotiation'.

Ryutaro Komiya reported a very positive Japanese view of APEC. From a Japanese perspective, the two worrying developments in trade policy through the 1980s were the difficult passage of the Uruguay Round and the spread of regionalism. APEC could be seen as providing an alternative path to progress on trade liberalization. Nevertheless, he cautioned that the meaning of 'free trade' in the Bogor Declaration remained unclear (a view shared by all symposium speakers).

He also foreshadowed difficulties with APEC trade liberalization in the future. Important APEC members were, in Komiya's view, likely to be opposed either to a most favoured nation (MFN) approach or to a reciprocity approach. Many Asian APEC members, including Japan, had benefited, and continue to benefit, from the global trade liberalization achieved under the GATT, and in particular the MFN rule which lay at its heart. The USA, on the other hand, was unlikely to support the MFN route to APEC's trade liberalization because it would allow EU members a free ride on the APEC liberalization wagon.

Arvind Panagariya argued that APEC was likely to encounter difficulties in the medium term in implementing trade liberalization beyond existing member commitments. In the long term, however, APEC member countries were likely to become so influential globally that the forum could drive multilateral liberalization. Whether APEC will play such a role will depend crucially on the US attitude, both towards trade liberalization and to APEC itself. This last point was emphasized by Alan Winters in his remarks at the conclusion of the conference.

Trade Policy and Growth

A remarkable feature of the South-East Asian countries has been their extraordinary growth rates over the last two decades. There has been considerable debate as to whether these high growth rates are the result of trade policies, of a high propensity to save out of income leading to high growth rates in capital stocks, or of improvements in their technologies. This growth has also partly contributed to renewed interest by theorists in growth modelling, and hence to the development of the idea of endogenous growth models. Some of the questions that naturally arise are: why is it that growth rates for developing nations seem to differ so much, the South-East Asian growth rates being very high and those of many countries in Africa and South America being much lower? Are differences a result of active policy choices on the part of national governments? Are growth rates related to the openness of countries? Are they convergent or permanently different?

The neoclassical growth theory that dominated thought on dynamics in the 1960s and 1970s paid little attention to the nature of technical change. In this theory, growth rates are generally not 'endogenous' – they are constant in the long run if the economies converge to the steady state. By contrast, the modern growth literature has generated models that concentrate on the production of new technologies for existing or new goods, and yield growth rates that do not necessarily converge to constant rates. By focusing on these issues, this new literature may be better placed than the old neoclassical paradigm to explain empirical observations on growth rates and to provide a framework for trade policy analysis.

Accordingly, the final group of papers was concerned with the linkage between trade and growth. The first of these was devoted to a survey of the topic of endogenous growth and trade policy. Scott Taylor provides an overview of the theoretical literature on endogenous growth models and on the linkage between this literature and international trade policy. This account of the literature is cast in terms of a taxonomy, borrowed from Rivera-Batiz and Romer (1991), and Grossman and Helpman (1993), of ways by which trade can affect the rate of growth: growth is affected by scale, allocation, spillover and redundancy effects. These effects on growth relate to the consequences of the crucial assumption of external economies of scale and operate though the gains from having bigger economies; from the allocation of resources between the production and research and development (R&D) sectors; the spillover effects or diffusion of new knowledge into related areas; and through redundancies of R&D expenses, when technological improvements can be obtained indirectly.

In addition to reviewing these effects, Taylor also addresses the question of how ongoing endogenous growth may affect national incentives to restrict or liberalize trade through time. Using recent developments by Michael Devereux (1997), endogenous growth is shown to have clear effects on nations' choices of optimal (Nash equilibrium) tariffs: balanced spillover effects leading to balanced growth have no effect upon these tariffs, while unbalanced spillovers yield increasing tariffs over time.

One of the crucial elements in the diffusion of new knowledge, and hence in the ability of countries to benefit from technological advances, lies in the international spillover effects. Not all countries are at the forefront of research and development, which require massive resources and highly trained labour. Accordingly, many countries rely on their ability to learn, in a variety of ways, about new technologies developed elsewhere. The chapters in this volume by Pham Hoang Van and Henry Wan, and by Motoshige Itoh address explicitly the question of how knowledge is transmitted between countries.

According to Van and Wan, technology is transferred between countries as a result of foreign direct investment and emulation of the products and techniques of the parent company by workers and contractors. This process is modelled using a game-theoretic approach. Van and Wan, after reviewing the stylized facts of South-East Asian technology transfer contained in the 'Wong–Watanabe case', formulate a model in which the foreign firm sets up production operations in the host country in the first stage of the game. In the second stage, local workers in this and local supplying firms learn (imperfectly) about the technology and the product; and in the third stage the local workers and firms decide whether to set up their own operations and to go into competition with the foreign multinational firm. Through this modelling and examples, Van and Wan show how this form of emulative technology transfer can work. Their modelling is suggestive of important technology linkages that require further theoretical examination and empirical testing.

By contrast to the theoretical approach taken by Van and Wan, Motoshige Itoh uses a case study approach to try to identify, by empirical observation of Japanese companies operating in South-East Asia, the mechanisms by which technology transfer occurs through trade and investment. Itoh's paper complements that of Van and Wan: both concentrate on technology transfer through worker training, but differ in the way the technology transfer manifests itself in the host country. Itoh focuses on the electrical and electronic industry in South-East Asia, looking in particular at the operations of one major Japanese company, Sony, in the region. He points out the importance of foreign direct investment (much of it Japanese) in the region, and in the electronics industry in particular, and notes the relationship between FDI and subsequent exports. Of special importance is the observation from the case study of eight Sony subsidiaries in Singapore, Malaysia and Indonesia of the technology spillover effects. These occur through the improvements in knowledge of the local workers through their contact with Japanese engineers and products, and manifest themselves at several different levels: spillovers to other parts of the subsidiary, to other local firms through job-hopping, and to local suppliers of parts (the latter possibly being in other countries in the region). These are important avenues of technology transfer and suggest valuable questions and topics for future theoretical and empirical research, as indicated by Ethier.

Overviews

The conference concluded with a round-table discussion of a variety of issues that arose at various points during the preceding three days. This discussion was preceded by brief conference summaries and evaluations by Alan Winters and Elhanan Helpman. Space limits prevent us from summarizing the extensive and informative discussions from the floor in either this final session or the commentary periods following each paper. The final comments by Winters and Helpman, while reflecting their own views on the chapters in this book, summarize incisively and effectively the flavour of the general discussion. Readers are simply directed to their contributions.

4   EMERGING ISSUES

Conference organizers always like to imagine that the events they arrange will amount to more than the sum of individual contributions, and that the conference will be of importance in shaping future research. But it is always risky to say what this is. Accepting this risk, however, we have identified three related but distinct research programmes that we believe are likely to be particularly fruitful over the next period. Not surprisingly, they are related through a common link to the evolution of trade policy in a regional context.

First, the notion of regionalism itself seems to be changing, partly in response to the much more open multilateral trade policy stance that most countries, even those heavily engaged in regional initiatives, have adopted. Traditional analyses, such as the Vinerian insights into trade creation and trade diversion, will need to be supplemented with theoretical advances seeking to capture the essence of regional agreements, which are more subtle in their nature than the EU, or, more recently, NAFTA. Are new theoretical structures necessary to explain the nature and implications of a regional agreement whose central tenet on trade policy appears to be 'concerted unilateralism'? Will they fall within the 'policy impact' rubric identified earlier, or will they be of the 'policy choice' type, canvassing issues such as the political choice to surrender some sovereignty to give impetus to an international political process that is in that nation's longer-term interest?

These questions, not always articulated during the conference itself, were suggested in part by the attention given to APEC as a regional forum with a strong trade liberalization focus, but lying outside special multilateral categories, such as the Article XXIV GATT concessions. Conventional classifications of trade agreements (for example, free trade areas, customs unions, and 'deep' integration) may need to be modified, or even recast, in the light of such developments.

Second, researchers may need to pay much more attention to the 'nitty gritty' of trade negotiations than they have in the past. Perhaps regional trade negotiators devote so much of their time to the specification of common standards, and other industry-level regulatory issues, because they are aware, as some more analytic researchers are not, that it is at this level of trade negotiation that agreements succeed or fail.

Wolfgang Mayer's separation of trade policy initiatives from their implementation, and the discretion he accorded the latter process, seems especially enlightening as an approach to this question. Broad policy parameters can be set in the knowledge that all parties to an agreement have at their disposal an array of administrative instruments that can be used to assuage domestic interests, or to pose credible threats to other parties. As the world trading system becomes more open, and as countries with more diverse belief systems become more comprehensively and intimately engaged in trade with each other, this distinction will increase in importance. For example, the complexities associated with monitoring trade through the Internet is likely to require a high degree of 'implementation' type negotiation. The importance of implementation issues following the conclusion of the Uruguay round negotiations, as highlighted by Greenaway, underlines implementation as an emerging issue.

Our third nomination for a fruitful future research programme highlighted by the conference is the linkage between foreign investment and technology transfer. In recent times, the traditional emphasis on complementarity of endowments as an explanation for trading patterns has been overtaken by theories relying on externality capture of one kind or another. Such theories enjoy empirical support – there appears to be more trade between countries with similar endowments and technology than there is between countries where they differ sharply. These theories also provide the underpinning to our understanding of the links between trade and growth, and are borne out by membership of regional trade agreements. To some extent, this leaves the traditional idea of endowment complementarity without a home – in spite of its great intuitive appeal, it seems not to explain much international trade action. The nature and role of technology transfer via foreign investment arose in various places throughout the conference. To some extent the APEC arrangement is more concerned with such things as foreign investment, technology transfer and the rules of trade than about trade reform itself. At a different level, in Ethier's paper on the 'new regionalism', returns to investment figure prominently as a motivating factor explaining international relations between countries. This notion is intimately related to technology transfer. One of the major pay-offs to a nation experiencing inward foreign investment is that some technology is in fact transferred through its presence and operation (typically with domestic labour) in the host country. Technology transfer was also prominent in the growth part of the conference. Economists' understanding of technology transfer, and of the channel of foreign investment through which such transfers flow, is relatively undeveloped, and the contributions in this volume which focus on this question open up an important area for future research, both theoretical and applied.

5   CONCLUDING COMMENTS

The conference aimed to shed light on a number of trade policy issues of special relevance to the Pacific Rim region, by bringing theorists and policy analysts together in a single forum. We believe that, through the efforts of both authors and discussants, this objective has been achieved. But the issues discussed here have their echoes in world-wide trade policy debate. More broadly, therefore, we hope that all those concerned with the theory and practice of international trade policy will find the volume of interest.

References

Bhagwati, J. (1991) *The World Trading System at Risk* (Princeton, NJ: Princeton University Press).

Bhagwati, J. and A. Panagariya (1996) 'The Theory of Preferential Trade Agreements: Historical Evolution and Current Trends', *American Economic Review*, vol. 86, pp. 82–7.

Bliss, C. J. (1994) *Economic Theory and Policy for Trading Blocks* (Manchester University Press).

Brander, J. A. (1981) 'Intra-Industry Trade in Identical Products', *Journal of International Economics*, vol. 11, pp. 1–14.

Brander, J. A. and P. Krugman (1983) 'A Reciprocal Dumping Model of International Trade', *Journal of International Economics*, vol. 15, pp. 313–22.

Devereux, M. (1997) 'Growth, Specialisation and Trade Liberalization', *International Economic Review*, vol. 38, no. 3.

Grossman, G. and E. Helpman (1993) *Innovation and Growth in the Global Economy* (Cambridge, Mass.: MIT Press).

Grossman, G. and E. Helpman (1994) 'Protection for Sale', *American Economic Review*, vol. 84, pp. 833–50.

Hillman, A. L. (1993) *The Political Economy of Protection* (Chur: Harwood).

Kemp, M. C. and H. Wan (1976) 'An Elementary Proposition Concerning the Formation of Customs Unions', *Journal of International Economics*, vol. 6, pp. 95–7.

Lipsey, R. (1960) 'The Theory of Customs Unions: A General Survey', *Economic Journal*, vol. 70, pp. 496–513.

Rivera-Batiz, L. and P. Romer (1991) 'International Integration and Endogenous Growth', *Quarterly Journal of Economics*, vol. 106, pp. 531–56.

Romer, P. (1994), 'New Goods, Old Theory, and the Welfare Costs of Trade Restrictions', *Journal of Development Economics*, vol. 43 no. 1, February, pp. 5–38.

The World Bank (1993) *The East Asian Miracle: Economic Growth and Public Policy* (Oxford University Press).

Viner, J. (1950) *The Customs Union Issue* (New York: Carnegie Endowment for International Peace).

.

Part I
Regional Experience

1 Current Issues in Trade Policy and the Pacific Rim[1]

David Greenaway
UNIVERSITY OF NOTTINGHAM

1 INTRODUCTION

The purpose of this chapter is to set the context for those that follow. It is *not* a comprehensive survey of 'current issues in trade policy', nor is it an overview of the trade policies of the full range of Asia-Pacific economies.[2] The sheer number and diversity of Asia-Pacific economies, and, for that matter, of current trade policy issues, would make either task infeasible except at the most superficial level. Rather, it begins from the following questions: why should the countries of the Asia-Pacific 'region' be contemplating closer regional co-operation; and what trade policy issues are germane to the trade-offs between more or less regional co-operation? This seems like the logical starting point of any discussion, and certainly much more logical than thinking deeply about the details of trade policy co-ordination in the context of any particular (actual or potential) regional trading arrangement. In addressing these questions I shall not only review what appear to be the key issues, but also refer to and contextualize later chapters in this volume.

Thus the issues on which this chapter focuses are selective: multilateralism and minilateralism; trade reforms, liberalization and growth; the World Trade Organization (WTO); the agenda following the Uruguay Round (UR) of negotiations under the General Agreement on Tariffs and Trade (GATT); and regulatory interventions. Section 2 begins to set the context by overviewing trade patterns and growth in the Asia-Pacific region. Section 3 continues by reviewing the forces that have driven so many countries to enter into regional trading arrangements (RTAs) of one form or another. It also sets out the range of RTAs in the Asia-Pacific region and questions the objectives behind and prospects for greater co-operation between the Asia-Pacific economies. In the fourth section the unilateral trade reforms in developing/emerging economies, which have been a distinctive feature of the 1980s and 1990s, are discussed, with particular reference to the Asia-Pacific region. In addition it reviews the pattern of trade policy regimes of the region's economies. Section 5 concentrates on the WTO and emerging post-Uruguay Round issues. Many commentators have spoken at length of the 'onion skin' phenomenon: peel away one layer and another is exposed. In the case of barriers to trade and investment, peel away border measures and you expose the importance of non-border measures. Section 6 takes this up, in focusing on the regulation of trade and investment. Finally, the seventh section concludes by evaluating the implications of these issues for the Pacific Rim.

2 TRADE PATTERNS AND GROWTH IN THE ASIA-PACIFIC REGION

We shall turn to the definition of what constitutes the Asia-Pacific region shortly. Before doing so, it is helpful to fix some markers relating to global trade, the changing relative importance of the key regional groupings in global trade and the balance between inter- and intra-regional trade.

Table 1.1 provides details of world merchandise exports and imports by region for 1994, with 1980 as a comparator year. Of the three largest trading groups shown, North America's share in world trade rose only modestly from 1980 to 1994, though with a larger rise in the share of world imports than of exports. Western Europe's share of world exports rose somewhat, while the region's import share actually fell. In contrast, Asia's share of world exports increased from 15.6 per cent to 27 per cent, and its share of imports from 16.7 per cent to 24.3 per cent. Asia has had the fastest growth of trade of any region over these years and, as the table indicates, it continues to show the fastest growth in the 1990s.

Table 1.2 shows intra- and inter-regional trade shares in 1994. Two points are worth noting. First, the Asian intra-regional share is second only to that of the intra-European share, whether expressed as a proportion of intra-regional trade or world trade. Thus, intra-regional trade within the Asia-Pacific region is as well developed as that within Western Europe. Second, the inter-regional trade between North America and Asia amounts in each case to over 25 per cent of total trade.

Two obvious questions then arise, one of which is of particular interest in the context of this chapter. The first is, to what extent has this growth of trade driven, or been driven by the dramatic growth of output that has been recorded in East Asia over the last quarter of a century? There is a substantial literature that addresses this question, although, it has to be said, without quite resolving it. For our part, we merely note that trade growth and output growth are correlated, without worrying for the time being about the direction of causality. The second question is, to what extent has the growth of intra-regional trade been stimulated by RTAs? Certainly in the European context, formal integration arrangements are seen as a key driver. Can the same be said of Asia-Pacific trade?

Table 1.3 lists the participants in RTAs in the Asia-Pacific region. The arrangement of longest standing is the Association of South East Asian Nations (ASEAN), which dates from the Bangkok declaration of 1967. The

Table 1.1 World merchandise exports and imports by region, 1980–94

(a) **Exports**

	Value ($ billions) 1994	Percentage share		Annual percentage change 1990–4
		1980	1994	
World[a]	4090	100.0	100.0	5
North America	678	14.5	16.6	7
Latin America	184	5.4	4.5	6
Western Europe[b]	1797	40.2	43.9	2
C/E Europe and the former USSR[b,c]	118	7.8	2.9	3
Africa	91	5.9	2.2	−3
Middle East	121	10.6	2.9	−2
Asia[a]	1103	15.6	27.0	11

Notes:
[a] Excluding Hong Kong re-exports.
[b] Comparisons between 1980 and other years are affected by German unification.
[c] Comparisons between 1980 and other years are affected by the changes in trade valuation in Central and Eastern Europe and the former USSR.
The statistics are affected by changes in the methods of collecting trade data in EU member states, beginning 1993.

(b) **Imports**

	Value ($ billions) 1994	Percentage share		Annual percentage change 1990–4
		1980	1994	
World[a]	4210	100.0	100.0	5
North America	845	15.5	20.1	7
Latin America	218	5.9	5.2	15
Western Europe[b]	1974	44.8	42.6	1
C/E Europe and the former USSR[b,c]	114	7.4	2.7	0
Africa	99	4.7	2.3	1
Middle East	121	5.0	2.9	5
Asia[a]	1021	16.7	24.3	10

Notes:
[a] Excluding Hong Kong re-exports.
[b] Comparisons between 1980 and other years are affected by German unification.
[c] Comparisons between 1980 and other years are affectcd by the changes in trade valuation in Central and Eastern Europe and the former USSR.
The statistics are affected by changes in the methods of collecting trade data in EU member states, beginning 1993.

Table 1.2   Intra- and inter-regional trade flows, 1994

	North America	Latin America	Destination Western Europe	Central and Eastern Europe and former USSR	Africa	Middle East	Asia	World[a]
Origin								

Percentage share of intra- and inter-regional trade flows in each region's total merchandise exports

	North America	Latin America	Western Europe	Central/Eastern	Africa	Middle East	Asia	World
North America	36.9	14.1	18.9	0.8	1.5	2.6	25.2	100.0
Latin America	48.4	20.2	17.8	0.8	1.2	1.0	9.4	100.0
Western Europe	8.2	2.5	68.1	4.2	2.8	3.0	9.5	100.0
C/E Europe and the former USSR	5.2	1.7	59.5	15.9	1.6	1.8	13.7	100.0
Africa	14.6	2.2	52.7	1.1	9.7	1.4	12.1	100.0
Middle East	13.0	2.8	23.2	1.5	1.9	9.1	45.6	100.0
Asia	25.9	2.5	16.3	1.0	1.3	2.5	48.5	100.0
World	19.8	5.2	41.8	2.8	2.2	2.8	23.9	100.0

Percentage share of intra- and inter-regional trade flows in world merchandise exports

	North America	Latin America	Western Europe	Central/Eastern	Africa	Middle East	Asia	World
North America	6.1	2.3	3.1	0.1	0.2	0.4	4.2	16.6
Latin America	2.2	0.9	0.8	0.0	0.1	0.0	0.4	4.5
Western Europe	3.6	1.1	29.9	1.8	1.2	1.3	4.2	43.9
C/E Europe and the former USSR	0.2	0.0	1.7	0.5	0.0	0.1	0.4	2.9
Africa	0.3	0.0	1.2	0.0	0.2	0.0	0.3	2.2
Middle East	0.4	0.1	0.7	0.0	0.1	0.3	1.3	2.9
Asia	7.0	0.7	4.4	0.3	0.4	0.7	13.1	27.0
World	19.8	5.2	41.8	2.8	2.2	2.8	23.9	100.0

Notes:
[a] Includes unspecified destinations. Exports to unspecified destinations are important in the case of Africa.
Source: World Trade Organization, International Trade: Trends and Statistics 1995.

South Asian Preferential Trading Arrangement (SAPTA) dates from 1971, and the Asia-Pacific Economic Co-operation forum (APEC) from 1989. The East Asian Economic Caucus (EAEC), effectively an expanded ASEAN, is still very much on the drawing board. ASEAN is not widely regarded as having been a success in promoting intra-regional trade/co-operation (see, for example, Balasubramanyam, 1989). The fact that the existence of SAPTA is so little known speaks for itself. This clearly suggests that the dramatic growth in Asian trade in general, and intra-regional trade in particular, has little, if anything, to do with RTAs. It has occurred despite the absence of well entrenched, broad RTAs striving to promote deep integration.

This may, of course, change with the creation of APEC, which is very broadly based in terms of its country coverage and geographical spread, and

Table 1.3 Regional trading arrangements in Asia

ASEAN	SAPTA	APEC
Brunei	India	Brunei
Indonesia	Bangladesh	Indonesia
Malaysia	Nepal	Malaysia
Singapore	Pakistan	Philippines
Philippines	Sri Lanka	Singapore
Thailand	Maldives	Thailand
	Bhutan	Japan
		South Korea
		United States of America
		Canada
		Australia
		New Zealand
		China
		Papua New Guinea
		Hong Kong
		Taiwan
		Mexico
		Chile

if one takes seriously the targets for free trade and investment by the year 2020 laid down by the Bogor Declaration in 1994, is also ambitious. Before looking in detail at the prospects for APEC, however, we need to address the issue of why, given the growth in intra-regional trade alongside an absence of RTAs, there has been a resurgence of interest in regional integration in Asia. This in turn is bound up with the more general question of the recent interest in regionalism on a world-wide scale.

3 MULTILATERALISM AND MINILATERALISM

Since the early 1980s there has been a wave of interest in regional trading arrangements (RTAs), often referred to as the 'new regionalism'. Like its analogue, the 'new protectionism', 'new' can be taken as a chronological reference: the new regionalism is a feature of the 1980s and 1990s, just as the 'old regionalism' was of the 1950s and 1960s. However, 'new' also refers to a number of distinctive characteristics of the phenomenon. First, whereas the old regionalism typically involved RTAs which were 'North–North' or 'South–South' in their membership, the new regionalism has been typified by 'North–South' arrangements (the North American Free Trade Area (NAFTA) and APEC being excellent examples). This feature certainly offers considerable potential for gains from trade. However, it also creates the potential for adjustment problems and trade tensions. Second, RTAs in the new regionalism are less 'geographically challenged' than in the old regionalism. The latter typically involved contiguous countries or near neighbours. Some recent or proposed RTAs are, quite literally, intercontinental. A priori, this too could be a good thing from a gains-from-trade perspective; but it also raises interesting co-ordination issues. Third, many agreements do not seem to be exclusive: multiple membership does not seem to be a problem. This may turn out to be an aid to promoting multilateralism; perhaps, however, it also suggests a greater commitment to the process of multilateralism than of regionalism on the part of participants in the RTA. Finally, whereas all the agreements in the 'old regionalism' focused on shallow integration (that is, liberalization of border measures), a number of recent agreements have aspired to deep integration, with commitments to harmonization of regulatory measures, freeing factor movements and so on. The European Union (EU) has gone furthest down this road, though the Australia–New Zealand Closer Economic Relations Agreement (CER) has also moved in this direction.

A particular spur to the new regionalism has been its interaction with multilateralism in the form of the Uruguay Round (UR) negotiations. In the late 1980s and early 1990s, when it looked for a time as though the UR negotiators might be unable to secure an agreement, a recurring theme among commentators was the so-called superbloc scenario. This was on the lines that an inevitable by-product of failure would be a fragmentation of the global economy into three blocs, crudely Europe, North America and East Asia. This would be threatening not only to the economic welfare of the members of those blocs but also, more importantly, to those many (small) countries that were excluded. This may have been a contributory factor to the signing of some twenty-seven regional agreements between 1991 and 1993. Although the successful conclusion of the Uruguay Round may have altered the focus of this debate a little, it has certainly not diminished interest in regional trade arrangements. Considerable energy continues to be expended by policy-makers in efforts directed at market widening and market deepening. Asia-Pacific is not immune to this: why?

Economists, in thinking about RTAs, generally focus on the issue of whether they will be a step towards or a step away from free trade. In principle, either could apply, depending on the arrangements pertaining to third-party access. In practice, influential commentators such as J. N. Bhagwati argue that they are almost inevitably a step away from free trade because of their discriminatory nature.[3]

Article XXIV of the GATT is, of course, intended to 'quality control' RTAs in order to ensure that they are more likely to be steps forward rather than backward; but it is hard to argue that compliance with this has been much of a hurdle. So why the interest in regional integration among the Asia-Pacific countries?

A generation of European economists has been preoccupied on and off with regional integration in their own region, especially in the last decade. After a period of quiescence and lack of momentum where European integration was concerned, the 1980s and 1990s have seen a flurry of sustained activity directed at both market widening and market deepening. The former has seen the EU expand in a southerly direction, to incorporate Greece, Spain and Portugal, as well as to the north, incorporating Finland, Sweden and Austria. Alongside this, deepening has occurred with the commitment to and implementation of the Single Market Programme. The momentum the latter generated has added possible economic and monetary union (EMU) to the agenda. If we ignore EMU, on the grounds that the economic arguments are different and the prospects of it being realised in even a sub-set of the EU are questionable (let alone such a possibility in other parts of the world) and focus on the former, the arguments for real integration are quite well known. First, there is the issue of static effects: under what conditions will trade creation exceed trade diversion? These are well known – it all depends on the number and similarity of countries involved and the pre- and post-union structure of tariffs. Then there are dynamic effects: will integration unlock growth potential by eroding X-inefficiencies, delivering pro-competitive gains and stimulating investment? In the case of Western Europe, the verdict of the European Commission (1988) seemed to be a qualified 'yes', while Baldwin (1989) saw spectacular gains.

But what is the relevance of this to Asia-Pacific? Do these countries in some sense comprise an obvious 'natural' trading bloc of complementary trading partners which would benefit from some kind of regional integration arrangement? The Asia-Pacific economies appear to comprise an extraordinarily diverse group. The most extensive Asia-Pacific set is that defined by APEC. APEC's eighteen member countries, listed in Table 1.3, span three of the five continents; include the most populous country in the world and some of the least populous; and bring together city states and continental economies, post-industrialized and developing countries, economic superpowers and economic minnows. The only thing most, but not all, have in common is a shared 'border' with the Pacific Ocean!

Despite this extraordinary diversity, it has been argued by some that there are features of a 'natural' bloc present. Thus, for example, using a standard type gravity model, Frankel, Stein and Wei (1994) have recently argued that it does constitute a 'natural' bloc on the grounds that the countries of the region at present trade more than they should, with the benchmark trade flows being predicted by the gravity equation. In fact, they argue that the trade-enhancing power of APEC is considerably in excess of that of the EU. Thus they conclude that 'it may be time for the official institutions to catch up with private sector realities', that is, to formalize regional co-operation to a greater extent. This is a powerful argument that APEC comprises a 'natural' bloc.

Polak (1996) has challenged both the findings and the conclusions. He argues that the gravity model is mis-specified and that the authors have in fact discovered 'a phantom APEC preferential trade area'. That result is echoed by Dhar and Panagariya in Chapter 5 in this volume. They show that when gravity equations are estimated on an individual country basis, East Asian exports exhibit, if anything, a statistically significant bias *away* from rather than towards intra-regional markets.

Given this evidence and the sheer diversity in structure and location of the countries concerned, it is hard for an outsider to see anything 'natural' about APEC as a candidate for an RTA. More fundamentally, the Asia component of Asia-Pacific has for the last decade or so been the fastest-growing region globally. Moreover, while over the period since the mid-1960s intra-regional trade in North America has declined and in Western Europe it has increased by around 25 per cent, in Asia it has more than doubled. As we saw earlier, this has occurred despite the absence of RTAs (unless one regards ASEAN and the CER as important drivers). Rapidly expanding intra-regional trade has been largely driven by rapid economic growth in the region and significant cross-border investment. In the light of that, one is bound to ask what, if any, value can be added by a formal RTA in the form of the EAEC, an expanded ASEAN or APEC? Since APEC is the most comprehensive, let us attempt to answer the question by reference to that.

APEC began as a consultative forum in 1989. In the period since then it has set out principles for liberalization (as in the Osaka Action Plan), as well as setting target dates for complete liberalization of trade among members. Thus, the year 2010 is the target for free and open trade between developed country members, and 2020 the target for all members – the dates set at the 1994 Bogor summit. Precise modalities for reaching these targets have not been agreed, beyond the fact that agreements will be reached by consensus. The difficulty with this is that there is great diversity of interests and expectations within the group. Some flavour of that diversity comes out of the chapters in this volume. Komiya, in Chapter 13, interprets Japanese interests in the agreement as being, at least in part, defensive: a possible counterweight in international negotiations; a device for defusing pressure in bilateral negotiations with the USA; and a mechanism for subverting bilateral agreements between the USA and other Asian countries. In reflecting on the US position, Panagariya argues in Chapter 14 that, where recent administrations are concerned, it is a logical component of the US battery of market opening instruments. In promoting aggressive export expansion, minilateralism has a role to play alongside multilateralism and unilateralism – any liberalization adds to economic welfare in a vision of RTAs that is fundamentally pre-Vinerian. Thus APEC complements the Canada/US Trade Agreement (CUSTA), NAFTA, the Transatlantic Free Trade Area (TAFTA), Special 301, Super 301 and so on, and in this vision there is no inconsistency between them.[4]

Where the smaller countries are concerned it is tempting to conclude that their enthusiasm for APEC is driven by concerns about discrimination in trade with Europe and North America. Lloyd, in Chapter 3 in this volume, certainly concludes that this is so where Australia and New Zealand are concerned. Ethier argues in Chapter 6, however, that where the smaller developing countries are concerned there may be more to it than that. He argues that regionalism helps small countries to continue to exploit the benefits of multilateralism. He also argues that the interaction between unilateral liberalization and regional integration can have important investment creation and maintenance effects as investment is drawn in from the 'large' countries – in this case, Japan and the USA. This may provide an additional incentive for small countries to participate in RTAs.

It is not immediately obvious how APEC will evolve, given these diverse interests and objectives. Making a public commitment to open trade and investment by a specified period and actually delivering it are quite different things. As Panagariya points out in Chapter 14, to deliver reciprocated liberalization consistent with GATT would mean an APEC free trade area or customs union. Neither seems likely at this stage. Wonnacott (1996) explores a third option, namely APEC liberalization on an MFN basis relying on the dominant supplier approach to minimize free rider problems. This may be more feasible.

Viewing the process from afar, it is hard to avoid the conclusion that, from an economic perspective, APEC is essentially a defensive reaction to two processes. First, the signals that are sent from Western Europe by the market widening and deepening in that region and from the parallel process of market widening in North America. Second, the signals associated with so-called results-orientated trade policy, in the USA in particular. Both are motivated by fears of market exclusion, though the optimal response to each may be different. The 'Fortress' scenarios have been most seriously voiced in connection with Fortress Europe but have also been raised in connection with North America. Clearly, the risk of market exclusion is non-zero, though serious analysis suggests that it is negligible. Thus, for example, Anderson (1991) looked specifically at the impact of European integration on Western Pacific economies and the threats and opportunities associated with faster European growth, changes in comparative advantage and a more discriminatory trade policy. He concludes that the complementarity of trade structures between the regions and the flexibility of Asian producers in adapting to changing market conditions are such that these developments pose no major threats. Kreinin and Plummer (1992) look at the impact of both EU and North American integration on Asian exports to those regions and conclude that they have had very little impact and are unlikely to have much of an impact in the future.

In so far as there is any threat, it comes from specific instruments targeted at specific countries. For example, the pattern of anti-dumping actions in the EU is non-random and targeted at a relatively small number of countries, among them some of the APEC states; US Super 301 and Special 301 action has been similarly targeted. There is no obvious protection from this kind of action associated with membership of APEC.

4   TRADE REFORMS, LIBERALIZATION AND GROWTH

One of the most distinctive and widely commented upon features of the trade policy landscape over the last two decades and especially since the 1980s, is the extensive trade liberalization that has been undertaken in developing countries.[5] What is distinctive about this liberalization is that it has been unilateral; in other words, the trade reforms have been outside the cycle of GATT rounds of multilateral tariff reductions. Unilateral liberalizations have been associated primarily with developing countries but are not exclusive to this group. Both Australia and New Zealand implemented ambitious trade reform programmes in the 1980s, which are still ongoing; the emerging economies of Eastern Europe have undergone profound change in the 1990s.

The motives for, and the extent and economic effects of, these liberalizations have been analysed extensively. Motive is partly a reflection of growing evidence that inward-orientated trade regimes are tainted with 'failure', and partly an outcome of the prominence which trade reforms have been assigned in lending programmes linked with policy adjustments (see Greenaway and Morrissey, 1993). The balance between these varies from country to country, and indeed region to region. Policy conditionality has been far more important in Africa, Latin America and South Asia than in Pacific Asia. Indeed, from the standpoint of Korea, Malaysia, Thailand and Singapore it has been largely irrelevant. It has played a more important role in the Philippines, Indonesia and China: of the APEC developing countries, these three, together with Papua New Guinea and Mexico, remain the most heavily protected. The importance of motive links in to the potential for regional integration: if there is to be any movement in this direction, it will surely require as a prerequisite further unilateral liberalization. Indeed, the US negotiating position within APEC calls for unreciprocated liberalization by other members. In some countries this may only be possible with the involvement of the multilateral lending agencies; in others, it may be that the lure of preferential access to 'large' countries is a sufficient inducement.

But this is to run ahead somewhat: has the unilateral liberalization which has occurred resulted in those countries that are, or have been, developing economies having tariff structures more similar to those of the developed market economies in APEC? Papageorgiou, Michaely and Choksi (1991) evaluate liberalization episodes in six Asia-Pacific countries (Korea, Indonesia, New Zealand, the Philippines, Chile and Singapore). Whalley (1991) focuses on four (Korea, the Philippines, China and Mexico). For the most part, both of these studies concentrate on the 1950s, 1960s and 1970s. Dean (1995) looks at more recent evidence for the 1990s. Table 1.4 provides summary data on nominal tariffs and the coverage of quantitative restrictions (QR) for eight recently liberalizing APEC countries.

Defining 'liberalization' is not straightforward. At its simplest it can be described as import liberalization. However, at least two other representations are widely used: a move towards neutrality; and a substitution of more efficient for less efficient instruments. The former merely acknowledges that protection is a relative concept. In a two-sector model, import protection means anti-export bias and can be reversed by introducing (symmetric) export incentives. This, of course, is the famous Lerner symmetry result. However, as Milner (1995) shows, once a non-tradable sector is present the resource allocation effects of offsetting protection become more complicated. Harris and Schmitt, in Chapter 8 in this volume, identify other reasons for questioning the symmetry between import taxes and export subsidies: anti-competitive effects and price-signalling effects. Both are potentially relevant and caution against relying too heavily on the 'neutrality' notion of trade liberalization.

Table 1.4 Protection levels in Pacific Asia developing countries

	Average nominal tariff[a]		QR coverage[b]	
	Pre-reform[c]	Current[d]	Pre-reform[c]	Current[d]
China (1986, 1992)	38	43	n.a.	70[e]
Indonesia (1985, 1990)	27	22	32	10
Korea (1984, 1992)	24	10	23	<5
Malaysia (1993)	n.a.	14	<5[f]	<5[f]
Philippines (1985, 1992)	28	24	100[g]	<5
Thailand (1986, 1990)	13[e]	11[e]	<5	<5
Chile (1984, 1991)	35	11	Minimal	0
Mexico (1985, 1990)[f]	24	13	92	20

Notes:
[a] Unweighted percentage rates, rounded to the nearest integer.
[b] Percentage of tariff lines covered by quantitative restrictions and licensing requirements. Rounded to the nearest integer.
[c] Prior to the most recent trade reform. First date in parentheses.
[d] Second date in parentheses.
[e] Data are import weighted.
[f] 'Pre-reform' is 1985; 'current' is 1992.
[g] 'Pre-reform' is 1983.
Source: Compiled from Dean (1995).

Despite its limitations, the average nominal tariff continues to be used as an indicator of protection/trade policy orientation. All the developing countries listed, with the exception of China, have average tariffs in the mid-1990s that are less than those prevailing in the 1980s. However, the rates still range from 10 per cent (Korea) to 43 per cent (China). In other words, they continue to have higher average levels of nominal protection, and probably also effective protection, than the economic superpowers of the region (USA and Japan) and the smaller developed market economies of Canada, Australia and New Zealand. With the exception of China, the picture of QR coverage looks more promising, with average coverage ratios generally less than 10 per cent and often less than 5 per cent. Since one widely held conception of liberalization is the substitution of less efficient (quotas) by more efficient (tariffs) instruments, this pattern is consistent with the notion that genuine trade reforms have been implemented.

Clearly, however, an issue remains of significant differences in trade structure and trade orientation across the countries of the region. Figure 1.1 shows tariff rates, and Figure 1.2 reports evidence on the frequency of non-tariff barriers. As is obvious, the differences in both the mean and variance of tariffs are considerable, so too are the differences in the frequency index. If one sees integration as involving a convergence in average tariffs and a reduction in their spread, together with a reduction in the use of non-tariff barriers, then these are differences of an order of magnitude to make integration commitments of the type being promoted in Western Europe or even North America ambitious without considerable unilateral liberalization. It could be argued that a formal commitment to integration is a useful anchor for further unilateral liberalization as in Mexico and its association with NAFTA, and perhaps this will turn out to be the case. However, a much more plausible scenario is that further trade reforms will be linked to policy conditionality or be wholly voluntary. With respect to the former, trade policy conditions continue to figure prominently in World Bank and IMF Adjustment Lending programmes; with respect to the latter, East Asia is a part of the world where the demonstration effects of an apparent association between outward orientation and economic performance are at their strongest. It is also a region, however, where 'outward orientation' can be consistent with alternative trade policy scenarios, ranging from free trade in Hong Kong to the dirigiste 'neutrality' of Korea. The pluralism this has engendered is unlikely to be much affected by APEC discussions, nor are APEC consultations likely to be much affected by the need to promote trade liberalization in the region.

Where unilateral liberalization is concerned, sustainability is obviously critical. Important aspects of sustainability are addressed by Anderson and Taylor in Chapters 9 and 15 of this volume. Anderson focuses on an important but neglected component, namely the fiscal dimension. Developing countries are heavily dependent on trade taxes. Tariff liberalization may result in fiscal

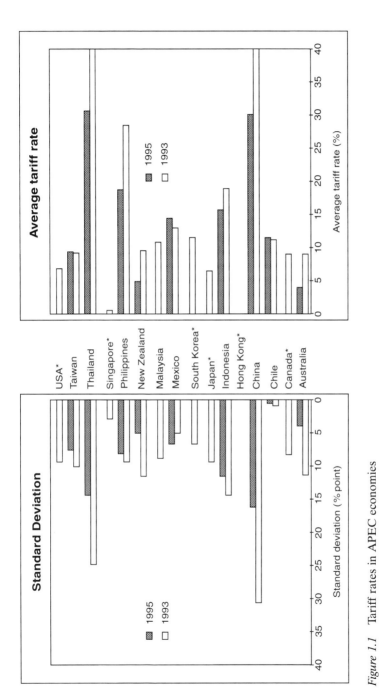

Figure 1.1 Tariff rates in APEC economies
Notes:
* Average tariff rates not available.
Source: Pacific Economic Co-operation Council, *Annual Report* 1995, p. 40.

16

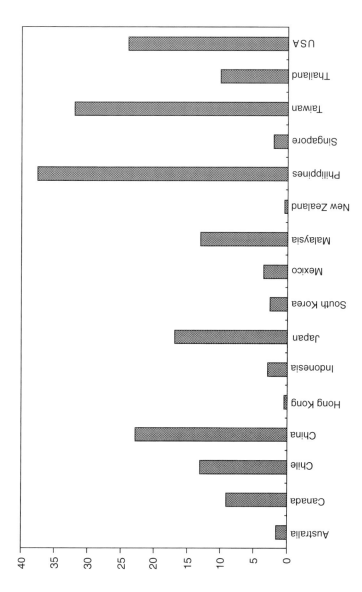

Figure 1.2 Frequency ratios of core non-tariff barriers, APEC economies, 1993 (percentages)

Source: Pacific Economic Co-operation Council, *Annual Report 1995*, p. 47.

depletion or fiscal enhancement. As Falvey (1994) has shown, the welfare economics of this is rather complicated. Empirically, both fiscal enhancement and depletion have been recorded following trade reforms (see Greenaway and Milner, 1991). The crucial point is that there is often a belief on the part of reforming governments that tariff reductions must mean fiscal depletion. In turn, this has an impact on the willingness of governments to reform and on the components of any reform package. What Anderson does is to integrate the trade reform and public finance literatures in setting out conditions for revenue-neutral (first and second best) liberalizations. In the process he develops some intuitively appealing and transparent expressions for depicting welfare-improving reforms. Given the centrality of fiscal dimensions to the commitment to and sustainability of reforms, this is a useful direction in which to have taken the literature.

A further preoccupation in the unilateral trade reform literature has been the relationship between trade reforms and economic growth. Despite the assertions of Papageorgiou, Michaely and Choksi (1991) the experience (even within their own sample is mixed (see Greenaway, Leybourne and Sapsford 1997). Some trade reforms have been associated with subsequent accelerations in growth, and others with decelerations. Until now this has typically been explained by reference to shake-out effects, to credibility problems having adverse impacts on investment, or to slippage in implementation. Taylor points to another possible explanation arising from the endogenous growth literature. In an international context knowledge spillovers are critical. Taylor shows how the impact of trade policy is very sensitive to whether knowledge diffuses slowly over time or instantaneously.

5 THE WORLD TRADE ORGANISATION (WTO), URUGUAY ROUND ISSUES AND POST URUGUAY ROUND AGENDA

Much has been written about the Uruguay Round and the agreements that resulted from it. The Round has been completed and the agreements are now being implemented. There are, however, UR implementation issues and post-UR issues that are still 'live issues'. Perhaps this is an area where APEC could be an important driver?

Take, first of all, implementation. Table 1.5 sets out the UR outcomes by negotiating area. Some of these will prove to be relatively straightforward – for example, tariff cuts, given that the approach is fairly transparent. The same cannot be said of those provisions applying to non-tariff barriers, in particular the prohibition of grey area measures and the associated revisions to the safeguard clause. The difficulty here will be in the detail of implementation, and potential for conflict within the region certainly exists, most notably between the USA and Japan, and the USA and the newly industrialised economies (NIEs). The same can be said of those provisions relating to contingent protection. The agreements make dispositions on both CVDs and anti-dumping actions. The evidence suggests that both have been used in a discriminatory fashion. It is unlikely that the new protocols will reduce the scope for discriminatory action and contingent protection will continue to be a source of trade policy tensions within the region, and between countries in this region and others.

Of the sectoral agreements, those relating to agriculture and to textiles and clothing are of greatest importance. Both, but especially agriculture, were very controversial subjects during the UR. Both, but again particularly agriculture, offer the potential for future trade policy conflict. Japan continues to have the most heavily protected of agricultural sectors, and the possibilities for tensions between Japan and the key promoters of agricultural liberalization in the region (the USA, Australia and New Zealand) are obvious.

The 'new issues': trade related investment measures (TRIMs), trade related intellectual property rights (TRIPs) and services were also complicated in part because they were new, in part because of the intrinsic difficulty of negotiating on non-border measures such as the protection of intellectual property. The general provisions and principles do include national treatment and MFN. Specific provisions relate to copyrights, trademarks, geographical indications, industrial designs, patents, layout designs of integrated circuits,

Table 1.5   Uruguay Round agreements

Negotiating area	Outcomes
Market access	
Tariffs	Average tariffs on industrial products cut by 38 per cent
	Elimination of duties in eleven sectors
	Increase in proportion of bound duties in developed market economies (DMEs) and less-developed countries (LDCs)
Non-tariff measures	Prohibition of grey area measures
	Tariffication of non-tariff barriers (NTBs) in agriculture
Sectors	
Natural-resource based Products	Tariff reductions
Tropical products	Tariff reductions
Textiles and clothing	Four-stage phase-out of Multi-fibre Agreement
	Transitional safeguards
	Constraints on circumvention

Agriculture	Tariffication of NTBs and gradual reduction thereof
	Constraints on non-decoupled domestic support
	Reduction in value and quantity of products subject to export subsidies
	Affirmation of rights and obligations in sanitary and phytosanitary measures
	Concessions for less developed and least developed countries

GATT System

Safeguards	Prohibition of grey area measures
	Explicit sunset arrangements
	Tighter criteria for application
	Limited provision for discrimination
Subsidies and countervailing duties (CVDs)	Traffic light system introduced
	Disciplines on use of CVDs
	Exemptions for least developed countries (LLDCs)
GATT Articles	Requirement that interventions under Articles XVIII$_B$ and XII be price based
	Clarification and reinforcement of Article XXIV criteria
	Strengthening of procedures for calculating dumping margin under Article VI; as well as strengthening injury test and dispute settlement
	Strengthening of provisions on rules of origin and pre-shipment inspection
MTNs	New procedures for negotiation of compensation when bindings are modified to assist LDCs in negotiations
Functioning of the GATT system	Commitment to sustain Trade Policy Review Mechanism (TPRM)
	Creation of WTO and shift to biannual ministerial meeting

New issues

Trade-related investment measures (TRIMs)	Prohibition of TRIMs inconsistent with Articles III and XI
	Phase out of existing TRIMs
	Concessions for LDCs
Trade-related intellectual property (TRIPs)	General commitment to MFN where possible
	Specific provisions on copyrights, trademarks, geographical indications, industrial designs, patents, layout designs of integrated circuits (ICs), trade sectors
	Phased transition for LDCs
Services	General commitment to MFN where possible
	Arrangements for progressive liberalisation
	Specific institutional provisions for air transport, financial services, telecommunications.

and trade secrets. Governments are obliged to ensure that enforcement in each area is effective, with phasing-in periods of one year (DMEs), five years (LDCs), or eleven years (LLDCs). Again, as with other areas, intellectual property had been a source of trade friction, primarily between the USA and East Asian trading partners. As the gains and losses of the intellectual property code become apparent, so too will the scope for trade frictions.

Services were controversial from the launch of the UR. Given the diversity of philosophies and regulatory regimes, it was also a complicated area on which to negotiate. The General Agreement on Trade in Services (GATS) is more limited in scope than appeared possible at the outset but takes an important first step in bringing discipline to the area. The agreement specifies a range of basic obligations which, as with TRIPs, include MFN and national treatment. A schedule was established for progressive liberalization; for a number of sectors (financial services, telecommunications, air transport services) detailed schedules are provided.

Implementation of the UR Agreements will therefore prove to be a live issue for the region for some time yet. Implementation will inevitably lead to some intra-regional trade tensions of a sort that do not appear to prevail within the EU. There, trade-offs across many of the issues were confronted during the negotiations, with the EU as a whole signing up for the package. (This is not to suggest, of course, that conflicts within the EU do not exist; they do. It merely makes the point that they tend not to spill over into wider trade discussions.) The trade-offs across Asia-Pacific contracting parties are sharper, in part because they did not negotiate as a group, and in part because of the greater diversity of interests among the members. It could be argued, of course, that co-operation through APEC will help to defuse potential tensions and facilitate implementation. That is certainly possible, especially if the signatories see the potential for additional welfare gains. Some work on a computable general equilibrium model (CGE) has evaluated alternative APEC scenarios. What this shows is that if an APEC trade agreement reinforces the UR outcomes there are net welfare gains for almost all Asia-Pacific countries. If, however, an agreement were discriminatory it would work against those outcomes with negative welfare effects. Not too surprising perhaps, but useful in setting parameters.

Then, of course, there is the post-Uruguay Round agenda. What are the key issues? What are the likely negotiating positions of APEC members? Is there scope for co-operation on those issues? Three things stand out: environment, labour standards and regulation. The first two we shall comment on here; the final one, which is broader in scope and in some sense systemic, will be dealt with in the next section.

Trade and the environment is a sensitive and analytically complex issue. Environment-related disputes have from time to time surfaced at GATT, and it is widely acknowledged that the WTO has a more proactive role to play here. A useful attempt to define the agenda within GATT is set out in Anderson and Blackhurst (1992). The studies in that volume set out in full the complexity of what is in practice a very fuzzy interface. Anderson and Blackhurst distil the key issues as first of all a recognition of the importance of indirect effects. Specifically, fiscal or regulatory interventions aimed at a particular environmental problem will have ripple effects on tradeable goods/services markets and these may trigger feedback effects. This leads to a second crucial point: there is an obvious need for multilateral co-operation, given the absence of a supranational regulatory authority. Put simply, co-operation is more likely to generate outcomes which minimize ripple and backwash effects. Third, the principles of optimal intervention that guide (or, to be more accurate, are *intended* to guide) the formulation of trade policy should similarly inform the formulation of environmental policy. Not only does this ensure that by-product distortions are minimized, it also ensures that trade liberalization is welfare-enhancing rather than welfare-reducing. It follows from the foregoing that trade policy will rarely, if ever, be the first best form of intervention. Finally, given the emotive nature of the environmental area it is especially susceptible to capture by special interest groups.

The WTO clearly has a job to do. Common sense tells one that it is not a job which will be prosecuted quickly or easily. This is an area where regional co-operation could pay dividends. The APEC group is the largest economic grouping globally and contains the fastest growing sub-region world-wide. Moreover, it also embraces countries with potentially very different interests in, for example, control of greenhouse gas emissions (USA and China), exploitation of non-renewable resources (Malaysia and Australia), protection of endangered species (USA and Japan) and so on. As with trade-related issues, the sheer diversity of interests creates considerable potential for conflict; however, in the absence of well-founded multilateral agreements, this is also diversity that can be exploited in developing protocols and agreements to be further developed by the WTO.

In a sense, the issue of labour standards is not a new one: the Havana Charter contained statements on labour standards and, as far back as 1953, the USA proposed a GATT provision on unfair labour standards. Recently, however, the issue has become rather more prominent. Part of the reason is, as with environmental issues, altruism. There are genuine concerns with issues such as exploitation of child labour, prison labour, repression of rights to organize, and so on. In addition, however, there are pressures originating from labour market rigidities in the major developed market economies (DMEs). Finally, there is the possibility, which Maskus and Holman (1996) develop, that the major DMEs 'need' something on which to negotiate in future multilateral trade negotiations, and this is it.

The links between labour standards and international trade are complex. Moreover, it is highly unlikely that trade policy represents a 'first best' form of intervention. The fact is, however, that labour standards are very much on the agenda now. Maskus and Holman (1996) consider alternative modalities for introducing labour standards into the WTO. These include an expansion of general exceptions under Article XX; establishing a legal framework along the lines of the TRIPs Code; and introducing an explicit 'social dumping' clause. None are straightforward, and all beg questions of appropriateness of intervention, potential for capture and adverse side effects on developing countries. As with environmental issues, one can pose the question whether protocols are more likely to be negotiated at the regional level. Again, this is an area where the region that has advanced furthest is the one that has gone the furthest in the direction of deep integration, namely the EU. However, the EU's progress thus far has been limited and not straightforward. Given the much greater diversity of interests in APEC, it is hard to see potential for moving more quickly here than on the WTO front.

6   REGULATORY ISSUES IN TRADE AND INVESTMENT

GATT's success in the liberalization of (nominal) tariffs served to emphasize the importance of non-tariff barriers in general, and grey-area measures in particular. As the circumstances in which grey-area and contingency measures can be used have become further constrained, so the importance of differences in regulatory regimes and competitive conditions has been given greater prominence. This, however, is only part of the story: it is crucial to remember that with the globalization of economic activity has come the involvement in international commerce of sectors where regulatory issues are far more important than border measures – tradable services is an obvious case. Moreover, with growing 'Allyn Young specialization' (Young, 1929), or what Krugman (1994) has recently relabelled 'slicing up the value chain', the boundary between international trade and investment has become more blurred. It is also the case that, to an increasing extent, international trade and cross-border investment are complements rather than substitutes. The extent to which commerce related to foreign direct investment (FDI) has come to dominate international transactions can be gauged by the following: sales through US affiliates overseas are now twice the value of US cross-border exports, and purchases from foreign-owned affiliates in the USA are now twice the value of US cross-border imports; intra-firm trade accounts for 23 per cent of US exports; and global sales of all multinationals exceed total global exports by some 40 per cent (Feketekuty and Rogowsky, 1996).

What all this means is that it is increasingly difficult to define the 'nationality' of firms and to read across to 'national interests'; it is increasingly difficult to implement trade rules based on origin; and the distinction between a domestic-policy instrument and a foreign-policy one is becoming increasingly blurred. Thus competitiveness of markets is determined by, *inter alia*, regulation, industrial policy and anti-trust provisions. Some hints at the ways in which this might have an impact on multilateral trade negotiations can be gleaned from the negotiations on services in the UR. There the negotiators eventually agreed a framework intended to encompass trade and factor movements. In turn, the schedules of contracting parties are meant to cover trade barriers, licensing arrangements, regulatory measures and so on. A more broadly-based, competition-orientated approach would extend this model across all areas of cross-border activity.

This is a major issue with which the WTO will have to grapple in due course. It is worth noting, however, that it is an issue that has been confronted at the minilateral and bilateral level. With respect to the former, the EU has gone the furthest, through its Single Market Programme together with its competition provisions, in at least thinking about a holistic approach to the competitiveness of markets. It has been more successful in some areas than in others, but the combination of mutual recognition, national treatment and, where appropriate, harmonization of regulations, has promoted some deep integration. At the bilateral level, the Structural Impediments Initiative negotiations between the USA and Japan were much more a discussion about the competitiveness of markets than about the narrower issue of market access.

This then raises the question whether progress to deep integration is more likely to be made at the minilateral rather than the multilateral level. Experience in the EU suggests that this could be so. Embryonic as it is, if APEC is to discuss liberalization seriously it is unlikely to be able to avoid discussing these issues. At the subregional level a start has been made in the Australia–New Zealand CER Agreement.

7 CONCLUDING COMMENTS

In this chapter we have focused on a range of 'current issues' in trade policy in the Pacific Rim. Following a scene-setting overview of trade patterns in the region we have concentrated on minilateralism and multilateralism; unilateral trade reforms; and post-UR issues. The connecting thread is the attention currently being paid to the potential for further regional integration. RTAs are not a new phenomenon to the region, with ASEAN and the South Asian Agreement on Regional Co-operation (SAARC) being examples of long-standing arrangements. In terms of scope and ambition, the agenda has shifted by an order of magnitude in the last five years, with proposals for a broader and deeper ASEAN, an ASEAN Free Trade Area (AFTA), an East Asian Economic Caucus (EAEC) and, of course, APEC. The potential evolution of Asian-Pacific integration will not hinge solely on APEC. However, APEC's success or failure will have a critical bearing on regional developments.

APEC is in many respects a unique phenomenon. It has the appearance of a regional trading arrangement but is not yet quite that. It embraces a remarkably diverse group of countries, some of which are members of other free-trade areas; some of which have bilateral accords; some are economic powerhouses; some economic minnows; some are developed; and some less developed. It has the potential to be a trading arrangement of enormous significance, yet its diversity must limit that potential. That diversity could be seen as being consistent with a natural trading bloc, in the sense that it offers great potential for gains from trade. On the other hand however, diversity could be seen as being inimical to integration, given that the range of trade policy issues that concern APEC members is probably wider than one would find in any other sub-set of seventeen of the world's economies. APEC has set itself trade policy objectives for the years 2010 and 2020. If it is to realise those objectives, the nature of the arrangement will probably have to change, and if it is to change, the issues outlined above will have to be addressed: What exactly is the purpose of APEC? How are the inevitable tensions between unilateral and minilateral liberalization to be handled? Can APEC contribute to the implementation of the WTO's post-UR agenda? How will the organization shape the post-UR agenda, in particular the need to focus liberalization efforts on the competitiveness of markets rather than on the narrower issue of removal of border measures?

Notes

1.   Comments on the first draft of the chapter from conference participants, especially the chapter's discussant, Kym Anderson, two anonymous referees and the editors, are gratefully acknowledged, as are comments from Chris Milner. This chapter draws upon work funded by the ESRC under its Asia-Pacific Programme; the author gratefully acknowledges ESRC support.
2.   Detailed reviews of trade policies can be found in the WTO's excellent series of Trade Policy Reviews. Assessments of these are published annually in the 'Global Trade Policy' issue of *The World Economy*.
3.   An interesting dimension to the debate is added by Bagwell and Staiger (see Chapter 7 in this volume). They show that the impact of RTAs for multilateral cooperation depends on the interplay of three effects: a tariff complementarity effect; a punishment effect; and a discrimination effect. As in the more conventional trade creation/trade diversion models, these can go either way. One interesting conclusion they reach is that when the multilateral system is not working effectively and countries are impatient, RTAs can have their most desirable effects on the multilateral system.
4.   Special 301 and Super 301 respectively refer to powers that can be initiated by the US Special Trade Representative against alleged contravention of intellectual property rights, and alleged unfair trade.
5.   Recent surveys/studies include: Papageorgiou, Michaely and Choksi (1991), Whalley (1991), Greenaway and Morrissey (1993), Dean, Desai and Reidel (1994), and Dean (1995).

References

Anderson, K. (1991) 'Europe 1992 and the Western Pacific Economies', *Economic Journal*, vol. 101, pp. 1538–52.

Anderson, K. and R. Blackhurst (eds) (1992) *The Greening of World Trade Issues* (London: Wheatsheaf).

APEC (1995) *Survey of Impediments to Trade and Investment in the APEC Region*, Report prepared by the Pacific Economic Cooperation Council (PECC) for APEC (APEC 95-CT-01-2).

Balasubramanyam, V. N. (1989) 'ASEAN and Regional Trade Cooperation in South East Asia', in D. Greenaway, T. Hyclak and R. Thornton (eds), *Economic Aspects of Regional Trading Arrangements* (London: Wheatsheaf).

Baldwin, R. (1989) 'The Growth Effects of 1992', *Economic Policy*, no. 9, pp. 248–91.

Dean, J. (1995) 'The Trade Policy Revolution in Developing Countries', in World Trade Organisation, *The World Economy: Global Trade Policy 1995*, pp. 173–90.

Dean, J., S. Desai and J. Riedel (1994) 'Trade Policy Reform in Developing Countries Since 1985', *World Bank Discussion Paper No. 267* (Washington, D.C: World Bank).

European Commission (1988) 'The Economics of 1992', *European Economy*, No. 35.

Falvey, R (1994) 'Revenue Enhancing Tariff Reform', *Weltwirtschaftliches Archiv*, vol. 130, pp. 175–90.

Feketekuty, G. and R. Rogowsky, (1996) 'The Scope, Implications and Economic Rationale of a Competition-Oriented Approach to Future Multilateral Trade Negotiations', *The World Economy*, pp. 167–82.

Frankel, J., E. Stein and S. J. Wei, (1994) 'Trading Blocs: The Natural, the Unnatural and the Super-Natural', CIDER Working Paper C94–034 (Berkeley, Calif.: University of California Press).

Greenaway, D. and C. R. Milner (1991) 'Fiscal Dependence on Trade Taxes and Trade Policy Reform', *Journal of Development Studies*, vol. 27, pp. 95–134.

Greenaway, D. and W. O. Morrissey (1993) 'Structural Adjustment and Liberalisation in Developing Countries: What Lessons Have We Learned?', *Kyklos*, vol. 46, pp. 241–62.

Greenaway, D., S. J. Leybourne and D. R. Sapsford (1996) 'Exports, (Liberalisation) and Growth Using Smooth Transitions Analysis', *Economic Inquiry*, vol. 34, pp. 798–814.

Kreinin, M. and M. Plummer (1992) 'The Effectiveness of Economic Integration in Industrial Countries on ASEAN and the NICs', *World Development*, vol. 20, pp. 1345–66.

Krugman, P. R. (1994) 'Growing World Trade: Causes and Consequences', *Brookings Papers*, no. 1, pp. 327–77.

Maskus, K. and J. Holman (1996) 'International Labour Standards and the WTO', mimeo (World Bank).

Milner, C. R. (1995) 'Relative Incentives and Trade Strategies: Typologies and Possibilities', *Economic Record*, vol. 71, pp. 230–9.

Papageorgiou, D., M. Michaely and A. Choksi (1991) *Liberalising Foreign Trade* (Oxford: Basil Blackwell).

Polak, J. J. (1996) 'Is APEC a National Trading Bloc? A Critique of the "Gravity Model" of International Trade', *The World Economy*, vol. 19, pp. 533–43.

Whalley, J. (1991) 'Recent Trade Liberalisation in Developing Countries'. What Is Behind It and Where Is It Headed', *Global Protectionism* (ed. D. Greenaway) (London), pp. 225–52.

Wonnacott, P. (1996) 'Merchandise Trade in the APEC Region: Is there Scope for Liberalisation on an MFN Basis?', *The World Economy, Global Trade Policy 1995*, pp. 33–52.

Young, A. (1929) 'Increasing Returns and Economic Progress', *Economic Journal*, vol. 38, pp. 527–42.

Comment

Kym Anderson
SCHOOL OF ECONOMICS, UNIVERSITY OF ADELAIDE

This chapter addresses several questions, upon two of which I wish to comment. One is: why are countries in the Asia-Pacific region seeking closer economic co-operation, given the rapid intra-regional trade growth that has taken place in the absence of a formal regional trade agreement? The other is: what roles are domestic regulatory policies going to play in trade policy discussions and negotiations? These questions are being thought about in a world that, in the past decade or so, has taken several quantum leaps towards the internationalization of national economies, largely because of:

(i) the widespread lowering of international trade barriers unilaterally, especially in developing and transition economies;

(ii) the deregulation of financial and foreign exchange markets and lowering of barriers to foreign direct and portfolio investment, including investment in the utilities and service sectors;

(iii) decreasing transport and communication costs of doing business internationally, facilitating rapid growth in intrafirm trade;

(iv) other microeconomic reforms of an intranational kind, partly to ease the adjustment burden for previously protected industries;

(v) the proliferation of regional integration agreements;

(vi) and, most recently and still ongoing, the implementation of the Uruguay Round (UR) agreements.

While some worries remain (for example, the closedness of the European bloc and aggressive unilateralism on the part of the USA), this is a context of global economic growth and structural adjustment and, hence, changing comparative advantages not only in the economies undertaking reform but also – via international market changes – in those economies that have not yet embraced reform.

Given that context, why is the Asia-Pacific region seeking still more economic co-operation? It was understandable in the late 1980s/early 1990s, when a conclusion to the UR remained elusive; but even following the UR's conclusion it continues to be sought. Greenaway is puzzled by this, partly because he does not see Asia-Pacific as a 'natural' economic region, and partly because he considers the region relatively open already. However, neither of these perceptions is quite correct. From an economic (as distinct from cultural) viewpoint, Asia-Pacific comprises countries with a wide diversity of endowments per worker of farm land, minerals, and physical and human capital, and hence great scope for gains from specialization in production and trade. These countries still have very substantial barriers to trade and investment in selected goods and services, so that there is still considerable scope for gains from further trade liberalization within the Asia-Pacific region; and APEC members have committed themselves to this on a MFN basis ('open regionalism'), with the objective of free trade in the region by the year 2010 for developed countries and 2020 for developing economies (Garnaut, 1996).

More than that, APEC together with the related Pacific Economic Cooperation Council (PECC) and Pacific Basin Economic Council (PBEC), is not concerned only with trade liberalization. Also involved are foreign investment liberalization, trade and investment facilitation, and technical co-operation (see Pangestu, in Chapter 12 in this volume). Moreover, the decline in border protection has raised the relative importance of domestic regulatory policies and standards as determinants of international competitiveness, so that APEC spends much time on relatively mundane, but none the less growth-enhancing, activities such as sharing information on policies, negotiating mutual recognition of technical standards, and seeking to expose protectionist motives behind excessive environmental standards or quarantine restrictions on imports. APEC also serves as a coalition to pressure other members of the global trading system to adopt liberal policies, as was done at the WTO's first ministerial meeting, in Singapore in December 1996. Hence APEC is not simply a defensive reaction to trade bloc formation in Western Europe and North America. That being so, only part of the answer to the question why the co-operation process is alive and well in the APEC region can be found in models that focus only on national and regional trade policies.

Certainly it is possible to be cynical about targets such as free trade by 2010 or 2020, but the reality is that those targets are already serving useful political purposes: national governments cite them when rejecting protectionist pressures at home and when justifying further liberalization unilaterally, to better position investors and exporters to take advantage of emerging opportunities abroad.

The fifth section of Greenaway's chapter correctly points to the fuzziness in many UR agreements and their long implementation periods, which could result in disappointed expectations and hence trade disputes over the next few years. The most contentious area is likely to be textiles and clothing. Recent empirical studies suggest that as much as a fifth of the expected global welfare gains from UR liberalization could be lost if textile import quotas are not removed (see, for example, Anderson, Dimaranan, Hertel and Martin, 1997).

Greenaway points also to the unfinished UR negotiations still in train for some services, and to the considerable scope for further progress in the next multilateral round in agriculture, textiles, services and trade-related investment. Then he touches on the so-called 'new' issues on, or mooted for, the WTO's agenda, namely, trade's relationship with environmental and labour standards and with competition policy.

The trade and environment issue is already part of the WTO work programme, and it and the labour standards issue are unlikely to go away because groups in some rich countries see them as the key to ensuring that trade is 'fair' (Bhagwati, 1996). Greenaway suggests that APEC might be a useful laboratory for sorting out these issues prior to their consideration by the WTO's much larger membership. But that raises the same question as for the WTO: that is, would it weaken APEC's capacity to achieve its more substantive objectives?

In the sixth section of the chapter the point is made that the European Union (EU) has faced these types of issues as part of the overall demand for harmonization of regulatory standards to ensure a 'level playing field' for competition. But one should keep in mind that the EU members would always be able to agree on harmonizing regulatory policies much more easily than would APEC or WTO members. This is because the EU has more capacity to compensate those who lose because of upward harmonization of standards. In the WTO context, the only compensation mechanism is liberalization 'concessions', and that possibility diminishes as trade barriers are lowered. Even that mechanism would be unavailable to APEC members if they really were to achieve free trade during the next 15–25 years.

To conclude, it seems clear to this observer that formal and informal regional integration arrangements are not going to disappear rapidly. On the contrary, ASEAN is looking to expand to ten members before the end of the 1990s, MERCOSUR now has a free-trade agreement with Chile and is looking to expand its membership further, and talks are going on between other groups of countries (for example, USA–EU, ASEAN–EU, and ASEAN–ANZCER). Thus, understanding more about the political economy of regionalism and its relationship with multilateralism and with unilateral trade and domestic policy reforms seem very appropriate items on our agenda for research, both conceptual and empirical (Winters, 1998). Finally, more thought also needs to be given by policy analysts to what the countries of the Asia-Pacific and elsewhere should be focusing on – and should be trying to exclude – at the 1999 WTO ministerial conference to prepare for the next comprehensive round of multilateral trade negotiations. Part of that task involves thinking about the possible consequences of the different forms that the next round of negotiations might take. If it becomes a series rather than a single event, because negotiators cannot cope with a single agenda larger than that of the UR, how can intersectoral and interissue trade-offs be arranged? And how will negotiations be affected by the fact that by the turn of the century the WTO might well have 150 members, including large economies in transition, such as China and Russia?

References

Anderson, K., B. Dimaranan, T. Hertel and W. Martin (1997) 'Economic Growth and Policy Reform in the APEC Region: Trade and Welfare Implications by 2005', *Asia Pacific Economic Review*, vol. 3, no. 4, pp. 1–18, April.

Bhagwati, J. N. (1996) 'The Demand to Reduce Domestic Diversity Among Trading Nations', ch. 1 in J. N. Bhagwati and R. E. Hudec (eds), *Fair Trade and Harmonization: Prerequisites for Free Trade?*, vol. 1 (Cambridge, Mass: MIT Press).

Garnaut, R. (1996) *Open Regionalism and Trade Liberalization* (Singapore: Institute for Southeast Asian Studies).

Winters, L. A. (1998) 'Regionalism versus Multilateralism', in R. Baldwin, D. Cohen, A. Sapir and A. Venables (eds), *Regional Integration* (Cambridge: Cambridge University Press).

2 China's Dual Trading Regimes: Implications for Growth and Reform

Barry Naughton
UNIVERSITY OF CALIFORNIA

1 INTRODUCTION

The dramatic growth of Chinese foreign trade since 1985 has attracted world-wide attention. Rapid growth of manufactured exports has come predominantly from the southern coastal regions, and foreign invested enterprises (FIEs) have played a prominent role in this growth. This chapter stresses the less-well-known fact that export-orientated enterprises operate in a trade policy regime that is very different from the regime faced by most Chinese firms, as well as by potential exporters *to* China. Export-orientated firms operate in an extremely open policy environment that can be characterized as an export promotion regime; the rest of the economy operates under a trade regime that is still best characterized as one of import substitution, with very substantial barriers to trade. To an unusual degree, China thus operates a bifurcated trade regime. This perspective provides a good framework for analyzing Chinese achievements to date, as well as providing an insight into the challenges still facing the reform of Chinese trade policy, including entry into the World Trade Organisation (WTO).

This chapter is divided into two main sections. The first section primarily describes the existing Chinese trade regime. Here I stress that the export-orientated sector of southern China is predominantly characterized by a trade policy that is quite liberal and open. The first sub-section describes that trade regime, and contrasts it with the less open, and less reformed, parts of the Chinese economy. Here I marshal the available data on the relative size and performance of these different trade sectors. Subsequently, I examine the interaction between the trading regime and the other factors that have been noted in describing Chinese trade performance: ownership and region. I argue that the trading regime is at least as important as ownership or region when analyzing China's export success. In fact, all three factors are intertwined, but the trading regime has up to now received the least attention in the literature. A few of the implications of this analytical framework are pointed out.

The second part of the chapter examines the current and future prospects for Chinese trade liberalization in light of the arguments in the first part. Concentrating on the demands of the WTO, I discuss three challenges: national treatment, exchange rate management, and unification and liberalization of the tariff system. There is a brief conclusion.

2 EXISTING CHINESE TRADE REGIMES

In the past, China, like other socialist economies, operated a foreign-trade monopoly designed to keep the domestic economy rigorously separated from the world economy. The foreign trade monopoly served as an 'airlock', insulating the domestic economy and price system from any influence from the world economy, while allowing a few trade goods to pass through it in accord with planners' preferences. The monopoly was enforced by the inconvertibility of the currency, and by a system that assigned trading rights for any specific commodity to one of only eight national foreign trade corporations (FTCs). However, from 1978, China has gradually liberalized and opened this system. Policy-makers viewed trade reform as a process that should advance gradually, more or less in tandem with domestic reforms, particularly price reform. Initial external policy reforms, especially the Special Economic Zones (SEZs), signalled a dramatic rupture with past socialist principles, but they were also carefully designed to have the minimum possible impact on the domestic economy. Despite this cautious beginning, successive waves of reform saw China realign its currency, establish conditional trade-related convertibility and decentralize control over foreign trade corporations. Trade reform was followed by an acceleration of China's exports: in 1978, China accounted for only 0.75 per cent of total world exports; whereas by 1995, China accounted for 3.0 per cent. Rapid growth of trade combined with substantial devaluation pushed up the ratio of total trade to gross domestic product (GDP) from 10 per cent in 1978 to 44 per cent in 1994.

By the early 1990s, China had established what were, in essence, two separate trading regimes. The first was an export promotion regime, dominated by FIEs, which simply *bypassed* the old centralized monopoly. This regime has achieved a surprisingly high degree of openness: goods are today imported and exported with a minimum of administrative interference and usually without tariffs. However, most domestic firms do not have access to this trading regime. The second regime existing today was created by the reform, decentralization and realignment of the old centralized monopoly, and it defines the rules that apply to most firms in the domestic economy. There have been important reforms under this regime, but elements of the pre-reform monopoly also remain in place and the system remains predominantly one of import substitution, characterized by a wide variety of tariff and non-tariff barriers.

The difference between the two regimes was at a maximum around 1993. At that time, not only were legal provisions different but, in addition, firms under the two regimes converted currencies at different rates. Firms operating under the 'export processing' regime (see below) could use their foreign exchange earnings to purchase *yuan* (the domestic currency, also called *renminbi*) at the cheaper swap-market rate, while most firms under the import substitution regime converted foreign exchange to *yuan* at the overvalued official rate. As a result, the former firms had more profitable opportunities to export than did the latter. On 1 January 1994, the official exchange rate was devalued, and the exchange rate unified; firms under both regimes have since converted foreign exchange at the same rate. Moreover, some tax exemptions for foreign investors have been scaled back in the past few years, so that the difference between the two regimes has narrowed in other respects also. Nevertheless, as of late 1996, the fundamental features that defined the separate regimes were still in place, and the dualistic system still intact. However, it is most striking that as China has attempted to move towards a more transparent and open trading regime in recent years, in order to enter the WTO, issues related to the harmonization of the two trading regimes have assumed prominence in Chinese domestic policy debates. Outside China, most attention has been focused on China's promises to reduce tariff rates, but within China as much attention has been paid to attempts to reduce the separation between the two trading regimes, in order to move towards a more integrated trading system. Thus, while the trade regime today is not quite as bifurcated as it was in the early 1990s, the need to overcome that bifurcation is still among the most pressing requirements for a move to a more open economy.

The Export Promotion Regime

FIEs have played a key role in the growth of China's exports (Lardy 1992, 1995). Table 2.1 shows the rapid growth of Chinese exports and the share generated by FIEs, which reached 41 per cent during the first half of 1996. What is perhaps less frequently appreciated is the extent to which FIEs have operated under an entirely different set of institutions and regulations from those applied to most domestic enterprises. Most crucial is the simple freedom the FIE possesses to import and export on its own account: it is not required to use a state-owned FTC as an intermediary. In addition, FIEs enjoy a variety of tax exemptions and concessionary tax rates and are able to import raw materials, components and (until 1996–7) production machinery duty-free, as long as they are engaged in export production. They experience little interference with specific import and export decisions, and enjoy extremely favourable regulatory treatment.

Table 2.1 Exports: total value and share of foreign invested enterprises (FIEs)

Year	Total exports ($US billions)	Share of FIEs (percent)
1985	27.4	1.1
1986	30.9	1.9
1987	39.4	3.1
1988	47.5	5.2
1989	52.5	9.4
1990	62.1	12.6
1991	71.9	16.8
1992	85	20.4
1993	98	25.8
1994	121	28.7
1995	148.8	31.5
1996 – first half	64.06	40.8

Source: 1994 China Foreign Economic Statistical Yearbook, p. 164; *China's Customs Statistics*.

More specifically, the major characteristics of the export promotion regime include the following:

(i)   The authority to engage directly in import and export.
(ii) Duty-free import of raw materials and components for export production.
(iii) Duty-free import of investment goods (partially phased out between July 1996 and year-end 1997 but reinstated in modified form in 1998).
(iv) Concessionary income tax rates. The statutory income tax rate in China is 33 per cent (30 per cent national plus 3 per cent local income tax), but FIEs qualify for a variety of concessionary tax rates based on location (15 per cent in the five SEZs, and 15–18 per cent in approved development zones in other regions; 24 per cent in very large 'Open Coastal Zones' or the old urban districts in the fourteen 'Open Coastal Cities'). Moreover, firms designated as 'export orientated' are eligible for a further 50 per cent reduction in income tax rates, irrespective of location.
(v)   Significant tax holidays. Taxes are regularly remitted for the first two years of *profit-making operation*, and levied at 50 per cent of the final rate in the third to the fifth profitable year. (Losses made during start-up can be credited against profits to delay the onset of the first profit-making year.)
(vi) Competition among local jurisdictions to attract investment leads frequently to significant overt or implicit subsidies. Local jurisdictions have

been known to guarantee subsidized prices for land, utilities and certain kinds of inputs, and regularly collude with potential foreign investors to minimize central government taxation (Zweig, 1995).

None of these provisions is novel. All have been used elsewhere in East Asia, and around the world. However, the sheer scale on which these provisions were introduced in China is unprecedented. In most countries, such concessions have been circumscribed within a designated and strictly policed export-processing zone. In essence, China created a kind of gigantic export-processing zone, initially in the provinces of Guangdong and Fujian. Although China's 'Special Economic Zones' (SEZs) attracted a lot of attention and were located near important economic centres in southern coastal China, it was not the SEZs *per se* that defined this export processing area. Its boundaries were determined not geographically, but rather primarily by the juridical status of the enterprise. Export-orientated FIEs qualified, whether located in SEZs or elsewhere.

Indeed, the crucial policy innovation that led to the creation of this trade regime was not the SEZs, but rather the development of 'export processing' arrangements. Over almost twenty years, these arrangements have grown to be extremely important, and have evolved into two variants. The earliest variant, which can be traced back as far as 1978, I label 'processing materials' (*lailiao jiagong*). Under this variant, foreign businesses, usually based in Hong Kong, ship raw materials and components into China duty-free. Chinese enterprises are paid 'processing fees', and the completed goods are then shipped back to Hong Kong for any additional processing, packaging and re-export. In this variant, the Hong Kong business retains ownership over the commodities and makes all the arrangements. The Chinese production enterprises are usually domestically owned (accounting for 86 per cent of the export value under this provision in 1995), and simply sign contracts with the Hong Kong firm. The second variant developed in the 1980s, when FIEs were allowed to import their own materials duty-free if they were used for export production. This variant, which I label 'processing imports' (*jinliao jiagong*) is distinct in that the production firm within China assumes ownership of the materials and arranges its own import, export and production. FIEs accounted for 74 per cent of the export value under this provision in 1995. I will refer to both variants together as 'export processing'.

Export processing has grown rapidly, and accounted for 56 per cent of China's exports during the first half of 1996. Moreover, the 'processing imports' variant has grown in relative importance, and is now two and a half times as large as the 'processing materials' variant (see table 2.2). As a result, the categories of FIE exports and export processing exports now overlap to a considerable extent, although they are not identical. In the first half of 1996, export processing (of both variants) accounted for 86 per cent of FIE exports,

Table 2.2   Exports under export processing provisions (percentage of total value)

Year	Processing materials	Processing imports	Total
1988	13.7	13.5	27.2
1991	18.0	27.2	45.1
1993	17.4	30.8	48.2
1994	15.0	32.1	47.1
1995	13.9	35.7	49.5
1996–6 mos.	16.1	40.3	56.4

Source: World Bank, 1994, p. 12; *China's Customs Statistics*, 1993, no. 12, 1994, no. 12, 1995, no. 12, 1996, no. 6, p. 12.

Table 2.3   Percentage share of total Chinese imports brought in under concessionary terms

	Export processing		Subtotal: export processing	FIE investment goods	Other concessionary imports	Total concessionary imports
	Processing materials	Processing imports				
1988	13.4	11.5	24.9	5.1	n.a.	30.0
1991	17.1	22.1	39.2	7.4	1.4	48.0
1993	12.5	22.5	35.0	16.0	4.3	55.2
1994	13.1	28.0	41.1	17.5	3.5	62.1
1995	12.3	31.9	44.2	14.2	0.9	59.3
1996–6 m	12.6	32.5	45.1	15.3	0.9	61.3

Source: World Bank (1994), p. 59; *China's Customs Statistics*, 1993, no. 12, 1994, no. 12, 1995, no. 12; 1996, no. 6, p. 12.

and FIEs produced 63 per cent of all export processing exports (see *China Customs Statistics*, 1996, no. 6, p. 13). Imported materials and components brought in duty free accounted for 45 per cent of total imports in the first half of 1996, while investment equipment or materials brought in duty free as part of foreign investment accounted for another 15 per cent of imports (see table 2.3).

Pioneered in Guangdong during the early 1980s, export processing provisions were extended to most of China's coastal provinces after 1987 as part of Zhao Ziyang's 'coastal development strategy'. This policy was a response to China's economic challenges and opportunities at that time. The success of the East Asian newly industrializing economies was creating an immense opportunity for China. Both Hong Kong and Taiwan had become established as major exporters, and by the mid-1980s, export success was creating major new economic pressures. Domestic costs were already rising while persistent export surpluses began to create upward pressure on their currencies. As exporters in Hong Kong and Taiwan began to search for alternative production sites with lower costs, in particular, lower labour costs, a liberal investment and trade regime allowed China to emerge as the preferred alternative site for export-orientated production. At the same time, given the semi-reformed nature of the economy of the Peoples' Republic of China (PRC) during the mid-1980s, the government had to allow exporters exceptional latitude to import components and raw materials. The domestic supply system was unreliable and unable to adapt to the needs of foreign investors. Chinese policy sometimes called 'both ends outside' (*liangtou zaiwai*) because it implied that FIEs would find both suppliers and markets abroad, allowed exporters maximum freedom to import and export, and at the same time minimized the links between these new export-orientated factories and existing supply capacity in the Chinese economy.

Thus the creation of a separate export promotion regime should be seen as a pragmatic adaptation to the limitations and opportunities facing Chinese policy-makers during the 1980s. By minimizing the links between the externally-orientated sector and the bulk of the domestic economy, policy-makers allowed the export sector to surge ahead while maintaining their preferred strategy of gradualism in domestic economic reforms. Most domestic firms were at least partially insulated from world markets through the maintenance of the dual trading regime.

Import Substitution Regime

The trade regime, contrasting with that described above, consists of what the Chinese call 'ordinary trade'. Ordinary trade accounts for about half of China's exports but only a third of imports. Thus, ordinary trade is considerably smaller than might normally be supposed. China's ordinary imports in 1995 were $43 billion, or only 6 per cent of GDP in 1995, converted at official exchange rates. In this extremely restricted sense, then, the Chinese 'export market' for other countries is not very large. The moderate size of China's ordinary trade imports is plausibly connected to the significant tariff and non-tariff barriers; while these barriers have been reduced in recent years, they are still formidable.

A World Bank (1994) analysis of the Chinese tariff structure prevailing in 1992 reveals that China had one of the largest numbers of different tariff rates of any developing country (sixty-nine), as well as a relatively high average tariff level. The unweighted mean tariff was 43 per cent, and the trade-weighted mean tariff 32 per cent. These tariffs are high enough to classify the ordinary trade regime as one of import substitution. In April 1996, China brought down its unweighted mean tariff to 23 per cent; but despite the significant reductions, China still has the highest tariffs of any APEC member other than Thailand.

There are also significant non-tariff barriers (NTBs) that apply to transactions in the ordinary trade regime. On the surface, such barriers would appear to have been substantially reduced in recent years. In 1992, fifty-three large product categories, covering about 50 per cent of total imports, were subject to one or more of four different overlapping NTBs. By mid-1996, this had been formally reduced to twenty-eight large product categories subject to compulsory quotas and eight categories subject to compulsory canalization.[1] Today, roughly 20 per cent of China's imports are subject to these two formal controls, including most important raw materials and virtually all transport equipment. Despite substantial reduction in NTB coverage since 1992, any assessment of the extent of change remains ambiguous.

In part, this ambiguity is due to the fact that the Chinese have replaced formal NTBs with a variety of arrangements, including 'automatic registration' of some categories of imports, that have the potential to restrain trade informally. The impact of these informal arrangements must be considered in light of the institutional organization of the ordinary trade regime. Most important, ordinary trade transactions are still controlled by state-owned enterprises, usually foreign trade companies (FTCs), which accounted for 92 per cent of ordinary trade exports and 86 per cent of ordinary trade imports in 1995. These state-run FTCs have inherited some of the characteristics of the old state-run trade monopoly. On the one hand, there has been an enormous decentralization and diversification of FTCs, such that the number has increased to between six and seven thousand. On the other hand, each FTC has a specifically authorized scope of business, with designated product lines and regions of operation. Authority to import is carefully controlled and, to a certain extent, tariffs and NTBs are used in complementary fashion. Thus, many FTCs retain elements of market power over imports within their authorized scope of business.

For example, Dickson (1996) examines the way the import system works for finished steel, after the abolition of formal NTBs in early 1994. There are fifty-five local and three national FTCs authorized to import steel, but each of the local FTCs is restricted to one of forty-two specific localities. As a result, no locality has more than two FTCs authorized to import steel (the national FTCs do not generally supply 'local' users). Moreover, these local FTCs are in many cases the former affiliates of the national FTCs, spun off as independent businesses during the trade reforms of the 1980s. Informal co-ordination among local FTCs would be easy, and in any case all steel imports must now be 'registered'. Each local FTC thus possesses a degree of market power which is contingent upon its privileged ability to import steel, which is potentially revocable. Clearly, such trading companies have substantial incentives to accept informal guidance from national authorities on import quantities in exchange for continued monopoly-like privileges. Perhaps as a result, despite the abolition of NTBs in early 1994, finished steel imports fell in both 1994 and 1995, when they were less than half the 1993 level.

For certain imports, control of trade is still managed in a relatively centralized fashion. Large centrally-run FTCs that are direct descendants of the
former national monopoly companies still play a big role. Thus, in 1993, the
most recent year for which such a breakdown exists, ordinary imports were $38
billion, and FTCs directly subordinate to central government ministries
accounted for exactly half: $19 billion.[2] An American or Australian exporter
selling goods, particularly bulk goods and raw materials, to China may well be
forced to deal with a single customer: an FTC run by the central government.
The situation with regard to crucial raw materials and intermediate goods such
as steel is not typical of all imports, since these are large and closely monitored
imports, considered by the Chinese government to affect economic security.
For other commodities, there may be more competing FTCs with import rights,
and fewer NTBs. However, these commodities are often labour-intensive
manufactures, where relatively high – in some cases prohibitively high – tariffs
are sufficient to restrain imports. In any case, a constant feature of the ordinary
trade import regime is that state-owned FTCs play a gatekeeper role, maintaining an institutional barrier that separates the domestic and world markets.

The barriers on the import side inevitably affect the environment for
potential exporters in China. Production enterprises generally are poorly
informed about world market conditions, and must rely on information con-
veyed to them by FTCs. Competition among FTCs is much greater for exports
than for imports, and in regions and commodities in which competition
among FTCs is fierce, production enterprises can get a good price simply by
selling to the highest FTC bidder. But in many regions, and for many commodities, markets will not achieve this level of efficiency. More generally,
because the ordinary trade regime constrains exporters to a single organizational form, competing and potentially more efficient organizational arrangements are forgone. Some indication of the extent of the problem is given in an
(admittedly old) survey of exporters in 1988 (He, 1989). This survey reported
that among production enterprises considered important export producers,
the proportion of enterprises reporting that they 'basically do not know' certain
facts was as shown in Table 2.4. The survey was undertaken in a region of China
in which access to information about the world economy is relatively good.

The final element necessary for an assessment of the ordinary trade regime
is the fact that actual tariff collections are a small proportion of nominal
tariffs. That is, even after account is taken of the large proportion of imports
entering China on concessional terms, the actual tariff collection rate runs
substantially below what the nominal tariff schedule would seem to indicate.
As Table 2.5 shows, the actual tariff take has been a small and declining
proportion of import values. Comparison with Table 2.3 indicates that, under
plausible assumptions about the distribution of the tariff burden, the share of
concessional imports, though large, is not large enough to account for the
entire difference between nominal and actual tariff revenues (see p. 35 above).

Table 2.4   Results of survey 1988

	Shanghai	Jiangsu
	Percentage of total respondents without information on:	
Competitors' foreign market price	88	90
Foreign market price of own product	69	76
Competitors' technology	78	73
Competitors' quality	91	95
Own world market share	92	95
Changes in world demand	88	81

Notes: Number of enterprises questioned: Shanghai 545; Jiangsu 145.

Table 2.5   Actual duty collection rate
(all duties as percentage of total value of imports)

Year	Percentage
1986	9.7
1989	8.4
1990	6.3
1991	5.6
1992	5.6
1993	5.9
1994	4.0

Source: World Bank, 1994, p. 60; Wang, 1996, p. 23.

No breakdown of tariff concessions by product category is available, but there is abundant anecdotal evidence of tariff concessions given to domestic investment projects, particularly those with central government support. It appears that a significant proportion of capital goods enter China without significant duties, even though they do not fall into formal concessionary categories. In these cases, the import decision is made administratively, based on government agencies' determination of need. More generally, the conclusion is unavoidable that Chinese imports are not regulated primarily by tariffs, but rather by a combination of tariffs, quotas for some items, and administrative guidance exercised over state-owned trading companies.

Interactions between Trading Regime and Ownership or Region

The fundamental principle according to which trade transactions are apportioned to one trade regime or another is the identity of the trading enterprise.

All FIEs are able to take advantage of the more liberal provisions. Some domestic enterprises are also eligible, but eligibility for domestic enterprises is both less common and less automatic: that is, less subject to a clear set of eligibility requirements. Moreover, access to the liberal trading regime differs significantly by province. There are thus a complex set of interactions among trading regimes, ownership of firms, and regional factors.

Trading Regime and Ownership

Because of the connection between ownership and access to the export promotion regime, there is a strong correlation between trading regime and firm ownership. We have already noted the prominent role that FIEs have played in China's export drive. Other authors have noted that China's township and village enterprises (TVEs) have played increasingly prominent roles in China's foreign trade. One particularly impressive set of statistics shows TVEs selling export commodities equivalent in value to 9.3 per cent of exports in 1986, increasing to 32.6 per cent in 1994 (*Township and Village Enterprise Yearbook*, 1995, p. 100). The success of these ownership forms has been contrasted with the less prominent role of State-owned Enterprises (SOEs) to produce an explanation of China's export success. For example, Lardy (1992, pp. 129–30, 143) argues that 'entrepreneurial firms', including FIEs and TVEs, but excluding SOEs, have been responsible for most of the export growth. By contrast, China's existing SOEs have not been able to take advantage of export opportunities to a commensurate extent.

There is an important element of truth in this explanation, but the emphasis on entrepreneurial firms can also be misleading. In the first place, the data on TVE exports that have been used are misleading, and can be better interpreted in light of the preceding discussion. Taking the numbers at face value would imply that TVEs were responsible for about 40 per cent of the increment in exports between 1986 and 1994. Corresponding numbers for FIEs (given in Table 2.1) imply that FIEs were responsible for 38 per cent of incremental exports. It is on such comparisons that the argument for entrepreneurial firms is based.

However, closer inspection of the numbers reveals a picture of much greater institutional complexity. The numbers for TVE exports include production carried out by foreign-invested TVEs (which will already have been included in FIE export data), as well as export-related production carried out by TVEs that are sub-contracting for SOEs. Available data enable us to calculate roughly the shares of each of these types of export production. Of total TVE export production in 1994, more than half came through these co-operative relations: about 30 per cent was produced by foreign-invested firms, and 22.5 per cent was produced under sub-contracting arrangements.[3] Moreover, each of these arrangements has grown considerably more rapidly than TVE exports as a whole. We can use these data to calculate rough shares of contributions to export growth by ownership and institutional form. Between 1986 and 1994, TVEs on their own accounted for about 18 per cent of incremental exports (not counting foreign-invested TVEs or sub-contracting with SOEs); TVEs sub-contracting with SOEs accounted for 9 per cent, while foreign-invested TVEs accounted for 13 per cent. This last figure, in turn, equals about a third of the FIE contribution to incremental exports. Indeed, the total FIE contribution breaks down neatly into thirds: a third joint ventures with TVEs (13 per cent of the increment); a third wholly-owned subsidiaries of foreign companies (12.5 per cent of the increment); and a third joint ventures with SOEs (12 per cent of the increment). By subtraction, and assuming that private urban businesses do not export, SOEs on their own accounted for 35 per cent of incremental exports (or 44 per cent if we include the value sub-contracted to TVEs). All forms of ownership have contributed to China's export success, in patterns that are consistent with their degree of access to liberal trading regimes. SOEs, in particular, have played an important role in supporting export growth, as they have in other areas of China's transitional economy.

The figures in the preceding paragraph are of more than purely academic interest, because they illuminate one of the key features of China's trade reform. Liberalization of the ordinary trade regime was limited, as stressed in the previous section; but liberalization proceeded far enough to create substantial incentives to export. Export-oriented SOEs and FTCs found themselves in significant competition, and with real incentives. Under pressure to control costs, they turned increasingly to TVEs, which faced real factor costs much more in line with China's underlying endowments than did SOEs. A key feature of the increasing prominence of TVEs has been the remarkable institutional flexibility which the growth of the sector permitted. Engaging in joint ventures, co-production, and sub-contracting with urban SOEs *and* foreign investors, TVEs contributed to the emergence of an array of hybrid institutional forms that were able to exploit the provisions of the existing system, and grow 'through the cracks'. We miss this institutional diversity if we simply attribute all export growth in which TVEs are involved to a generalized entrepreneurial impulse.

This perspective can also illuminate the behaviour of SOEs under the dual trading regime. SOEs in general have never had anything like the access to export markets that FIEs routinely have. In fact, for those SOEs that are attracted to export opportunities, the dual system creates a peculiar set of incentives. In essence, the rational course of action for a domestic firm that seeks to export is to establish a joint venture (JV) subsidiary with a foreign partner. This has tremendous benefits for Chinese domestic firms. Automatically, the subsidiary JV achieves access to all the trading privileges described above, including favourable financial treatment and the ability to import and export fairly freely. In addition, in the Chinese legal context, the JV has a presumption of managerial autonomy, giving it much more freedom from bureaucratic overseers than the SOE is ordinarily entitled to expect. Indeed, this combination of domestic and foreign trading flexibility has important benefits for the parent enterprise. Consider, as an example, a domestic garment factory visited in the early 1990s in the greater Shanghai region. This SOE had direct-export authority, but was subject to obstacles and delays in importing good quality zippers for its export clothing. Its strategy to escape from this and numerous other obstacles was to establish a JV subsidiary in Shenzhen. The subsidiary could freely import zippers, which were then easily diverted to the parent enterprise, enabling it to produce export-quality garments. In turn, the SOE diverted resources and markets to the Shenzhen subsidiary, in order to enjoy lower profit taxes and greater managerial autonomy. The JV option allowed the SOE to meet world quality standards and probably allowed it to increase its own exports. At the same time, the SOE had strong incentives to channel the bulk of the increase in exports into its JV subsidiary. Similar incentives are at work for nearly all domestic Chinese enterprises. Indeed, the benefit of being a joint venture has been significant enough that there are reports of domestic enterprises granting 25 per cent stakes to their contacts in Hong Kong merely to qualify as joint ventures (25 per cent is the minimum required foreign stake).[4]

The same incentive structure stimulates 'round-tripping', in which Chinese firms establish Hong Kong subsidiaries that invest back in China. There is no doubt that this is a significant phenomenon, though few hard data are available. One fragmentary piece of data (reported in Tian, 1994, pp. 335–56) is that 15 per cent of realized foreign investment in Shanghai during 1980–92 came from Chinese firms' subsidiaries in Hong Kong. This was just under a third of total Hong Kong investment in Shanghai.[5] If Chinese subsidiaries account for anywhere near this share of total Hong Kong investment in China, tens of billions of dollars would be involved in round-trip investment.

The behaviour of SOEs represents a special case of the general observation that trade promotion policies of the type the Chinese have adopted combine trade creating and trade diverting elements. In addition to their obvious utility in creating new trade opportunities, concessionary measures have also tended to divert trade growth from existing SOEs towards the new JV sector. At the same time, the flexibility provided to the enterprises eligible for concessionary treatment unquestionably enhanced the flexibility and productivity of the economy as a whole. Domestic enterprises learned to 'work the system' and to obtain many of the benefits of the export promotion policies.

Trading Regime and Region

There are also significant interactions between the trading regime and regional development. Guangdong and Fujian provinces participate in the more liberal trading regime to a much greater degree than other provinces. Conceptually, this is true, for three reasons. First, these two provinces were granted significant autonomy early in the reform process. This gave them the ability to expand the number of trading companies, and to interpret eligibility for concessional treatment in an extremely liberal fashion. Second, these two provinces were the sites of the four initial Special Economic Zones (SEZs), which enjoyed additional concessionary benefits. Since the SEZs were large and relatively loosely policed, benefits from the SEZs tended to spill over into the surrounding region. Finally, these two provinces were, of course, selected for special treatment precisely because of their proximity to potential investors in Hong Kong and Taiwan. Thus, even without special treatment, foreign investment would have been more important in these provinces than in other parts of China.

Early autonomy had a significant impact on the evolution of the Guangdong economy. Guangdong had the authority to set up its own FTCs, and in fact set up many more provincial FTCs than any other province. It had fewer central government constraints on overall imports, and more authority to determine its own import targets, including imports of consumer goods (generally restricted in the rest of China). Finally, the province's obligation to turn over foreign exchange to the central government was quite modest given the scale of the province's trade (Tian, 1994). Foreign exchange circulated much more freely in Guangdong than elsewhere, with the Hong Kong dollar serving as a quasi-official currency through much of the late 1980s.

Moreover, the impact of the liberal legal provisions prevailing in those provinces has been increased by the ease with which they can be abused. Goods can be moved into China under concessionary provisions, even when they are not strictly eligible. Such goods can then be diverted to other enterprises or sold on the open market. On occasion, local customs officials have a great deal of discretion over effective duty rates, and there may be bargaining over tax rates and attempts to influence the outcome. Many foreign businessmen have reported their surprise at seeing goods produced by their own companies for sale in China, through unauthorized distributors, at prices substantially below the international price plus nominal tariff duty on the good. There are even businesses in Hong Kong – called 'channel providers' – that specialize in providing these low-cost import services. One side-effect of the relatively porous system is that Chinese statistics on imports of materials and components for export processing are probably substantially overstated, and include a significant amount of goods subsequently diverted to other uses.

Smuggling is also significant. An official Hong Kong government estimate from the early 1990s was that goods smuggled into China equal about 15 per cent of the value of legal trade from Hong Kong to China (Huang, 1993, p. 39). Given that legal exports from Hong Kong to China in 1995 totaled

US$58 billion, that would imply a smuggling trade of over $8 billion. Virtually all foreign cigarettes sold in China are smuggled, and one reasonably well-educated guess of the value of smuggled cigarettes in 1990 was $500 million. A similar situation prevails for video cassette recorders (VCRs). In the first half of 1991, China produced 60 000 VCRs. None were legally imported, but 1.19 million were sold domestically (Huang, 1993, pp. 36, 38). Other consumer electronics products also are widely smuggled, with personal computers being a particular focus of interest in recent years.

The preceding factors imply that the separation between the liberal trading regime that FIEs enjoy and the import substitution regime under which most domestic enterprises labour is not absolute. There is substantial leakage from the open economy to the remainder of the domestic economy, and this leakage is especially important in Guangdong and Fujian. Indeed, these provinces, particularly Guangdong, can almost be said to operate predominantly under the open export-processing regime. One result is that the importance of foreign trade in the most open provinces is qualitatively different from that in the remainder of China. Figure 2.1 shows the export ratios of China's provinces for 1994 and each province's share of national GDP is shown after the province's name. Guangdong is quite unlike the rest of

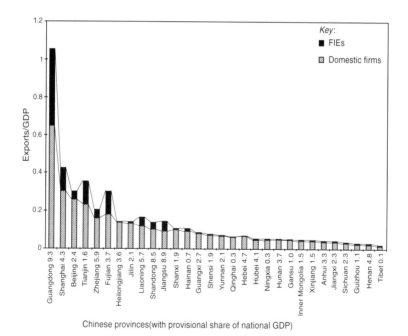

Figure 2.1   Provincial exports ratios, 1994

China: exports were 106 per cent of GDP, compared with 14 per cent in China excluding Guangdong.

At the same time, the concentration of foreign investment and export potential in Guangdong has already peaked, and will probably continue to decline. In 1990, Guangdong accounted for fully 70 per cent of all FIE exports; by the first quarter of 1996 notwithstanding spectacular growth, the share had declined to 52 per cent. Fujian has similarly seen a decline, from 12 per cent to 7 per cent. Foreign investment has moved up the coast, and two regions have expanded their shares of FIE exports noticeably during the same period: the *Jiangnan* or Greater Shanghai region, which has increased its share from 9 per cent to 19 per cent; and the provinces around the Bohai Gulf (Liaoning, Shandong and Tianjin) which have increased their share from 6 per cent to 16 per cent, largely because of Japanese investment.

Some Implications of the Analytical Framework

China's dramatic export growth becomes more understandable if we understand its development in light of the dual trade regime. Exports responded to dramatic policy liberalization, but this was a liberalization that the Chinese regime was willing to adopt precisely because it remained circumscribed by region and by enterprise status (primarily ownership status). Moreover, the export success was possible because external conditions were ripe for a rapid transfer of export production, from Hong Kong and Taiwan especially, to the Chinese mainland.

If these institutional considerations are not taken into account, aggregate statistics tend to give a misleading impression of China's openness to foreign trade. The argument here is distinct from, and complementary to, that of those who argue that China's trade ratio is overstated because GNP is understated from a purchasing power parity standpoint. (Rough purchasing power parity conversions yield a much larger US dollar GNP than do exchange-rate conversions: see Lardy, 1995, for discussion). Here, the argument is not that the numbers are inaccurate, but simply that they could easily be misleading. Simple calculation of China's export/GDP ratio (using prevailing exchange rates) in 1994 yields a ratio of 22 per cent; but, as noted above, if Guangdong is excluded the ratio drops to 14 per cent. Of course, Guangdong is part of China and ought to be included in the calculation – but our interpretation of the phenomenon will be altered if we take into account the wide regional variation; and this is even more true when we recognize that the regional variation is itself deeply entwined with variation in trading regimes and ownership patterns. The more important generalization may be that, if the export promotion regime is put to one side, China's openness to foreign trade remains modest and still subject to numerous restrictions.

The particular set of policies that led to dramatic export success, have also limited the benefits and brought some associated problems. First, of course, is that the particular form of export expansion has meant somewhat fewer (though still considerable) benefits to the Chinese domestic economy than could have been realised. Margins on export production under the export promotion regime are quite modest: Chinese sources regularly argue that only 10–20 per cent of the value of 'processing' exports represents value added within China. Since import content is high, and marketing networks are controlled by Hong Kong, Taiwan and developed-country firms, the argument is at least plausible. (As indicated above, however, the figures on which such assertions are based are suspect: there are clear incentives to overstate values of imported inputs and to understate values of resulting exports.) Moreover, linkages from the export sector to the remainder of the Chinese economy remain modest, precisely because the incentives to source from outside China are so favourable. Additionally, the tax take from the export sector is very small.

Finally, the combination of rapid export growth and moderate import growth has created large trade surpluses with the USA, and resultant trade tension (see Fung and Lau, 1996, for an analysis of the trade figures). In fact, the US deficit with China has virtually no direct economic impact in the USA, since almost no domestic US producers have been displaced by Chinese exporters – the USA long ago stopped producing most of the goods currently imported from China, and imports from China are now mainly replacing earlier imports from Hong Kong and Taiwan (Noland, 1996). But the current configuration of trade has had the ironic, and largely undesirable, effect of a redistribution of US deficits from Hong Kong and Taiwan, with which the USA has generally smooth relations, to China, with whom relations have been consistently troubled since 1989. To the extent that there are political concerns with the deficit in the USA, they seem to be driven largely by fears about the future: a worry that China will emerge as a huge 'neo-mercantilist' state piling up enormous global trade surpluses (Mastel, 1995). Such concerns seem to reflect the contrasting experiences from China's two different trade regimes: on the one hand, rapid Chinese export growth from the export promotion regimes and, on the other hand, continued difficulties in expanding US exports under the still significantly protected import substitution regime. These perceptions undermine the political benefits that ought to flow from the enormously mutually beneficial exchange between China and the USA.

2 FUTURE CHALLENGES AND PROSPECTS

As China moves to further liberalize and open its economy, and particularly as it seeks to enter the WTO, it is clear that it needs to address not only the general problems associated with trade liberalization, but also some specific issues associated with the existing bifurcated trade regime. Future trends can best be considered under three headings: national treatment, exchange rate management, and an effective system of tariffs.

National Treatment

Entry into the WTO includes the acceptance of the principle of national treatment, which requires that foreign firms be treated no less favourably than domestic firms. Clearly, there is significant tension between the principle of national treatment and the principles on which the Chinese trading regime is founded, since full access to the export promotion regime is granted only to foreign-invested firms. The preceding discussion has emphasized the privileges FIEs receive under the dual trading regime, but it is certainly true that the preferences FIEs receive in many areas are also offset to some extent by a series of restrictions on their autonomy and on the areas in which they may operate. Whole areas of the Chinese economy are off-limits to foreign firms. Compliance with WTO rules will require the removal of numerous discriminatory regulations that restrict FIEs. The most important of these are:

(i)   The right to establish an FIE is strictly guarded by the Ministry of Foreign Trade and Economic Co-operation (MOFTEC). Foreign investment projects are approved on a case-by-case basis, and only in line with policy guidelines established by the government.

(ii) All FIEs are subject to a number of explicit requirements with respect to foreign exchange earnings, access to the domestic market, and local content of production.

(iii) Access to the legal system is quite difficult in general, and systematically different for FIEs; there are a large number of 'internal' regulations to which FIEs do not have regular access (Zhu, 1996).

Changing these provisions will require a very large change in the way the Chinese government is accustomed to doing business. In theory, China could join the WTO under a regime in which FIEs enjoyed only privileges and no handicaps. But, in practice, this is inconceivable: in China, as in any country, a legal regime that discriminated across the board against domestic firms would not be politically acceptable.

Exchange Rate Management

The devaluation and the unification of exchange rates in January 1994 have been a huge, and unexpected, success. Equilibrium was established in the market for foreign exchange, and the currency has been subject to a managed float since 1994. Current-account convertibility was achieved by the end of 1996. The massive inflow of foreign investment since 1992, has combined with devaluation to create a new environment within which Chinese policy reform can proceed. On the one hand, foreign investment has been responsible for both a large increase in exports and a very substantial upgrading of the quality of import-competing goods in the Chinese economy. Early in the reform period, it appeared that demand for foreign goods was insatiable, and reformers acted as if no exchange rate could equilibrate supply and demand for foreign currency. However, the quality differential between domestic and world-market goods is no longer as large as it once was, as any repeat visitor to China can readily attest. Allowing for the continuing import restrictions, the 1994 devaluation unexpectedly created a price for foreign currency that emerged as a stable equilibrium; and now, the continued influx of investment, combined with successful export growth, is even beginning to create problems of currency *appreciation* for China.

Figure 2.2 displays the long-range development of the Chinese real exchange rate: very substantial real depreciation between 1980 and 1987 underlies the Chinese export expansion, and the 1994 devaluation brought the official rate to its lowest real value ever. Figure 2.2 also shows the swap market rate for the 1987–93 period, and that the devaluation of 1994 brought

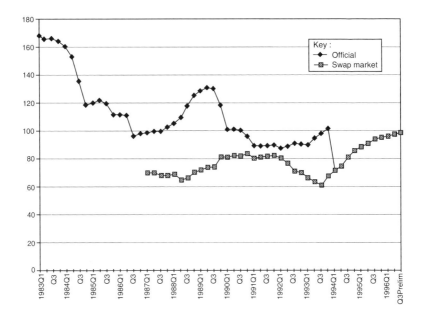

Figure 2.2   Real bilateral exchange rate: US$ per yuan, 1987 = 100

Percentage increase over one year earlier (3-month moving average)

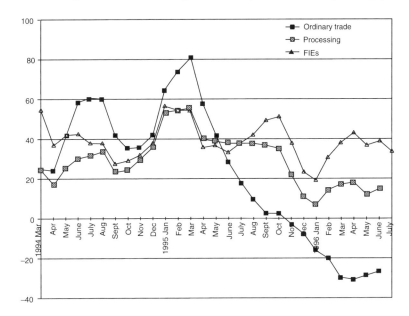

Figure 2.3 Export growth rates: by trade regime and ownership

the unified rate down to the swap market rate, at least initially. Ordinary trade responded sharply: during 1994, ordinary exports surged by 42.5 per cent, well above trend (see Figure 2.3). However, enterprises under the export promotion regime are relatively insensitive to currency fluctuations and since links with the domestic economy are attenuated and local costs are a small part of total export costs, currency fluctuations have a very modest impact. The 1994 unification of the exchange rate was in any case not a devaluation for the export promotion sector, since it already transacted predominantly on the secondary 'swap market'. In fact, exports produced by processing imports did not deviate from their long-run growth trend, posting a 37 per cent increase in 1994. Imports under both regimes responded in mirror image: ordinary trade imports fell by 6.6 per cent, while export processing imports maintained their rapid long-run growth trend.

By 1996, real appreciation was affecting export performance – again asymmetrically by regime. Cumulative domestic inflation of more than 40 per cent has led to a substantial real appreciation of the exchange rate. Despite substantial accumulation of reserves by the government (which were expected at the time of writing to surpass US$100 billion at end-1996), the nominal value of the renminbi (RMB) has drifted slightly upward, further contributing to real appreciation. Indeed, the real exchange rate is now higher than the secondary market rate has ever been, by a substantial margin, and equal to the official rate in 1987. Again, ordinary trade has shown itself to be highly sensitive: ordinary exports declined by 29 per cent in the first half of 1996. The effect on FIE exports, as Figure 2.3 shows, was barely perceptible. Even though the effective appreciation – relative to historic patterns – has been more pronounced for processing exporters, they are relatively insensitive because of the limited share of domestic currency costs in total costs.

More broadly, the experience with exchange rate management since 1994 throws into relief both the accomplishments of Chinese policy-makers and the continuing challenges facing them. While import substitution remains substantial, access to domestic markets granted to FIEs is now also significant. Foreign capital inflows combined with import restrictions unavoidably create upward pressure on the currency that undermines the competitiveness of exporters. While processing exporters have been immune to this effect so far, they have certainly experienced cost increases that have reduced their margins. As the trade regime is progressively unified and the exchange regime opened, fluctuations in capital flows will create difficulties in exchange-rate management. Since the inflow of investment to China is large, variations in the rate of flow are also likely to be large. Even more crucially, China is still a long way from having a stable set of monetary institutions. Inflation has been moderately high and fluctuating during the past few years, and most observers see continuing fragility in the financial system. If financial problems emerge, they will certainly spill over on to the exchange rate. China is unlikely to be able to maintain the extremely focused and stable exchange rate policies that characterized the East Asian 'miracle' economies during their export expansion phases.

Tariff System

With respect to tariffs, China faces a dual challenge. Nominal tariffs must be reduced and made more uniform; but the actual tax take should probably be increased through the elimination of special exemptions and the gradual phasing out of some (but not all) of the concessionary programmes. In fact, since 1995, China has adopted a series of measures designed gradually to unify the two trading regimes. In a number of cases, these changes have had the effect of reducing the preferences available to encourage foreign investment and exports. This can usually be explained by the need to increase tax revenues, to the sense that exports have grown enough in recent years and perhaps to the fear that further accumulation of reserves could exacerbate trade tensions with the USA.

The most important of these measures include:

(i) Eliminating the exemption from duty of capital goods brought in for foreign investment (To be phased out in 1996–7).
(ii) Requiring improved auditing of materials imported for export production (early 1996).
(iii) Lowering nominal tariffs from a trade-weighted average of 35.9 per cent to 23 per cent (April 1996).
(iv) Reducing the VAT drawback rate for exports (1995 and 1996).
(v) Establishing the principle that import duties should not be remitted (April 1996).

Some of the measures may prove to have been driven more by short-term revenue considerations than by the vision of an optimal trade-policy reform. However, they do throw into relief fundamental facts about Chinese reform in the run-up to WTO membership. Tariff reductions will need to be matched with increases in the extent to which tariffs are collected, and in the extent to which they regulate the volume of imports. Unification of China's bifurcated trading regime will be part of future trade-policy reform. While this reform generally will increase China's integration into the world economy, many of the specific measures may reduce incentives to export in the short term, and may tend to bring the rate of export growth down somewhat from the explosive growth of the late 1980s and early 1990s. This is particularly important given that real exchange rate appreciation between 1994 and 1996 has already begun to eat into export growth rates.

3 CONCLUSION

The dual trading regime is an effective framework within which to analyse both the past experience of Chinese trade growth and the prospects for future reform. That framework helps to explain the relevant institutional facts, including the differential performance of different ownership systems, and the enthusiasm which Chinese firms show for joint ventures and 'round-trip' investments through Hong Kong. In this sense, it is an analytic framework superior to one based on 'entrepreneurial firms', which implies that microeconomic characteristics related to ownership are sufficient to explain differential success, but neglects the differential access to trading opportunities, which varies systematically with ownership. The dual regime framework also performs well when changes in exchange rates and export response elasticities are being examined: the very different behaviour of flows under the two trade regimes indicates that this is the appropriate framework for analysis.

In a different fashion, the dual trading regime framework is also superior to interpretations that see China as an emerging neo-mercantilist power. For example, Mastel (1995) sees the combination of import restrictions and export promotion as indicating a regime in which the government systematically builds trade surpluses and protects strategic domestic industries. This viewpoint gives insufficient importance to the fact that the Chinese system – unlike those of Japan or Korea in their rapid growth periods – relies on FIEs to play a crucial role, not only in producing exports but also in importing and exporting commodities and, increasingly, in producing for the Chinese market. The Chinese government in some respects has less control over physical trade flows than did the earlier-developing East Asian 'miracles'. It makes more sense to see the coexistence of export promotion and import protection in the Chinese case as a transitional stage, designed to open an economy that was initially highly distorted, than as the opening stage of a emerging neo-mercantilist state.

China's movement towards an integrated, more liberal, trading regime must obviously proceed from within the context of the existing dual trade regime. Because of the unique institutional characteristics of China's current regime, outside observers should monitor progress in a number of different areas. Even with good intentions, trade liberalizations often fail, and it is useful to have benchmarks for measuring the progress of Chinese reforms. At the current stage of reform, reduction in nominal tariff rates is less sensitive (and therefore less useful as a benchmark) than it would be in an alternative regime where tariffs really governed imports. By contrast, more attention needs to be paid to NTBs, and especially to the preservation or dismantling of a monopoly framework for imports. In this context, one of the most important developments in 1996 was that China agreed to the formation, in Shanghai's Pudong Special Zone, of three foreign-invested FTCs. Investors from Japan, Korea and Germany are thus allowed to form joint ventures with existing Chinese FTCs. While it remains to be seen how much leeway these FIEs will have in practice, this is a potentially important crack in the institutional barriers separating the Chinese and world markets.[6]

Finally, it should be stressed that China's future trade reform will certainly lead in the direction of a more integrated trading regime. However, the extent to which movement in this direction will be accompanied by an across-the-board increase in the openness of the Chinese economy is still uncertain. In principle, it is conceivable that integration of the trading regimes could occur in a way that actually reduces the overall level of openness, if too much stress is put on scaling back the privileges that FIEs enjoy under the export promotion regime. In any case, the integrated system will not *necessarily* take on the highly open characteristics of the existing export-processing regime. In practice, government revenue considerations are likely to play an important role in shaping the specific pattern of trade reform. Because foreign trade is already large, growing rapidly, and lightly taxed, it is a tempting target for a Chinese government that is undergoing a serious fiscal crisis. In 1994, actual import duties in China were only 11.4 per cent of central government revenue. This compares with a developing country average of 29 per cent (and an Asian developing country average of 31 per cent) in the sample of Burgess and Stern (1993). If China does adopt a regime in which trade is moderately taxed, but in which investment inflows continue to keep real exchange rates high, we may expect export growth to decelerate significantly. Within China, in addition to the usual interest groups that seek the maintenance of protection, there are also political and economic groups that express resentment about special privileges enjoyed by foreign investors and coastal regions. Demands for a 'level playing field' will make the impetus for an integrated trade regime stronger, but also make it harder to predict the degree of openness into which the system will evolve. The most desirable outcome from an economic standpoint would come from a political alliance between groups favouring a level playing field and groups confident that they can exploit opportunities in the world market. In this case, an integrated trade regime could achieve a high degree of openness and lead to further integration of China into the world economy.

Notes

1. Canalization refers to the requirement that a given import be handled only by specific FTCs designated by the central government: this could be a monopolist ('single desk') or a larger number. For 1992, see World Bank (1994), especially pp. 63–7 and 82–84. Two categories of formal NTBs have been eliminated between 1992 and 1996: compulsory import planning and a separate list of machinery products for which importation was forbidden. For 1996, see 'China Adjusts Catalogue of Import Licensing', *China Economic News* (1996) Supplement No. 7 (19 August), pp. 1–16. Compare the discussion in United States Trade Representative (1996), pp. 47–8.
2. *China Customs Yearbook* (1993), pp. 150–1 and 157. The largest importers in 1993 were the Metal and Ores Import Export Corporation ($3 bn); the Chemical Import Export Corporation ($2.5 bn); the Technology Import Export Corporation ($1.4 bn); and Cearoils, the grain monopoly trader ($0.88 bn).
3. The basic data are collected by the township and village enterprise division of the Ministry of Agriculture, based on reports by production enterprises. Moreover, data are reported as domestic currency sales. As a result, the connection with actual export flows is considerably looser than is the case with the other trade data used in this chapter, which come from Customs Offices. The *Township and Village Enterprise (TVE) Yearbook* (1994), p. 376, reports 73.7 billion yuan as production of export commodities by foreign-invested TVEs. For all TVEs, export commodities sold to FTCs or directly exported (219.3 billion yuan) were 85.6 per cent of total production of export commodities (256 billion yuan).

Assuming the same ratio holds for foreign-invested TVEs, and that foreign-invested TVEs do no indirect exporting, foreign-invested TVEs accounted for 29 per cent of total TVE exports in 1993, and, given the extremely rapid growth of FIE exports, assuming 30 per cent for 1994 is quite conservative. Figures for 'indirect exports,' which refer to subcontracting relationships are given in *TVE Yearbook* (1995), p. 101. See also Zhang (1996), p. 36.

4. But this argument should not be exaggerated. In the aggregate, the foreign partners hold 63 per cent of the registered capital in the JV sector nationwide; and 71 per cent in Guangdong (*Statistical Yearbook of China*, (1995) p. 558). Overall, then, FIEs are predominantly foreign-managed, notwithstanding the presence of significant numbers of domestically-managed firms with minority foreign investment.

5. It should be noted that some Chinese firms have been resident in Hong Kong since 1949, and have a strong economic presence there. These firms have followed other Hong Kong firms in extending operations back in the PRC. Thus, not all such investment is covert round-tripping by any means. However, all export production from such investments is included in the FIE total.

6. 'See China Opens a New Possibility of Joint Venture Trading Companies', *China Economic News* (1996), no. 23 (24 June), pp. 15–16. One of the motivations for China to engage in such joint ventures is that they hope to develop some of their FTCs into global actors, like the Japanese general trading companies.

References

Burgess, R. and N. Stern (1993) 'Taxation and Development', *Journal of Economic Literature* vol. 31, June, pp. 762–830.

China's Customs Statistics, monthly (Beijing: Haiguan Zongzhu).

China Customs Yearbook [*Zhongguo Haiguan Tongji Nianjian*] (Beijing: Haiguan Zongzhu).

China External Economics Statistical Yearbook [*Zhongguo Duiwai Jingji Tongji Nianjian*] (Beijing: Zhongguo Tongji).

Dickson, I. (1996) 'China's Steel Imports: An Outline of Recent Trade Barriers', University of Adelaide, Chinese Economic Research Unit, Working Paper 96/6.

Fung, K. C. and L. Lau (1996) 'How Large is the US Deficit with China?', Stanford University Asia Pacific Research Center, Working Paper.

He, Peihai (1989) 'A Tentative Discussion of Light Industry's Role in the Structural Adjustment of the Coastal Development Strategy', *Gongye Jingji Guanli Congkan*, no. 2, p. 13.

Huang, W. (1993) *Zhongguo Yinxing Jingji* [*China's Hidden Economy*] (Beijing: Zhongguo Shangye).

Lardy, N. (1992) *Foreign Trade and Economic Reform in China, 1978–1990* (New York: Cambridge University Press).

Lardy, N. (1995) 'The Role of Foreign Trade and Investment in China's Economic Transformation', *The China Quarterly*, no. 144, December, pp. 1065–82.

Mastel, G. (1995) *Trading with the Middle Kingdom* (Washington, DC: Economic Strategy Institute).

Noland, M. (1996) 'US–China Economic Relations', (Asia Pacific Economic Cooperation Working Paper 96–6, Institute for International Economics, Washington, DC).

Pomfret, R. (1991) *Investing in China: Ten Years of the Open Door Policy* (Hemel Hempstead: Harvester Wheatsheaf).

Statistical Yearbook of China, [*Zhongguo Tongji Nianjian*] (Beijing: Zhongguo Tongji).

Tian, G. (1994) 'Shanghai's Role in China's Economic Development 1979–1992', Unpublished Ph.D. dissertation, Macquarie University, Sydney.

Township and Village Enterprise (TVE) Yearbook [*Zhongguo Xiangzhen Qiye Nianjian*] (Beijing: Zhongguo Nongye)

United States Trade Representative (1996) *1966 National Trade Estimate Report on Foreign Trade Barriers* (Washington, DC: US Government Printing Office).

Wang, Y. (1996) 'Analysis of Foreign Trade Trends in 1996 and Appropriate Policies', *Guoji Maoyi Wenti* [*Problems of International Trade*], 1996, no. 4, pp. 21–5, 32.

World Bank (1994) *China: Foreign Trade Reform* (Washington, DC: World Bank).

Zhang, Wei (1996) 'Trade Liberalisation and the Development of China's Township and Village Enterprises', *Guoji Maoyi Weni* [*Issues in Foreign Trade*], 1996, no. 2, pp. 34–40.

Zhu, L. (1996) 'Inward Foreign Investment and National Treatment', *Guoji Maoyi* [*Intertrade*] 1996, no. 1, pp. 27–9.

Zweig, D. (1995) ' "Developmental Communities" on China's Coast: The Impact of Trade, Investment, and Transnational Alliances', *Comparative Politics*, April, pp. 253–74.

Comment

Wen Hai
BEIJING UNIVERSITY

A part of China's successful reforms is due to its 'open door' policy. In less than twenty years China has grown from the 32nd to the world's tenth largest trading country and has been the second largest (after the USA) recipient of foreign direct investment (FDI) in recent years. On the other hand, China has often been criticised for being a highly protected economy that discriminates against foreign goods, services and investment. China's inability to join the WTO – as not satisfying membership requirements – is an illustration of this international criticism.

Why does China have such different policies towards its external economic sectors? What are the reasons that it is not an 'open economy'? Barry Naughton's chapter provides some answers to these questions. He argues that China operates under a bifurcated trade regime of export promotion and import substitution. The chapter provides detailed and up-to-date information about China's trading policies. He also relates the trade regime to ownership and regions, in analyzing China's achievements and challenges in its external reforms. However, there is not much discussion of the reasons why China has established these 'two separate trading regimes'.

What is the rationale for this bifurcated trade regime? It is not difficult to understand if we relate this issue to the general approach of China's economic reforms. While reforms in its external sector appear to be more rapid than in the internal sector, policies on trade and foreign investment are, in fact, consistent with the domestic industrial reforms. The principle of policies in both the export and import sectors is basically the same: to develop the economy without damaging domestic state-owned enterprises (SOEs).

As a former planned economy, China has a large but inefficient state sector. Although China has been in economic transition since 1978, social and political stability still have very high priority on the government's agenda, especially after the 1989 Tiananmen Square incident. To avoid rapid social and political changes and possible turmoil, the government has adopted a gradual approach in its economic reforms and, in the external sector this has led to a dual trading regime. Rather than establish a new bifurcated trade system, China has, in fact opened some sectors of its economy and kept other sectors closed in order to maintain employment levels. In tandem with efforts to maintain employment is the desire for capital and technology to fuel

56

economic development. As in most countries in East Asia and elsewhere, China has adopted policies to attract foreign investment.

Attracting Foreign Investment

In analyzing China's external reforms, it is useful to separate foreign investment policy from the trade regime. The main objective of policies favourable to foreign-invested enterprises (FIEs) is to attract capital, technologies and managerial skills. These policies apply to all FIEs, no matter in which industrial sectors they are investing. Although many of these firms are in the export sector, there are also large numbers of FIEs operating in 'import substitution' sectors such as the automobile industry.

Adjustments to policies towards foreign investment are based on the needs for foreign capital in different sectors. In the past, most foreign capital was invested in the 'processing' export sectors from which China received few benefits. The Chinese government has adjusted its policy towards these FIEs accordingly, even though they are under the export promotion regime. On the other hand, foreign investment in some import-competing sectors, such as high technology (telecommunications, automobiles, computers), is still encouraged. The objectives of China's foreign investment policies have shifted from merely attracting foreign capital to developing certain sectors.

Dual Trading Regime

Rather than dividing the Chinese trade regime into 'export promotion' and 'import substitution', I would describe the current Chinese trade regime as a 'dual trade regime' or a 'gradually-opened trade regime'. Part of the trade regime has been liberalized, while the rest has remained unchanged. It is not difficult to see that the most open sectors in China are those dominated by non-state-owned enterprises, including FIEs and township and village enterprises (TVEs). Aside from foreign investment policies, the Chinese government does not provide much protection for these sectors (textiles, toys, and light industries), though both import and export policies in these sectors are now less restricted. The most protected industries are those dominated by SOEs. The protectionist policies in these sectors include both import restrictions and explicit or implicit export subsidies. Like the dual-track price system and the dual exchange rate regime, China's dual trade regime is also a transitional form which reflects the approach via piecemeal and phased reforms.

Reform and the WTO

Thus, the dual trading regime is a result of China's 'gradual' reform strategy. As China further integrates into the world economy, it has to reform the protective part of the trade regime along the lines of WTO principles. However, the speed of China's external reforms is subject to the success of the internal reforms of the SOEs. As long as the SOEs still dominate the industrial sector, free trade in that sector is unlikely.

Currently, about a third of Chinese industries will face international competition once China lifts all trade protection. These sectors account for almost 40 per cent of the total value of industrial output and for about 30 per cent of industrial employment. Furthermore, most of the firms in these sectors are state-owned with very low labour efficiency. Because of political and social concerns, the Chinese government is currently hesitant to introduce more direct competition to the SOEs. International pressures and motivation to join the WTO will have a positive impact on the speed of reform in China's external sector. Yet failure to reform and privatize the SOEs will remain the major obstacle to unification of the dual trading regime. China will eventually liberalize its trade system and become a member of the WTO, but it may take an even longer time than Western countries have expected, because of the slow pace of the much needed reforms of the SOEs.

3 Unilateral and Regional Trade Policies of the CER Countries

Peter J. Lloyd
UNIVERSITY OF MELBOURNE

1 INTRODUCTION

While Australia and New Zealand are sovereign states, they have in the 1980s and 1990s pursued sets of trade policies which share many elements and which together represent a style of trade policy that is distinctive. Among the common elements are a fast rate of unilateral reductions in barriers to trade with other nations, a sharp movement away from reliance on quantitative restrictions and other non-tariff instruments of trade restriction, membership of a regional trading arrangement that has achieved virtually complete freedom of bilateral trade and deepened the integration of the two economies, and a strong commitment to multilateralism.

These policies were quite different from those followed by Australia before the mid-1970s and by New Zealand in the period before the 1980s. Yet, from a long-term point of view, the trade policies of Australia and New Zealand also exhibit remarkable similarities. By the 1920s, both countries had average tariffs that were high compared with those of other high-income countries (see Anderson and Garnaut, 1987, table 2.1) and they were increased for many manufacturing industries in the following decades. Given these initial levels and a low level of participation in the early rounds of tariff-cutting under the General Agreement on Tariffs and Trade (GATT), Australia and New Zealand by 1970 had average tariff rates which were the highest of the member countries of the Organisation for Economic Cooperation and Development (OECD). In addition, Australia and New Zealand introduced comprehensive import licensing in 1939 and 1938 respectively, and used them as wartime measures, but they extended and continued these schemes long after the end of the war. In Australia, import licensing continued until 1962, and selective tariff quotas and quotas were reintroduced after 1973. In New Zealand, import licensing continued until the mid-1980s. While no exactly comparable statistics are available for protection from both tariff and non-tariff measures in other countries, we can safely say that, among the OECD countries, Australia and New Zealand had the highest average levels of protection for their import-competing manufacturing producers during the 1970s and early 1980s.[1] Thus the history of trade policies in Australia and New Zealand in the last two decades or so represents a triumph of anti-protectionist or pro-free-trade views over a long-standing and deeply rooted protectionism.

This chapter reviews these policies. It is necessary to review the events in Australia and New Zealand separately as the timing and nature of their reforms differ in some respects. The first and second sections provide a potted history of these policies in Australia and New Zealand, respectively, emphasizing the movement away from high trade barriers as a result of unilateral reductions; and Section 2 includes the first estimates of the Trade Restrictiveness Index (TRI) (that is, true utility-constant levels of trade barriers) for Australia. The third section then examines the regional aspects of trade policies, and the fourth examines multilateral aspects of trade policies in the two countries, including the approach of both countries to the Asia Pacific Economic Co-operation Forum (APEC). Section 5 offers some concluding remarks and hypotheses concerning the trends in these trade policies and their convergence.

2   INDUSTRY ASSISTANCE IN AUSTRALIA[2]

One of the features of the Australian debate about protection is the availability of excellent data measuring the extent of the distortions caused by government border interventions. Under the influence of Max Corden, the report of the government-appointed Vernon Committee (1965, app. L) produced the first official estimates of effective protection (and subsidy equivalents) for the manufacturing sector in Australia. These related to the year 1961–2 and were made for seven industry groups and for some sub-groups and individual commodities within these groups. Beginning with its Annual Report for 1969–70, the Tariff Board (Tariff Board, 1970, app. 2) and its successors, the Industries Assistance Commission and the Industry Commission, have produced annual estimates of nominal and effective assistance for the Manufacturing sector and later for the Agricultural and the Mining sectors. The estimates cover the major Commonwealth Government interventions, which apply selectively to some activities only. The instrument coverage is quite comprehensive; it includes assistance provided by tariffs, and the major non-tariff border instruments (quantitative import restrictions, production bounties, local content schemes and certain export incentives) and, for agricultural commodities, domestic pricing arrangements and tax concessions from the Commonwealth government and from state government interventions of national significance. For this reason, the term 'rates of assistance' has been preferred in Australia to the term 'rates of protection'.

Consistent times series for these rates are now available for the Manufacturing sector from the year 1968–9, for the Agricultural sector from 1970–1 and for the Mining sector from 1986–7. For the Manufacturing sector, these estimates are available at the 2-, 3-, and 4-digit classifications of industries and for the Agricultural sector for twenty-six commodity groups (for the latest series see Industry Commission, 1995) and for the Mining sector for 16 subindustry groups (Industry Commission, 1992). Indeed, for more than 25 years, the Australian Government has had in this area of policy-making the best data available to any government.

Figures 3.1 and 3.2 show the average nominal and effective rates of assistance for the manufacturing and agricultural sectors, respectively, from the beginning of these series. For the manufacturing sector, the discontinuities reflect the periodic rebasing of the estimates to account for changes in the structure of activities in this sector, and the figures include forecasts based on the announced phased reductions upto the year 2000–1. These figures show a downward trend for assistance to the manufacturing sector from 1973 which is strong and continues steadily to the year 2001. There is a downward trend for the agricultural sector which holds for the period as a whole, but this is due to the sharp reductions in 1970 and 1971 and is subject to wide annual

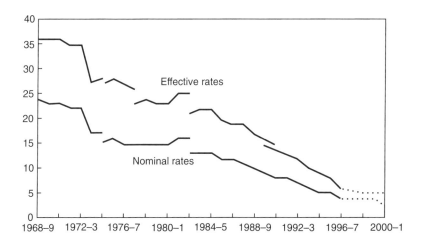

Figure 3.1 Average nominal and effective rates of assistance for the manufacturing sector:[a] 1968–9 to 2000–1 (per cent)

Notes:
[a] The discontinuities in the series reflect the periodic rebasing of the estimates to account for changes in the structure of the manufacturing sector.

Sources: As indicated in text.

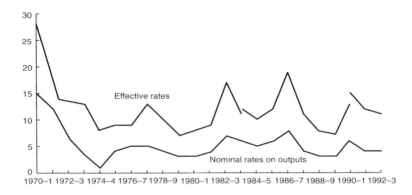

Figure 3.2 Average nominal and effective rates of assistance to agriculture: 1970–1 to 1992–3 (per cent)

Source: As indicated in text.

fluctuations because many of the instruments giving assistance to agricultural producers vary with prices or incomes and are, therefore, not constant in *ad valorem* terms.

The estimates of assistance to the mining sector relate to 1990–1 and selected earlier years (Industry Commission, 1992, table K10). These show that the mining sector has had negative average assistance, since mining outputs receive almost no assistance and many of the inputs are subject to tariffs and other forms of assistance which raise their prices above world prices. There are no estimates of rates of assistance for the services industries, though the Australian Government imposes substantial impediments to international trade in services, chiefly through the regulation of industries such as coastal shipping, banking and civil aviation (Industry Commission, 1995, app. G).

Thus the effect of assistance in Australia over the period has been to penalize exporters in the agricultural and mining sectors (and probably also in the services sector). There is a long tradition of the analysis of the costs of protection, and their burden on exporters in particular, which dates back to the 1929 Brigden Report. This analysis will not be reviewed here; instead, I shall present at the end of this section new estimates of the TRI for Australia.

The reductions in assistance to manufacturers have resulted from an almost continuous programme of reform.[3] This began in a systematic way with the Tariff Review, which was a review of the highly protected areas of manufacturing. It was proposed by the Tariff Board in its 1966–7 Annual Report but was not implemented until the Minister for Trade and Industry, in May 1971, finally forwarded to the Board the references it had requested to begin it. On 19 July 1973, without any notice and following a report from a confidential committee appointed a month earlier, the Government cut by 25 per cent all tariffs except those applying to goods which were subject to excise duties. This is the largest single reduction in levels of assistance in Australian history and marks the beginning of the period of reduced levels of assistance. It lowered the average effective rate of assistance for the sector by about eight percentage points. (There were only a few imports subject to quantitative restrictions at that time.) The chief concern of the Government that appointed the committee was to reduce aggregate excess demand and the rate of inflation, not to reform the pattern of assistance to industry. After the event there was vigorous debate as to whether this tariff cut was responsible for the subsequent rise in the unemployment rate, and this led to speculation that there could never again be an across-the-board cut in rates of assistance in Australia.

Piecemeal reforms of the assistance to some industries which received above-average assistance, such as the passenger motor vehicles (PMV), the textile, clothing and footwear (TCF), and the whitegoods industries, continued under references sent by the Government to the Industries Assistance Commission. Then, in the May 1988 Economic Statement, the Government announced a programme of tariff reductions for most imports, to continue until 1992. The method of cutting tariffs applied greater percentage cuts to higher rates. With some exceptions, tariffs greater than 15 per cent were phased down to 15 per cent and those between 15 and 10 per cent to 10 per cent by 1992. In addition, the 2 per cent revenue duty, which had applied to all imports from January 1980, was removed from 1 July 1988. One must note, however, the exceptions to the tariff cuts related to certain imports covered by industry plans for PMV and TCF products and also to tariffs on some agricultural products subject to commodity stabilization or other schemes. These were the most highly assisted product groups. Under the April 1988 amendments to the motor vehicle plan, tariffs were reduced and import quotas abolished on these products.

In its Industry Policy Statement of March 1991, the Government announced the continuation of this programme of tariff reductions beyond 1992. Most tariffs were phased down to 5 per cent by July 1996. In this programme, the tariffs on both PMV and TCF industry products, the two areas with relatively high rates of assistance remaining in the 1990s, are to be reduced annually to levels of 10, 15 or 25 per cent by the year 2000. Despite efforts by these industries to slow down this timetable, the Labour Government that instituted the programme stuck to it. The coalition government elected in 1996 has not yet revealed its policies with respect to the substantive tariffs. In the election campaign it had announced that the Tariff Concession Scheme, which gives duty-free entry to most imported business inputs not made in Australia and to some consumer goods for which there is no close substitute made in Australia, would be abolished. This change was proposed as a revenue measure but in May, following strong pressure from industry lobby groups, the Government announced that concessions would be reduced to 40 per cent of the tariff costs rather than being eliminated.

Almost all these reductions in assistance, shown in Figures 3.1 and 3.2, were carried out unilaterally. Widespread tariff reductions were introduced in January 1977 as the Australian commitment to the Tokyo Round of multilateral trade negotiations (MTN). These tariff reductions were not across-the-board but were instead designed specifically to cause minimal disruption to Australian industries and mainly represented the removal of unused assistance to lightly-assisted industries. They did not, therefore, lessen the dispersion in rates of assistance; and even these reductions were made in part as a response to the devaluation of the Australian dollar in November 1976. It has been estimated that these 1977 MTN reductions lowered the average effective rate for the manufacturing sector by three percentage points during the 1976–7 and 1978–9 years (Industries Assistance Commission, 1979, p. 80). Hence, of the reduction in the average effective rate of assistance to the manufacturing sector from 36 per cent in 1968–9 to 8 per cent in 1995–6, the MTN reductions have contributed only three percentage points (that is about 11 per cent of the total) and the corresponding contributions to the reductions in the agricultural sector would be proportionately less.

Two other features of the reduction in tariff assistance are noteworthy. These are the trend to substitution of tariff for non-tariff measures of assistance since the early 1980s, and the reduction in the inter-industry variation in nominal and effective rates.

Quantitative restrictions on imports, chiefly under the regime of import licensing, were the main instrument of assistance to the import-competing industries after the Second World War. Import licensing ended in Australia in the early 1960s and tariffs again became the instrument of protection for all but a few highly regulated industry groups. Beginning in December 1974 and continuing in 1975 tariff quotas, quotas and other quantitative restrictions were reintroduced in Australia for several commodity groups. Although originally applied as temporary measures for periods of one or two years, they became the main instruments of protection for the two industries receiving the highest levels of assistance, the PMV and the TCF groups. In the early 1980s the government moved to reform some aspects of the administration of these quotas and later to dismantle them. Imports of motor vehicles ceased to be subject to quotas from 13 April 1988. From 1 March 1989, assistance for TCF products by means of quotas was reduced, through the device of gradual reductions in the rate of penalty duty applying to imports outside quotas. This programme was accelerated under the March 1991 Statement and all TCF products became free of quotas on 23 February 1993. Moreover, the local content scheme for motor vehicles manufactured in Australia, which was a part of the agreement reached in 1945 between the Australian Government and General Motors Holden to promote the local production of chassis and engines and was formalized in 1965, terminated at the end of 1988, and that for the tobacco industry, which was a part of the marketing arrangements for growers and dated back to 1936, terminated on 1 January 1995. The area of production now assisted by content-based schemes is the services industries such as television and films (see Industry Commission, 1996, app. G) but there are no measures of the incidence of these restrictions.

It was this return to assistance by means of tariffs that made it possible to project accurately the rates of assistance until the year 2000 shown in Figures 3.1 and 3.2.

The Industries Assistance Commission has split up the assistance provided to manufacturing industries by 'form': that is, by instrument. This was done by calculating the subsidy equivalents of each instrument. In 1983–4, quantitative restrictions accounted for 15 per cent of the total assistance to outputs, and tariffs for 84 per cent. This statistic understates the significance of quantitative restrictions, as the assistance for the two highly protected industry groups, TCF and PMV, came mainly from quotas. By 1992–3, tariffs accounted for 97 per cent of the assistance to manufacturing industries (Industry Commission 1995, table 4.2). Today, the remaining non-tariff barriers affecting the manufacturing sector consist of a few bounties (mainly on ships, computers, textile yarn and books) and selective export subsidies (mainly the Export Market Development Grants Scheme and the Automotive Export Facilitation Scheme), but the agricultural sector still receives support from a variety of schemes, most of which are commodity-specific (see Industry Commission, 1995, Appendix F). Australia has also been one of the main users of the anti-dumping provisions of Article VI of the GATT, which is sometimes classified as a non-tariff barrier because of the protective effect of these duties, but the number of new cases has declined considerably since the early 1990s.

In substituting tariffs for quotas, Australia introduced one major modality of reform that is noteworthy. It was the first country, to my knowledge, to auction import quotas. In 1980 the Government of Australia introduced a tender for about 11 per cent of the quota for imports of passenger motor vehicles. It reverted to an historical allocation of import quotas for 1981 but, in January 1982, the Government introduced a similar scheme for tendering for 15 per cent of the quotas for imports of TCF products. Quota tenders were introduced partly in order to reveal the structure of protection implicit in quotas which covered broad categories of goods and partly to collect rent otherwise accruing to the quota-holders; the rent earned from property rights inherent in quota allocations became more transparent when transferability of quotas was allowed and large transfer prices were paid. The tender premiums that were paid for the TCF commodity groups in each category varied widely in any one year from zero to well over 100 per cent and, within the tender categories, they varied widely over the years.[4] These were on top of the basic duty rates applying to the same goods, which were generally high, most being 50 per cent or more. Thus they revealed implicit rates of assistance which were very high and unstable over time.

Regarding the inter-industry variation in effective rates, the Tariff Board and its successors have been aware that it is the variation around the average of the rates of nominal and effective rates of assistance for different groups of producers that imposes distortions on the economy. They have used the standard deviation as the measure of variation. While there is no measure of variation that is a predictor of the magnitude of welfare losses from inter-industry variation in these rates in general, Anderson (1995) has shown that a mean-preserving reduction in the variance of nominal rates is welfare-improving under certain conditions.

For the manufacturing sector, time series of the standard deviation of the nominal and effective rates of assistance, measured at the 4-digit level, is available from 1968–9 (Industry Commission, 1995, table A6.7–8). This shows that the reductions in the average nominal and effective rates of assistance for this sector were generally, but not always, accompanied by reductions in the variances of this assistance. Having remained constant at around 30 per cent from the beginning of the series in 1968–9, the standard deviation of the effective rates fell in 1973–4 as a result of the across-the-board tariff cut to 23 per cent; with a 25 per cent cut, the variance after the cut was only 9/16 $(= [3/4]^2)$ of the level before the cut. The measure then rose with the introduction of highly selective quotas in the mid-1970s to a peak of 48 per cent in 1984–5, although the average nominal and effective rates in this sector were falling over this period. It fell after the reduction in quotas and has fallen steadily since the phased reductions in tariffs began in 1991, though not after the 1988 programme, because of the exemptions for some highly assisted industries (Industry Assistance Commission Report 1989, Table A7.8). The results in 1973 and 1991 illustrate that a widespread reduction in (nominal) rates reduces the variance.[5]

There are estimates of the variance of nominal and effective rates of assistance to the Agricultural sector in Australia. These show again that the variance of the effective rates is much higher than that of the nominal rates. Intra-sectoral variance in the agricultural sector is higher than that in the manufacturing sector and has not declined over the period. Given that the manufacturing sector has been the most assisted of the sectors throughout the period, and that the variance of rates in this sector has fallen, the inter-activity variance across all sectors has almost certainly fallen.

Since, in some periods, the trends in the average levels of assistance to the manufacturing and agricultural sectors and in the standard deviations of the assistance for these sectors have moved in opposite directions, the overall trend in the extent of distortions in the economy is ambiguous. This problem of measuring the height of restrictions to international trade has long been recognized in Australia (sec, for example, Crawford, 1934). It is an index number problem in a general equilibrium context.

Anderson and Neary have recently resolved this problem. In a series of papers (see, in particular, Anderson and Neary, 1994; and Anderson 1995), they constructed the Trade Restrictiveness Index (TRI). The index is derived from the Trade Expenditure Function for a distorted economy which was first developed by Lloyd and Schweinberger (1988). This function provides a money metric for welfare changes in the economy. The function is $B(p^*, p, v, u)$ where p^* and p are the vectors of world prices and domestic prices respectively, v is the vector of primary endowments, which are assumed constant, and u is the vector of household utilities. If all border interventions are *ad valorem* tariffs/export subsidies or equivalents, p can be replaced by the vector of these tariffs, t. The Trade Restrictiveness Index, τ, is then given from the equation:

$$B(p^*, t, v, u) = B(p^*, 1\tau, v, u) \qquad (3.1)$$

where $1\tau = (\tau, \ldots, \tau)$ is the vector of uniform tariff rates. This index is a true utility-constant index of the distortions. It captures all the general equilibrium demand and supply responses to changes in the structure of border interventions. It has the desirable property that, for a given economy, a decrease in the index must increase the welfare of the economy in the sense of a Pareto improvement.

This index has been calculated from the Monash general equilibrium model of the Australian economy. Table 3.1 reports the results for the year 1986–7, which is roughly in the middle of the period represented in Figures 3.1 and 3.2. For all sectors, the index is the solution to Equation (3.1). This shows that the pattern of border interventions in the Australian economy in 1986–7 was equivalent to a uniform *ad valorem* tariff of 21.80. This compares to an imported-weighted index of the actual non-uniform distortions of 13.69. Thus, the latter conventional index is a considerable understatement of the true utility-constant index.

The same utility-constant calculation has been done for the subset of border interventions relating to the manufacturing sector only. This shows

Table 3.1 A comparison of average levels of trade restriction, Australia, 1986–7

Sector	Import-weighted average	Trade restrictiveness index
Manufacturing	16.98	24.62
All sectors	13.69	21.80

that the TRI for this sector was 24.62, which is higher than that for all sectors as the manufacturing sector was the most heavily assisted sector. Again, the TRI is much higher than the import-weighted index of 16.98. The Industry Commission also calculates the average nominal rate of assistance to output of the manufacturing sector using the (unassisted) value of production as weights. In 1986–7 the average nominal rate of assistance was 12 per cent (Industry Commission, 1995, table A6.4), which is an even greater underestimate.

Evidently the weighting of the index used to calculate the height of trade restrictions is extremely important. It has been shown that, in the neighbourhood of the initial tariffs, the TRI is an arithmetic mean of the individual tariff where the weights are the marginal welfare weights given by the effects of the changes in each tariff on the value of the function B relative to the effects of changing all border prices (Anderson, 1995, equ. 6), namely:

$$\tau = \sum_{i}^{n} t_i \left[(\partial B / \partial p_i \, p_i) \right] \tag{3.2}$$

These weights may be positive or negative in a distorted economy. These marginal weights were calculated for the Australian economy at the 2-digit level. A few of the export industries had negative weights. The industries with the highest weights are reported in Table 3.2, together with the import weights

Table 3.2 Import weighted average and the weights in the import trade restrictiveness index

	Import-weighted average	Trade restrictiveness index
Motor vehicles and parts	0.184	0.351
Footwear	0.031	0.198
Clothing	0.053	0.169
Knitting mills	0.028	0.048
Electronic equipment	0.142	0.043
Manufacturing machinery and equipment	0.078	0.042
Construction machinery	0.026	0.030
Wire products and other metal products	0.024	0.016
Wine and spirits	0.006	0.016
Electrical machinery and batteries	0.045	0.016
Rubber products	0.022	0.015
Man-made fibres, yarns and broadwoven fabrics	0.044	0.015
Cotton yarns and household textiles	0.031	0.015
Sporting equipment and other manufacturing	0.020	0.014

for comparison. The results are very clear. Sub-industries in the TCF and PMV industries with high rates of assistance have much higher marginal welfare weights; indeed, the first three sub-industries alone account for 70 per cent of the weights in the TRI. All the heavily weighted sub-industries are in the manufacturing sector. These results show the high costs imposed on the economy from the extremely high rates of assistance given to a few producers.

3   INDUSTRY ASSISTANCE IN NEW ZEALAND

New Zealand is the only developed country in the last thirty years to have used quantitative restrictions, in the form of a comprehensive import licensing system, as the primary instrument of protection for its manufacturers. This system led to a structure of effective rates of protection characterized by very high average levels of assistance to import-competing activities, very wide variations among and within industries, and an unstable structure.

For New Zealand, unlike Australia, there is no annual time series of these effective rates. Hampton (1965) and Candler and Hampton (1966) made among the first estimates anywhere of the nominal rates of protection for goods subject to import licensing (by making direct price comparisons) for the year 1955, and also estimated a version of effective rates, following Max Corden. They found nominal rates of protection ranging from zero to 177 per cent for a selection of commodities that were items in the Consumer Price Index. The Economic Monitoring Group of the New Zealand Planning Council (1984) constructed a fragmented time series of rates of protection from 1955 to 1985. These series showed nominal and effective rates of protection for import-competing producers which were consistently very high over the thirty years. The average nominal rate peaked in 1964–7 at 54 per cent and the average effective rate in 1981–4 at 50 per cent. They estimated that the 'clothing' industry received an effective rate of protection of 1105 per cent at its peak in 1964–7 and the 'vehicle assembly' industry 2428 per cent during the period 1955–8. Other estimates of nominal and effective protection were made, but they are limited in commodity and instrument coverage.

Syntec Economic Services (1988), following the methods of the Industries Assistance Commission in Australia and employing some IAC staff as consultants, provided the first set of measures of assistance in New Zealand which were comprehensive in terms both of covering all manufacturing and most agricultural producers and of including all tariffs, identifiable subsidies and import licensing instruments of assistance. In the manufacturing sector, they estimated rates of assistance down to the 5-digit level. Some estimates have been made subsequently, but they used a different classification of industries and method of estimation.

Table 3.3   Nominal and effective percentage rates of assistance in New Zealand

	1981–82	1985–86	1987–88
Manufacturing			
Average nominal rate	20	19	14
Average effective Rate	39	37	26
Pastoral Agriculture			
Average nominal rate	13	4	1

Source: Syntec Economic Services (1988).

The Syntec Economic Services estimates are of particular value as they cover the years in which the major reforms occurred and are directly comparable with the Australian estimates. They made detailed estimates of the average nominal and effective rates for three years: 1981–2, 1985–6 and 1987–8 (see Table 3.3).

In 1981–2 the average nominal rate of assistance to manufacturing industries was 20 per cent and the average effective rate 39 per cent.[6] The comparable figures for Australia in the same year were 16 per cent and 25 per cent, respectively.) Some manufacturing industries received very high levels of assistance, largely due to the import licensing system. In 1982, some 22 per cent of total merchandise imports were subject to import licensing. At the 2-digit level, 'textiles, wearing apparel, leather industries' and 'fabricated metal products, machinery and equipment' had effective rates of assistance of 90 per cent and 69 per cent respectively. The average rates had fallen to 14 per cent and 26 per cent respectively by 1987–8. (The comparable figures for Australia in that year were 11 per cent and 19 per cent.)

On the other hand, the rates of assistance for agricultural producers were much lower than those for producers in the manufacturing sector. In 1981–2 the average nominal rate of assistance to the main pastoral group of agricultural commodities – meat, wool and milk products – was only 13 per cent. This fell to a mere 1 per cent in 1987–8 after the elimination of most agricultural subsidies in New Zealand.

The New Zealand experience in reducing protection is remarkable for the speed of the reforms and for the modality of the shift from reliance on quantitative restrictions to reliance on tariffs. The trade liberalization reforms began in 1979 with the announcement of the intention to allocate quotas by tender, and some other minor reforms, but it was the election of the Labour government in 1984 that began the process in earnest. In April 1984, the government adopted an import liberalization programme centred on the conversion of the import licensing regime into a regime of *ad valorem* tariffs (see Rayner and Lattimore (1991) for a review of the early reform years).

As with the Australian schemes in the PMV and TCF industries, the central idea was to use the tenders to provide information on the price distortions. The method of implementing the liberalization of quantitative restrictions differed from that used in Australia. In addition to existing licences, further licences were issued under the Import Licensing Tendering System, up to 5 per cent of the annual domestic production less exports (by value) and, as a general rule, import licences were to be removed when the tender premiums fell to 7.5 per cent or less over a two-year period. The method of allocating the tender quotas resembled that in Australia except that the duty levied was equal to the individual bids and, therefore, at non-uniform rates within the tender quotas.

In fact, New Zealand accelerated and liberalized this timetable in a number of ways. In July 1984 it increased global import access for goods subject to licensing to a minimum of 10 per cent (previously a maximum of 5 per cent) of the estimated domestic production less exports, and future annual allocations of licences were set at 5 per cent (previously 2.5 per cent). A year later, in September 1985, extra tenders equal to a 5 per cent increase in access were granted. The import licensing system ended on 1 July 1988 for industries that were not subject to industry plans, which constituted about 70 per cent of the manufacturing sector. The remaining import licences were to be removed by 1992 but were in fact removed in 1990, six years after the import liberalization programme began.

Over the same period that import licensing was being liberalized, the tariff rates on all commodities were liberalized by across-the-board cuts in rates, 5 per cent on 1 July 1986 and 10 per cent a year later. These were the first (unilateral) reductions in New Zealand tariff history, according to Rayner and Lattimore (1991, p. 98). There were some additional cuts in tariffs on non-competing imports. In 1987 the New Zealand Government conducted the first comprehensive review of the country's tariffs. As a result, a programme of phased annual tariff cuts over the period 1 July 1988 to 1 July 1992 was announced in the General Tariff Reduction programme. This programme used the 'Swiss formula' devised in the Tokyo Round of multilateral trade negotiations and which results in a greater proportionate reduction of higher tariff rates.[7] It leads, therefore, to a more rapid narrowing of the dispersion of rates than does an across-the-board uniform percentage cut. In addition, all specific duties were converted to *ad valorem* rates by 1 July 1992. (In Australia many specific rates, once commonly applied to the TCF goods, have been replaced by *ad valorem* rates. Specific rates now apply mainly to excisable commodities. These rates collected 3.6 per cent of all import duty in 1994–5, compared, for example, to 19.1 per cent in 1979–80.) Since 1992 phased tariff cuts have continued but, as in Australia, special provisions have been necessary for delayed cuts to industries subject to industry plans. This includes the groups of footwear, carpet and apparel, and motor vehicles – the same two groups as in Australia. New Zealand committed itself to reducing the maximum tariff on most products to 10 per cent by 1996. Performance-based export incentives and the export market development incentive were phased out in 1990 and most assistance to agricultural producers, including the important Supplementary Minimum Prices schemes for meat and wool producers and input subsidies for fertilizers, were ended. On 16 December 1994, the New Zealand Government announced a further unilateral tariff reduction plan for the period 1 July 1997 to 1 July 2001. By the year 2000, the maximum tariff will be 15 per cent.

Following the method of the IAC in Australia, Syntec Economic Services estimated the share of total assistance provided by each form of assistance. In 1981–2, import licensing accounted for 22 per cent of the gross-subsidy-equivalent measure of assistance to the manufacturing sector and tariffs for 78 per cent, but by 1987–8 the share of import licensing had fallen to 1 per cent for the year (Syntec Economic Services, 1988, table 2.1).

By the end of 1992 the only major form of assistance to New Zealand's industry was *ad valorem* tariffs. Thus it had radically reformed the form of assistance at the same time as it had rapidly reduced assistance. Indeed, New Zealand now probably has the purest system in the world in terms of almost total reliance on (*ad valorem*) tariffs for assistance to merchandise commodities,[8] (apart from Singapore and Hong Kong which are free ports). Even the US Trade Representative, in his annual review of foreign trade barriers facing US exporters, found little to complain of and concluded 'New Zealand's increasingly open trade and investment policy is a bellwether for regional and global trade and investment liberalization' (United States Trade Representative, 1996, p. 251).

Syntec Economic Services also estimated the standard deviation of the nominal and effective rates for the manufacturing sector. For the three years surveyed in the 1980s, these were 122, 110 and 94 per cent respectively (Syntec Economic Services, 1988, table A.2.3) These standard deviations are 4 and 5 times higher than those in Australia. They also find very high standard deviations within the 2-digit industries. It was this extreme inter-and intra-industry variability in rates of assistance, largely due to the import licensing system, that created such large distortions in the incentives to produce commodities in the New Zealand economy. These extreme distortions persisted until 1990. However, the dispersion of these rates as measured by the standard deviation had declined substantially by 1987–8 and must have fallen sharply since that time. The sweeping and extremely rapid trade reforms carried out since 1983 have greatly improved national resource allocation.

It is possible to compare (unweighted) average tariffs and the frequency index of non-tariff barriers in New Zealand with those in Australia and other APEC countries using data recently collated by the Pacific Economic Co-operation Council (PECC) (1995b). The data relating to 1993 show that both average tariffs and non-tariff barriers to imports have declined more rapidly in New Zealand and Australia over the five-year period 1988 to 1993 than those of other APEC countries. (Chile is the one country that broadly matches the rate of reform in the CER countries.) This five-year period omits the substantial reforms in both countries in the early 1980s. At the end of this period, the unweighted average tariffs of 9 per cent and 8 per cent in Australia and New Zealand, respectively, were a few percentage points higher than those in the USA (6.8 per cent), Canada (6.7 per cent) and Japan (6.5 per cent). The index of non-tariff barriers in New Zealand was much lower than the indices of these countries and less than those of other APEC countries, with the exceptions of Hong Kong, Singapore and Chile; and the same is true of Australia, though again its index is higher than that of New Zealand. Both countries have reduced tariffs considerably in the years since 1993, to levels that are now about the same as those of other OECD countries. Overall, therefore, the levels of import restrictions are less in New Zealand and Australia than the OECD average.

While no internationally comparable measures of disparities in rates of assistance are available, it is possible to compare the standard deviations of applied tariff rates in Australia and New Zealand with those of other APEC countries in 1993 and 1995. For all sectors, the standard deviations of these rates in the CER countries were about the average of the APEC countries (PECC, 1995b, Fig. 4.1). Some data on the standard deviations are also available for OECD countries (OECD, 1996). The standard deviations of tariff rates in Australia and New Zealand were above the OECD average in 1993 but lower than those in Japan and Switzerland. Given the elimination of most non-tariff barriers in the CER countries, it may be that the disparities in nominal rates of assistance are now less than the OECD average.

4 THE CLOSER ECONOMIC RELATIONS AGREEMENT

On 1 January 1983 the Closer Economic Relations Agreement between Australia and New Zealand (CER) replaced the 1966 New Zealand Australian Free Trade Area (the original NAFTA). In a short time, the provisions of the agreement have been substantially widened and deepened so that the area is now more closely integrated than any regional trading arrangement other than the European Union (EU). This section will concentrate on the main features of the Agreement and the relationships between the bilateral freeing of trade and the unilateral actions described in the sections above. Recent reviews of the progress of CER are provided by Lloyd (1995), PECC (1995a), and Holmes (1996).

CER was planned to bring about a complete free trade area by 1995 – that is, all border restrictions were to be ended within twelve years. Tariffs were to be phased out by 1988, performance-based export incentives by 1987, and quantitative import restrictions and tariff quotas by 1995. In fact, this target for the ending of these forms of assistance was achieved on 1 July 1990, some five years ahead of the schedule. In addition, anti-dumping actions against the trans-Tasman partner ceased from the same date.

The first Review of the Agreement in 1988, among other extensions, widened the liberalization of border trade to trade in services, including national treatment in relation to all laws, regulations and practices as well as free market access. This took effect from 1 January 1989. There was a 'negatives list' of services not covered. Although the number of services on this list has been reduced as a result of annual reviews and the 1992 and 1995 reviews, some significant areas are still inscribed, mainly in Australia, where the telecommunications, aviation and shipping industries are still subject to a high degree of domestic regulation. Complete equality of access for government purchases of goods was achieved when New Zealand joined the Australian National Preference Agreement between the Commonwealth and Australian States on a nil preference basis from 1 June 1989, with New Zealand reciprocating the benefits. This was extended to all government purchases of services in July 1991. From this time, all trans-Tasman trade in goods and most trade in services has been completely free of border barriers.

CER has also resulted in a substantial reduction of non-border barriers. The most notable and important of these is that, as a part of the 1988 Agreed Minute on Industry Assistance, the two countries have ceased to pay bounties and other production subsidies that would affect international trade. There has also been a growing harmonization of policies in several areas, including customs and quarantine procedures, technical and food standards and, most notably in this context, competition law and some other areas of business law. Following the example of the EU the Australian Commonwealth and State Governments have implemented a Mutual Recognition regime for standards and occupations from 1 March 1993. As a result of the 1995 review of CER, a Trans-Tasman Mutual Recognition Arrangement for both goods and occupations was added, with effect from 1 January 1997.

In 1992, from an initiative by the then Australian Prime Minister, Mr Paul Keating, a Memorandum of Understanding on Air Services was signed on 1 August 1992. This was to establish a single aviation market covering the two countries from 1 November 1994, but it lapsed when the Australian government withdrew from the agreement a week before it was due to take effect. The new coalition government, which came to power in 1996, has stated its intention to resume negotiations on the single aviation market. In May 1996, the Australian and New Zealand stock exchanges have reached an agreement in principle to establish a single trans-Tasman market covering share options and derivatives. This is intended as the first step towards a single securities market. It will require enabling legislation in both countries; and there are some outstanding areas that negotiations have been unable to resolve, chiefly the tax treatment of trans-Tasman equity and the incorporation of foreign investment into the agreement. There are no provisions in the CER agreement relating to factor movements between the two countries. (Residents move without restriction between the two countries under a separate Trans-Tasman Travel Arrangement dating back to the 1920s.) Thus the free trade area is moving unevenly towards a single market form of integration.

One feature of this progress is that it has been achieved with simple rules and no formal institutions, not even a secretariat. This is in marked contrast to the EU, with its complex structure of institutions and large bureaucracy, and NAFTA, which has a growing set of institutions, and even the Association of South East Asian Nations (ASEAN), which has a secretariat. CER was planned as an agreement that would require low maintenance and a minimum of bureaucratic resources.

Another notable feature of the Agreement is that it has been accompanied by strong unilateral movements towards free trade (and deregulation) in both countries. As noted in the previous sections, both Australia and New Zealand have achieved substantial unilateral liberalization since the Agreement came into effect in 1983. CER is the most outstanding example of 'open regionalism', interpreting that term in the sense of a regional liberalization of trade in goods and services, accompanied by a liberalization *vis-à-vis* countries outside the region. The only other regional trading arrangement in the world that has achieved substantial regional liberalization accompanied by substantial unilateral liberalizations is ASEAN.

The dual liberalization by means of unilateral and regional action is no coincidence; and in New Zealand's case its unilateral liberalization almost coincides with the period of CER regional liberalization. Fundamentally, both countries have sought to open their economies to increased trade with the rest of the world and have followed both the bilateral and the unilateral route.

There have been some positive interactions between these two routes to liberalization. Both Australia and New Zealand see the bilateral freeing of trade in goods and services as a way of making the countries more competitive in world markets. There has also been a desire, especially in New Zealand, to reduce possible trade diversion to the trans-Tasman partner. Australian irritation with import licensing restrictions on access to New Zealand markets after tariffs had been reduced led the two countries to put a firm timetable for the elimination of quantitative restrictions on bilateral trade into the CER Agreement, thus paving the way for the New Zealand decision two years later to phase out the import licensing system. Similarly, the realization by both countries that their export incentive schemes and subsidies distorted bilateral trade led them in general to reduce these incentives substantially. In these ways, bilateral liberalization has aided the unilateral liberalisation *vis-à-vis* all trading partners.

5 AUSTRALIA AND NEW ZEALAND IN THE GATT

The multilateral trading system is very important to Australia and New Zealand, as two trading countries which are small and not members of a larger economic group, and they were foundation members of the GATT in 1947 and the WTO in 1994. The multilateral trade policies of the two countries are reviewed briefly, followed by some comments on APEC.

Australia has generally abided by the rules of the GATT as it believed that the multilateral organization provided protection for smaller trading countries against aggressive unilateral actions by larger and more powerful countries. Although its tariffs have been higher than those of most other developed countries, it has made relatively little use of non-tariff barriers for most of the last 25 years and has therefore come closer than many other GATT contracting parties to the GATT principle that countries should use tariffs rather than quantitative restrictions or other measures to restrict trade. During the period between 1974 and 1993, when quantitative restrictions were again used in Australia to protect major industries, it preferred to use the more transparent quotas and tariff quotas rather than the voluntary export restraints and orderly marketing agreements used by many other countries. It has taken complaints about other contracting parties to the GATT, principally in the area of agricultural trade; and sometimes in concert with New Zealand. But the Australian record in abiding by the rules of the GATT and the WTO is not unblemished. In the first eleven months of the existence of the WTO, two of the twenty-one complaints to the organization were against Australia, both against quarantine measures applying to imports of Atlantic salmon, brought by the USA and Canada jointly (WTO, 1995).

The Australian record in relation to tariff bindings has not been good. Prior to the Uruguay Round, Australia had bound only about 20 per cent of its tariff lines, which was a much lower percentage than for any of the other OECD countries, most of whom had bound 90 per cent or more. Historically, the non-binding of tariffs has been important as it has given Australian governments the freedom to raise tariffs when they wished to increase protection of producers of certain goods.

Its record in subscribing to those parts of the GATT that were voluntary is also not particularly good. When the Tokyo Round introduced nine supplementary and voluntary Codes and Agreements in 1979, Australia did not accede to those relating to technical barriers to trade, subsidies and countervailing duties, trade in civil aircraft, and to government procurement. It signed the subsidies code later in 1981. Australia has still not acceded to the WTO Agreement on government procurement, which is the most important of the four remaining voluntary agreements.

In terms of the reduction in Australia's own border barriers, the GATT multilateral trade negotiations have been less important than either unilateral or regional policies. In the earlier rounds, Australia made few concessions and received a largely free ride from the USA and other major industrialized countries in relation to tariffs restricting its access to foreign markets. The last two rounds, the Tokyo Round and the Uruguay Round, were by far the most important of the multilateral negotiations during the life of the GATT. As the major part of its participation in the Tokyo Round, Australia made widespread tariff reductions in January 1977 but, as noted in section 1, these did not reduce the rates of assistance to the most highly assisted industries.

The Australian contribution to the Uruguay Round, signed in April 1994, included an average tariff cut of 44 per cent relative to the 1986–7 levels, and changes to tariffs in the local content scheme and stabilization plan in the tobacco industry, along with minor changes to non-tariff restrictions – the tariff quota on cheese imports and sales-tax concessions on fruit and vegetable juices – and the termination of export subsidies for the dairy industry. These tariff cuts compare with the cuts under the announced phased programmes of 70 per cent. They do not, therefore, add to the scheduled unilateral reductions over this period. On the other hand, Australia did agree to bind 95 per cent of the tariff lines; and although, in many cases, the bound rates are above the levels that will apply after the implementation of the present schedule of tariff cuts, this is an historic change.

Australia made at least one significant contribution to the success of the Uruguay Round as a whole. It created the Cairns Group, so named because the first meeting was held in Cairns in 1986. The Cairns Group was a coalition within the GATT of agricultural exporting countries (but not including the USA and the European Community) whose agricultural sectors were generally low-cost and lightly assisted compared with those in the USA, the EC and Japan. It insisted that, as laid down in the Punta del Este Declaration, the world agricultural trading system should be reformed through a reduction in border protection and subsidies, and it targeted especially the major industrial nations. Australia chaired all sessions of the Group. The Group is generally credited with having had a major influence on the Agreement on Agriculture and the outcome of the Uruguay Round in general, though the extent of the reforms in the Agriculture Agreement fell well short of proposals put forward by the Cairns Group during the multilateral negotiations (see Tyers 1993).

The history of New Zealand activities in the GATT is rather different from that of Australia, until the liberalization of the 1980s. As a small country whose exports have been heavily concentrated in primary products, chiefly temperate foodstuffs, New Zealand had a high stake in the observance of GATT rules by other countries which were potential importers of these products or competitors in third-country markets. Indeed, it is likely that, between the time of the accession of the UK into the EEC in 1973 and the present, New Zealand exports have been more severely restricted than those of any other GATT contracting party by import barriers in the major markets of the industrial countries and by export subsidies which reduced its markets in third countries. Not surprisingly, New Zealand was a strong supporter of the Cairns Group during the Uruguay Round; and New Zealand and Australia were the major proponents of the extended Trade Policy Review Mechanism of the WTO.

New Zealand's own observance of the GATT rules was, however, far from exemplary until the mid-1980s. During the long continuous period of comprehensive import licensing, New Zealand was the outstanding example of a developed country which relied on quantitative restrictions rather than tariffs as the main instrument of industry assistance and it made no reductions in tariff rates. However, this situation changed dramatically and swiftly after 1984, to the point that New Zealand is now the outstanding example among the developed countries of a country which relies almost entirely upon tariffs as the instrument of industry assistance and which has reduced its import trade barriers and its subsidies to export industries unilaterally.

Because the binding constraint on most restricted-import commodities was quantitative controls during the period of import licensing, the small tariff concessions that New Zealand made in multilateral negotiations before the Uruguay Round did not significantly reduce assistance to the highly protected industries. In the Uruguay Round, New Zealand cut tariffs on some product groups, but this concession was dwarfed by the programme of phased unilateral tariff cuts which it announced at the conclusion of the Round.

Prior to the Uruguay Round, the New Zealand Government had bound only 48 per cent of tariff lines. This was the lowest percentage of the OECD countries apart from Australia. However, as a part of its commitments in this Round, New Zealand agreed to bind all tariff lines, except those for used motor vehicles and used clothing.

Another important part of the external trade strategies of both Australia and New Zealand is APEC. This organization was an Australian initiative, having been first proposed by the former Prime Minister, Mr Bob Hawke, in a speech in Seoul in January 1989, and the first ministerial meeting was held in Canberra later that year. The Eminent Persons Group (EPG), which proposed a goal of free trade in Asia-Pacific and introduced the concept of 'open regionalism' into APEC discussions of trade liberalization, also followed from an Australian suggestion. The proposals for regional trade liberalization contained in the Bogor Declaration and the Osaka Action Agenda have been very strongly supported by the Australian and New Zealand Governments. My own interpretation of this support in Australia is that the government has seen APEC as a counter to the formation of large continent-based regional trading arrangements in Europe and the Americas, and possibly also in East Asia, and to the dangers of discrimination against the exports of countries which are not members of these emerging blocs. New Zealand has an explicit purpose of pursuing unilateral, regional and multilateral trade liberalization.

It remains to be seen whether and, if so, how APEC proposals for trade liberalization will be implemented. At the time of writing, they are due to be discussed again at the Manila Meeting of Economic Leaders in 1996, and it is too early to make a definite judgement about the contribution of APEC to regional and global trade liberalization. Yet APEC has already had a major influence on the debates in the Asia-Pacific region and elsewhere, with its vision of ultimate complete free trade and its discussion of new modalities of trade negotiations such as 'concerted unilateral actions'. It should also be remembered that it is still less than three years since the appearance of the First Report of the EPG which precipitated the present proposals.

6 CONCLUDING REMARKS

This brief history of the trade policies of the CER countries in the last 25 years or so reveals a number of interesting features and raises some questions.

First, while the assistance to import-competing producers in the manufacturing sector in Australia and New Zealand has been the highest of the OECD countries, this comparison overstates the importance of trade distortions in these economies relative to other economies. In heavily protecting some uncompetitive producers in this sector, Australia and New Zealand behaved no differently from the European, North American and Japanese governments in protecting their uncompetitive producers of some high-cost agricultural commodities and, one should note, many mineral products (such as coal), which are very heavily protected in Europe and some other OECD countries. All countries have concentrated their assistance on industries or sub-industries in which the national producers have a strong comparative disadvantage. The misfortune of Australia and New Zealand is that they reduced international trade and specialization in the commodity group for which international trade and technology developed most rapidly.

Second, one observes a frequent imitation of trade policies initiated by the trans-Tasman partner. During the period reviewed in this chapter, New Zealand imitated Australia several times; across-the-board tariff cuts, the auctioning of quotas, the introduction of industry plans (which was a strategy first used by the Whitlam Government for the Steel industry), the measurement of rates of assistance in the Manufacturing and Agricultural sectors.[9] This borrowing has been a major factor in the formation of trade policies, especially since the early 1980s, and it has produced convergence of Australian and New Zealand trade policies.

Third, both Australia and New Zealand have become fairly aggressive trade reformers. The sharp and rapid reductions in average levels of assistance and in the dispersion of these rates among industries has led to the opening up of these economies once more to higher levels of international trade in goods and services (and, one should note, to cross-border capital flows). The trade ratios of these countries have increased since the new opening of their economies, but they are still not high relative to those of many other countries of comparable size and income.

This fundamental reversal of protectionist policies raises the basic question of why it has taken place. Consider first Australia. While the structure of the economy and the associated pattern of rents received from the structure of assistance have changed somewhat, the changes have not been great. The relative importance in production and exports of agricultural producers, who historically have been a coalition calling for lowering of assistance to manufacturers, has declined, and the importance of mining and service-sector exporters has increased. Although the Mining and Service sectors have been discriminated against, and this effect has increased towards the end of the period studied here as these sectors have become more important in the Australian economy, they have had little to say about assistance policies. By the 1990s the average rate of assistance to manufacturers barely exceeded that given to agriculture producers on average. This may have weakened the historical opposition of the Agricultural sector to assistance for the manufacturing sector. But it is difficult to explain much of the decline of protectionism in terms of these changes.

My own explanation of the historic shifts that have occurred relies more upon two non-coalition factors. The first is the slow but eventually dominant influence of a steady drip of anti-protectionism. This came initially from academics, percolating to the civil servants and eventually transforming public attitudes towards differential industry assistance policies. It began with the 1929 Report of the Brigden Committee, but the major debates can be dated from the work of the Tariff Board and of Max Corden on effective protection in the 1960s. This represents one area where the contribution of academic economists in Australia has been profound. Sound ideas are eventually irresistible. The second factor is the growing transparency of the pattern of assistance and its effects on exporters, consumers and other groups who have been adversely affected. In Australia, the Industry Commission and its predecessors have played a very honourable part, constantly pointing out, in a number of reports since 1968–9, the implications of complex patterns of assistance to the PMV and TCF industries in particular, and providing systematic measures of this assistance.

The New Zealand history is somewhat different. While an increasing number of economists in the New Zealand Treasury, the Reserve Bank and outside the New Zealand public service challenged the traditional protectionism from the late 1970s, the critical factor was a financial crisis coupled with a deep disillusionment with reliance on state assistance in many areas: the welfare state, government-owned enterprises, overseas marketing and other areas as well as industry assistance. If New Zealand had had a Tariff Board and a more vigorous academic group of trade analysts, the reforms might have come earlier, but they might not have been as far-reaching.

There are lessons to be learnt from Australian and New Zealand experiences, I believe, for other countries with slower rates of reform of trade policies, especially in relation to the role of independent enquiries, transparency and changes in the instruments of assistance. Similarly, the CER is the cleanest regional trading arrangement in the world, with virtually no exceptions to free trade in goods and services and an absence of bureaucracy, and both countries are now model members of the WTO in terms of their observance of both its rules and its spirit.

Notes

1. Mancur Olson (1982, p. 135) cited Australia and New Zealand as two slow-growing countries with high levels of protection and an inability to adjust to changes. In 1981, the prime minister of Singapore described the Australian government as 'more restrictive, conservative and backward-looking [in its industrial protection policies] than the meanest of the EEC countries' (cited by Anderson and Garnaut, 1987, p. 1).

2. The part of the second section (on the TRI) is taken from a joint paper with Professor Peter Dixon and Dr Philip Adams of Monash University.

3. For a review of the earlier post-war history of protection and the tariff debate, see the excellent survey by Corden (1963). For the period from the mid-1960s to the mid-1970s, which includes the period of the Tariff Review and the 1973 tariff cut, see Lloyd (1978). For the period up to 1985, see Woodland (1992). The best source of information for later years is the annual reports of the Industries Assistance Commission and the Industry Commission.

4. The tender quotas were offered for sale by a tender in which the bidders indicated the *ad valorem* premium over the base tariff rates which they were prepared to pay, and the number of units bid. The tender quotas were then allocated to the highest bidder, the second highest bidder and so on until the total bids equalled the total tender pool available. The duty paid by all successful bidders is the sum of the basic rate applicable and the tender premium, the bid rate at which the total bids equal the total tender pool available.

   When only a portion of the quota is sold by tender, the tender premium is an upper bound of the true *ad valorem* equivalent – that is, the *ad valorem* tariff which, if substituted for the quota, would yield the same quantity of imports (Gibbs and Konovalov, 1984). The Australian experience is that the *ad valorem* equivalents derived from tender premiums correspond closely with estimates based on other methods such as direct price surveys and quota transfer sale prices (Industries Assistance Commission (1985, Appendix 6)).

5. Strictly speaking, this proposition applies to the variance of the nominal rates and holds only if all rates of assistance are cut equi-proportionately. This was the case in the 1973 reductions. It does not hold exactly in the later phased reductions

because of some exemptions and, offsetting this, the somewhat uneven extent of the reductions in those tariffs that were cut. While the variance of effective rates depends on the pattern of input–output coefficients as well as the variance of the nominal rates, the pattern of the variance of the effective rates follows that of the variance of nominal rates.

6. Syntec followed the IAC in using as weights the unassisted value of production. Consequently, the New Zealand estimates are lower than their TRI but no estimates have been made of the TRI in New Zealand.

7. Let t^0 and t^1 be the tariff rates before and after the cut and α the parameter determining the size of the cut. With the Swiss formula $t^1 = \alpha t^0 / (\alpha + t^0)$.

8. The only blot on the New Zealand copybook is the continued use of anti-dumping actions. Along with Australia and a small number of other countries (chiefly the USA, the EU and its member countries, Canada and Mexico), New Zealand has been a frequent user of anti-dumping measures.

9. In more recent years, New Zealand has made a number of policy innovations in areas outside trade policies; for example, the Reserve Bank Act of 1989, the Employment Contracts Act of 1991 and the Fiscal Responsibility Act of 1992, all of these in the area of the macro-management of the economy. Australia, the Big Sister, seems reluctant to admit the wisdom of its Little Sister in any of these areas.

References

Anderson, J. E. (1995) 'Tariff Index Theory', *Review of International Economics*, vol. 3, June, pp. 156–73.

Anderson, K. and R. Garnaut (1987) *Australian Protectionism: Extent, Causes and Effects*, (Sydney: George Allen & Unwin).

Anderson, J. E. and J. P. Neary, (1994) 'Measuring the Restrictiveness of Trade Policy', *The World Bank Economic Review*, vol. 8, pp. 151–69.

Candler, W. and P. Hampton (1966) 'The Measurement of Industrial Protection in New Zealand', *Australian Economic Papers*, vol. 5, June, pp. 47–58.

Corden, M. (1963) 'The Tariff', in A. Hunter (ed.), *The Economics of Australian Industry* (Cambridge University Press).

Crawford, J. G. (1934), 'Tariff Level Indices', *Economic Record*, vol. 11, pp. 213–21.

Gibbs, I. and V. Konovalov, (1984) 'Volume Quotas with Heterogeneous Product Categories', *Economic Record*, vol. 60, September, pp. 294–303.

Hampton, P. (1965) 'The Degree of Protection Accorded by Import Licensing to New Zealand Manufacturing Industries', Agricultural Economics Research Unit Report No. 12, Lincoln College, Christchurch, New Zealand.

Holmes, Sir F. (1996) *The Trans-Tasman Relationship* (Wellington: Institute of Policy Studies).

Industries Assistance Commission (1979) *Annual Report for 1978–79*, (Canberra: Australian Government Publishing Service).

Industries Assistance Commission (1985) *Annual Report for 1984–85* (Canberra: Australian Government Publishing Service).

Industry Commission (1992), *Annual Report 1991–92* (Canberra: Australian Government Publishing Service).

Industry Commission (1995) *Assistance to Agricultural and Manufacturing Industries*, Information Paper (Canberra: Australian Government Publishing Service).

Industry Commission (1996) *Annual Report 1995–6* (Canberra: Australian Government Publishing Service).
Lloyd, P. J. (1978) 'Protection Policy', in F. H. Gruen (ed.), *Surveys of Australian Economics* (Sydney: George Allen & Unwin).
Lloyd, P. J. (1995) 'The Future of Trans-Tasman Closer Economic Relations', *Agenda*, vol. 2, pp. 267–80.
Lloyd, P. J. and A. G. Schweinberger (1988) 'Trade Expenditure Functions and the Gains from Trade', *Journal of International Economics*, vol. 24, pp. 275–97.
New Zealand Planning Council, Economic Monitoring Group (1984) *Strategy for Growth* (Wellington: New Zealand Planning Council).
Olson, M. (1982), *The Rise and Decline of Nations: Economic Growth, Stagflation, and Social Rigidities* (New Haven: Yale University Press).
OECD (Organisation for Economic Co-operation and Development) (1996) *Indicators of Tariff and Non-tariff Barriers to Trade* (Paris: OECD).
PECC (Pacific Economic Co-operation Council) (1995a) *Milestones in APEC Liberalisation: A Map of Market Opening Measures by APEC Economies* (Singapore: PECC).
PECC (Pacific Economic Co-operation Council) (1995b) *Survey of Impediments to Trade and Investment in the APEC Region* (Singapore: PECC).
Rayner, A. C. and R. Lattimore (1991) 'New Zealand', in D. Papageorgiou, M. Michaely and A. M. Choksi (eds), *Liberalizing Foreign Trade*, vol. 6 (Oxford: Basil Blackwell).
Syntec Economic Services (1988) *Industrial Assistance Reform in New Zealand* (Sydney: Syntec Economic Services).
Tariff Board (1970) *Annual Report for Year 1969–70* (Canberra: Commonwealth Government Printing Office).
Tyers, R. (1993) 'The Cairns Group and the Uruguay Round of International Trade Negotiations', *Australian Economic Review*, First Quarter, pp. 49–60.
United States Trade Representative (1996) *1996 National Trade Estimate Report on Foreign Trade Barriers* (Washington, D.C: US Government Printing Office).
Vernon Committee (Committee of Economic Enquiry) (1965) *Report of the Committee of Economic Enquiry* (Melbourne: Wilke and Co.).
Woodland, A. D. (1992) 'Trade Policies in Australia', in Salvatore, D. (ed.), *National Trade Policies* (New York: Greenwood Press).
WTO (World Trade Organization) (1995), 'WTO's First Year: "An Encouraging Start"', *WTO Focus*, December.

Comment

Richard G. Harris
SIMON FRASER UNIVERSITY

This chapter is an interesting overview of trade policies in Australia and New Zealand during the last three decades offering four important observations on the character and evolution of these policies. The first is that Australia and New Zealand both had historically high levels of protection, but there has been a steady reduction in these in the last two decades in Australia, and since 1984 in New Zealand. Second, these policy changes have occurred as a consequence of unilateral actions rather than through a multilateral process. Third, tariffs have been the preferred instrument of protection relative to non-tariff barriers. Fourth, the CER is one of the most successful and open forms of regional trading agreement in the world economy.

As one who comes from neither Australia nor New Zealand, and given the historical nature of the paper, there is little that I found to disagree with directly. My comments focus on some political economy questions regarding the interpretation of this history, and on the way in which some of the arguments are presented.

To a North American, the most noticeable characteristic of this history is the unusually high level of protection of manufacturing that persisted at a time when the rest of the OECD had long abandoned such high levels, with the notable exception of the motor vehicle and textiles, footwear and clothing (TFC) sectors. Why did neither Australia nor New Zealand participate more vigorously in liberalization under GATT during the earlier period? To answer these questions, I believe one needs a political-economy model of trade policy. Historically, protection has been used either as a means of promoting industrialization, or as a means of income redistribution. Which of these was relatively more important in Australia and New Zealand? Both countries have had, for example, strong labour unions, and the concept of the 'just wage' is deeply rooted in their history. If this is the dominant explanation of the use of protection, one might want to enquire why other instruments of income redistribution were not used. If industrialization was the motivating factor, then it is ironic that they moved so late, given that it became fashionable in the rest of the industrialized world to promote increased integration as a means of developing technologically advanced manufacturing.

One suspects that perhaps the answers lie elsewhere. Both countries were large primary exporters and perhaps the commodity boom of the 1970s resulted in a false sense of economic security, that tended to delay the date

84

of reckoning. Alternatively, it might be argued that the distance from the large markets in Europe and North America was the dominant factor. In the absence of reasonable proximity to the large industrial markets there may well have been a sort of policy fatalism, in that both countries perceived themselves to be inevitably destined to be importers of manufactures. A corollary to this argument would be that little advantage was seen as likely to accrue from the liberalizations resulting from the negotiations under GATT.

It is noteworthy that while the CER countries show some substantive differences from other industrialized countries in the evolution of their trade policies, there were also important similarities. Both motor vehicles and the TFC sector were important exceptions to the general liberalization in other sectors and this occurred in almost all industrial countries. Second, the timing of the turn to regionalism in trade policy is not very different from that in other countries. The CER was really born in the late 1980s and both the NAFTA and the 1992 EU Single Market initiative were under discussion in the same period.

Much of the chapter is concerned with changes in the level and pattern of protection and will prove a useful survey of these developments for those interested in the history of trade policy in the region. The remarkable and rapid removal of barriers in the 1980s is the striking fact to this reader. The author also covers the reduced dispersion of effective and natural rates of protection, and the shift from other instruments of protection to *ad valorem* tariffs. In all cases these are viewed as favourable developments, but some new estimates of the Trade Restrictiveness Index (TRI) suggest that in the middle 1980s the degree of protection was much higher than averaged tariff equivalent rates would suggest. As the author points out, the TRI index weights sectors by marginal welfare gain; hence the most restricted sectors are weighted the most heavily.

Reduction in the dispersion of tariff rates is viewed as a good thing by the author and we know from the literature on piecemeal reform that this is true in some simple neoclassical models. However, one must be careful in drawing too strong a policy conclusion. If economies of scale, or technology transfer via imported intermediate inputs, are important an escalated tariff structure (with lower tariffs the further upstream the good in the production process) can be optimal as compared with one without escalation. To restore tariffs on intermediate inputs in order to reduce tariff dispersion is hardly a sensible policy prescription.

It would have been useful to present some results-oriented aspects of the trade reforms in the CER countries. For example, what has happened to the growth rates of manufactured exports? What has happened to productivity in manufacturing? What has been the impact on intra-industry trade and flows of foreign direct investment? Critics would argue that evidence of reductions in tariff and non-tariff barriers, while indicative of the success of the *proponents* of liberalization, does not document the economic success of the policies themselves. One is left wondering whether support for the policies is based on their distributive effects rather than on their efficiency consequences.

The next part of the chapter deals with the Australia–New Zealand regional trading agreement (CER). Generally this is judged to be highly successful, although again some evidence on trade flows would be helpful to the reader in supporting this judgement. I was left with some queries as to how the CER is dealing with problems that other regional trading agreements are encountering. For example, how is the CER dealing with rules-of-origin? The use of content-based rules or of rules based on changed tariff classification has led to a number of administrative problems in the NAFTA, to the point that it is argued that many firms do not bother to attempt to achieve the cost gains to be had from sourcing regionally. In the area of services, the chapter discusses some of the initiatives such as those affecting air transport. More generally, however, how has the CER dealt with harmonisation of regulatory standards? I could list other problem areas. The point is that regional trade agreements among industrialized countries are as relevant to services and investment as to commodity trade. Would the CER also be judged to be a success in these areas? My guess is that the answer is 'yes', but it would be useful to have more information.

In summary, this an interesting and useful survey of the history of the trade policy of the CER and a useful marker of the development of trade policy in Australia and New Zealand. The Pacific Rim and APEC are increasingly the focus of attention in a large number of countries. For policy analysts outside Australia or New Zealand, attempting to achieve a deeper understanding of the APEC region as a whole, the trade-policy history of Australia and New Zealand is a crucial component of that larger picture, and this chapter is an excellent starting point.

4 External Trade and Economic Growth: The Malaysian Experience

Eu Chye Tan and Mohammed Ariff
UNIVERSITY OF MALAYA

1 INTRODUCTION

Conventional wisdom suggests that exports linked with the expansion of the Malaysian manufacturing sector have brought about impressive rates of economic growth (and hence economic development) for Malaysia. The notion that export expansion could serve as an engine of growth in both developed and developing economies has been explored by economists since the late 1950s. Kindleberger (1962), Beckerman (1962), Lamfalussy (1963) and Chen (1977) have attempted to provide some theoretical links between an expansion of exports and economic growth. Kindleberger argues that an export expansion could promote investment, and cost-reducing innovations and economies of scale in production. Beckerman hypothesizes that, faced with the prospect of an export expansion, entrepreneurs will be motivated to invest more, resulting in greater output and productivity. In stressing the importance of the balance-of-payments position of a country, Lamfalussy maintains that a surplus external payments position arising from increased exports could spur the government to adopt expansionary policies that could encourage domestic investment. Chen (1977) contends that a surge in exports could aid in the financing of imports of capital goods that augments capital formation or accumulation.

On the other hand, other economists have expressed reservations about the notion of exports as an engine of growth. Nurkse (1959) argues that, contrary to what had happened in the nineteenth century, trade was not an engine of growth in the twentieth century. Kravis (1970), criticizing the 'trade engine theory' shows that trade should be viewed as a handmaiden, rather than an engine, of growth. There also exists the belief that some basic level of development is necessary for a country to benefit most from export-orientated growth, especially that involving manufactured exports (Tyler, 1981).

In general, empirical evidence of the relationship between exports and economic growth is mixed. For example, while Michaely (1977) maintains strong support for the view that rapid growth of exports has accelerated economic growth since the late 1970s, empirical studies by Ballance, Anfari and Singer (1982), Batchelor, Major and Morgan (1980), and Jung and Marshall (1985) have cast doubts on this view. However, a cursory look at the development experience of advanced East Asian countries, namely Japan, Korea and Taiwan, would lead one to conclude that exports have a significant bearing on economic growth and development. Though these countries began with a period of import substitution with a strong bias against exports, they have subsequently adopted a pro-export regime sooner than other developing countries because of the compelling need for foreign exchange (World Bank, 1993). While Japan modified its trade policy to encourage manufactured exports in the 1950s and early 1960s, the Asian 'tigers' (South Korea, Taiwan, Singapore and Hong Kong) acted similarly in the late 1960s. Instead of attempting to conserve foreign exchange by imposing stricter import controls, they resorted to export promotion. To sustain export growth, currencies were devalued and a number of other instruments were employed such as export credit, duty-free imports for exporters and their suppliers, export targets and various tax incentives. They have all welcomed technology transfers through licensing, capital goods imports and foreign training. However, Japan, Korea and Taiwan did restrict inflows of foreign direct investment and this is probably the main difference between Malaysia and these countries.

This chapter seeks to discuss the growth and development experience of Malaysia against the backdrop of its trade, investment and industrial promotion policies, particularly since the early 1970s, when export-oriented industrialization was initiated; and, in an attempt at corroboration, it then submits the relationship between Malaysia's external trade performance and economic growth to a formal econometric treatment. The Engle–Granger (1987) cointegration technique is used to establish the long-run relationship between exports and, interchangeably, the merchandise trade balance on the one hand and income on the other. Granger causality tests are also conducted to ascertain whether exports and movements in the merchandise trade balance do precede changes in income. The econometric analyses are couched in both nominal and real terms to enhance the robustness of the results, as one may argue that the unit values of exports and imports, inevitably used to deflate nominal exports and imports, are inappropriate deflators.

The rest of the chapter is organized as follows. Section 2 discusses the growth and development experience of Malaysia with a general reference to its trade, investment and industrial promotion policies, and the elements of these policies are highlighted in the third section. Section 4 discusses the results of the econometric analyses, and the fifth section offers concluding remarks.

2   OVERVIEW OF THE ECONOMIC DEVELOPMENT OF MALAYSIA

Malaysia is a relatively small country situated in South-East Asia, with an area of 330 000 square kilometres and a population of 20 million people. Rich in natural resources, it has a multiracial population comprising Malays and other indigenous people (62.4 per cent), Chinese (29.1 per cent), Indians (8 per cent) and others (0.5 per cent). Essentially based on private enterprise, with the government assuming an active role in mapping out national development strategies, the Malaysian economy is one of the fastest growing in Asia. With a per capita income of US$4000 in 1995, it ranks third in terms of economic prosperity in South-East Asia after Singapore and Brunei.

Malaysia has maintained a favourable annual rate of economic growth with relative price stability since achieving independence in 1957. Growth of real gross domestic product (GDP) accelerated from an average annual rate of 4.1 per cent in the latter half of the 1950s to 8.1 per cent in the 1970s. However, there was a considerable deceleration in the growth rate in the early 1980s, because of a protracted global economic recession, and this culminated in a decline of Malaysia's real GDP by 1.1 per cent in 1985. A strong recovery was staged subsequently by the Malaysian economy, with annual real GDP growth averaging 8.5 per cent over the 1987–95 period.

Fundamentally, Malaysia is an increasingly trade-orientated economy, with exports and imports of goods and services each accounting for about 74 per cent of GDP during 1990–4 compared to 46 per cent in 1980–4. Its share in total world exports expanded from 0.75 per cent in 1980–4 to 1.1 per cent in 1990–4, while its share in total world imports also expanded from 0.66 per cent to 1.1 per cent. In 1995, it was the world's nineteenth largest exporter and the seventeenth among importers. During the same year, its per capita exports stood at US$3895. This was higher than those of other major exporters such as Australia (US$2944) and the USA (US$2237). Its per capita imports of US$4090 were also higher than those of the USA (US$2953), Australia (US$3328) or Japan (US$2687).

All these achievements may be attributed to the trade and industrial investment policies Malaysia adopted, if one adheres to the 'trade-engine' theory. Initially based on agricultural and other primary commodities, such as rubber and tin, Malaysia has transformed itself over the years into a dynamic industrial economy. During its formative years, Malaysia depended heavily upon natural rubber and tin as foreign exchange earners and was then the world's leading producer and exporter of these commodities; 60 per cent of its export earnings represented rubber and 11 per cent tin. Hence, with 71 per cent of its foreign trade earnings hinging upon these two materials the Malaysian economy was highly susceptible to the vicissitudes of international trade. This warranted programmes to diversify primary commodity exports and to promote industrial development. Consequently, oil palm, logs, sawn timber and petroleum gained significance in the list of exports, with the share of rubber and tin in the total contracting from 69.1 per cent in 1960 to a mere 2.2 per cent in 1993. In contrast, logs, sawn timber, palm oil and petroleum (crude and partly-refined) collectively accounted for 27.9 per cent of total exports in 1990, against 20 per cent in 1960. This relatively modest expansion in the share of these latter major commodity exports over the period is explicable by the burgeoning share of manufactures in the total.

The main ambition of the Malaysian government since the 1960s has been to develop a vibrant manufacturing sector in order to boost the resilience of the economy. It embarked upon an industrialization policy that initially emphasized import substitution, followed by a switch of emphasis to export promotion in the early 1970s. In fact, as suggested by Table 4.1, the growth of manufacturing output has always outpaced the growth of total national output since the 1960s, except during the 1981–5 period. These policy developments did have a bearing on the evolution of Malaysia's external trade structure. From pre-Independence days until the late 1960s, imports largely comprised consumption goods, as the domestic consumption goods industry had yet to develop to an extent capable of serving domestic needs adequately. Hence import substitution was then the main theme of the industrialization programme. The programme succeeded in scaling down the share of imports of consumption goods in total imports from 50.7 per cent in 1961 to 32 per cent in 1970. The momentum of import substitution continued, and by 1994 the share of consumption goods in total imports had further slackened, to a mere 14.6 per cent. In fact, most of the existing consumer products marketed domestically can be attributed to this decade of import substitution.

At the dawn of the 1970s, it was felt that industrialization based on import substitution alone would be inadequate to serve national development needs. Further import substitution was also constrained by the limited size of the domestic market and the fact that import-substituting industries could no longer absorb the growing labour force. Overseas market ventures, and hence export-oriented industrialization, were then perceived as a force for employment generation and as a catalyst for meeting the socioeconomic redistribution objectives of the government, embodied in the New Economic Policy (NEP) promulgated in 1970. The socioeconomic restructuring programme under the NEP was to be implemented within the context of an expanding economy such that no particular group in Malaysian society would be deprived. The export-oriented industrialization programme was first implemented with the creation of export processing free trade zones (EPFTZs), and the creation of these zones seemed successful in terms of employment and export growth.[1]

In the early 1980s, the planners felt that it was time for the country to move on to a more advanced stage of industrialization. The stage for heavy

Table 4.1 Malaysia–GDP, exports and foreign direct investment

	1961–65	1966–70	1971–75	1976–80	1981–85	1986–90	1991–95
GDP annual percentage growth							
Total[a]	6.3	5.52	7.1	8.6	5.8	5.0	8.1
Manufacturing[a]	11.1	9.95	11.6	13.5	4.9	6.4	12.2
Exports							
Total (M$m)	—	—	7333.70	19573.70	32930.50	56654.90	131659.70
Annual percentage growth	—	—	14.94	25.84	6.56	16.7	18.5
Manufacturing (M$m)	—	—	1231.42	4000.86	9716.24	29191.58	98003.76
Annual percentage growth	—	—	28.7	26.1	15.3	30.4	25.9
Foreign direct investment[c]							
Net inflow (M$m)	200	185	651.80	1282.80	2539.4	3007.60	11765.20
Annual percentage growth	3.91[b]	28.38	46.14	20.98	0.23	42.80	14.24

Notes:
[a] Figures from 1961–5 to 1976–80 are based on 1970 prices, while those for subsequent periods are based on 1978 prices.
[b] 1962–5.
[c] Proxied by net inflows of long-term corporate investment.

Source: Computed from various Five-Year Plans of Malaysia and Bank Negara Malaysia, *Quarterly Economic Bulletin* (various issues).

industrialization in the country, at times referred to as a second round of import substitution, was set with the establishment of the Heavy Industries Corporation (HICOM) in 1980. This was despite doubts expressed by some commentators about the viability of the programme, given the limited size of the domestic market, the attendant need to accord heavy industries a high level of protection to ensure their survival, and the global over-capacity of industries involved in the production of cars, steel, cement and oil-refining (Ariff and Tan, 1994). The reasons given by the government in its pursuit of heavy industrialization were:

(i)   the need to reduce the nation's dependence on imports of capital and intermediate goods to sustain the growth process;
(ii) to foster both forward and backward linkages in the manufacturing sector in order to promote the growth and development of a host of ancillary industries; and
(iii) a strong heavy industries sector had been a vital factor contributing to the economic success of the newly-industrialized countries.

In a way, this represented an adoption of some part of the Korean and Japanese industrialization strategy. Heavy and chemical industries were strongly encouraged by Korea, which was lavished with financial incentives (Park and Westphal, 1986; and Westphal, Rhea and Pursell 1988). In the first decade and a half after the Second World War, a host of weak industries was also promoted by Japan, and they too were lavished with protective tariffs and financial incentives to adopt advanced technology. However, a timetable was usually set for the industries to develop their viability.

   Foreign direct investment (FDI) has played the key role in Malaysia's industrialization process. Arguably, Malaysia would not have experienced a rapid growth of export-orientated industries had there been an absence, or only weak presence, of FDI. In fact, net inward flows of direct investment expanded steadily, from M$185m in 1966–70 to M$11765.2m in 1991–5. Interestingly, the growth pattern of manufactured exports has followed that of net inflows of direct investment, as periods of decelerated and accelerated growth in manufactured exports have tended to coincide with those in investment flows (see Table 4.1). Foreign investors have cited political and economic stability as the prime attraction for locating their operations in Malaysia. Most developing countries face in their early stage of economic development a serious shortage of domestic savings to meet investment needs. Hence they need to rely on foreign capital. In Malaysia, there is no such serious resource gap. Foreign direct investment has been relied upon mainly as a source of technology and employment creation, and as a foreign exchange earner. While Malaysian people have had investable funds, they lacked the technology and market outlets to succeed industrially. But both the internal and external constraints on exports have been overcome to some extent.

It seems apt to characterize the export growth experienced by Malaysia thus far as foreign-investment-led. Investments, especially in export-orientated industries, could precipitate foreign-investment-led export growth (Lloyd, 1996) and foreign investors have indeed broadened the array of Malaysia's exportables, thus contributing to the export volume. The success of export-orientated industrialization is manifest in the rising share of manufactures in total exports. From about 16.8 per cent in 1970–5, it rose to about 74.4 per cent in 1990–5, outstripping the growth of aggregate exports, as indicated by Table 4.1. This is consistent with the findings of many that a significant relationship exists between industrial development and growth of manufactured exports (James, 1996). In 1995, the manufacturing sector contributed about 33 per cent of GDP, against 20 per cent in 1980 and 14 per cent in 1970. Employment in the sector accounted for two million people or 26 per cent of total national employment by 1995, compared with 9 per cent in 1960.

While Malaysia has been according protection to its industries, the degree of protection has been mild by developing country standards. Thus Malaysia has been enhancing its image as a country with a liberal trade regime while maintaining a protective stance towards its heavy industries. Except for the motor vehicle, iron and steel, and petrochemical industries, other industries have generally experienced decreased tariff protection over time. There has been a series of abatements and abolitions of import duties on a broad range of products, especially since 1987 and these tariff liberalizations have been carried out unilaterally on a most favoured nation (MFN) basis. All this may also be construed as part of a programme preparing Malaysia for the challenges posed by the full implementation of the ASEAN (Association of South-East Asian Nations) Free Trade Area (AFTA).

Be that as it may, there is one other attribute of the Malaysian structure of protection that is praiseworthy, which is the sparing use of quantitative restrictions. Such restrictions are widely practised by less developed countries and are potentially far more trade-distorting than tariff protection, so that they can cause a severe misallocation of resources. In Malaysia, quantitative restrictions are chiefly applied to imports from certain countries as a result of political differences and to imports deemed a threat to national security or consumer safety.

None the less, Malaysia is conscious of the challenges posed by the new international economic environment to its ability to sustain its industrial progress. While Malaysia has yet to establish a comparative advantage in capital-intensive industries, it has already faced challenges from labour-surplus countries such as India, Vietnam and China. Its industrialization drive has arrived at a crossroads as its attractiveness as a low-cost labour-intensive production base for multinational corporations (MNCs) has already been eroded by labour shortages. Nor does the country have an adequate technologically-based workforce that would allow it to compete more effectively with the Asian tigers.

In fact, the government has been stressing human capital development and research and development (R&D) in recent years. There is, in fact, an urgent need to upgrade the skills of the workforce, given that Malaysia is fast losing its comparative advantage in labour-intensive industries. It has to foster greater automation of the manufacturing sector. There is no cause for promoting labour-intensive industries further as there is already an over-dependence on foreign workers. The continued use of immigrant labour contributes to a deficit in the current account of the balance of payments, as these workers repatriate their incomes. What is even more fundamental is that the use of them implies lower domestic value-added in Malaysian manufactured products. It is estimated that, in 1995, two out of every ten workers in Malaysia was foreign.

Since the early 1980s, in fact, the manufacturing sector has been experiencing shortages of technically skilled workers. This cast doubts on the utility of the education system except as a provider of general education (Gan and Soon, 1996). Enrolment rates and the amount of public expenditure on education are by no means indicative of the quality of education, an important aspect of human capital formation. It was estimated that in 1986–9, Malaysia had only four R&D scientists and technicians per 10 000 people, while Singapore and Japan had 18.7 and 60 respectively. Currently, there are only 7000 full-time research scientists in Malaysia, equivalent to a ratio of 400 per million population. This pales in comparison with the equivalent ratios of Japan (6500), the UK (3200), Germany (3000) and Republic of Korea (1300). It is projected that the country will experience a shortage of 17000 engineers and 53000 technicians by the year 2000. A national human resource development programme to transform the country into a high-tech, value-added and skills-intensive economy is thus called for.

Studies on East Asian success also show that the accumulation of physical and human capital has been a prime mover of growth, as those countries which have invested more in physical and human capital have grown faster (see, *inter alia*, Becker, 1993); and this is consistent with the prediction of neoclassical growth models. Human capital formation complements investment in physical capital, rendering the latter more productive. Apart from the high-performing economies of East Asia, remarkable progress in the leading economies of North America and Western Europe has also been been largely the result of substantial stress on human capital formation. Moreover, investment in education and training also assists in coping with changing technologies and thus leads to improved utilization of physical capital.

Human resource development could also complement the efforts of the government to intensify R&D within the country. This could alleviate the need to import capital goods as Malaysia engages more in capital-intensive industrial activities. The government has stressed that it is necessary for Malaysians not to be mere users of products but also to be suppliers and developers of technology and its applications. An inventive culture is needed to lay a strong foundation for the country's development. In 1993, Malaysia's total R&D expenditure was only 0.17 per cent of GDP, compared with Japan (3 per cent), the USA (2.77 per cent), the UK (2.11 per cent), and Australia (1.36 per cent). However, the limited size of the Malaysian market may constrain R&D activities. A larger domestic market could induce importers of technology to invest in R&D for the purposes of adapting or creating new technology (Findlay, 1978) and large economies such as Brazil and India have, in fact, laid more stress on developing their own technology. However, if Malaysian entrepreneurs are able to find more outlets for their products, especially in non-traditional markets, then R&D may become more feasible for them.

Both human resource development and R&D have now become even more important as most of the fiscal incentives at present offered by Malaysia will have to be rescinded by the year 2003, in the spirit of the General Agreement on Tariffs and Trade (GATT).

3   INDUSTRIAL INVESTMENT AND EXPORT-DEVELOPMENT POLICIES

Malaysia's investment promotion and industrialization policies have been closely interwoven with its export promotion policy. Its policy of attracting foreign direct investment (FDI) has hastened its industrialization process and boosted the stability and diversity of its export earnings. In fact, the government's main policy ventures since the late 1960s have been directed to attracting FDI, export promotion and diversification and liberalization of imports of investment and intermediate goods.

The establishment of export processing free trade zones (EPFTZs) in Malaysia in the early 1970s marked the start of export-orientated industrialization. A vast majority of firms in these zones are foreign-owned. The rationale for the creation of such zones for specific export-orientated industries was to minimize customs formalities related to imports of raw materials and components and to exports of finished products. Licensed manufacturing warehouses (LMWs) for the manufacture of export-orientated goods were also allowed to be set up under Customs Bond. Akin to firms located in EPFTZs, LMWs also enjoy duty-free access to imported intermediate goods and capital equipment. The main distinction between EPFTZs and LMWs is that, while the former are physically concentrated in designated areas, the latter are geographically dispersed.

The principal investment incentives are enshrined in the Promotion of Investments Act 1986 and the Income Tax Act 1967. The tax incentives offered under these Acts provide either partial or total relief from income tax payment and include pioneer status, investment tax allowance (ITA) and double deduction of expenses for export promotion. Pioneer status is applicable to companies undertaking promoted activities, and such companies could enjoy partial exemption from income tax for a period of five years. As an alternative to pioneer status, companies producing promoted products or engaged in promoted activities may apply for the ITA, which provides an allowance of 60 per cent of qualified capital expenditures incurred within five years from the date of approval.

To boost the growth of exports, certain expenses incurred in promoting exports of manufactured products are eligible for double deduction; these include, *inter alia*, overseas advertising, offer of free samples abroad, export market research, preparation of tenders for the supply of goods overseas, participation in approved trade or industrial exhibitions, maintenance of overseas sales offices for export promotion, and export credit insurance premiums. All intermediate and capital goods used as inputs in the production of exports are exempted from import duty (or excise duty if they are locally produced) and sales tax, and if tariffs have already been paid, drawbacks are allowed. Export credit refinancing, insurance and guarantee schemes have also been introduced to smooth the flow of exports.

As part of its efforts to foster trade with 'South' countries, the Malaysian government has offered financial aid to four general trading companies (GTCs), to enable them to embark upon programmes to promote the country's exports (including services), and in particular Malaysian branded products, as well as to identify possible competitive sources of raw materials and other inputs needed by Malaysian industries.

In recognition of the need to upgrade industrial efficiency and promote industrial modernization, many other incentives have been offered. These include reinvestment allowances, industrial building allowances, incentives for R&D and training, incentives for small-and medium-scale industries and incentives for the storage, treatment and disposal of toxic and hazardous wastes.

To further enhance the attractiveness of Malaysia in the eyes of foreign investors, 100 per cent foreign ownership is allowed of companies that export at least 80 per cent of their output; and for other export-orientated projects with lower export ratios, the maximum permissible level of foreign equity participation is correspondingly lower, though still substantial. To facilitate the process of investment application and approval for prospective investors, the Malaysian Industrial Development Authority (MIDA) has been designated as the co-ordinating centre since 1 October 1988. Investors need only approach MIDA for the approvals required at the federal level in respect of manufacturing activity and the granting of tax incentives. Thus the administrative procedure has been somewhat simplified.

The 'tax barrier' to international trade and investment has also been lowered by the conclusion of double taxation agreements between Malaysia and a number of other countries, providing for the avoidance of double taxation on international income such as business profits, dividends, interest and royalties derived in one country and remitted to another. They entail taxation of business profits only in the country in which the enterprise is situated and, in the case of dividends paid by companies exempted from tax under the Promotion of Investments Act 1986, foreign recipients are also exempt from Malaysian income tax on such dividends. To date, Malaysia has concluded double taxation agreements with about forty countries and, in addition, investment guarantee agreements (IGAs) with a number of developed and developing countries, which tend to enhance confidence among investors. An IGA assures foreign investors against risks of expropriation and nationalization, and provides for free repatriations of capital.

The liberal exchange control regime is also welcoming to foreign investors. Permission from the Controller of Foreign Exchange is not needed for a non-resident to undertake direct or portfolio investment in Malaysia and all payments to non-residents for any purpose – including repatriation of capital, profits and dividends, fees, royalties and proceeds from the sales of assets in Malaysia by foreign investors – are readily permitted. Though foreign investors are generally expected to bring in a reasonable amount of their own funds, they can also secure domestic credit, almost freely, to finance their businesses in Malaysia.

4 ECONOMETRIC ANALYSIS: COINTEGRATION AND GRANGER CAUSALITY

Having descriptively linked Malaysia's economic growth to its trade and industrial development, an attempt is now made to provide a formal econometric treatment of this relationship. This first involves testing for the existence of the long-run relationship between exports and, interchangeably, merchandise trade balance on the one hand and income on the other, both in nominal and in real terms, using the Engle–Granger (1987) technique, and then testing for Granger causality. The Engle–Granger test for cointegration can be construed as a preliminary verification of the theory of trade as an engine or handmaiden of growth. If income is indeed cointegrated with exports or the visible trade balance, it would suggest such a possibility. An endogeneity test may then be pursued to determine the direction of causation. The deployment of the Granger causality test represents merely a supplementary attempt to establish the empirical relevance of the engine–handmaiden theory to Malaysia. Quarterly data for the 1970–94 period used in this analysis are drawn from various issues of Bank Negara Malaysia's *Quarterly Economic Bulletins*. Since quarterly income figures are not available, they are interpolated from annual figures based on the industrial production index.

In order to avoid spurious regressions, Dickey–Fuller (DF) and augmented Dickey–Fuller (ADF) tests are first administered to the individual data series. The augmented Dickey–Fuller test for unit root involves running the following regression:

$$\Delta z_t = \alpha_0 + \alpha_1 T + \alpha_2 z_{t-1} + \sum_{i=1}^{n} \gamma_i \Delta z_{t-i} + \mu_t$$

where z is the natural logarithm of a variable, T is the time trend and μ is a white noise stationary error term. If α_2 assumes a zero value, then z is non-stationary and z is deemed to have a unit root. The null hypothesis that $\alpha_2 = 0$ can be tested by referring to its usual t-statistic computed as the ratio of α_2 to its estimated standard error. This statistic is referred to as the augmented Dickey–Fuller (ADF) statistic. However, the distribution of ADF does not follow the usual student's t. Its approximate critical values can be found originally in Fuller (1976). The number of lags (n) chosen is such that the regression yields non serially-correlated errors. If $n = 0$, the t-value is just referred to as the Dickey–Fuller (DF) statistic, though its critical values are similar to cases requiring augmentation. The tests confirmed that the variables are integrated of order one, $I(1)$.

Table 4.2 provides the cointegration test statistics of up to twelve lags between real income and real exports, nominal income and nominal exports, real income and real merchandise trade balance, and nominal income and nominal merchandise trade balance, respectively. They are obtained by running an ordinary least squares (OLS) regression for each of the above pairs of variables, as follows:

$$y_t = \beta_0 + \beta_1 x_t + \eta_t$$

where y = national income in nominal or in real terms; and
$\quad\quad x$ = exports or visible trade balance in nominal or in real terms.
y and x are said to be cointegrated if η_t is stationary or integrated of order zero, $I(0)$. It is interesting to note that this cointegration test consistently rules out any long-run relationship between exports or visible trade balance on one hand, and income on the other.

Given the absence of cointegration, perhaps it is of supplementary interest to verify whether movements in exports and/or visible trade balance do

Table 4.2   Dickey–Fuller (DF) and augmented Dickey–Fuller (ADF) tests for cointegration

Test	Real income versus real exports[a]	Nominal income versus nominal exports[b]	Real income versus real trade balance[c]	Nominal income versus nominal trade balance[d]
DF	−2.597 (−3.414)	−3.315 (−3.399)	−0.938 (−3.435)	−1.151 (−3.399)
ADF(1)	−2.430 (−3.415)	−2.672 (−3.400)	−0.634 (−3.436)	−1.033 (−3.400)
ADF(2)	−2.709 (−3.416)	−2.415 (−3.400)	−0.501 (−3.438)	−0.898 (−3.400)
ADF(3)	−2.174 (−3.417)	−2.092 (−3.401)	−0.463 (−3.440)	−1.357 (−3.401)
ADF(4)	−2.598 (−3.418)	−2.739 (−3.402)	−0.302 (−3.441)	−1.440 (−3.402)
ADF(5)	−2.239 (−3.419)	−2.270 (−3.402)	−0.456 (−3.443)	−1.127 (−3.402)
ADF(6)	−2.339 (−3.420)	−1.960 (−3.403)	−0.226 (−3.445)	−1.085 (−3.403)
ADF(7)	−1.945 (−3.421)	−1.479 (−3.404)	−0.252 (−3.447)	−1.144 (−3.404)
ADF(8)	−2.068 (−3.422)	−1.096 (−3.404)	−0.861 (−3.449)	−1.432 (−3.404)
ADF(9)	−1.654 (−3.424)	−0.887 (−3.405)	−0.699 (−3.451)	−1.278 (−3.405)
ADF(10)	−1.367 (−3.425)	−1.005 (−3.406)	−0.886 (−3.454)	−1.211 (−3.406)
ADF(11)	−1.523 (−3.426)	−0.975 (−3.407)	−0.627 (−3.456)	−1.172 (−3.407)
ADF(12)	−1.632 (−3.427)	−0.896 (−3.408)	−0.895 (−3.458)	−0.534 (−3.408)

Notes:
[a]   1972Q1–1992Q1–Unit values of exports are not available after 1992Q1.
[b]   1970Q1–1994Q4.
[c]   1972Q1–1987Q4–Unit values of imports are not available after 1987Q4.
[d]   1970Q1–1994Q4.
Figures in parantheses refer to 95 per cent critical values.

precede income movements or vice versa or whether the movements are simply contemporaneous via Granger causality tests. A data series p does not Granger-cause m if in a regression of Δm on lagged Δm's and lagged Δp's, the coefficients of the latter are zero. Consider, for example,

$$\Delta m_t = \sum_{i=1}^{k} \theta_i \, \Delta m_{t-i} + \sum_{i=1}^{k} \lambda_i \, \Delta p_{t-i} + \varepsilon_t$$

in which p is then indicated as not causing m if $\lambda_i = 0 (i = 1, 2, \cdots k)$. The results of the causality tests are presented in Table 4.3. With regard to the relationship between real income and real exports, it can be discerned that real income is not Granger-caused by real exports, as the null hypothesis to the contrary can only be accepted at the marginal significance level of 0.290. Real income also does not appear to Granger-cause real exports, with a marginal significance level of 0.404. Hence the notion that real exports precede real income or vice versa can be dispelled. This is true also with regard to real income in relation to merchandise trade balance. The real trade balance does not Granger-cause real income with a marginal significance level of 0.266, and that real income does not Granger-cause real trade balance is also true, with 0.539 as the marginal significance level. In nominal terms, there is no Granger causality running from trade balance to income or vice versa at marginal significance levels of 0.498 and 0.297, respectively. Only a bi-directional causal relationship is found between nominal exports and nominal income, with marginal significance levels of 0.003 and 0.001.

Hence these econometric results do not seem to support the trade engine theory. This is somewhat consistent with the empirical studies of Ballance, Anfari and Singer (1982), Batchelor, Major and Morgan (1980) and Jung and Marshall (1985), but is inconsistent with that of Michaely (1977) as cited in the Introduction, above. The results thus do not support our earlier descriptive links of Malaysia's economic growth and development to its export, investment and industrial promotion policies. Hence the question arises whether credence should be lent to the descriptive approach or to the econometric approach.

The outcome of the econometric approach may be qualified as being a result of probably unreliable data. First, the data mobilized could be inappropriate since the quarterly real gross national product (GNP) figures are interpolations from annual figures. Moreover, the unit values of exports and imports used to deflate nominal exports and imports may not yield accurate real figures. Thus, it might be concluded that the 'trade engine theory' can be upheld on the basis of the descriptive approach alone. However, if the econometric results are indeed valid, then there exist a number of factors that could have frustrated the relationship.[2] Factors that could render the contribution of exports to economic growth ineffective include:

Table 4.3 Granger causality tests, F-statistics

	Real income	Real exports	Nominal income	Nominal exports	Real trade balance	Nominal trade balance
Real income		1.060 (0.404)			0.883 (0.539)	
Real exports	1.245 (0.290)					
Nominal income				4.810 (0.001)		1.249 (0.297)
Nominal exports			3.963 (0.003)			
Real trade balance	1.311 (0.266)					
Nominal trade balance			0.850 (0.498)			

Note: Figures in parentheses below F-statistics refer to the marginal significance level.

(i) The high level of foreign direct investment. There is no doubt that FDI has contributed to the industrial development and export growth. However, the benefits of export growth to the domestic economy might have been truncated. There is substantial FDI in the resource-based and non-resource-based industries, particularly beverages and tobacco, chemicals and chemical products, petroleum refineries/products, textiles and textile products, fabricated metal products, machinery manufacturing, electrical and electronic products, and scientific and measuring equipment. Annual repatriation of profits, as a result, can be quite high. Net investment income outflows alone constituted on average about 9.52 per cent of merchandise export earnings annually during 1971–90 as opposed to 6.09 per cent in 1961–70. However, in 1991–5, the percentage declined to 6.8 per cent, presumably in response to the government's call upon foreign investors to plough back their profits locally. Moreover, it is estimated that for every ringgit invested in the country, 85–90 sen are spent on imports of capital goods.

(ii) Low domestic value-added of manufactured exports. Manufactured exports, as opposed to primary exports, have low value-added. The share of non-manufactured exports in total exports in fact contracted steadily from 83.2 per cent in 1970–5 to a mere 25.6 per cent in 1990–5, while that of manufactured exports rose from 14.1 per cent to 69 per cent. Given the limited indigenous technological capability, massive amounts of intermediate and capital goods have to be sourced from abroad. While imports of investment and intermediate goods only constituted about 51 per cent of total imports in 1961–5, they constituted about 84 per cent in 1990–4 (see table 4.4). It is also estimated that for every ringgit of manufactured goods exported, Malaysia needs to import 50–60 sen of intermediary goods. In general, since the bulk of FDI has accrued to export-orientated industries, it is not surprising to see foreign firms generating both exports and imports concurrently for Malaysia via their international investment and trading networks. For example, a

Table 4.4 Gross imports of goods by economic function (percentage share)

Period	Consumption	Investment	Intermediate
1961–5	49.1	20.8	30.1
1970–4	28.2	31.4	40.4
1980–4	19.6	31.3	49.1
1985–9	19.5	32.0	48.5
1990–4	16.1	40.4	43.5

Source: Computed from Bank Negara Malaysia, *Quarterly Economic Bulletin* (various issues).

number of Japanese and American firms in the electronics industry are maintaining complex production networks that span a number of countries in the Asia-Pacific region.

(iii) High freight and insurance payments. Apart from outflows of investment income, freight and insurance payments constitute another major leakage from the domestic economic system. Generally there is a tendency for the total value of such payments to vary directly with the volume of exports, given the underdeveloped nature of the domestic shipping and insurance industries. Though the net loss of freight and insurance payments as a percentage of the total deficit in the services account declined from 36.6 per cent in 1971–5 to 23.1 per cent in 1986–90, it rose again to 38.8 per cent in the 1991–5 period.

5   CONCLUDING REMARKS

The purpose of this chapter has been to relate the growth and development experience of Malaysia to its trade and industrial promotion policies descriptively and to corroborate the descriptive evidence with some formal econometric analysis. While a casual observation of developments would suggest the important contribution of exports to Malaysia's economic growth, and hence development, the econometric analysis seems to suggest otherwise. No cointegration is found between exports and, interchangeably, merchandise trade balance on the one hand or income on the other. Moreover, there is no unidirectional causality running between these variables. These conflicting positions could probably, but only probably, be due to the limitations of the data employed. However, if the econometric results are indeed valid, then the non-relationship may be a matter worthy of policy-makers' concern. Exports might not have been able to contribute effectively to economic growth because of leakages from the domestic economic system, as pointed out in section 4. Since the econometric results do not accord with the idea that exports have constituted an engine of economic growth, the growth and development achieved so far could have been foreign investment-led instead of export-led *per se*.

Regrettably, this notion of foreign investment-led growth and development is not amenable to econometric analysis because of the absence of quarterly investment figures. None the less, this chapter could serve as a useful policy lesson for other developing countries in Asia that see high promises in export orientation. A more discriminating export-orientated policy is perhaps needed. Maintaining high value-added exports and enhancing the capacity of a country to retain export earnings may be important policy considerations.

Notes

1. However, the performance of these zones in terms of backward linkages and contribution to the development of skills and technology transfer have not been significant (Ariff, 1989; Warr, 1983, 1987; Castro, 1984).
2. In fact, a visual inspection of the composition of the national accounts over the period 1971–94 reveals that economic growth had been domestic-led in fifteen out of the twenty-four years, led either by the growth of the public sector or by private sector expenditure, or even both. Import growth was also relatively high in four out of the nine years when economic growth could be considered as being export-led. The most notable years are 1974 and 1994. In 1974, when exports of goods and services grew by 42.2 per cent, imports grew by 63.7 per cent. And in 1994, when exports rose by 25.7 per cent, imports rose by 27.7 per cent.

References

Ariff, M. (1989) 'Export Processing Zones: The ASEAN Experience', in Chia Siow Yue and Cheng Bifan (eds), *ASEAN–China Economic Relations: Developments in ASEAN and China* (Singapore: Institute of Southeast Asian Studies).

Ariff, M. and E. C. Tan (1994) 'Trade and Development', in National Institute of Public Administration, *Malaysian Development Experience: Changes and Challenges*, (Malaysia).

Ballance, R., J. A. Anfari and H. W. Singer (1982) *The International Economy and Industrial Development: Trade and Investment in the Third World*, (Brighton: Harvester).

Batchelor, R. A., R. L. Major and A. D. Morgan (1980) *Industrialization and the Basis for Trade* (Cambridge University Press).

Becker, G. S. (1993) *Human Capital: A Theoretical and Empirical Analysis with Special Reference to Education* (Chicago: University of Chicago Press).

Beckerman, W. (1962) 'Projecting Europe's Growth', *Economic Journal*, vol. 72, December.

Castro, J. S. (1984) 'The Bataan Export Processing Zone', in E. Lee (ed.), *Export Processing Zones and Industrial Employment* (Bangkok: International Labour Organization).

Chen, K. Y. (1977) *Export Expansion and Economic Growth in Some Asian Economies: A Simultaneous Equation Model*, Paper presented at the Fifth World Congress of the International Economic Association, Tokyo, 29 August–3 September.

Engle, R. F. and C. W. J. Granger (1987) 'Cointegration and Error Corrections: Representation, Estimation and Testing', *Econometrica*, vol. 55, no. 2.

Findlay, R. (1978) 'Some Aspects of Technology Transfer and Direct Foreign Investment', *Papers and Proceedings of the 19th Annual Meeting of AER*, May.

Fuller, W. A. (1976) *Introduction to Statistical Time Series* (New York: John Wiley).

Gan, W. B. and L. Y. Soon (1996) 'Explaining the Malaysian Economic Growth', Paper presented at the Twentieth ACAES Conference on Asian Economies, Selangor, Malaysia, 14–17 May.

James, W. E. (1996) 'Sustaining Growth of Exports of Manufactured Goods and Industrialisation in Indonesia: Competition and Technology Issues', Paper presented at the Twentieth ACAES Conference on Asian Economies, Selangor, Malaysia, 14–17 May.

Jung, W. S. and P. Marshall (1985) 'Exports, Growth and Causality in Developing Countries', *Journal of Development Economics*, vol. 18.

Kindleberger, C. P. (1962) *Foreign Trade and the National Economy* (New Haven, Conn.: Yale University Press).

Kravis, I. B. (1970) 'Trade as a Handmaiden of Growth: Similarities between the Nineteenth and Twentieth Centuries', *Economic Journal*, vol. 80, December.

Lamfalussy, A. (1963) *The United Kingdom and the Six: An Essay on Economic Growth in Western Europe* (Homewood, Ill.: Irwin).

Lloyd, P. J. (1996) 'The Role of Foreign Investment in the Success of Asian Industrialisation', Paper presented at the Twentieth ACAES Conference on Asian Economies, Selangor, Malaysia, 14–17 May.

Michaely, M. (1977) 'Exports and Growth: An Empirical Investigation', *Journal of Development Economics*, vol. 4.

Nurkse, R. (1959) *Patterns of Trade and Development* (Stockholm: Almquist and Wiksell).

Park, H. and L. E. Westphal (1986) 'Industrial Strategy and Technological Change: Theory vs. Reality', *Journal of Development Economics*, vol. 22.

Tyler, W. G. (1981) 'Growth and Export Expansion in Developing Countries: Some Empirical Evidence', *Journal of Development Economics*, vol. 9.

Warr, P. G. (1983) 'The Jakarta Export Processing Zone: Benefits and Costs', *Bulletin of Indonesian Economic Studies* vol. 19, no. 3, December.

Warr, P. G. (1987) 'Malaysia's Industrial Enclaves: Benefits and Costs', *The Developing Economies* vol. 25, April.

Westphal, L. E., Y. E. Rhee and G. Pursell (1988) 'Korean Industrial Competence: Where It Came From', *World Bank Staff Working Paper*, no. 469 (Washington DC: World Bank).

World Bank (1993) *The East Asian Miracle: Economic Growth and Public Policy* (New York: Oxford University Press).

5 Is East Asia Less Open than North America and the EEC? No[1]

Sumana Dhar
WORLD BANK

Arvind Panagariya
UNIVERSITY OF MARYLAND

1 INTRODUCTION

Two interrelated issues have attracted much attention from policy-makers and economists in recent years: (i) Is there intra-regional bias in trade flows of countries in Europe, North America and East Asia? and (ii) Are markets in East Asia and or the European Union (EU) relatively closed to outsiders? Within the USA there is widespread belief that, despite low formal trade barriers, both EU and East Asian markets are less open to outsiders than are markets in North America.[2]

The claims of intra-regional bias and lack of openness are often based on simple measures, such as the extent of intra-regional trade and import penetration ratios respectively. Because bilateral trade flows depend on many factors other than regional bias (for example, gross and per capita income levels of trading partners and distance), one cannot equate a high intra-regional trade ratio with regional bias, or a low import penetration ratio with closed markets. Recently, economists have begun to subject at least the issue of regional bias to a more careful scrutiny. Among the authors who have attempted to control for other variables are Krugman (1991), Frankel (1993) and Saxonhouse (1993), who have employed the so-called gravity model in different forms to address the issue of regional-bias.[3]

Krugman runs a rough-and-ready regression using bilateral trade data of the G7 countries and finds evidence of intra-regional bias in trade in North America and Europe. Frankel pursues this analysis more systematically, enlarging the sample to more than sixty countries. Based on the gravity equations for total trade, he finds evidence of intra-regional bias not only in the EU and the Western Hemisphere but also in East Asia. Indeed, comparing the relative size of the coefficients measuring regional bias, the bias is strongest in East Asia. On the other hand, Saxonhouse, who estimates factor-endowments-based gravity equations for bilateral trade flows of twenty-nine manufacturing sectors, concludes against the presence of regional bias in East Asia's trade patterns. He tests whether within- and outside-region exports of East Asia deviate from the general pattern of exports of the rest of the world, and he finds that East Asia's intra-regional exports are well explained by gravity equations estimated for thirty-five countries outside East Asia. Thus, he concludes that East Asia's trade pattern no different from that of other countries.

In this chapter, we subject the twin issues of regional bias and openness to a more careful and detailed econometric analysis than has been done to date.[4] Purely in terms of the quality of estimation, we contribute to the literature in three important ways. First, we work with a much larger data set than anyone has used so far. Second, with the sole exception of Thursby and Thursby (1987), authors estimating the gravity model have pooled the data for different countries and then fitted the same equation to the trade flows of all the countries in the sample.[5] We perform detailed statistical tests and reject unequivocally the hypothesis that the coefficients across countries are identical. We then estimate the equation separately for twenty-two countries located in North and South America, Europe and Asia. Finally, most investigators have estimated the equation using total trade rather than exports and imports separately (Aitken, 1973, Frankel, 1993, and Bergstrand 1985, 1989). We test the hypothesis of equality of coefficients for exports and imports for all countries and overwhelmingly reject it. We then estimate separate equations for exports and imports.

Our main findings are as follows. First, and not surprisingly, the results based on individual country equations are very different from those obtained from pooled, cross-country equations. In some cases, the results are qualitatively different. A good example is the coefficient associated with distance, which shows that bilateral trade does not respond uniformly to the proximity of countries.

Second, if there is intra-regional bias in trade, it is to be found more in North America and the EEC than in East Asia. This result, from country-specific equations, is different from that reached by Frankel (1993) on the basis of the pooled cross-country equations.[6] All countries in the EEC show intra-regional bias in exports as well as imports. The same holds true for the USA and Canada. For six out of nine countries in East Asia, exports have a statistically significant bias *away from* intra-regional markets.

Third, we are able to go one step beyond the existing literature by testing for the openness of each region to outside countries. Out of the forty-four countries in our sample, those outside North America, the EEC and East Asia – twenty seven in all – serve as the control countries. The openness of each of the three regions can be compared with this control group. Our results do not support the hypothesis that East Asian markets are closed to outside countries. For example, in the export equation of the USA, controlling for other variables, exports to East Asia are larger than to countries in the control group; and this conclusion holds true for all countries except Mexico.

Finally, in the same vein, we can consider the openness of the EEC and North America. We find that, *ceteris paribus*, for countries outside the EEC, exports to the EEC are larger than to countries in the control group (that is, outside the three regions). For example, controlling for other variables, exports of Indonesia to EEC countries are larger than to countries in the control group. Most surprisingly, and contrary to conventional wisdom, many countries show exports to North America less than to countries outside the three regions! This is true for all EEC countries and Australia.

The paper is organized as follows. In Section 2, we discuss the basic gravity equation, its rationale and the diagnostic tests performed to arrive at the particular form in which we estimate it. In Section 3, we estimate the equation for a group of twenty-two countries and discuss its implications, and the fourth section gives our concluding remarks.

2 RATIONALE AND DIAGNOSTIC TESTS

Gravitational force between two bodies is directly proportional to the mass of those bodies and inversely proportional to the distance between them. By analogy, the gravity equation postulates that bilateral trade flows are directly proportional to the mass of the two nations, represented by their gross domestic products (GDPs), and inversely proportional to the distance between them. This basic relationship is often augmented by the inclusion of other variables, such as per capita GDPs of the two countries, a dummy variable for a common border, and other dummy variables to represent memberships in different regional arrangements.[7] Because a key issue we wish to address concerns the regional trading blocs in Europe, North America and East Asia, we can represent this relationship by:

$$
\begin{aligned}
\ln T_{jt}^i = {} & \beta_0 + \beta_1 \ln (\text{DISTANCE}_j^i) + \beta_2 \ln (\text{GDP}_t^i) + \beta_3 \ln (\text{GDP}_{jt}) \\
& + \beta_4 \ln (\text{PCGDP}_t^i) + \beta_5 \ln (\text{PCGDP}_{jt}) + \beta_6 (\text{EC6}_j^i) \\
& + \beta_7 (\text{NA}_j^i) + \beta_8 (\text{EA}_j^i) + u_{jt}^i
\end{aligned}
\tag{5.1}
$$

$$
i = 1, \ldots n_i, \quad j = 1, \ldots n_j; \quad i \neq j; \ n_i < n_j
$$

where i denotes the reporter country, j the partner country, t the year of observation, n_I the total number of reporter countries in the sample, and n_J the total number of partner countries. T_{jt}^i stands for either the value of exports from country i to country j, or the value of imports into country i from country j or the sum of the two (that is, total value of trade between i and j) in year t. $DISTANCE_j^i$ denotes the distance between countries i and j, and GDP_t^i and $PCGDP_t^i$ the total and per capita GDP of country i in year t, respectively. GDP_{jt} and $PCGDP_{jt}$ are the corresponding variables for country j. The last three variables are dummy variables. $EC6_j^i$ takes a value of 1 if i and j are both in the EU, but 0 otherwise. NA_j^i and EA_j^i have a similar interpretation, where the former stands for North America and the latter for East Asia.[8]

According to the definitions we have used, EC6 consists of the original six members of the EEC, NA comprises Canada, USA and Mexico, and EA includes ten major countries in East Asia.[9] To some extent, these choices of regional groupings are arbitrary. For example, instead of EC6, one could choose EC9, which would include Denmark, Ireland and the UK, who joined the EEC (now EU) in 1973.[10] Similarly, instead of NA we could define a broader grouping comprising the entire Western hemisphere, and replace EA by the members of Asia-Pacific Economic Co-operation forum (APEC).[11] In making our choices of groupings, we have given the foremost consideration to the fact that the groupings are those where *ex ante* regional effects are the strongest.

A different, albeit related, issue is that neither NA nor EA has existed as a formal regional arrangement over the sample period. Our justification in the case of NA is that an element of preferential trading has existed via offshore assembly provisions between Mexico and the USA, and the special relationship in the automobile sector between the USA and Canada. The justification for EA is that trade preferences have been given by Japan to its Asian trading partners under the GATT's Generalized System of Preferences (GSP). More importantly, there are frequent assertions that through foreign investments that favour intra-regional trade over extra-regional trade, Japan has created an effective bloc in East Asia.

Equation (5.1) does not have a strong theoretical foundation and the reasoning behind the explanatory variables is largely intuitive.[12] Distance is expected to have a negative coefficient because transport costs rise and access to information may decline as distance rises. Controlling for per-capita GDP, total GDP is thought to have a positive effect on the absolute level of trade and this can be shown with the help of a multi-country, multi-good Ricardian model (Anderson, 1979). But it is possible (though not plausible), for the reporter country's GDP to have a negative effect on the *value* of its trade. For example, in the Heckscher–Ohlin model, if all factors expand proportionately in the reporter country, the latter's per capita GDP remains unaffected while total GDP rises. If the elasticity of foreign demand for the country's exports is sufficiently low, even though the *quantities* of exports and imports rise, their *value* may decline.[13] Per capita income is generally hypothesized to have a positive effect on trade because, controlling for total GDP, the higher the per capita income the greater the demand for differentiated products, and the greater the degree of specialization in production. Here again, the argument is not watertight. According to the Linder hypothesis, trade expands with a reduction in differences in per capita incomes. This suggests opposite signs for per capita incomes of the two countries. The last three dummy variables test for possible regional bias and are expected to have positive signs.[14]

All estimation and results in this chapter are based on annual data for forty four countries for the years 1980–91.[15] The sample includes all OECD countries, and all the countries with significant amounts of trade in East Asia, South Asia and Latin America. We exclude countries in Africa, primarily because the quality of data in that region is much poorer than elsewhere and because the distance variable in that region does not capture the same factors as elsewhere, generally because of poor accessibility. We also exclude the countries of Eastern Europe and the Soviet Union.[16]

We subject the data to three diagnostic tests, described in the Appendix to this chapter (pp. 119–20). First, we find that the Cook and Weisberg (1983) test of heteroscedasticity rejects the hypothesis of homoscedasticity at the 99 per cent confidence level; and to obtain robust standard errors and covariance matrices, we use Huber's (1967) formula, discovered independently by White (1980).[17]

Second, we formally test the hypothesis of equality of coefficients across countries. Equation (5.1) is traditionally estimated by pooling the data for all reporter countries for one or more years. This pooling amounts to the restriction that exports of, say, Italy, follow the same relationship to the explanatory variables as exports of, say, Germany. Because this seems unlikely to us, we choose to test formally the hypothesis that the coefficients in equation (5.1) are identical across countries. Like Thursby and Thursby (1987), we overwhelmingly reject this hypothesis.

Finally, we test for the equality of coefficients across exports and imports for each of the twenty-two countries for which we estimate the gravity equation whereas most investigators have implicitly assumed equality by estimating the gravity equation for total trade. We reject the null hypothesis of equality of coefficients with a probability of 95 per cent or higher in every case.

3 ESTIMATION

Based on our diagnostic tests, we estimate separate export and import equations for each of the twenty-two countries using Huber's (1967) formula to ensure that the coefficients and t-ratios are heteroscedasticity consistent. For the purposes of comparison, we also estimate the gravity equation by pooling data from these same twenty-two reporter countries.

One modification we make to equation (5.1) while estimating it at the country level is to drop the per capita GDP of the reporter country. For a particular reporter country i, GDP_t^i and $PCGDP_t^i$ show an extremely high correlation. For most of the twenty-two countries for which we estimate the gravity equation, the correlation exceeds 0.9. Because such a high correlation is bound to give rise to multicollinearity, we choose to drop $PCGDP_t^i$ as a separate variable. For comparability, we also drop this variable in the pooled equation, but, because of cross-country variation, multicollinearity is not a serious problem in this larger sample.

Overall Evaluation of the Results: the Pooled Equation

Table 5.1 presents the estimates for the pooled gravity equation for exports and imports. The first two equations correspond to Equation (5.1) with the omission of per capita GDP of the reporter country, as noted above. The last two equations redefine each regional dummy variable so that it takes a value of 1 if the partner country is in the region, and 0 otherwise. Thus, EAP takes a value of 1 if the partner is in East Asia, and 0 otherwise. EC6P and NAP are defined analogously. Recall that in Equation (5.1), the regional dummy takes a value of 1 if both the reporter and partner are in the region, and measures the *ex post* intra-regional bias in trade after controlling for other determinants of trade. The alternative regional dummy (in the last two equations in Table 5.1) measures whether, in general, the region trades more relative to countries outside the three regions, after we have controlled for other variables.

All coefficients in all the four equations have the expected signs and high t-ratios. Only the t-ratio associated with NA in the first equation is low, but even in this case the coefficient is statistically significant at the 90 per cent (though not at 95 per cent) level of confidence. Increases in the two GDPs and in per-capita GDP of the partner all lead to increases in exports as well as imports. Because the variables are in log form, the coefficients represent the percentage changes in exports or imports due to a 1 per cent change in the two GDPs or in the per capita GDP of the partner. Distance has a negative effect on both imports and exports. All regional dummies have a positive effect on both exports and imports, indicating intra-regional bias in the first two equations and openness relative to countries outside the three regions in the last two equations.

Remarkably, the coefficients relating to the basic gravity variables (GDPs and per capita GDPs of the reporter and partner and distance) show very little variation across equations. The coefficients associated with the reporter and partner-country GDPs vary from 0.733 to 0.886. Those associated with the partner country's GDP vary from 0.20 to 0.22 in the export equations and between 0.365 and 0.390 in the import equations. The coefficient of distance variable varies between 0.750 and 0.973.

Table 5.1 Pooled equation for all reporter countries

	CONST	LGDP_i	LGDP_j	LPCGDP_j	LDIST	EC6	EA	NA	EC6P	EAP	NAP	ADJR2	RT MSE
Reporter and partner in the region													
Log of total exports	−13.615	0.864	0.825	0.200	−0.918	0.153	0.740	0.143				0.59	1.774
	−36.2	77.7	53.3	11.5	−37.3	2.0	10.6	1.7					
Log of total imports*	−17.193	0.886	0.843	0.365	−0.751	0.362	1.283	0.343				0.62	1.780
	−44.7	77.4	55.3	21.3	−30.7	4.8	19.5	3.7					
Only partner in the region													
Log of total exports	−11.286	0.833	0.733	0.220	−0.973				0.722	0.859	0.466	0.60	1.747
	−27.8	73.5	42.4	12.4	−39.7				17.1	20.6	8.2		
Log of total imports*	−14.267	0.829	0.786	0.390	−0.890				0.387	0.999	0.267	0.62	1.763
	−35.4	72.6	46.4	22.4	−36.6				10.1	22.6	5.6		

Notes:
* N = 11419.
Variables with prefix 'L' are in log form. All others are dummy variables.
Sample period is 1980–91. *t*-ratios are given below the coefficients.
For data and statistical tests see Appendix on pp. 119–20.

Comparing the magnitudes of the coefficients of regional dummies in the first two equations, we see that, as in Frankel (1993), East Asia shows the greatest intraregional bias. On the other hand, because the coefficient of EAP in the last two equations is also the highest among regional dummies, East Asia also appears to be the most open region. We could estimate the pooled gravity equation with both sets of regional dummies included but, as we see immediately below, the issues of regional bias and openness are more transparent once we switch to country-specific gravity equations.

Country-specific Equations: Assessing the Intra-regional Bias

When we estimate the gravity equation by country, there is only one reporter country. For example, in Hong Kong's export equation, that country is the only exporter, with the remaining forty-three countries in the sample being importers. Because Hong Kong is in East Asia regional dummies in its equation, NA and EC6, always take a value of 0 (recall that regional dummies EA, NA and EC6 take a value of 1 only when *both* reporter and partner are in the region, and 0 otherwise). Effectively, NA and EC6 variables drop out of Hong Kong's and, indeed, from all East Asian countries' equations. In the same vein, EA and NA drop out of equations for all countries in EC6, and EA and EC6 drop out of equations for all countries in NA. For countries outside all these regions, such as Argentina and Australia, all three regional dummies drop out.

A main message that comes out of country-specific equations with respect to the conventional variables GDP^i, GDP_j, and $PCGDP_j$ and $DISTANCE^i_j$ is that their coefficients vary considerably across countries. Thus, the picture of robustness of the magnitudes of the coefficients emerging out of the pooled equations is misleading. To economize on space, we do not report these coefficients here and, instead, refer the reader to the longer version in Dhar and Panagariya, 1995. But it is worthwhile to consider one example here. Recall that in the pooled equation, the coefficient of $DISTANCE^i_j$ varies from -0.75 to -0.97. In the country-specific equations for exports alone, this coefficient varies from -0.60 for Great Britain to -4.4 for Thailand.

Even more interesting are our results with respect to the regional dummy variables whose coefficients are presented on the leftside of Table 5.2. The first column in this table shows the coefficient associated with the relevant regional dummy, while the second gives the adjusted R^2. Recall that the only regional dummy which does not take a value of 0 all the time is that associated with the region in which the country is located. Because the regions are mutually exclusive, any given country lies in only one region. Therefore, we have at most one coefficient of a regional dummy to be reported.

The key question we want to address is whether East Asia exhibits significantly different characteristics with respect to intra-regional trade when compared with other regions included in the analysis. According to pooled equations, when both the reporter and partner are located in either East Asia or the EEC, there is a positive and statistically significant effect on exports and imports at the 95 per cent or higher level of confidence. The same also holds true for North America in the case of imports. In the case of exports, the statistical significance of the coefficient of NA is in doubt: it is significant at the 90 per cent level of confidence but not at 95 per cent. If we go by the magnitude of the coefficients in each equation, the intraregional bias is largest in East Asia. These results lend some support to claims of intraregional bias in East Asia, and an absence of such a bias in North American trade.[18]

The picture alters substantially when we estimate the equation at the level of the country. For the EEC, both for exports and imports, location of the partner in the same region has a positive and statistically significant effect. The magnitude of the coefficient is uniformly larger than that in the corresponding pooled equation and comparable with the coefficients on which we based the claim of intra-regional bias in East Asian trade. These results contradict the common belief that the coefficient in a pooled equation is a weighted average (with positive weights) of corresponding coefficients estimated from unpooled samples. Based on the pooled equation, we would accept the hypothesis of low intra-regional bias in EEC trade, especially exports. But individual country equations lead us to exactly the opposite conclusion.

For countries in East Asia, differences between results obtained from cross-section and country equations are even more stark. In the country equations, the regional dummy tells different stories for exports and for imports.[19] In the export equation, the dummy is positive and statistically significant for only three (Japan, Korea and Taiwan (China)) out of nine countries. For the remaining six, the coefficient is negative and, in five cases, statistically significant at the 90 per cent or higher level of confidence. These results contradict the positive, large and statistically highly significant coefficient of EA in the pooled equation. On the import side, the story from the pooled equation generally holds. Broadly, the bias is larger for the more developed economies of the region – Japan, Korea and Taiwan (China).

In North America, the story is similar to that in the EEC for the developed countries, but not for Mexico. The regional effect as captured by the NA dummy is quite large and statistically highly significant in both the export and import equations of the USA and Canada. In both cases, the coefficients are far larger than those in the pooled equations. In the case of Mexico, for which fits have generally been poor, the coefficient of NA in the export equation remains stubbornly negative.

To summarize, the results so far suggest an intra-regional bias in both exports and imports in the EEC and North America. Contrary to popular

Table 5.2 Equations for various reporter countries

| Reporter (i) | Reporter and partner in the region | | | | Only partner in the region | | | | | | | |
| | Log of total exports | | Log of total imports* | | Log of total exports* | | | | Log of total imports* | | | |
	Same region	ADJ R2	Same region	ADJ R2	EC6P	EAP	NAP	ADJ R2	EC6P	EAP	NAP	ADJ R2
Countries in EA	EC6 & NA = 0		EC6 & NA = 0						EA & EC6 = 0			
Hong Kong	-0.835	0.68	0.295	0.76	0.670	-0.727	0.679	0.69	0.605	0.254	-0.533	0.77
	-3.2		1.1		4.3	-2.9	2.8		4.1	0.9	-3.1	
Indonesia	-0.701	0.73	0.675	0.75	1.333	-0.391	1.178	0.74	0.280	0.715	-0.301	0.75
	-2.2		2.8		5.7	-1.2	5.5		1.6	3.0	-1.8	
Japan	0.927	0.86	1.479	0.80	0.192	1.010	0.387	0.86	-0.299	1.681	0.589	0.81
	8.1		7.2		1.9	8.5	3.3		-3.7	7.8	5.3	
Korea	2.816	0.33	4.452	0.49	0.423	3.033	1.568	0.35	-0.199	4.641	1.178	0.50
	5.0		8.3		2.8	5.2	5.1		-1.3	8.4	4.8	
Malaysia	-0.306	0.79	1.160	0.67	0.767	-0.164	-0.130	0.80	0.568	1.276	0.051	0.67
	-1.7		7.4		4.0	-0.9	-0.7		3.6	7.4	0.2	
Taiwan (China)	1.068	0.38	2.818	0.46	1.132	1.356	1.987	0.41	0.579	3.004	1.328	0.47
	2.6		7.0		7.8	3.2	6.5		4.3	7.1	5.5	
Philippines	-0.118	0.73	1.541	0.66	1.306	0.090	0.858	0.75	0.639	1.639	0.393	0.67
	-0.3		3.5		5.9	0.2	3.3		3.0	3.7	1.5	
Singapore	-0.960	0.35	0.122	0.45	-0.003	-0.977	-0.241	0.35	-0.009	0.072	-0.671	0.45
	-3.0		0.4		0.0	-2.9	-1.3		-0.1	0.2	-3.7	
Thailand	-2.958	0.80	-1.065	0.78	1.316	-2.667	0.330	0.81	0.003	-1.069	-0.156	0.78
	-11.8		-4.0		5.8	-10.9	1.3		0.0	-3.9	-0.9	
Countries in NA	EA & EC6 = 0		EA & EC6 = 0									
Canada	0.859	0.80	1.497	0.78	0.187	0.985	0.722	0.84	-0.084	1.283	1.159	0.84
	3.5		8.5		1.6	12.7	3.6		-1.1	15.5	7.6	
Mexico	-0.490	0.52	0.895	0.46	0.439	-0.360	-0.295	0.52	0.628	-0.686	1.174	0.47
	-2.0		4.2		2.7	-1.0	-1.1		4.6	-2.0	4.7	
USA	2.004	0.75	2.472	0.71	0.471	1.315	1.368	0.84	0.185	1.854	1.339	0.86
	11.5		11.1		5.3	17.5	9.3		2.5	23.6	7.7	

Countries in EC 6 — EA & NA = 0   EA & NA = 0

	EA & NA = 0	R²	EA & NA = 0	R²	(model 3)	R²	(model 4)	R²
Belgium	0.699 (9.4)	0.87	1.029 (11.9)	0.90	0.494 (6.4); 0.801 (8.6); −0.381 (−3.4)	0.89	0.902 (10.7); 0.228 (3.5); −0.514 (−4.6)	0.91
Luxemburg	0.314 (4.6)	0.91	0.600 (9.0)	0.86	0.176 (2.4); 0.599 (9.7); −0.374 (−4.1)	0.93	0.364 (5.3); 0.881 (13.7); −0.790 (−8.4)	0.92
West Germany	0.463 (6.5)	0.91	0.804 (12.4)	0.92	0.319 (4.8); 0.660 (9.5); −0.008 (−0.1)	0.92	0.638 (10.2); 0.698 (12.7); −0.139 (−1.6)	0.94
France	0.663 (10.9)	0.90	1.172 (21.3)	0.91	0.625 (9.3); 0.305 (4.1); −0.328 (−3.8)	0.91	1.054 (17.7); 0.072 (1.2); −0.751 (−7.1)	0.92
Italy								
Netherlands	0.734 (9.74)	0.88	0.559 (5.30)	0.82	0.525 (6.4); 0.739 (9.9); −0.442 (−4.1)	0.90	0.324 (3.9); 1.228 (17.9); −0.027 (−0.2)	0.89

Countries outside regional groups

	EC 6 EA NA = 0	R²	EA & NA = 0	R²	(model 3)	R²	(model 4)	R²
Argentina	0	0.44	0	0.46	1.657 (8.6); 0.796 (4.8); 0.856 (4.3)	0.50	1.215 (6.8); 0.179 (0.7); 1.040 (4.2)	0.47
Australia	0	0.74	0	0.70	1.055 (6.7); 0.917 (7.6); −0.514 (−2.6)	0.77	0.393 (2.6); 1.124 (8.3); −0.479 (−2.4)	0.73
Brazil	0	0.65	0	0.56	0.826 (8.1); 1.071 (10.2); 0.441 (4.2)	0.72	0.529 (4.4); 1.672 (7.7); 1.161 (6.8)	0.61
Great Britain	0	0.75	0	0.75	0.199 (2.0); 0.790 (6.4); 0.164 (1.0)	0.78	0.005 (0.1); 1.098 (9.2); −0.221 (−1.4)	0.79
India	0	0.80	0	0.73	1.116 (7.3); 0.883 (6.8); 1.074 (5.6)	0.83	0.402 (1.7); 0.839 (5.6); −0.022 (−0.1)	0.74

Pooled equation (as reported in Tables 5.1) N = 11419

	EC 6 EA NA	R²	EC 6 EA NA	R²	(model 3)	R²	(model 4)	R²
Pooled equation	0.15 (2.0); 0.74 (10.6); 0.1 (1.7)	0.59	0.36 (4.8); 1.28 (19.5); 0.34 (3.7)	0.62	0.722 (17.1); 0.859 (20.6); 0.466 (8.2)	0.60	0.387 (10.1); 0.999 (22.6); 0.267 (5.6)	0.62

Notes:
*   Exports : N = 527, except the Philippines 439, West Germany and India 484.
*   Imports : N = 527, except India 439, the Philippines and West Germany 484.
Only RHS variables reported here are the regional dummies. Other independent variables used are the same as in Table 5.1.
Sample period is 1980–91. *t*-ratios are given below the coefficients.
For data and statistical tests see Appendix on p. 119.

claims, the bias is weaker in East Asia than in the EU and North America. On the export side, six out of nine countries show a negative bias which is statistically significant. On the import side, the positive bias is not peculiar to East Asia, being also present in the EU and North America.

'Other Region' Effects

So far, we have allowed for trade effects that are purely intra-regional. We did not control for the bias arising from the location of a partner in another bloc – for example, the effects on the exports of a North American country of the location of a partner in the EEC or East Asia. It may be argued that if East Asia or the EEC is a closed bloc, *ceteris paribus*, the USA will be able to export less to countries in this region than to countries not belonging to any bloc. Controlling for this bias, we can also compare intra-regional bias with extra-regional bias. For example, we can consider the possibility that North America may be more open than other regions to all countries or that East Asia may be closed to outside countries. To capture such effects, we now introduce dummies for the three regions. Formally, our equation now takes the form:

$$
\begin{aligned}
\ln T^i_{jt} = {} & \beta^i_0 + \beta^i_1 \ln (\text{DISTANCE}^i_j) + \beta^i_2 \ln (\text{GDP}^i_t) \\
& + \beta^i_3 \ln (\text{GDP}_{jt}) + \beta^i_4 \ln (\text{PCGDP}_{jt}) + \beta^i_5 (\text{EC6P}_j) \\
& + \beta^i_6 ((\text{NAP}_j) + \beta^i_7 (\text{EAP}_j) + u^i_{jt} \\
& j = 1, \cdots, \quad n_J, \quad t = 1980, \cdots, 1991; \quad i \neq j
\end{aligned}
\tag{5.2}
$$

where we add a 'P' at the end of the symbol for each regional dummy to distinguish it from the corresponding dummy variable in equation (5.1). EC6P_{jt}, EAP_{jt} and NAP_{jt} take the value of 1 when the reporting country's trading partner belongs to the EEC, East Asia and North America, respectively. If the partner does not belong to the region, the value is 0.

Note that the interpretation of the coefficients of these dummy variables is different depending on whether the reporter also belongs to a given region or not. When the reporter is in the same region, the dummy coincides with that in the previous sub-section and captures intra-regional effects. If the reporter country is outside the region, the dummy measures the general openness of the region. For example, in an East Asian country's equation, EAP measures intra-regional bias, but in a North American country's equation, it measures East Asia's openness to outside countries. If intra-regional bias is present, for a country located in East Asia, the coefficient of the EAP dummy will be positive. If East Asia is more open than the countries outside that region, the coefficient of EAP in equations of countries outside East Asia will be positive.

The right side of Table 5.2 reports the results of our estimation relating to the three dummy variables. Once again, to save space, we do not report the coefficients of other variables.

The first point to note is that compared with the left side of the table, the adjusted R^2 is marginally higher. This means that the addition of partner dummies increases the explanatory power of the model. Because the results of the dummies capturing intraregional effects (that is, the reporter lies in the region represented by the dummy) remain qualitatively unchanged, we here focus on dummies capturing the effects of outside regions (that is, when the reporter does not lie in the region represented by the dummy).

Consider first the export equation. For countries outside East Asia, with the sole exception of Mexico, EAP has a positive and statistically significant coefficient at well above the 99 per cent level of confidence. For countries outside the EEC, the same holds true for EC6P, except in the cases of Japan and Singapore. For Japan, the coefficient is positive and statistically significant at the 95 per cent level of confidence, while for Singapore, it is negative and statistically insignificant. For countries outside North America, the coefficient of NAP shows more ambiguity. For four out of five countries in the EEC, NAP has a negative and statistically significant coefficient at the 99 per cent level of confidence. The same also holds true for Australia, though not for countries in East Asia. In the latter case, the coefficient is positive and statistically significant at the 99 per cent level of confidence for seven out of nine countries, and negative and statistically insignificant for the remaining two countries. In sum, controlling for other variables, countries export more to East Asia and the EEC than to countries outside the three regions represented in Equation (5.2). Countries in the EEC export less to North America than to countries outside the three regions in the sample.

A closer examination of the export equations on the right side of Table 5.2 reveals that for four out of five countries in the EEC, the coefficient of EAP is *larger* than that of EC6P. In other words, relative to countries outside the three regions, the bias in exports in favour of East Asia is larger than the intra-regional bias! This also holds true for Canada. For the USA, the coefficient for EAP (1.32) is virtually the same as for NAP (1.37), implying that the bias in favour of East Asia is not much less than the intra-regional bias. For the majority of countries in East Asia, the bias in favour of the EEC is the largest. For Japan and Korea, the intra-regional bias, and for Taiwan (China), the bias in favour of North America predominates, when compared with exports to countries outside the three regions.

In the import equations we see some evidence supporting the hypothesis of a bias against imports from North America. Oddly, the evidence points not to Japan or much of East Asia but to the EEC as the culprit. Relative to countries outside the three regions, there is a favourable bias for North

America but it is less than the intra-regional bias. The region that has most reasons to complain against Japan and Korea is the EEC, whose coefficient is negative.

To conclude, for countries in the EEC, on the whole, the bias in both exports and imports is positive when the partner is in the EEC or East Asia, while it is negative when the partner is in North America. In the export equation, except in the case of Italy, the coefficient of EAP is consistently larger than that of EC6P, contradicting strongly the hypothesis that East Asian markets are closed to outside countries. Oddly enough, it is towards North America that exports show a negative and statistically significant bias for four of the five countries in the EEC.

4   CONCLUSIONS

Intra-regional bias in trade is to be found more in North America and the EEC than in East Asia. Canada, the USA and all countries in the EEC show intra-regional bias in exports as well as imports. In East Asia, exports of six out of nine countries have a statistically significant bias *away from* intra-regional markets.

We also compare the openness of each of the three regions with a control group of twenty-seven countries outside North America, the EEC and East Asia. Our results do not support the hypothesis that East Asian markets are closed to outside countries. *Ceteris paribus*, for countries outside the EEC, exports to the EEC are larger than to countries in the control group. Most surprisingly, and contrary to the conventional wisdom, controlling for other variables, exports to North America are less than to countries outside the three regions for all EEC countries and Australia!

We have also argued that conclusions drawn from individual country equations are very different from those obtained from traditional pooled, cross-country equations. In virtually all cases, not surprisingly, the cross-country equation masks large differences across countries. For example, in the export equations, the coefficient associated with distance varies between -4.4 and -0.60. More importantly, while in the pooled equation exports of East Asia show a strong intra-regional bias, when considered individually, exports of six out of nine countries show *extra-regional* bias.

Appendix: Data and Statistical Tests

Data

Years:	1980–91.
Trade:	$X_j^i(M_j^i)$ – average annual US dollar value of exports (imports) between each reporter and partner for 1980–91 from the COMTRADE database of UN Statistical Organization, Geneva.
GDP:	GDP^i, GDP_j – GDP in US dollars of the reporter and partner for 1980–91 from the National Accounts database of the World Bank, which uses the Atlas Method. The data in current prices are converted from the local currency into US dollars when the exchange rate is highly distorted.
Population:	From Social and Demographic Indicators database of the World Bank.
Distance:	Distance$_j^i$ – the straight-line distance between major ports of entry of reporter and partner, from Linneman (1966) complemented by Fitzpatrick and Madlin (1986).
Regions:	EC6, EA, NA: dummy = 1 if both reporter and partner are members of a regional block, 0 otherwise; EC6P, EAP, NAP: dummy = 1 if partner is a member of a regional block, 0 otherwise.

Partner countries in the sample which do not appear in Tables 5.1 and 5.2:

Asia	Bangladesh, China, Pakistan, Sri Lanka.
Europe	Ireland, Spain, Greece, Portugal, Turkey, Austria, Switzerland, Finland, Norway, Sweden.
Oceania	New Zealand.
South America	Bolivia, Chile, Colombia, Peru, Paraguay, Uruguay, Venezuela.

Statistical Tests

The Cook–Weisberg (1983) test of heteroscedasticity searches for the existence of increasing or decreasing variation in the residuals in relation to the fitted values by modelling variance as a function of the fitted values. Letting $\hat{y}_j$ be the fitted value of y_i and defining vector $\mathbf{z_j} = (\hat{y}_j^2, \hat{y}_j^3, \hat{y}_j^4)$, heteroscedasticity is modelled as var $(u_j) = \sigma^2[\exp(\mathbf{z_j t})]$ where $\mathbf{t}$ is a vector with the same dimension is $\mathbf{z_j}$. The test involves estimating the model $\hat{u}_j^2 = a + \mathbf{z_j t} + v_j$ and testing $\mathbf{t} = 0$.

To test for the equality of coefficients across countries, suppose the countries in the sample are numbered 1, 2, ..., 44 and the total number of explanatory variables is K. Let the explanatory variables be $x_1, \ldots x_k$. Taking two countries at a time, say 1 and r, we estimate the following equation.

$$\ln T_{jt}^i = (\beta_0 + \gamma_0\,D_0^r) + (\beta_1 + \gamma_1\,D_1^r)\,x_{1t}^i + \cdots + (\beta_k + \gamma_k\,D_k^r)\,x_{kt}^i + u_{jt}^i$$
$$i = 1, r; \quad j = 1, \cdots, 44; \quad i \neq j; \quad t = 1980, \cdots, 1991 \tag{A1}$$

where T_{jt}^i is the relevant trade flow between i and j in year t, $(\beta_0\ \beta_1 \ldots \beta_k)$ and $(\gamma_0\ \gamma_1 \ldots \gamma_k)$ are coefficients to be estimated, $x_{1t}^i \ldots x_{kt}^i$ are values (in log if appropriate) of the explanatory variables associated with country i in period t, and $D_0^r, D_1^r, D_2^r \ldots D_k^r$ are dummy variables which take a value of 1 if the observation relates to country j and 0 otherwise. Under the hypothesis that the coefficients associated with each explanatory variable for country 1 and r are the same, we have $\gamma_0 = \gamma_1 = \ldots = \gamma_k = 0$. We used the standard F-test to check the validity of this null hypothesis. Because the test is done on a pairwise basis, it must be applied to all possible pairs of countries. That is to say, country 1 must be checked against all $r = 2, \ldots 44$, country 2 against all $r = 1, \ldots, 44$ and $r \not\equiv 2$, etc. To limit the number of cases, we chose to apply the test to exports from a total of 22 countries whose equations are eventually estimated. Even then, we have 231 pairs of countries to compare. We rejected the null hypothesis of the equality of coefficients across countries in every one of these cases with 99% probability. Indeed, in a large number of cases, the much stronger hypothesis of equality of individual coefficients (i.e., $\gamma_k = 0$) was rejected with a 90% or higher probability using the t-test.

Finally, to test for the equality of coefficients for exports and imports, we estimated Equation 5.1 for a given country. Because the error terms in the export and import equations are likely to exhibit contemporaneous correlation, we used SUR method. We then applied the standard F-test for equality of coefficients in the two equations. Once again, the test was repeated for each of the 22 countries. In each case, the null hypothesis of the equality of coefficients was rejected.

Notes

1. Findings, interpretations and conclusions in this chapter are entirely those of the authors and should not be attributed to the World Bank, its affiliated organizations, or to members of its Board of Executive Directors or the countries they represent. We thank the editors of the volume and a referee for extensive comments which led to a major revision of the original version of the chapter. We also acknowledge helpful comments from Junichi Goto, Paul Armington, Ann Harrison, Lant Pritchett, Maurice Schiff and Sethaput Suthiwart-Narueput on earlier drafts of the chapter.
    The choice of title may appear surprising, since the EEC has become the EU. We justify it on the basis that the 'EEC bloc' in our statistical analysis is the six original members of the EU.
2. The view is expressed most strongly with respect to Japan. See Krugman (1993) and Dornbusch (1993).
3. The history of the gravity model goes further back. The model was pioneered by Tinbergen (1962) and Poyhonen (1963) independently, and extended by Linneman (1966). To our knowledge, Aitken (1973) was the first to use the gravity equation to evaluate regional effects. Subsequently, Thursby and Thursby (1987) and Bergstrand (1985, 1989) also allowed for regional effects.
4. At one level, it may be argued that openness should be measured in terms of trade barriers rather than trade-to-GDP ratio or any other *ex post* measure. Some policy-makers and economists contend, however, that the effect of lower trade barriers on trade may not be realized, because of restrictive regulatory policies or oligopolies.
5. Thursby and Thursby include several short-run variables such as the exchange-rate variability and prices in the equations. This mixing of short-run and long-run variables inevitably influences their results. In this chapter, we follow closely the pure gravity equation as, for example, in Aitken (1973) and Frankel (1993), and include only the long-run variables.
6. As noted earlier, Frankel found the intraregional bias to be stronger in East Asia than in the EEC and Western hemisphere.

7. Rationale for the inclusion of price and exchange rate variables by Thursby and Thursby (1987) and Bergstrand (1985, 1989) is derived from essentially partial equilibrium models. Bergstrand lays out a general equilibrium model but then chooses not to solve for equilibrium prices. As illustrated in Anderson (1979) and Markusen (1986), once we solve for prices, only income or endowments variables should appear in the equation. This is particularly true if we are interested in the determinants of long-run trade flows.

8. It is customary to include a dummy variable representing a common border between i and j. Because we found that variable to be often highly correlated with the regional dummies, we did not include it in our analysis.

9. These are: China, Hong Kong, Indonesia, Japan, Malaysia, the Philippines, Singapore, South Korea, Taiwan and Thailand.

10. The case for including the remaining five members of the EU is less compelling, since they began the implementation of the customs union with the EC9 after 1981 and our sample period begins in 1980. But even here one can argue that since NAFTA was not even voted on by the US Congress until December 1993, and that is included here as a separate regional grouping, we could justify including the last five members of the EU also.

11. Frankel (1993) and Frankel and Wei (1997) experiment with a variety of group-ings. Their broad conclusions are not affected by the choice of groupings.

12. *Ex post* rationalizations of the gravity equation include Anderson (1979) and Bergstrand (1985, 1989) and, most recently, Deardorff (1995).

13. For more on this, see Thursby and Thursby (1987) and Bergstrand (1985, 1989).

14. Frankel (1993) is the main author who uses the *traditional* gravity equation to address the issue of an East Asian trading bloc. The equation he employs is slightly different from ours. In effect, Frankel restricts Equation (5.1) such that coefficients associated with the reporter- and partner-country GDPs and those associated with the two per capita GDPs are identical. Since theory does not give a clear guidance on even the *signs* of the reporter-country GDP and per capita GDP, let alone their magnitudes, such a restriction is unwarranted.

15. Technically, there are forty-five countries in the sample. But since trade data are reported jointly for Belgium and Luxemburg, this reduces the number of obser-vations in any one year to forty-four. In addition, data are missing for China for certain years.

16. A complete list of the countries can be found in the longer version of the paper (Dhar and Panagariya, 1995).

17. We used the econometric package 'STATA' for all our computations. The Cook–Weisberg test and Huber formula were chosen because of their ready availability in STATA. The latter does not require that errors be homoscedastic or that the observations follow an assumed distribution and produces robust standard errors and covariance matrices.

18. The intraregional bias shown in our cross-section equations is similar to that obtained by Frankel (1993) for total trade. He finds the coefficients for the East Asian block to be the largest at 1.84. For the EU the coefficient takes the value 0.4. The coefficient associated with NA is statistically insignificant as in our pooled export equation.

19. Note that there is no contradiction between a positive intra-regional bias in exports and a negative bias in imports, or vice versa. Because trade is not balanced bilaterally, and controlling for other variables, Japan may export more to its East Asian partners than to outside countries but import less from them than from the latter.

References

Aitken, N. D. (1973) 'The Effect of the EEC and EFTA on European Trade: A Temporal Cross-Section Analysis', *American Economic Review*, vol. 63, no. 55, pp. 881–92.

Anderson, J. E. (1979) 'A Theoretical Foundation for the Gravity Equation', *American Economic Review*, vol. 69, March, pp. 106–16.

Bergstrand, J. H. (1985) 'The Gravity Equation in International Trade: Some Microeconomic Foundations and Empirical Evidence', *Review of Economics and Statistics*, vol. 67, August, pp. 474–81.

Bergstrand, J. H. (1989) 'The Generalized Gravity Equation, Monopolistic Competition, and the Factor Proportions Theory in International Trade', *Review of Economics and Statistics*, vol. 71, pp. 143–53.

Cook, R. D. and S. Weisberg (1983) 'Diagnostic for Heteroscedasticity in Regression', *Biometrika*, vol. 70, pp. 1–10.

Deardorff, A. V. (1995) 'Determinants of Bilateral Trade: Does Gravity Work in a Neoclassical World?', National Bureau of Economic Research Working Paper no. 5377.

Dhar, S. and A. Panagariya (1995) 'Is East Asia Less Open than North America and the EEC? No.', Center for International Economics, University of Maryland at College Park, Working Paper no. 10.

Dornbusch, R. (1993) 'Round Table Discussion', in J. de Melo and A. Panagariya (eds), *New Dimensions in Regional Integration* (Washington DC: The World Bank).

Fitzpatrick, G. L. and M. J. Madlin (1986) *Direct Line Distances* (London: Scarecrow).

Frankel, J. A. (1993) 'Is Japan Creating a Yen Bloc in East Asia and the Pacific?', in J. A. Frankel and M. Kahler (eds), *Regionalism and Rivalry: Japan and the United States in Pacific Asia* (Chicago: University of Chicago Press for NBER), pp. 53–87.

Frankel, J. and S.-J. Wei (1997) 'The New Regionalism and Asia: Impact and Options', in A. Panagariya, M. Quibria and N. Rao, *The Global Trading System and Developing Asia* (Hong Kong: Oxford University Press).

Huber, P. J. (1967) 'The Behavior of Maximum Likelihood Estimates under Non-Standard Conditions', *Proceedings of the Fifth Berkeley Symposium on Mathematical Statistics and Probability*, vol. 1, pp. 221–33.

Krugman, P. (1991) 'The Move Toward Free Trade Zones', in *Policy Implications of Trade and Currency Zones* (Jackson Hole, Wyoming: Federal Reserve Bank of Kansas).

Krugman, P. (1993) 'Regionalism vs. Multilateralism: Analytical Notes', in J. de Melo, and A. Panagariya (eds), *New Dimensions in Regional Integration* (Washington DC: The World Bank).

Linnemann, H. (1966) *An Econometric Study of International Trade Flows* (Amsterdam: North-Holland).

Markusen, J. R. (1986) 'Explaining the Volume of Trade: An Eclectic Approach', *American Economic Review*, vol. 76, December, pp. 1002–11.

Poyhonen, P. (1963) 'A Tentative Model for the Volume of Trade between Countries', *Weltwirtschaftliches Archiv*, vol. 90, no. 1, pp. 93–100.

Saxonhouse, G. R. (1993) 'Trading Blocks and East Asia', in J. de Melo and A. Panagariya (eds), *New Dimensions in Regional Integration* Washington DC: The World Bank).

Thursby, J. G., and M. C. Thursby (1987) 'Bilateral Trade Flows, the Linder Hypothesis, and the Exchange Risk', *Review of Economics and Statistics*, vol. 69, pp. 488–95.

Tinbergen, J. (1962) *Shaping the World Economy: Suggestions for International Economic Policy*, (New York:).

White, H. (1980) 'A Heteroscedasticity-Consistent Covariance Matrix Estimator and a Direct Test for Heteroscedasticity', *Econometrica*, vol. 48, pp. 817–30.

Comment

Junichi Goto

KOBE UNIVERSITY AND YALE UNIVERSITY

This chapter compares the openness of East Asian countries with those of Europe and North America. The title succinctly summarizes the question posed and the answer to it, and we know everything about the chapter by just looking at its title. To the question 'Is East Asia Less Open Than North America and the EEC?' the authors clearly say 'No'.

The question is very important in the real world, because many outside countries, especially the USA, often complain that the markets of the East Asian countries are very closed to outside countries, although East Asia exports freely to the 'open' outside market. I agree with the authors' conclusion that East Asia is not less open than other regions, not because I am from Japan and supporting the view of the Ministry of International Trade and Industry but because after living in the USA for many years I have come to believe that, at least *ex-ante*, the openness of East Asia is similar to that of the USA. Hence this chapter gives me more supporting evidence for my belief.

In addition to its relevance to the real world debate, the paper makes an important methodological contribution. It utilizes gravity equations where export (or import) is regressed on size (GDP), distance, and several other variables, as Frankel and others did in their papers. However, the method of this chapter is different from the latter in two important aspects:

(i) While Frankel and others use pooled, cross-country gravity equations, the present chapter uses country-specific equations. Hence, the authors do not need to assume that the coefficients across countries are identical.

(ii) Unlike Frankel and others, the present chapter estimates export equations and import equations separately, so that they do not have to assume the equality of coefficients for exports and imports. As I discuss below, this separation of exports from imports reveals an interesting fact of the East Asian trade pattern.

My comments on this excellent and very informative chapter concern three points.

The first comment concerns the country selection for the three groups: East Asia, Europe, and North America. Although the European and North

American groups consist of very similar countries, East Asia is a very hetero-geneous group. But many studies suggest that greater similarity of trading partners tends to increase the amount of trade between them. For example, Linder's hypothesis implies that trade in manufactured goods between two countries will be inversely related to the difference in their per capita incomes. Further, the so-called New Trade Theory initiated by Krugman and others predicts, and the empirical study by Peter Lloyd suggests, that more intra-industry trade is created between similar industrialized countries in order to exploit the benefit of technology of increasing returns to scale. As Table 5A shows, the East Asian group in the chapter consists of very different countries, ranging from very poor (low-income) countries such as China and Indonesia, where per captia incomes are a mere $470 and $670, respectively, to one of the richest countries of the world, Japan, where per capita income is

Table 5A   Per capita GNP (constant US$)

East Asia				**Other EC12**		
China	470	L				
Japan	28 190	H				
Indonesia	670	L				
Malaysia	2 790	UM				
Philippines	770	LM				
Thailand	1 840	LM				
Hong Kong	15 360	H				
Korea, RP	6 790	UM				
Singapore	15 730	H				
EU6				**Other EC12**		
Belgium-Luxemburg	20 880	H		Denmark	26 000	H
Germany, FR	23 030	H		UK	17 790	H
France	22 260	H		Spain	13 970	H
Italy	20 460	H		Ireland	12 210	H
Netherland	20 480	H		Portugal	7 450	UM
				Greece	7 290	UM
North America						
Canada	20 710	H				
Mexico	3 470	UM				
USA	23 240	H				

Notes:
H – High income
UM – Upper middle income
LM – Lower middle income
L – Low income

Source: *World Bank: World Development Report 1994.*

more than $28 000. However, as the European group, this chapter considers only six EU countries. Per capita incomes of these countries are strikingly similar, at a little over $20 000, and all these countries are classified as high-income countries by the World Bank. In North America, per capita incomes of Canada and the USA are also very similar. Although that of Mexico is different, the estimation results in the paper show that Mexico is an outlier in the North American group in any case. When we speak of the European region today we mean more than the six founder-members of the original EEC; probably we mean the EC 12 or the EU15 or more. If we expand the members of the European group, the strong homogeneity of the EU six will not be maintained. For example, per capita incomes of Portugal and Greece are about a third of those of the six. I would like to see how the authors' conclusion is modified (or maintained intact) if the European group is expanded to the EC 12 or EU15.

My second comment concerns the interpretation of Table 5.2, where regional dummies are included in the estimation equations. Although the authors correctly estimate export and import equations separately, they do not distinguish between the two when they interpret the estimation results. On pp. 113–16 the authors say 'Contrary to popular claims, the (intra-regional) bias is weaker in East Asia than in the EU and North America. On the export side, six out of nine countries show a negative bias which is statistically significant. On the import side, the positive bias is not peculiar to East Asia, being also present in the EU and North America'. However, it seems to me that the difference between the analyses of exports and of imports in Table 5.2 supports the 'popular claims' (or US complaint) on the East Asian trade pattern. Table 5.2 suggests that most East Asian countries tend to export to outside countries (presumably to the USA), but also that most of them, except for Thailand, tend to import from other East Asian countries. Thus, the table suggests that while East Asia imports from the region, it is exporting all over the world, which summarises the popular (and especially the US) belief. In contrast, the EU six import from themselves but export to themselves also.

My third comment is a rather minor one. When we examine the tables in the chapter, Hong Kong and Singapore (and Thailand) are often outliers in the East Asian group. Although the reason for Thailand is unclear, Hong Kong and Singapore are different from other countries in that they are extremely open trading countries. When we look at the usual trade statistics published by the IMF and others, these data typically include the amount of imports for re-export, and the value of exports (or imports) of Hong Kong often well exceeds the GNP because many imports are just for re-export. In this sense, the attempt of Frankel to introduce dummy variables for Singapore and Hong Kong seems to be, to some extent, justified. In view of this, I would like to ask the authors first to check whether the value of re-exports is subtracted from the value of exports in their regression analysis. If not, the estimation results for the two countries will be distorted. And, even if this data problem does not arise, some accommodation seems to be needed for Hong Kong and Singapore, which are extremely small open economies.

Finally, I would like to point out an important characteristic of East Asian exports and its implication for regional trading arrangements in Asia and the Pacific, which is in conformity with the findings of this chapter, at least as far as the export market is concerned. Most East Asian countries are heavily dependent on the market on the other side of the Pacific Ocean, particularly on the huge US markets. Therefore, any regional arrangements which exclude the USA are unlikely. For example, in spite of the enthusiastic proposal for the EAEC by Prime Minister Mahathir of Malaysia, most East Asian countries did not buy the idea, which is now almost dead. In contrast to the EAEC, APEC emerges as a very promising arrangement. It is promising because:

(i)   it includes both side of the Pacific, which have already been close trading partners for many years (or 'natural' trading partners);

(ii) it will have considerable bargaining power in world trade negotiations, which arises from its size (the combined share of APEC in world GNP is almost 50 per cent); and

(iii) as the study by Koichi Hamada and I (using a CGE model for regional integration) suggests, the APEC very much increases members' welfare without harming non-members' welfare very much. Therefore, incentive-wise, APEC is, unlike EAEC and other regional trading arrangements, one of the most promising configurations of regional integration in the area.

Note

1.   Goto, J. and K. Hamada (1996) 'Regional Economic Integration and Article XXIV of the GATT', Economic Growth Center Discussion Paper (New Haven, Conn.: Yale University).

Part II
Trade Policy and the 'isms'

6 Multilateral Roads to Regionalism

Wilfred J. Ethier

UNIVERSITY OF PENNSYLVANIA

1 INTRODUCTION

Regionalism has returned. The 'old regionalism' initiatives of the 1950s and 1960s eventually petered out (except, of course, in Western Europe). But since the late 1980s a 'new regionalism' has run rampant, with dozens of new initiatives coming on the scene. As a result, well over a hundred regional arrangements, involving most nations, now exist.

Trade theorists have investigated two questions: (i) Will the formation of regional trading blocs raise or lower welfare? Answers are mixed;[1] (ii) Will regionalism help or hamper multilateral efforts for trade liberalization? Answers to this question are more negative, but still basically mixed.[2] Two features have been prominent in these investigations: the treatment of regional integration as being exogenous, and a Vinerian perspective on regional integration as a combination of trade creation and trade diversion.

The Vinerian perspective was developed in response to the emergence of the 'old regionalism' after the Second World War. But the international environment greeting the 'new regionalism' differs from that experienced by the old regionalism in two critical ways:

(i) The multilateral liberalization of trade in manufactured goods among the industrial countries is much more complete now than it was then.

(ii) Scores of economically less advanced countries have abandoned the basically autarkic, anti-market policies they followed during the days of the old regionalism and are now actively trying to join the multilateral trading system.

As a result, there may well be a *qualitative* distinction between the old regionalism and the new. For example, the Vinerian paradigm of trade creation versus trade diversion drove analysis of the former, but it is by no means clear that it should drive analysis of the latter.

This Chapter concerns attempts to describe what the qualitative new regionalism might be. I wish to treat regionalism as being *endogenous*, and I model several ways in which it might emerge in a world characterized by past

131

success in multilateral liberalization and currently by extensive reform attempts. Two common messages emerge from the various models: (i) regionalism is an endogenous response to the development of the multilateral trading system, and treating it as exogenous is misleading; and (ii) the primary purpose of the new regionalism is not to foster regional integration and trade diversion; rather, it is a response to such integration that allows the region to adapt to multilateral developments. Thus the paper suggests a presumption that regional integration facilitates multilateral liberalization.[3]

The next section describes the stylized facts of the new regionalism, and how they differ from those of the old regionalism that motivated the Vinerian perspective. The latter is briefly reviewed in section 3. Sections 4–7 then describe, with varying degrees of rigour and completeness, four alternative – but complementary – approaches that have been suggested as explanations of how regionalism could develop in a multilateral world.

2   THE STYLIZED FACTS OF THE NEW REGIONALISM

The following six characteristics do not apply to all current regional initiatives, which are quite diverse, but they do apply to most of the more important ones.

(i)   Contemporary regionalism typically involves one or more small countries linking up with a big country.

In the North American Free Trade Area (NAFTA) Mexico and Canada are each a small fraction, economically, of the USA; the new members of the European Union (EU) are tiny relative to the EU itself; the same is true of the Central European adherents to the Europe Agreements (EA) with the EU; Brazil is likely to play a dominant role in Mercosur and so on.

(ii)   Typically, the small countries have recently made, or are making, significant unilateral reforms.

This is dramatically true of the EA's central European participants, which had abandoned Communism, of the members of Mercosur (where it is also true of the big country, Brazil) and of Mexico. But it also characterizes, to a lesser degree, the small industrial-country participants in various regional initiatives. Canada had turned away from Trudeau-style economic nationalism as it negotiated a free trade agreement with the USA, and the Scandinavian applicants to the EU (except for Norway, which declined to join) had made significant reforms in some sectors (for example, agriculture).

(iii)   A dramatic move to free trade between members is *not* what it's all about: the degree of liberalization is typically modest. Thus the Vinerian paradigm is not a natural starting point.

For example, NAFTA in fact provides only modest liberalization: US tariffs were already low and NAFTA hedges sensitive sectors in all sorts of ways. Canada and Mexico have done somewhat more, but the most significant measures (largely Mexican) were unilateral and not part of NAFTA. The accession of new members to the EU is even more glaring: because of their prior arrangements, the trade relations of Austria, Finland and Sweden with the EU are virtually identical to what they would have been had they decided not to join! The EA provide for little in the way of concrete liberalization. Even with the more ambitious Mercosur, the liberalization involved is small relative to the unilateral liberalizations of the members.

(iv)   The liberalization that is achieved is due primarily to concessions by the small countries, and not by the large country: the agreements are quite one-sided.

The moderate liberalization achieved in NAFTA has resulted much more from 'concessions' by Mexico and Canada than from the US contribution. In negotiations over enlargement, the EU has been flexible with regard to financial responsibilities and periods of adjustment, but has always maintained a take-it-or-leave-it attitude regarding the nature and structure of the EU itself. The EA involve virtually no 'concessions' by the EU: indeed, the EU instituted anti-dumping measures against some of its new partners even as the initial agreements were coming into effect! In a sense, this asymmetry is a direct reflection of how the world has changed since the days of the old regionalism: one reason that the new small countries get only small tariff advantages is simply that the large countries have small tariffs to begin with. Mercosur is perhaps the exception that proves the rule: the big member country is also one of the reformers.

(v)   Regional arrangements often involve 'deep' integration: the partners seldom confine themselves to reducing or eliminating tariff barriers, but also harmonize or adjust diverse assortments of other economic policies.

The EU is a clear and dramatic example of this. The US – Canadian agreement and the subsequent NAFTA included a host of commitments to economic reform by Canada and Mexico. Sometimes partners in regional arrangements exempt each other from acts of administered protection (such as anti-dumping duties), but often they do not (for example, NAFTA). Sometimes partners are, in effect, granted rights of appeal denied to non-partners (NAFTA again). Of course, the last three rounds of negotiations under the General Agreement on Tariffs and Trade (GATT) tried, with significant success, to broaden the scope of multilateral arrangements. But a major attraction of the new regionalism seems to be that negotiations with a small number of partners broadens the range of instruments over which negotiation is feasible.

(vi)   Regional arrangements are regional in a geographic sense: the partici-
       pants are neighbours.

Unlike the other five stylized facts, this characteristic was probably just as true of the old regionalism as it is of the new.

In summary, regional integration often involves reform-minded small countries 'purchasing', with moderate trade concessions, links with a large, neighbouring country that involve 'deep' integration but confer relatively minor trade advantages.

3   THE VINERIAN PARADIGM

Suppose that the countries of the world all initially trade with each other and all have tariffs. Some countries then abolish all tariffs on each other's products, but maintain their tariffs on goods from the rest of the world (W), whose commercial policy is unchanged. The elimination of tariffs between the partners is a move towards free trade, which we might expect to generate beneficial *trade creation*. But now goods from W are subject to tax, whereas similar goods from the partners are not. We would expect this price discrimination to generate harmful *trade diversion*. Thus integration has on balance replaced one distortion (the tariff on partner trade) with another distortion (geographical price discrimination).[4]

Trade creation is presumably beneficial and trade diversion harmful. Which dominates depends upon circumstances; integration may or may not be a good thing. If, before integration, the partners trade mainly with each other, trade creation will be likely (but not certain) to dominate, because there is not much trade with W to divert. The larger the extent of the integration, the more likely it is to be beneficial: integration of the whole world can involve no trade diversion. But the welfare consequences are inherently indeterminate; this is basic to the Vinerian paradigm.

The above applies to trade based on comparative advantage, but analogous possibilities occur with imperfect competition or economies of scale. For example, if integration increases welfare in the partner countries by exposing firms there to intensified competition (*competition creation*), it may also reduce the competition faced by firms in the rest of the world (*competition diversion*), producing a possibly negative effect on welfare. Similarly, one can talk about *scale creation* and *scale diversion*.

A notable exception to this sea of ambiguity is the Ohyama–Kemp–Wan Theorem.[5] Suppose that, when the partners integrate, they adjust their external tariffs so that they together import and export to W exactly what they together did before integration. Then there is no net trade diversion, and integration is necessarily beneficial. Thus any group of countries can always integrate and harm no country in the world. This suggests the possibility of a *regional road to multilateralism*: a trading bloc might continue to expand by adding new members until the entire world is included.

Such a possibility is of practical relevance only if it is feasible and tempts the partners. Feasibility could be a problem if integration induces strategic behaviour by the rest of the world. And the theorem gives no reason why the partners should want to adjust external tariffs to prevent harm to non-partners. Article XXIV of the GATT requires only that external barriers be, on average, no higher after integration than before; this can be consistent with a lot of trade diversion.[6]

4 REGIONAL REGIONALISM

The first road to regionalism[7] is reflected in the stylized facts that regional arrangements are established by geographical neighbours and that they often involve 'deeper' integration. Countries tend to trade a lot with their neighbours, so it is sometimes said that current regional initiatives, often involving neighbours, are therefore likely to be benign, with trade diversion overwhelmed by trade creation.[8] The geographical nature of regional arrangements, like the arrangements themselves, has been treated as exogenous in the literature. The present approach, by contrast, will treat them as endogenous responses to multilateral liberalization.

The Model

The following comprise the basic building blocks of my model:

(i) Countries are identical, except that they are separated spatially. Assume that countries are grouped into N continents of n countries each; the distance between any two countries in the same continent is d, and the distance between any pair in different continents is D, with $d < D$.

(ii) Trade flows between pairs of countries are predicted by a *gravity equation*: the amount of bilateral trade is positively related to the economic sizes of the countries and negatively related to a measure of the gross distance between them.

The gravity equation consistently describes actual trade patterns well. In this model, gross distance is all that matters, since countries are otherwise identical.[9] Gross distance will be determined by geographic distance (as described above), and by tariff barriers. These barriers comprise tariffs and the tariff-equivalents of other instruments, and, initially, are given by past history. Assume that, if each of a pair of countries imposes a tariff-equivalent barrier of t on products from the other, the total trade between the two is given by $\alpha/(t+d)$ if they are in the same continent and by $\alpha/(t+D)$ if they are in different continents, for some parameter $\alpha > 0$.

(iii)   The government of each country may negotiate a mutual reduction in trade barriers with other governments, but each government is constrained by negotiating costs. In subsequent periods there will be new rounds of negotiations, with the governments constrained by the same costs in negotiating further reductions in trade barriers.

At the outset of each negotiating round, each government decides whether to negotiate *regionally* (only with other countries in the same continent) or *multilaterally* (with all other countries); because of the symmetry, all governments make the same choice. The negotiating costs relate to the government's political support, not modelled explicitly. I assume that larger reductions in trade barriers incur greater costs, as they further inflame adversely-affected special interests, and that a reduction in the number of negotiating partners lowers costs. The reason for the latter is twofold: (a) fewer negotiating partners means that the reduction in trade barriers applies to a smaller range of goods and so harms fewer special interests; and (b) the fewer the number of partners, the easier it is to reach agreement, enabling deeper integration – that is, agreement over a wider range of policies; this allows a country to achieve a given reduction of trade barriers in more alternative ways, enabling it to find a way that minimizes the harm done to powerful special interests.

I assume that the total cost a government is willing to incur in a negotiating round is exogenously given. Let γ denote the amount by which reducing the number of negotiating partners by one allows a government to increase the rate of trade-barrier reduction at unchanged cost.

(iv)   In its negotiations, each government strives to maximize, subject to the constraint on costs, an index of benefits. Benefits are greater the greater the reduction in trade barriers and the greater the number of partners to which those reductions apply.

Let δ denote the amount by which reducing the number of negotiating partners by one must be matched by an increase in the rate of trade-barrier reduction to leave unchanged the perceived benefit.

(v) The parameter δ is a decreasing function of the ratio of aggregate trade with negotiating partners to aggregate trade with non-partners.

The idea here is that the government, for political reasons, wants to reduce the 'tax' on as much trade as possible, and that existing trade matters more than trade that would exist if barriers were lower. Also, a higher partner-to-non-partner trade ratio may also imply a higher trade creation-to-trade diversion ratio.

Implications

Consider now how successive rounds of trade negotiations might develop in the framework described above. Let $T(t)$ denote the ratio of each country's intracontinental trade to intercontinental trade, if all countries impose the tariff equivalent t on all trade:

$$T(t) = \frac{(n-1)\frac{\alpha}{t+d}}{n(N-1)\frac{\alpha}{t+D}} \tag{6.1}$$

Now,

$$-\frac{t}{T}\frac{dT}{dt} = \frac{t}{t+d} - \frac{t}{t+D} > 0 \tag{6.2}$$

since $D > d$. Thus, if $t^0 > 0$ denotes the initial level of trade barriers, $T(t^0) < T(0)$. With δ a decreasing function of its argument, there are three possibilities:

(i) $\delta(T(t^0)) > \delta(T(0)) > \gamma$. Initially, multilateral negotiation is more tempting than regional negotiation, and remains so after each successive round. The world continues to approach free trade with regional blocs never emerging, so call this the *multilateral outcome*.

(ii) $\gamma > \delta(T(t^0)) > \delta(T(0))$. Initially, regional negotiation is more tempting than multilateral negotiation, and remains so after each successive round. The world splits up into continental regional blocs, and no multilateral negotiation can even begin until the regions all have free internal trade. Call this the *Vinerian outcome*.

(iii) $\delta(T(t^0)) > \gamma > \delta(T(0))$. Initially, multilateral negotiation is more tempting than regional negotiation, but eventually successful multilateral liberalization will cause regional negotiation to become more attractive. Regional blocs then emerge, and multilateral negotiation cannot resume until regional integration is complete. Call this outcome *induced regionalism*.

Imposition of an Article XXIV-style requirement that regional integration be substantially complete would add another constraint to the commencement of regional negotiations. This would have no effect on the multilateral outcome, but it could add a preliminary stage of multilateral negotiation to the Vinerian outcome, and it could prolong the multilateral phase of the induced-regionalism outcome.

The basic message of this section is an explanation of how the success of multilateral tariff reduction can generate regionalism. The explanation has used reduced-form representations of a trade model and of a political-economy model. The former – the gravity equation – is compatible with a sufficiently wide class of structural models to inspire hopes of generality, though structure would, of course, be needed to draw normative conclusions. The political-economy representation, though clearly meant to mimic historical experience in a crude way, is more special. For example, governments must choose either a multilateral strategy or a regional strategy; they are not allowed to pursue both simultaneously while choosing relative emphasis.

The assumption that δ is decreasing in the ratio of partner trade to non-partner trade plays a key role. It is not hard to build structural models with this property. But it is also possible (though not easy) to build structural models where the reverse is true. In this case, the outcome will involve the initial formation of regional blocs whose partial success (if partial integration is allowed) will eventually induce the commencement of multilateral negotiations. The multilateral and Vinerian outcomes will remain, but they will now correspond to cases (ii) and (i) respectively.

5   REFORM FACILITATION

The second road to regionalism[10] utilizes the stylized facts that the latter usually involves a big country linking up with one or more small ones that are making significant reforms, and that the degree of liberalization is modest but asymmetrical.

The Model

The model comprises N identical industrial countries, each endowed with H units of human capital, L skilled labour and U unskilled labour, and of M identical less-developed countries. Each developed country can produce one good, x, using human capital and skilled labour, and one service, z, requiring skilled labour and unskilled labour. Goods are tradable but services are non-traded; the goods produced by the respective countries are imperfect substitutes for each other.

Production

Production of each good is in two stages, with one stage, using only human capital, necessarily performed at home. The other stage, using only skilled labour, can be performed anywhere; that is, the home firm can employ labour located in any country (foreign direct investment) to perform this stage. If this stage is conducted abroad, the resulting unfinished goods must be exported from the foreign subsidiary. If b denotes the level of operations of this stage, final output is given by:

$$x = f(H, b) \qquad (6.3)$$

where f is a conventional neoclassical production function, H denotes the stock of human capital, and where:

$$b = kL_b \qquad (6.4)$$

with L_b the skilled labour allocated to stage b. I assume that $k = k(\sum_{i=1}^{N} L_{bi})$ with $k' > 0$ and with L_{bi} denoting the skilled labour allocated to stage b of the good of country i. The b-stage features increasing returns to scale that depend upon the size of global[11] b-stage activity for all N goods and that are external to the individual firm. I assume that goods are produced in perfectly competitive markets.

Production of the non-traded service, z, is by competitive firms operating under constant returns to scale and utilizing the total stock U of unskilled labour and the amount L_z of skilled labour. Thus,

$$L = L_b + L_z \qquad (6.5)$$

Protection in the Industrial World

I assume that each developed country levies an *ad valorem* tariff, t, on the imports of each foreign good (and it also levies a tariff t_b on its own b-stage production, if that stage is performed abroad). I assume all developed countries are identical, and I shall confine attention to symmetric equilibria, so t will be the same for all countries and all goods.

Commercial policy in each industrial country is determined by a political process in which unskilled labour attempts to secure rents. Instead of modelling this explicitly, I simply assume that the political process operates as if the country were maximizing a social welfare function that trades off labour's wage against aggregate welfare:

$$V = rw + (1 - r)u \qquad (6.6)$$

where w equals the marginal product of unskilled labour in producing services. The parameter r reflects the influence of unskilled labour over the political process.[12]

The Less Developed Countries

Each less developed country implements a commercial policy which is also the outcome of a political process, again not modelled explicitly, in which special interests attempt to secure rents. Because I am concerned with the possibility of fundamental economic reform, not with marginal changes in protection, I assume that the government must choose between just two possible policies: autarky or reform. With autarky, the special interests secure their rents. But if the social welfare benefit R of reform is expected to be sufficiently great, the government will attempt reform; let r^* denote the minimum the expected value of R must attain for the government to be tempted by reform. The parameter r^* thus reflects the influence of special interests over the political process.

The benefit of reform depends of course on the benefit of participating in the multilateral system, and this, in turn, depends on k. So I assume that R is an increasing function of $k : R = R(k)$. The less-developed country will be tempted to undertake reform if, and only if, the global economy is sufficiently productive that $\rho R(k) \geq r^*$, where ρ equals the probability that reform will succeed. The goal of reform is to modernize the country's economic structure and to bring it into the multilateral system. To capture this idea, I simply assume that reform is successful if, and only if, the country does, in fact, attract foreign direct investment (not permitted in autarky).

A developed-country firm that undertakes direct investment in a less-developed country employs labour there and pays for it with exports of its own finished good. I assume that the goods produced by developed countries have not been adapted for use by the less-developed, who therefore regard them as perfect substitutes for each other. Less-developed countries also benefit because their own non-traded sectors (not modelled here) benefit via spillovers.

I assume that the less-developed countries differ from each other in only one way: the propensity r^* to favour special interests. Let $M_R^*(\rho, k)$ denote the number of less-developed countries that, given ρ and k, would attempt reform. $M_R^*(\rho, k)$ is clearly increasing in each of its arguments.

A Symmetric Nash Equilibrium in Policy: Unilateralism

Next, consider an international equilibrium in which r and all the r^* are sufficiently large that *no* less developed country attempts reform (that is, $M_R^*(\rho, k) = 0$ in equilibrium), and each developed country sets an ad valorem tariff t on imports of each of the $N - 1$ foreign goods at a level that is optimal, given that every other developed country has chosen that t and that the less-developed countries all choose autarky. This characterizes unilateralism.

I assume that N is sufficiently large that each country behaves as though its actions have no effect on the world prices of traded goods or on the global k.[13] If P denotes the relative price, in terms of home services, of each of the $N - 1$ foreign goods, this small-country assumption is that the home government proceeds as though k and P/p are exogenous. Then a choice of t determines both p and L_b via equilibrium conditions. The effect on the government's objective of a change in t is $\dfrac{dV}{dt} = r\dfrac{dw}{dt} + (1 - r)\dfrac{du}{dt}$. Note that, with terms-of-trade effects and external scale effects both absent, the effect of a tariff change on utility is simply the change in import volume multiplied by tp, the excess of the social value of a marginal import over its social cost. Thus $\dfrac{dV}{dt} > 0$ if $t = 0$. The government will always wish to institute some protection because, with t initially zero, protection will produce a first-order increase in the wage of unskilled labour with no first-order effect on utility. The optimum (unilateral) tariff, as a function of L_b and p, is given by $\dfrac{dV}{dt} = 0$. The symmetric non-cooperative equilibrium simultaneously determines L_b, p and t.

Multilateralism

Assume the following sequence of moves:

(i) Initially, the developed countries are in a unilateral equilibrium and the less-developed countries have each chosen autarky.

(ii) Next, the developed countries, without participation by the less-developed, negotiate a multilateral equilibrium (described below) and implement it.

(iii) Then, the less developed countries observe t^M and the multilateral equilibrium value of k and *individually* decide whether to reform or not, taking t^M and k as given. The reform efforts are made, they succeed and/or fail, and a new international equilibrium emerges, with t still fixed at t^M but k is determined endogenously.

Suppose now that the developed countries undertake multilateral trade liberalization. In the resulting multilateral equilibrium, each developed country adopts the policy that is optimal, if all other developed countries adopt the *same* policy, given the policies adopted by the less developed countries. That is, the developed countries jointly choose a common t, denoted t^M.

The less-developed countries do not participate in the multilateral process and continue to choose policies of autarky. It should not be surprising that, subject to a technical condition, moving from a unilateral equilibrium to such a multilateral one produces a lower common tariff, larger b-stage production of each good (with, therefore, enhanced scale effects), and higher welfare for each developed country.

Note several distinctive features of this approach to multilateralism. First, no country attempts to manipulate the terms of trade to its advantage, reflecting a belief that such attempts have not been important in practice.[14] This implies a critical role for special interests: countries would otherwise adopt free trade unilaterally.

Second, national concern for social welfare provides countries with an incentive to enter into multilateral arrangements.

Third, the purpose of multilateralism here is to internalize an externality: The development of a multilateral trading system confers benefits of technological spillovers, external economies of scale, and so on, on all participants. Jointly setting their commercial policies allows countries to address this collectively.

Fourth, the theory assumes, unlike much recent literature,[15] that individual countries credibly commit themselves to the multilateral policy even though, *ex post*, each government will not be doing the best it can – according to its own objective function – given the policies of the other governments.

Implications of Multilateralism for the Less Developed Countries

Multilateralism lowers the tariff, and this will increase L_b, causing k to rise. Since $R(k)$ is increasing in k, R also increases. Multilateralism increases the temptation for the less-developed countries to reform. To consider the case in which R rises enough so that some countries embark on reform, make the following assumption:

$$R(k^U) < r_1^* < R(k^M) \qquad (A1)$$

where k^U and k^M respectively denote the value of k in the unilateral and multilateral equilibria, and r_1^* denotes the smallest r^*, that is, that of the country most receptive to reform. Then all less-developed countries choose autarky in the unilateral equilibrium, and some attempt reform in the multilateral equilibrium if ρ is sufficiently high.

A reform attempt will succeed if, and only if, some developed-country firms undertake direct investment there, so turn to this question next. Direct investment will introduce trade in b-stage products: imports of b into the developed countries are subject to protection at the rate t_b. I assume that each developed country sets t_b to optimize some criterion, given the multilateral equilibrium.[16]

International Equilibrium

Let M_R^* denote the number of less-developed countries that attempt reform and M_R the number that succeed. The developed countries will wish to undertake direct investment in the reforming less-developed countries if wages are sufficiently low there, which I assume. Let m denote the total employment of skilled labour by the foreign subsidiaries of each developed country. Market clearing conditions will determine the equilibrium value of m, but this model does not determine how the total direct investment Nm is distributed among the reformers. A symmetric equilibrium would allocate Nm among all M_R^* in equal amounts $F = Nm/M_R^*$, thus ensuring that $M_R = M_R^*$. But there is no reason to expect this outcome because, from the viewpoint of the investing firms, all less-developed countries are identical. So I assume that, when all potential hosts are equivalent, investing firms decide where to invest, among all potential hosts, by some random process.

Let L^* denote the maximum labour available in each less-developed country for employment by foreign subsidiaries. Then if $Nm > (M_R^* - 1)L^*$, some investment must go to each potential host, so $\rho = 1$ and $M_R = M_R^*$. But otherwise distributions of Nm that leave some potential hosts without foreign subsidiaries do exist. With the location of direct investment determined at random,

$$\rho(M_R^*, m) = \phi\left(\frac{Nm}{(M_R^* - 1)L^*}\right) \tag{6.7}$$

where ϕ reflects the random process by which investment is allocated. Assume that $\phi = 0$ if $m = 0$, $\phi = 1$ if $Nm > (M_R^* - 1)L^*$, and $\phi' > 0$ otherwise. Clearly ρ is decreasing in M_R^* and increasing in m whenever its argument is less than unity.

Equilibrium conditions determine k and m, and $M_R^* = M_R^*(\rho, k)$ and equation (6.7), then simultaneously determine ρ and M_R^*, and thus $M_R = \rho M_R^*$ also. Since ρ and M_R^* are positively related in $M_R^* = M_R^*(\rho, k$ and negatively related in (6.7), the solution is unique. Thus a switch from unilateralism to multilateralism induces some (M_R) less-developed countries to reform successfully, some $(M_R^* - M_R)$ to attempt reform and fail, and some to wish to reform but to refrain from trying because of the fear of failure. The condition for this is the following:

With multilateralism and no investment: $f_L(H, kL_b) > \alpha(1 + t_b)$

With multilateralism and investment: $\quad Nm < (M_R^* - 1)L^*$ $\qquad$ (A2)

Regionalism

Now introduce the possibility of regional arrangements between developed countries and less-developed countries. Such arrangements can be initiated after the developed countries switch from the unilateral equilibrium to the multilateral one, and while the less-developed countries are considering whether to reform or not. Define a regional agreement to be:

An agreement between one developed country and one less developed country in which:

The less developed country commits itself:

- To attempt reform;
- To levy a tariff of t^L on imports of goods from all developed countries other than those of its partner, whose goods will not be subject to duty.

The developed country commits itself:

- To make a marginal reduction, $dt_b < 0$, in the duty applicable to b-stage output imported from its partner country.

A less-developed country that attempts reform without entering into a regional initiative sets $t^L = 0$ without discrimination. Thus a country may choose between two roads to reform: unilateral, non-discriminatory free trade; or bilateral preferential trade.

A Regional Initiative

Will any such regional arrangements be negotiated? Suppose that the developed countries have moved from a unilateral to a multilateral equilibrium and all the assumptions hold. Then some less-developed countries will want to attempt reform, but $\rho < 1$. Consider how a regional arrangement would affect such a country.

Such an arrangement would commit the less-developed country to undertaking reform. The trade preference implies that all imports will come from the partner country, so that t^L will be prohibitive, regardless of its positive level; but this is of no consequence, since the less-developed country regards all goods as perfect substitutes. But the preferential reduction in t_b, though only marginal, is much more significant. From the point of view of firms considering direct investment to produce b-stage output for the partner country's good, all less-developed countries choosing reform are completely equivalent, except for this marginal preference. Thus it attracts all such investment.[17] This ensures that the reform will succeed: ρ becomes unity when the country signs the regional arrangement because of the 'investment diversion' it implies.

There will also be 'investment creation': a preferential reduction in t_b will increase m and cause a smaller fall in L_b, so that k increases, with the international spillovers this implies. These effects will not be large – the changes are marginal – but the direction is unambiguous.

Now consider the effect on a potential developed country partner. Such a country obtains a secure, less-developed country market for its good, but this is of no real consequence: in equilibrium its export of goods to all less-developed countries must equal the wage bill paid by its foreign subsidiaries, regional arrangement or not. The developed country benefits from investment creation. This has a favourable effect on social welfare, but the marginal change in t_b will have a zero first order effect on the government's objective function, since t_b has been assumed to have been optimally set. The principle gain to the government is merely the assurance that it will not find itself facing a tariff of t^L – and thus higher production costs for its good – in the event that all reforming less-developed countries conclude regional arrangements with other developed countries. Thus the government of a developed country may see little to gain from a regional arrangement. But it has nothing at all to lose, and its potential partner has much to gain. Thus it is reasonable to expect that, if necessary, a side payment by the latter would produce such an agreement. So I assume that a developed country would agree to a regional arrangement. And other developed countries should not object, because the only effect on them will be the rise in k.

But the regional arrangement will not be uniformly benign. Other less-developed countries desiring reform will suffer. Suppose one less-developed country, that would undertake reform in any case, enters into a regional arrangement. Then the direct investment producing b-stage output for that country's partner will all be diverted there. Thus the numerator of the argument of ϕ in equation (6.7) falls by m; the denominator is unaffected, since the less-developed country with the regional arrangement still remains a potential host for other direct investment. Therefore, each value of M_R^* now corresponds to a lower value of ρ in equation (6.7) than before: the function shifts down. Accordingly, both ρ and M_R^* are lower than without the arrangement. Regionalism produces 'reform destruction' by causing fewer countries to attempt reform and lowering the proportion of those who succeed.

Suppose instead that the less-developed country would not have attempted reform at all in the absence of the regional arrangement. This can be termed 'reform creation' and tends to nullify the fall in M_R^* but further accentuate that in ρ. Thus the probability of success falls even more than before, but the number of countries attempting reform may either rise or fall, depending on the balance between reform creation and reform destruction.

Regional Equilibrium

The above describes a single regional arrangement, which might be either good or bad for the world as a whole. But all developed countries would accept such an arrangement, and all less-developed countries that attempt reform will want one. So, consider the international equilibrium that would emerge if all countries were allowed freely to enter into such arrangements.

I have defined a regional arrangement as one between a single developed country and a single less-developed country. But one country might enter into several arrangements with different partners, thus, in effect, generating larger groupings.[18] Then, regardless of the relative number of developed and less-developed countries, all can potentially participate in some arrangement. But there are some constraints.

The first is that, if many less-developed countries enter into arrangements with a single developed country, each arrangement may no longer guarantee the success of each reform effort. Although the arrangements will divert investment from non-participants to participants, there is no guarantee that the investment will be distributed among all participants. Suppose that M_{RR} less-developed countries establish regional arrangements with one developed country. For these arrangements to guarantee the success of each country's reform effort, it is necessary that $m > (M_{RR} - 1)L^*$. A less-developed country will never enter into a regional agreement that violates this condition if an agreement with some other developed country would not violate it. Thus regional groupings would emerge to satisfy the requirement, if possible. The number of less-developed countries that would wish to undertake reform if they could be certain of its success is $M_R^*(1,k)$. Then the condition that guarantees that it is possible to accommodate all less-developed countries that so wish, with regional arrangements guaranteeing successful reform is the following:

$$N\left(\frac{m}{L^*}+1\right) > M_R^*(1,k) \tag{A3}$$

A second question is whether a country already in one regional arrangement would be willing to enter another also. Consider first a developed country. If its partner is not large enough to supply fully its need for b-stage goods from abroad, this country will want another partner. But with an interior solution, the developed country has nothing to gain from a second arrangement. It has nothing to lose either, and its potential partner has much to gain. Thus it is again reasonable to expect that a side payment by the latter would produce such an agreement, so I assume that developed countries would agree to enter multiple arrangements.

Would a less-developed country be willing to enter additional arrangements? These would attract more investment, but, with successful reform already guaranteed by one arrangement, this is no benefit. The country has nothing to gain, but nothing to lose either. The developed country, on the other hand, now has much to gain. With all less-developed countries linked to developed countries through regional arrangements, the developed country without such a link will find its exports of goods required to pay for the labour employed in its foreign subsidiaries subject to the tariff of t^L, even though it must pay the same wage as everyone else. Since one party has much to gain and the other nothing to lose, I again assume that such an arrangement would be negotiated.

The regional equilibrium should now be apparent. With luck, all developed countries, and all less-developed countries that wish to reform if $\rho = 1$, will enter regional arrangements that guarantee the success of all the reform efforts. Reform destruction will not occur, but reform creation will.

Note several features of this approach to regionalism. First, the major role of regionalism is to facilitate reform in the less-developed countries. A secondary role (because it is marginal) is to stimulate investment. Second, the relationship between multilateralism and regionalism is benign. Regionalism is the consequence of multilateral success, not failure, and it, in turn, strengthens rather than undermines the basis for a commitment to the multilateral order. Third, I used the terms 'investment creation' and 'investment diversion' to acknowledge an apparent parallel to the Vinerian paradigm. But trade diversion is the major negative influence there, whereas investment diversion is strongly positive here, as the force behind the major benefit of regionalism.

This section has assumed that a reforming country makes a once and for all choice between non-discriminatory tariff reduction and preferential trade. But combining the analysis of the previous section with that of this section introduces the possibility of a third approach. A reforming country might begin with non-discriminatory tariff reductions, which then increase the relative importance of trade with neighbours and thereby make preferential trade more attractive.[19] The following section supplies an additional reason why such a shift in the pattern of trade might induce regionalism.

6 REFORM COMMITMENT AND CREDIBILITY

While attracting foreign direct investment is crucial to the success of reform, so is sustained commitment by the reforming regime and its successors. Regional arrangements are useful here and, to the extent that the reform attempt is due to the success of the multilateral system, so too are the regional arrangements. The stylized fact important here is: reform-minded small countries linking up with a larger country in an arrangement featuring deeper integration.

The basic idea is to use the regional arrangement as an external commitment to reform that will bind the government to the reform measures in the future. Multilateral negotiations are of little use for this purpose, since they would not embody detailed reform measures by individual countries and because they provide no enforcement mechanism should a country backslide. Regional arrangements can address both problems.

Because such arrangements allow for deeper integration, they can contain obligations to undertake specific measures central to the reform effort. This is illustrated quite clearly by the free trade agreement between Canada and the USA, and by the subsequent NAFTA. The fact that the agreement is with a big country (often the dominant trading partner) adds a credible enforcement mechanism.

The previous section's discussion of the relationship between the success of a reform effort and the ability to attract direct investment is also relevant here. In practice, the credibility of the commitment of the government to its announced reform can, in fact, be very important in attracting direct investment and, in that way, ensuring the success of the reform. Even a regional arrangement with only modest preferences for the small country establishes an external commitment to reform that (weakly) binds future governments, thereby making the future preservation of reform (slightly) more credible. This, in turn, makes the country more attractive for direct investment, relative to similar countries without such external commitments. Thus the ability of a regional arrangement to bind a government to reform can be important for the success of that reform even when it confers only modest direct benefits.

7   INVESTMENT MAINTENANCE

The model of section 5 described the small-country participants as being less-developed, and modelled them differently from the 'large' industrial countries. But in many cases the small participants in regional arrangements can hardly be described as less-developed: Canada in NAFTA, and the new members of the EU, for example. And there are also the former Communist countries of Central Europe to consider.

The analysis of section 5 basically applies also to this last group. These countries are eager to attract direct investment, the ultimate success of their reform efforts remains both in doubt and dependent on their ability to attract such investment, and the Europe Agreements have given them a small advantage over other, similar, countries: not by trade preferences, but by a higher implicit likelihood of future integration into the EU.

For small industrialized nations, the model of the fifth section needs to be altered, because the objectives of these countries are different from those of the less-developed countries, but the basic analysis of the earlier section still applies. For the small countries joining the EU, the problem is not so much to attract new direct investment as to remain attractive sites, in an increasingly integrated world, for activities currently conducted there. The small advantage they obtain is not additional preference, but future participation in EU decision-making.[20] Thus the basic story applies.

These countries are also undertaking reform, but the reforms are not of the fundamental nature being attempted in the less-developed part of the world. These reforms in many cases make the countries more attractive sites for direct investment, but the success of the reforms can hardly be said to depend crucially on how much investment is attracted. The considerations discussed in section 6 are also pertinent here.

8 CONCLUDING REMARKS

The era of the new regionalism differs from that of the old in two fundamental ways: in the earlier period, multilateral liberalization of trade in manufactures among the industrial nations was just beginning, but now it is nearly complete; import substitution and Communism dominated the non-industrial part of the world then, but now reform is rampant. This chapter has discussed several alternative, but complementary, ways in which regionalism might develop. These approaches suggest the following relation of the new regionalism to multilateralism:

(i)   The new regionalism is a direct result of the success of multilateral liberalization.

(ii) Regionalism is the means by which new countries enter the multilateral system and a means by which small countries already in it continue to exploit its success.

(iii) Regionalism is creating new industrial groups with an interest in preserving the liberal trade order.

This chapter has assumed away the usual dangers associated with regional integration – harmful trade diversion and aggressive policies of large blocs. My purpose has been simply to focus clearly on what is new. I claim that changes in the world, especially multilateral liberalization, have produced a new regionalism qualitatively distinct from the old. I do not claim that the old regionalism has disappeared, nor that the Vinerian concerns do not remain relevant and important.

Of course, any changes – regional initiatives are no exceptions – offer protectionists new scope for their efforts. An argument that regional initiatives reflect causes much more benign than a tendency to divide the globe into several highly protected blocs does not establish that the latter will not, in fact, be the ultimate result. But this chapter suggests that the new regionalism reflects the success of multilateralism – and not its failure.

Notes

1. See Bhagwati and Panagariya (1996) and Krugman (1991).
2. See Bond and Syropoulos (1995) and Bagwell and Staiger (1993a, 1993b).
3. Chichilnisky (1994) also argues that, in the presence of economies of scale, regional integration may foster multilateral liberalization. But her argument is quite different from each of the four discussed below.
4. The classic reference is Viner (1950). See also Lipsey (1960), Ethier and Horn (1984), and Panagariya (1996).
5. See Ohyama (1972) and Kemp and Wan (1976).
6. See McMillan (1993) and Frankel *et al.* (1996).
7. See Ethier (1997) for a full account.
8. But see Bhagwati and Panagariya (1996) for a contrary view.
9. The gravity equation can be thought of as a reduced form consistent with many trade models, so that its empirical success reveals little about the underlying causes of trade. See Deardorff (1995).
10. See Ethier (1996) for a full account.
11. For international economies of scale, see Ethier (1979, 1982).
12. Detail of the political process is beyond the scope of this chapter. See Grossman and Helpman (1994) for a detailed derivation of behaviour much like that summarized by Equation (6.6) and Hillman (1989) for a broader discussion of political economy issues.
13. Each country conducts trade policy by separately choosing $N-1$ import constraints, symmetry assuring that the $N-1$ choices are all the same; no deliberate export policy is chosen. This is important: while the small country assumption can be appealed to as justification for each country perceiving no influence in each of its import markets or on global economies of scale, the country is none the less the sole supplier of its own good.
14. For an alternative view, see Bagwell and Staiger (1996a, 1996b).
15. For example, Bond and Syropolous (1995) distinguish multilateralism from regionalism by assuming that in the former countries cannot pre-commit. Kemp and Shimomura (1995) consider equilibria analogous to this chapter's multilateralism, but they do so by introducing another solution concept, not by relying on an exogenous commitment mechanism.
16. It does not matter for what follows *which* criterion the country optimizes – for example, it might be simply V, or V amended to give negative weight to foreign investment and so on.
17. Provided, of course, that L^* is large enough to accommodate all such investment. Boundary solutions will be ignored.
18. Such a situation is sometimes referred to as a 'hub-and-spoke' system. See Wonnacott (1996).
19. Garriga and Sanguinetti (1995) argue that something like this applies to Mercosur.
20. For more on this, see Baldwin and Flam (1994).

References

Bagwell, K. and R. W. Staiger (1993a) *Multilateral Tariff Cooperation During the Formation of Regional Free Trade Areas*, NBER (National Bureau of Economic Research), Working Paper.

Bagwell, K. and R. W. Staiger (1993b), *Multilateral Tariff Cooperation During the Formation of Customs Unions*, NBER Working Paper.

Bagwell, K. and R. W. Staiger (1996a) *Reciprocal Trade Liberalization*, Working Paper.

Bagwell, K. and R. W. Staiger (1996b) *Regionalism and Multilateral Tariff Cooperation*, NBER Working Paper; now ch. 7 in this volume.

Baldwin, R. E. and H. Flam (1994) *Enlargement of the European Union: The Economic Consequences for the Scandinavian Countries*, CEPR Occasional Paper no. 16.

Bhagwati, J. and A. Panagariya (1996) *Preferential Trading Areas and Multilateralism: Strangers, Friends or Foes?* University of Maryland Center for International Economics Working Paper no. 22.

Bond, E. and C. Syropoulos (1995) 'Trading Blocs and the Sustainability of Inter-Regional Cooperation' M. Canzoneri, W. J. Ethier and V. Grilli (eds), *The New Transatlantic Economy* (Cambridge: Cambridge University Press).

Chichilnisky, G. (1994) 'Trading Blocks with Endogenous Technology and Increasing Returns', unpublished manuscript.

Deardorff, A. V. (1995) *Determinants of Bilateral Trade: Does Gravity Work in a Neoclassical World?*, Discussion Paper no. 382, Research Forum on International Economics, University of Michigan.

Ethier, W. J. (1979) 'Internationally Decreasing Costs and World Trade', *Journal of International Economics*, vol. 9, no. 1, pp. 1–24.

Ethier, W. J. (1982) 'National and International Returns to Scale in the Modern Theory of International Trade', *American Economic Review*, vol. 72, no. 3, pp. 389–405.

Ethier, W. J. (1996) *Regionalism in a Multilateral World*, Working paper, Department of Economics, University of Pennsylvania.

Ethier, W. J. (1997) *Regional Regionalism*, Working Paper, Department of Economics, University of Pennsylvania.

Ethier, W. J. and H. Horn (1984) 'A New Look at Economic Integration', in H. Kierzkowski (ed.), *Monopolistic Competition and International Trade*. (Oxford University Press), pp. 207–29, reprinted in A. Jacquemin and A. Sapir (eds) (1989), *The European Internal Market: Trade and Competition* (Oxford: Oxford University Press).

Frankel, J. A., E. Stein and S. J. Wei (1996), 'Regional Trading Arrangements: Natural or Supernatural?', *American Economic Review*, vol. 86, no. 2, May, pp. 52–6.

Garriga, G. and P. Sanguinetti (1995) '*Es el Mercosur un bloque natural? Efectos de la politica comercial y la geografia sobre el intercambio regional*' Estudios, vol. 18, no. 73 pp. 59–68.

Grossman, G. and E. Helpman (1994) 'Protection for Sale', *American Economic Review*, vol. 84, pp. 833–50.

Hillman, A. L. (1989) *The Political Economy of Protection*, (Chur: Harwood Academic Publishers).

Kemp, M. C. and K. Shimomura (1995) 'The Apparently Innocuous Representative Agent', The Japanese Economic Review, vol. 46, pp. 247–56.

Kemp, M. C. and H. Wan (1976) 'An Elementary Proposition Concerning the Formation of Customs Unions', *Journal of International Economics*, vol. 6, pp. 95–8.

Krugman, P. (1991) 'Is Bilateralism Bad?', in E. Helpman and A. Razin (eds), *International Trade and Trade Policy* (Cambridge, Mass.: MIT Press).

Lipsey, R. G. (1960) 'The Theory of Customs Unions: A General Survey', *Economic Journal*, vol. 70, no. 279, pp. 496–513. Reprinted in R. E. Caves and H. G. Johnson (1968), *Readings in International Economics* (Homewood, Ill.: Richard D. Irwin).

McMillan, J. (1993), 'Does Regional Integration Foster Open Trade? Economic Theory and GATT's Article XXIV', In K. Anderson and R. Blackhurst (eds), Regional Integration and the Global Trading System (New York: Harvester Wheatsheaf).

Ohyama, M. (1972) 'Trade and Welfare in General Equilibrium', *Keio Economic Studies*, vol. 9, pp. 37–73.

Panagariya, A. (1996) *The Meade Model of Preferential Trading: History, Analytics and Policy Implications*, University of Maryland Center for International Economics Working Paper no. 21.

Viner, J. (1950) *The Customs Union Issue* (New York: Carnegie Endowment for International Peace).

Wonnacott, R. J. (1996) 'Free-Trade Agreements: For Better or Worse?', *American Economic Review*, vol. 86, no. 2, May, pp. 62–6.

Comment

L. Alan Winters
WORLD BANK

As we have come to expect from Wilfred Ethier, this is an original, exciting and clever chapter. It seeks to move the modelling of regionalism in three directions which, while prominent in political discussion, have not figured strongly in analytical endeavours: why regionalism is regional; regionalism and investment; and regionalism and the credibility of reform. It also captures, in places, the notion that regional liberalization is, in some sense, safer than multilateral liberalization.

I welcome the breaking of such new ground and will try to contribute to it by exploring the context of Ethier's results – specifically asking how much of the evidence on regionalism they do, in fact, explain – and by examining certain details of his models.

Ethier's stylized facts are useful for defining a concrete research agenda – a set of phenomena that have to be explained; but I would argue that they refer only to a subset of recent instances of new regionalism. For example, size disparities characterize EU enlargement, the EU's association agreements and the creation of NAFTA, but not other arrangements, such as those in Africa (for example, the CBI, UDEAC, UEMOA), the revival of the Andean Pact, the Group of Three (Colombia, Mexico and Venezuela) or the ASEAN Free Trade Area. Mercosur has a size disparity, but in this case the largest member, Brazil, is not the most advanced in reform. Neither is it really true that the EU has been more liberal than its recent Scandinavian accedants – they have had to become less liberal in some respects – for example, on the MFA. Thus we are looking here at one particular form of regional integration – sometimes known as North–South arrangements – not the whole range.

Turning to regional regionalism, we are confronted by something like the argument that regionalism among 'natural partners' is benign. This has been debated extensively – see Winters (1996) – but has, in the end, yielded no satisfactory insights. Ethier's results have no normative dimension, but he constructs his model so that trade barrier removal on larger trade flows is worth more than that on smaller flows. He does this essentially by the assumption 'that existing trade matters more than trade that would exist if barriers were lower': that is, by focusing on the direct distributional aspects of trade taxes rather than their allocative effects. It is possible that governments behave in this way, but it is not at all obvious that they do, still less that they should.

One application of this model that does seem relevant to me is in the area of 'deep integration'. One of the aspects of the EU's (then, the EC's) '1992' programme was the reduction of real transactions costs between member countries – for example, paperwork, queuing, money transfer costs, standards verification and so on. These essentially raise the real unit cost of internationally traded goods and their reduction saves resources proportional to the affected trade. These savings could easily dominate allocative effects (rectangles usually outweigh triangles) and this may explain why some elements of deep integration are regional.

The heart of the paper is the 'reform facilitation' model, which is highly original. It binds together credibility, fear of reform, investment and asymmetric regional deals to produce a very benign view of regionalism. A key building block of this view is a world in which regionalism can do no harm to its partners or, it later turns out, to anyone else. With identical industrial countries and identical developing countries there is no danger of picking the wrong partners – that is, no danger of trade diversion. Similarly, with no developing country trade initially, there is no scope for diversion here either, and with no intra-industrial country regionalism, the sorts of difficulties that Frankel, Stein and Wei (1995) identify in differentiated-goods worlds cannot arise. All this implies that regionalism can never impose costs – it is riskless – and therefore that anything it can achieve in other dimensions has no potential offsets.

The main model essentially uses regionalism as a co-ordinating mechanism. It ensures that developing countries which wish to reform and industrial countries which wish to invest are brought together. This view immediately poses the question: is co-ordination really necessary? First, as Ethier notes, if there is a sufficient supply of investment to meet all developing country aspirations, there is no co-ordination problem. Second, the assumption that industrial countries liberalize collectively and suddenly implies a step change in R – the return to reform for developing countries. As a result, several developing countries are persuaded suddenly and simultaneously to consider reform. Co-ordination is necessary because each fears that all the investment necessary for successful reform will go to other members of the group. However, if, equally reasonably, industrial country liberalization proceeded smoothly, R would decline smoothly and developing countries would enter the reform and investment race one at a time. Provided that the first n arrivals had been sated and investment supply were not exhausted, the $(n + 1)$th would face no uncertainty. Hence regionalism would not be necessary.

Third, in the real world there is much more to attracting investment than declaring oneself open. Many of these factors are endogenous or manipulable, so that countries could attract investment through means other than regionalism. If these were potentially harmful – for example, excessive investment subsidies – and if the Nash equilibrium in them were inefficient, some co-ordination would be desirable, but, except where it is costless as here, regionalism is not necessarily the optimal means.

The observation in the previous paragraph prompts me to note an element in Ethier's model that might make regionalism worse than multilateralism for developing countries as a whole. He notes that industrial countries gain little from regionalism and that side-payments may be necessary to persuade them to sign agreements. At the limit, these might shift nearly all the surplus from reform from developing countries to their industrial partners. In Ethier's world, if regionalism is permitted, any developing country that does not have a regional arrangement certainly cannot reform successfully. Thus, in bidding for partners, developing countries could end up giving away nearly all the benefits if their negotiating position is weak. If regionalism were precluded, on the other hand, a smaller number of developing countries would reform and only a sub-set might succeed, but at least these would reap the benefits of their efforts. On average developing countries could be better off!

A related question is what other means exist for co-ordinating international investment or ensuring successful reform? Policy credibility might be achieved by binding trade policy under the WTO, or through sustained political commitment. Regional arrangements are certainly not sufficient for credibility – for example, Greece's failure to attract FDI since joining the EEC – and neither are they necessary, (for example, Chile and Taiwan). Thus, while recognizing that regional arrangements can sometimes enhance credibility, as Ethier argues, I suspect that several other factors are at least as important. The sanctions that would accompany defection from a regional arrangement may offer credibility for policies *vis-à-vis* partners but they do not necessarily do so for policies *vis-à-vis* the rest of the world.

Ethier tells us that, in the 'reform facilitation' model, regionalism strengthens the multilateral order. Certainly it does not undermine it, for it takes us to an equilibrium equivalent to and supported by multilateralism. But neither does it lead to multilateralism, because in this model regionalism delivers most of what countries desire. All actual trade between industrial countries and developing countries is duty free under the regional arrangements and there is no incentive to open North–South trade between unrelated parties. Developing countries do not trade with each other. Thus all that is left for multilateralism to deliver is the 'non-issue' of intra-industrial country trade, and there is nothing in the model to encourage industrial countries to liberalize this. Indeed, if instead of being a one-off matter, developing countries had to attract a stream of investment, and if there were a finite probability that industrial country firms would switch from one developing country to another, the incentives for regionalism would be continuing. Of course, in this model that would not matter, but if there were any possible costs to regionalism it might.

To conclude, this is a fascinating and stimulating chapter. It clearly adds to our understanding of regionalism by modelling formally some factors that have previously been treated only informally. On the other hand, we should not take its very stark results too literally. The effects covered by the chapter clearly matter, but not to the exclusion of all else.

References

Frankel, J. A., E. Stein and S. J. Wei (1995) 'Trading Blocs and the Americas: The Natural, the Unnatural, and the Super-Natural', *Journal of Development Economics*, vol. 47, pp. 61–95.

Winters, L. A. (1996) 'Regionalism versus Multilateralism', Policy Research Working Paper, no. 1687, The World Bank.

7 Regionalism and Multilateral Tariff Co-operation[1]

Kyle Bagwell
COLUMBIA UNIVERSITY AND NATIONAL BUREAU OF
ECONOMIC RESEARCH

Robert W. Staiger
UNIVERSITY OF WISCONSIN-MADISON AND NATIONAL
BUREAU OF ECONOMIC RESEARCH

1 INTRODUCTION

In recent years, there has been a proliferation of regional trading agreements. What are the consequences of such agreements for multilateral tariff co-operation? Are regional agreements 'building blocks' or 'stumbling blocks' for the multilateral liberalization process? In this chapter, we develop a formal model that identifies important effects that regional agreements may have on multilateral tariff co-operation; and we find that the consequences of such agreements for multilateral tariff co-operation need not be clear-cut: regional agreements can produce effects which complement multilateral liberalization efforts, and can also produce effects which undermine the multilateral liberalization process. While we do not provide a conclusive answer to the questions posed above, we outline a framework of effects which can enable a better understanding of the possible impact of regional agreements on multilateral tariff co-operation. We also describe circumstances in which the net impact of the various effects can be determined.

We present our results in a 'competing exporters' model of trade. There are three goods and three countries, and each country imports one good that is supplied by each of the other two countries. We consider first a static model of trade, in which we allow that two of the countries enter into regional trading agreements. Here, we identify a *tariff complementarity effect*: when the two countries reduce their tariffs on one another to zero, they each find it attractive also to lower the tariff applied to imports from the non-member country. In the static model, therefore, regional agreements complement multilateral liberalization efforts. We show further that the extent of

157

multilateral liberalization is greater if the regional agreement takes the form of a free-trade agreement than if it takes the form of a customs union.

While the static model serves to illustrate the tariff complementarity effect, we argue that international trade agreements are best modelled as the outcome of a repeated game. The repeated-game approach puts enforcement at centre stage. Can countries use the threat of a trade war to enforce lower multilateral tariffs when regional agreements have taken place? To explore this question, we begin with the benchmark case in which no regional agreements have taken place and countries adopt *most favoured nation (MFN)*, i.e., non-discriminatory, tariffs. We allow that two of the countries are patient and thus willing to co-operate at very low tariffs, whereas the third country is less patient and unable to sustain reciprocal tariff reductions below a certain level. In this setting, we find that the former two countries act as hegemons (see, for example, Kindleberger, 1981), eventually offering to lower their tariffs to a degree greater than they request reciprocally from the impatient country. This is because, when tariffs are non-discriminatory, the patient countries can achieve further bilateral liberalization only if they also offer further multilateral liberalization. Accordingly, the MFN principle may benefit 'weak' countries that cannot sustain deep liberalization, since such countries are eventually allowed partially to 'free ride' on the liberalization activities of other countries.

We consider next the possibility that the two patient countries form a free-trade area. An understanding of the consequences of this regional agreement for the multilateral tariffs that are associated with the third country is facilitated by the identification of three key effects. First, as in the static game, there is a *tariff complementarity effect*: when two countries form a free-trade area, they are inclined to lower tariffs on imports from non-members. As before, this effect suggests that regional agreements complement multilateral tariff co-operation. A second effect is a *punishment effect*, which is in fact the flipside of the tariff complementarity effect. In particular, since the members of the free-trade area find high multilateral tariffs unattractive, the threat of a trade war from such a region is not especially worrying, and so the non-member country is less able to sustain a low multilateral tariff on its imports once the other countries have formed a free-trade area. The punishment effect, therefore, suggests that the formation of a free-trade area may harm multilateral tariff co-operation. Finally, a third effect is the *discrimination effect*. This effect describes the free-rider benefits of MFN liberalization that the impatient country loses once the patient countries form a free-trade area and select discriminatory tariffs. This effect suggests that regional agreements undermine multilateral tariff co-operation.

We demonstrate that the three effects can be ranked when the non-member country is sufficiently impatient. In that event, the non-member country is focused on the present, and the punishment effect is eliminated.

The tariff complementarity and discrimination effects remain, however, and the latter will dominate if and only if the two member countries are sufficiently patient, so that their multilateral liberalization under MFN is sufficiently deep. In this case, the formation of a free-trade area leads to an overall deterioration in multilateral tariff co-operation.

Finally, we consider the formation of a customs union, finding that the same three effects appear. With a customs union, the tariff complementarity and punishment effects are weakened, however, since a member of a customs union is less attracted to low multilateral tariffs than is a member of a free-trade area. When the non-member country is sufficiently impatient, so that the punishment effect is eliminated, we find again that the discrimination effect dominates if and only if the two member countries are sufficiently patient. In this circumstance, the formation of a customs union results in an overall deterioration in multilateral tariff co-operation. Furthermore, we find that the formation of a customs union is more likely to harm multilateral tariff liberalization than is the formation of a free-trade area, in that the former leads to increased multilateral tariffs of member countries for a wider range of patience levels of the member countries.

Our chapter contributes to a growing literature concerned with the impact of regional agreements on the multilateral trading system. For example, Richardson (1992, 1993) argues that the formation of free-trade agreements can initiate a competition for tariff revenue that leads member countries to reduce their external tariffs. Focusing on enforcement issues at the multilateral level, Bond and Syropoulos (1996) argue that customs union formation may make low multilateral tariffs more difficult to sustain. But Bond, Syropoulos and Winters (1996) also show that the deepening of regional integration within a customs union can enhance the ability of the multilateral agreement to secure low multilateral tariffs. Bagwell and Staiger (1997a, 1997b) focus on the period of transition during which regional agreements are formed, and show that the formation of customs unions is likely to lead to a temporary 'honeymoon' period of enhanced multilateral co-operation, while the formation of free-trade agreements is more apt to bring discord at the multilateral level. The present chapter contributes to this literature by identifying several new effects of regional agreements that have not previously been analyzed, and by exploring their implications for the enforcement of multilateral tariff co-operation.

2   THE STATIC MODEL

We consider a three-country, three-good partial equilibrium world in which each country's import market is served by competing exporters from its two trading partners. The three countries are denoted by A, B, and C, and we use

$J = \{A, B, C\}$ as a notational index for countries. In similar fashion, the three goods are represented as a, b and c, and we use $i = \{a, b, c\}$ as our notational index for goods. Finally, it is sometimes convenient to let j identify the good that corresponds to the lower case value of J (for example, if $J = A$, then $j = a$). We assume that country J is endowed with zero units of good j, while it is endowed with 3/2 units of each of the other two goods. Country J demands each of the three goods, however, and the demand for good i in country J is given by $D(P_i^J) = \alpha - \beta P_i^J$, with P_i^J denoting the price of good i in country J. Thus, country J must import good j to consume it, and can import good j from either trading partner.

Given the symmetry of the world as viewed from any one country, we can economize on the presentation of the static model by letting $L(J)$ denote J's 'left-hand' trading partner and $R(J)$ denote J's 'right-hand' trading partner. We then use $l(J)$ to denote the good that J exports to its left-hand trading partner, and we let $r(J)$ represent the good that J exports to its right-hand trading partner. Figure 7.1 illustrates the trading relationships as viewed by country A using this notation (that is, for $J = A$). Here, country A's left-hand trading partner is country B (that is, $B = L(A)$), and country A exports good b to country B (that is, $b = l(A)$).

As Figure 7.1 makes clear, we do not allow a country simultaneously to import a good from one source and export it to another. Given the symmetry of the model, this practice would never occur if tariffs satisfied the MFN principle and hence were non-discriminatory. In principle, however, it is possible that the tariff discrimination that emerges when countries enter into regional agreements could induce exporters to begin serving new markets that they had found unprofitable. In our analysis of regional agreements, we abstract from this possibility. We do so for two reasons. First, in practice, there are likely to be fixed costs associated with serving a new market, and so the corresponding new trading volume would need to be significant before

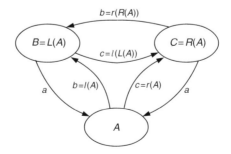

Figure 7.1   Trade relationships viewed from country A

such costs would be incurred. Second, this abstraction greatly simplifies the analysis, enabling us to offer a tractable framework within which to isolate and study important effects of regional agreements for multilateral tariff co-operation.

With this notation we let $\tau_j^{L(J)}$ denote country J's specific tariff on imports of j from its left-hand trading partner. Analogously, we denote country J's specific tariff on imports of good j from its right-hand trading partner by $\tau_j^{R(J)}$, and we denote by $\tau_{l(J)}^J$ and $\tau_{r(J)}^J$ the specific tariffs faced by country J's exporters from its left-hand and right-hand trading partners, respectively.[2] Focusing on tariffs that are non-negative and non-prohibitive to bilateral trade flows, we have the following arbitrage conditions relating the price of good j in importing country J and exporting countries $L(J)$ and $R(J)$:

$$P_j^J = P_j^{L(J)} + \tau_j^{L(J)} = P_j^{R(J)} + \tau_j^{R(J)}, \quad J = \{A, B, C\} \tag{7.1}$$

Import and export functions can also be defined as:

$$M_j(P_j^J) = D(P_j^J); \quad X_{i(J)}^J(P_{i(J)}^J) = \frac{3}{2} - D(P_{i(J)}^J), \quad i = \{l, r\}$$

respectively.[3] Finally, the market clearing conditions are given by:

$$M_j(P_j^J) = X_j^{L(J)}(P_j^{L(J)}) + X_j^{R(J)}(P_j^{R(J)}) \tag{7.2}$$

Using the arbitrage conditions in (7.1), the market clearing conditions in (7.2) can be solved to yield equilibrium prices in each country as a function of the chosen tariffs:

$$\begin{aligned} P_j^J(\tau_j^{L(J)}, \tau_j^{R(J)}) &= (\alpha - 1)/\beta + (\tau_j^{L(J)} + \tau_j^{R(J)})/3 \\ P_{i(J)}^J(\tau_{i(J)}^J, \tau_{i(J)}^{I(J)}) &= (\alpha - 1)/\beta - (2\tau_{i(J)}^J - \tau_{i(J)}^{I(J)})/3, \quad (I, i) \in \{(R, l), (L, r)\} \end{aligned} \tag{7.3}$$

Hence, as (7.3) indicates, the price in country J of import good j is increasing in J's tariff on imports from each of its trading partners. As for export goods, the price in country J of the good $l(J)$ that J exports to its left-hand trading partner is decreasing in the tariff faced by its exporters and increasing in the tariff imposed on competing exports of $l(J)$ coming from J's right-hand trading partner. Similar remarks apply for good $r(J)$.

Market clearing trade volumes are now given by:

$$\begin{aligned} M_j(\tau_j^{L(J)}, \tau_j^{R(J)}) &= 1 - \beta(\tau_j^{L(J)} + \tau_j^{R(J)})/3 \\ X_{i(J)}^J(\tau_{i(J)}^J, \tau_{i(J)}^{I(J)}) &= 1/2 - \beta(2\tau_{i(J)}^J - \tau_{i(J)}^{I(J)})/3, \quad (I, i) \in \{(R, l), (L, r)\} \end{aligned} \tag{7.4}$$

As expected, country J's import volume is decreasing in the import tariff that it selects for good j, and similarly country J's export volume of good $l(J)$ is decreasing in the import tariff levied upon this export good by country $L(J)$. Notice further that country J's export volume of good $l(J)$ increases when country $L(J)$ applies a higher tariff to the competing exporters in country $R(J)$. A similar interpretation applies to good $r(J)$. Finally, using (7.4) we have that tariffs will be non-prohibitive provided that:

$$\frac{3}{4}\beta + \tau_{l(J)}^{R(J)}/2 > \tau_{l(J)}^{J}; \quad \frac{3}{4}\beta + \tau_{r(J)}^{L(J)}/2 > \tau_{r(J)}^{J}, \quad for \quad J = \{A, B, C\} \quad (7.5)$$

We define the welfare of each country as the sum over each good of consumer surplus, producer surplus, and tariff revenue. With the functional dependence of market clearing prices and trade volumes on tariffs given in (7.3) and (7.4), respectively, country J's welfare is given by:

$$W^{J}(\tau_{j}^{L(J)}, \tau_{j}^{R(J)}; \tau_{l(J)}^{J}, \tau_{l(J)}^{R(J)}; \tau_{r(J)}^{J}, \tau_{r(J)}^{L(J)}) = \int_{P_{j}^{J}}^{\alpha/\beta} D(P)dP + \int_{P_{l(J)}^{J}}^{\alpha/\beta} D(P)dP$$

$$+ \int_{P_{r(J)}^{J}}^{\alpha/\beta} D(P)dP + 3P_{l(J)}^{J}/2 + 3P_{r(J)}^{J}/2 + \tau_{j}^{L(J)}X_{j}^{L(J)} + \tau_{j}^{R(J)}X_{j}^{R(J)}$$

The qualitative features of our results are unaltered if the producer-surplus terms are scaled with parameters representing political-economy considerations (Bagwell and Staiger, 1996).

With government welfare functions now defined, we first solve for the Nash tariff choices of countries A, B and C. Our partial equilibrium structure and our assumption that countries do not tax exports imply that each country's optimal tariff choices will be independent of those of its trading partners. However, we now show that a country's choice of tariff on imports from its left-hand trading partner will depend on the tariff it sets on imports of the same good from its right-hand trading partner. The first-order conditions that define country J's best-response tariffs on imports of good j from its left- and right-hand trading partners, denoted by $\tilde{\tau}_{j}^{L(J)}(\tau_{j}^{R(J)})$ and $\tilde{\tau}_{j}^{R(J)}(\tau_{j}^{L(J)})$, respectively, are given by:

$$\partial W^{J}/\partial \tau_{j}^{L(J)} = 0 \Rightarrow \tilde{\tau}_{j}^{L(J)}(\tau_{j}^{R(J)}) = 3/22\beta + 7\tau_{j}^{R(J)}/11$$
$$\partial W^{J}/\partial \tau_{j}^{R(J)} = 0 \Rightarrow \tilde{\tau}_{j}^{R(J)}(\tau_{j}^{L(J)}) = 3/22\beta + 7\tau_{j}^{L(J)}/11 \quad (7.6)$$

It is straightforward to check that second-order conditions are globally met.

Condition (7.6) reveals an interesting complementarity between a country's tariffs on imports of the same good from different trading partners. As the tariff on imports of j from J's right-hand trading partner rises, it becomes *more* attractive for J to raise the tariff on imports of j from its left-hand trading partner. The complementarity of import tariffs across trading partners reflects three reinforcing effects. First, with $\tau_j^{R(J)}$ higher, the volume of J's consumption of good j drops, and so the consumer surplus cost of the price increase associated with a rise in $\tau_j^{L(J)}$ is lower. Second, with $\tau_j^{R(J)}$ higher, imports from $L(J)$ rise, and so the increase in tariff-revenue collected on imports from $L(J)$ as $\tau_j^{L(J)}$ rises is larger. And third, with $\tau_j^{R(J)}$ higher, the increase in imports from $R(J)$ that comes with a rise in $\tau_j^{L(J)}$ generates a greater increase in tariff revenue. Therefore, as (7.6) indicates, higher import tariffs on one import source will encourage a choice of higher import tariffs on competing import sources.

Finally, it is direct to solve (7.6) for the Nash equilibrium tariffs. Exploiting the symmetry of the model, we set $\tau_j^{L(J)} = \tau_j^{R(J)}$ to find $\tau^N = 3/8\beta$. From (7.5), symmetric tariffs in excess of $3/2\beta$ are required to prohibit trade, and so the unique symmetric Nash equilibrium has each country setting a non-prohibitive tariff τ^N on imports from each trading partner.

As for the efficiency properties of the Nash equilibrium, it is straightforward to show that a country's welfare is negatively affected by a tariff on its exports (its terms of trade worsen), but positively affected by a tariff on its competitor's exports (its terms of trade improve). Nevertheless, the overall impact of an importing country's tariffs on exporting country welfare is negative, and hence each country's tariffs exert a negative externality on all its trading partners taken together. As such, from an efficiency point of view (maximizing the sum of W^A, W^B, and W^C), the Nash equilibrium involves too much protection and, indeed, efficiency requires free trade. Hence, countries face a Prisoner's Dilemma problem because of the terms-of-trade externalities associated with their tariff choices.

We complete this section by considering the impact of regional agreements on external tariffs in the Nash equilibrium. In so doing, we illustrate a *tariff complementarity effect* that regional liberalization will have on desired external tariff levels in the Nash equilibrium. This effect will play an important role in the following section, where we explore more fully the implications of regional agreements for multilateral tariff co-operation.

Consider, first, the impact of a *free trade agreement* between countries A and B on the external tariffs chosen by countries A, B and C in the Nash equilibrium. Under a free-trade agreement between A and B, we set $\tau_a^B = \tau_b^A \equiv 0$. However, countries A and B continue to set their remaining tariffs independently to maximize their respective welfares, while country C continues to set tariffs on imports from A and B to maximize its welfare. By condition (7.6), country C's tariff choices are independent of those of its trading partners, and so C continues to set tariffs given by $\tau_c^A = \tau_c^B = \tau^N = 3/8\beta$. However, country A chooses its optimal tariff on imports from C *given* its free trade agreement with B, which by (7.6) is given by $\tilde{\tau}_a^C(\tau_a^B = 0) = 3/22\beta \equiv \tilde{\tau} < \tau^N$. Similarly, country B chooses its optimal tariff on imports from C *given* its free trade agreement with A, which by (7.6) is given by $\tilde{\tau}_b^C(\tau_b^A = 0) = 3/22\beta \equiv \tilde{\tau} < \tau^N$. Comparing multilateral tariffs in the presence of a free-trade agreement between A and B to multilateral tariffs in the absence of such an agreement, we therefore find that C's tariff choices are unaffected by the agreement between A and B, but that A and B choose to liberalize their external tariffs as a result of the free-trade agreement between them. This reflects the tariff complementarity effect that regional liberalization has on desired external tariff levels in the Nash equilibrium: countries that eliminate tariffs against imports from a sub-set of their trading partners through a free-trade agreement will be inclined in a Nash equilibrium to reduce external tariffs against their remaining trading partners also.[4]

Finally, we observe that the tariff complementarity effect of a free-trade agreement is strong enough to ensure that C gains in the Nash equilibrium when A and B form a free-trade agreement relative to its Nash welfare in the absence of a free-trade agreement. Such an outcome is not ensured, since the free trade agreement between A and B has two opposing effects on C: given the tariff complementarity effect it ensures that C's exports are taxed less, but the agreement also implies that the exporters in A and B, with which C's exporters compete, face no tax. However, defining ΔW_{FTA}^C as the change in C's welfare under the Nash equilibrium following the creation of a free-trade agreement between A and B, it is straightforward to show that:

$$\Delta W_{FTA}^C \equiv W^C(\tau^N, \tau^N; \tilde{\tau}, 0; \tilde{\tau}, 0) - W^C(\tau^N, \tau^N; \tau^N, \tau^N; \tau^N, \tau^N) > 0$$

Hence, the outside country gains when its trading partners form a free-trade agreement.

Consider next the impact of a *customs union* between countries A and B on the external tariffs chosen by countries A, B and C in the Nash equilibrium. Under a customs union between A and B, we set $\tau_a^B = \tau_b^A \equiv 0$. However, countries A and B now set their remaining tariffs to maximize their joint welfare, while country C continues to set tariffs on imports from A and B to maximize its welfare. Notice that countries A and B do not import a common good, and so the customs union does not impose a direct constraint on each member's external tariff choices – that is, these choices need not be harmonized. However, external tariff choices are none the less affected by the joint welfare criterion adopted under a customs union.

Again, by condition (7.6), country C's tariff choices are independent of those of its trading partners, and so C continues to set tariffs given by $\tau_c^A = \tau_c^B = \tau^N = 3/8\beta$. However, country A chooses its optimal tariff on imports from C, *given* its customs union with B, to maximize $W^A + W^B$, the joint welfare of A and B. Country B chooses its optimal tariff on imports from C analogously. Defining $\bar{\tau}_a^C(\tau_a^B)$ $(\bar{\tau}_b^C(\tau_b^A))$ as the tariff on A's (B's) imports from C that maximizes the joint welfare of A and B, the first-order conditions for these problems yield $\bar{\tau}_a^C(\tau_a^B = 0) = \bar{\tau}_b^C(\tau_b^A = 0) = 3/10\beta \equiv \bar{\tau} < \tau^N$. Hence, as with a free trade agreement, a customs union exhibits a tariff complementarity effect which leads countries A and B to lower their Nash tariffs against C.

However, the tariff complementarity effect is weaker in a customs union than it is in a free-trade agreement, and we have $\tilde{\tau} < \bar{\tau} < \tau^N$. This is because members of a customs union are concerned about the negative externality imposed on other customs union members when they lower their external tariff and thereby reduce the tariff advantage offered to their customs union partners. Moreover, the tariff complementarity effect is sufficiently weakened under a customs union that C no longer gains relative to the Nash equilibrium with no agreement between A and B. Defining ΔW_{CU}^C as the change in C's welfare under the Nash equilibrium following the creation of a customs union between A and B, it is straightforward to show that:

$$\Delta W_{CU}^C \equiv W^C(\tau^N, \tau^N; \bar{\tau}, 0; \bar{\tau}, 0) - W^C(\tau^N, \tau^N; \tau^N, \tau^N; \tau^N, \tau^N) < 0$$

Unlike the case of a free-trade agreement, we find that the tariff complementarity effect under a customs union is therefore too weak to outweigh the negative effects of tariff discrimination on the outside country, which loses because of the tariff discrimination it now faces in serving the markets of the customs union.

The tariff complementarity effect associated with regional agreements that we have identified above suggests that regional agreements might be thought of as complementary to multilateral liberalization or, in Bhagwati's (1991) terminology, as *building blocks* rather than *stumbling blocks* to multilateral liberalization. However, we have maintained throughout this section the assumption that multilateral tariffs are set non-cooperatively in a Nash equilibrium. Effectively, this ignores the fact that regional agreements are occurring *within* the broader context of attempts at multilateral co-operation. In the next section, we extend our analysis to incorporate this important dimension.

3 REGIONALISM AND MULTILATERAL TARIFF CO-OPERATION

In this section we consider the fact that regional agreements occur within the broader context of attempts to maintain multilateral tariff co-operation. This requires that we acknowledge efforts to co-operate in tariff policy at the multilateral level. However, if these multilateral efforts were perfect in the sense that they implemented efficient trade policies from the perspective of countries A, B and C, then free trade at the multilateral level would be achieved and there would be no role for regional agreements. Therefore, we must introduce a reason why multilateral co-operation is limited.

Here we focus on enforcement difficulties at the multilateral level as a reason why the multilateral agreement cannot achieve full efficiency. In particular, we adopt the view that the multilateral agreement must be self-enforcing (see, for example, Dam, 1970), and model multilateral tariff co-operation as a repeated game among the three countries. The repeated game that we consider involves infinite repetition of the static game developed in the previous section. The three countries attempt to achieve tariffs below their static Nash levels and use infinite reversion to the static Nash tariffs as a credible (sub-game perfect) punishment that would be triggered if any country were to defect from its stipulated tariffs under the multilateral agreement. In this setting, we assume that limits to multilateral enforcement prevent the multilateral agreement from reaching global free trade. We then ask how preferential agreements affect the ability of countries to sustain low multilateral tariffs.

We proceed in three stages. First we consider the ability of countries to achieve low non-discriminatory tariffs. That is, we look for the lowest (non-negative) tariffs achievable by the multilateral agreement under the restriction that all tariffs conform to the MFN principle. This provides a multilateral benchmark from which to gauge the impacts of regional agreements on multilateral co-operation. Next, we consider how the degree of multilateral tariff co-operation is affected by the presence of a free-trade agreement between countries A and B. And, finally, we consider how the presence of customs unions affects the degree of multilateral tariff co-operation.

MFN

We begin by considering the ability of countries A, B and C to maintain low multilateral tariffs under the restriction that all tariffs conform to the MFN principle. The principle of MFN requires that $\tau_j^{L(J)} = \tau_j^{R(J)} \equiv \tau_j$ for $J = \{A, B, C\}$. We assume that the three countries attempt to maintain low MFN tariffs (τ_a, τ_b, τ_c) with the threat of infinite reversion to the Nash tariff τ^N in the event that any country deviates from its tariff as stipulated under the agreement. To solve for the *most co-operative* tariffs sustainable under the agreement (that is, the self-enforcing tariffs that maximize the joint welfare of the three countries) we must consider the incentive constraints under which countries operate.

When each country's tariff policy conforms to MFN, we represent country J's welfare by:

$$\hat{W}^J(\tau_j, \tau_{l(J)}, \tau_{r(J)}) \equiv W^J(\tau_j, \tau_j; \tau_{l(J)}, \tau_{l(J)}; \tau_{r(J)}, \tau_{r(J)})$$

In developing the incentive constraints faced by each country, we consider first the one-time payoff to country J in deviating from the multilateral agreement. Since punishment from both trading partners will follow any deviation, we consider the one-time payoff to J in deviating simultaneously against both its trading partners to its best-response tariff τ^N. Denoting this one-time payoff from defection by $\hat{\Omega}(\tau_j, \tau_{l(J)}, \tau_{r(J)})$, we note that:

$$\hat{\Omega}(\tau_j, \tau_{l(J)}, \tau_{r(J)}) \equiv \hat{W}^J(\tau^N, \tau_{l(J)}, \tau_{r(J)}) - \hat{W}^J(\tau_j, \tau_{l(J)}, \tau_{r(J)})$$

$$= \frac{4\beta}{9}[\tau_j - \tau^N]^2 \equiv \hat{\Omega}(\tau_j)$$

Observe that country J's incentive to defect depends only upon the import tariff that country J selects under the multilateral tariff agreement. Not surprisingly, when country J selects a lower import tariff τ_j as part of the agreement, it has a correspondingly higher incentive to defect. At the other extreme, country J's incentive to defect is zero when it already sets its Nash tariff under the multilateral tariff agreement (that is, when $\tau_j = \tau^N$).

Under the multilateral agreement, a deviation will be followed by infinite reversion to Nash tariffs for all countries. Thus, to see whether country J will indeed give in to the temptation to deviate as embodied in $\hat{\Omega}(\tau_j)$, we next consider the cost of the ensuing 'trade war'. We represent the per-period cost of a trade war by $\hat{\omega}^J(\tau_j, \tau_{l(J)}, \tau_{r(J)})$, and note that:

$$\hat{\omega}^J(\tau_j, \tau_{l(J)}, \tau_{r(J)}) \equiv \hat{W}^J(\tau_j, \tau_{l(J)}, \tau_{r(J)}) - \hat{W}^J(\tau^N, \tau^N, \tau^N)$$

$$= \frac{1}{3}\left\{\beta(\tau^N)^2 + \left[\frac{\beta}{6}((\tau_{l(J)})^2 + (\tau_{r(J)})^2) - \frac{1}{2}(\tau_{l(J)} - \tau_{r(J)})\right] - \left[\frac{4\beta}{3}(\tau_j)^2 - \tau_j\right]\right\}$$

$$\equiv \hat{\omega}(\tau_j, \tau_{l(J)}, \tau_{r(J)})$$

This function exhibits several intuitive properties. In particular, country J experiences higher welfare under the agreement, and thus recognizes a higher per-period cost of a trade war, when its agreed-upon tariff is higher and when the agreed-upon tariff of any other country is lower.[5] Also, when all countries select symmetric tariffs, the per-period cost of a trade war is maximized at free trade and is zero when the agreement itself calls for the Nash tariff.

Finally, to represent the discounted future cost that a country experiences when a trade war is initiated, we must describe the manner in which countries discount future welfare. We assume that countries are heterogeneous in the degree to which they value the future, as embodied in each country's discount factor $\delta^J \in [0, 1)$. In particular, we assume that countries A and B are relatively patient as compared with country C, so that:

$$\delta^A = \delta^B = \delta_H \geqslant \delta_L = \delta^C \tag{7.7}$$

We can now present the incentive constraints (IC) that must be satisfied for any set of MFN tariffs (τ_a, τ_b, τ_c) that are self-enforcing under the multilateral trade agreement. In particular, for each country, the one-time benefit in deviating from the agreement must be no greater than the discounted cost to that country of the ensuing trade war. Formally, we have:

$$
\begin{aligned}
ICA: \quad & \hat{\Omega}(\tau_a) \leqslant \frac{\delta_H}{1 - \delta_H} \hat{\omega}(\tau_a, \tau_b, \tau_c) \\[2mm]
ICB: \quad & \hat{\Omega}(\tau_b) \leqslant \frac{\delta_H}{1 - \delta_H} \hat{\omega}(\tau_b, \tau_c, \tau_a) \\[2mm]
ICC: \quad & \hat{\Omega}(\tau_c) \leqslant \frac{\delta_L}{1 - \delta_L} \hat{\omega}(\tau_c, \tau_a, \tau_b)
\end{aligned}
\tag{7.8}
$$

Any set of MFN tariffs (τ_a, τ_b, τ_c) satisfying (7.8) can be sustained as a self-enforcing multilateral trade agreement under our assumptions.

We first derive the lowest *symmetric* tariff satisfying (7.8). To this end we let $\tau \equiv \tau_a = \tau_b = \tau_c$ and note that (7.8) will be satisfied with equality at $\tau = \tau^N$. To explore the possibility that lower symmetric tariffs can be sustained, we note that, under (7.7), as τ is lowered from τ^N, country C's incentive constraint (ICC) in (7.8) will be the first to bind. We thus look for a tariff below τ^N that makes ICC hold with equality:

$$\hat{\Omega}(\tau) = \frac{\delta_L}{1 - \delta_L} \hat{\omega}(\tau, \tau, \tau)$$

Noting that $\hat{\omega}(\tau, \tau, \tau) = \beta[(\tau^N)^2 - (\tau)^2]/3$, we find that the lowest symmetric tariff, which we denote by $\underline{\tau}$, is given by:

$$\underline{\tau} = \left[\frac{4 - 7\delta_L}{4 - \delta_L} \right] \tau^N \tag{7.9}$$

Hence, as (7.9) indicates, under condition (7.7) multilateral free trade can be supported if and only if $\delta_L \geqslant 4/7$. Henceforth we assume that $\delta_L < 4/7$.

We next observe from (7.8) that countries A and B, being more patient than C, have 'slack' in their respective incentive constraints at $\underline{\tau}$, that is, *ICA* and *ICB* hold with strict inequality at $\underline{\tau}$, and thus A and B could sustain even lower MFN tariffs in a self-enforcing agreement. We therefore explore the 'hegemonic' role that could be played by countries A and B in a multilateral trading system by allowing them to liberalize further than $\underline{\tau}$ on an MFN basis. Having relaxed the restriction of overall symmetry, we maintain the restriction that A

and B impose symmetric tariffs $\tau_a = \tau_b$ and now look for the set of MFN tariffs (τ_a, τ_a, τ_c) that lie below the Nash level and satisfy (7.8).

To this end, we denote by $\tau_c(\tau_a)$ the lowest MFN tariff sustainable by country C when facing a tariff τ_a from both its trading partners A and B, and observe from (7.8) that $\tau_c(\tau_a)$ will be defined by the lower root of:

$$\hat{\Omega}(\tau_c) = \frac{\delta_L}{1 - \delta_L}\hat{\omega}(\tau_c, \tau_a, \tau_a) \tag{7.10}$$

Solving (7.10) explicitly yields:

$$\tau_c(\tau_a) = \tau^N - \frac{1}{2}\sqrt{\delta_L(7\tau^N - \tau_a)(\tau^N - \tau_a)}$$

We note that $\tau_c(\tau_a = \tau^N) = \tau^N$, $\tau_c(\tau_a = \underline{\tau}) = \underline{\tau}$, $\partial \tau_c(\tau_a = \tau^N)/\partial \tau_a = \infty$, and that $\tau_c(\tau_a)$ is increasing and convex over $\tau_a \in [0, \tau^N]$. Intuitively, country C is unable to sustain a tariff below the Nash level when countries A and B select their Nash tariffs, since C would be treated no less favourably by A and B in a trade war. As countries A and B lower their import tariffs, however, country C would now have something to lose in a trade war with A and B, and so country C can sustain a tariff below the Nash level despite the consequent positive incentive to defect.

Similarly, we denote by $\tau_a(\tau_c)$ the lowest MFN tariff sustainable by country A when facing a symmetric tariff from country B and a tariff τ_c from country C. We note from (7.8) that $\tau_a(\tau_c)$ will be defined by the lower root of:

$$\hat{\Omega}(\tau_a) = \frac{\delta_H}{1 - \delta_H}\hat{\omega}(\tau_a, \tau_a, \tau_c) \tag{7.11}$$

Solving (7.11) explicitly yields:

$$\tau_a(\tau_c) = \frac{3[2 - \delta_H] - \sqrt{\left(\frac{9}{4}\delta_H\right)^2 - 4\beta(8 - \delta_H)\delta_H(\tau_c - \tau^N)\left[\frac{9}{4} - \beta(\tau_c - \tau^N)\right]}}{2\beta(8 - \delta_H)}$$

We observe that $\tau_a(\tau_c = \tau^N) < \tau^N$, $\tau_a(\tau_c = \underline{\tau}) < \underline{\tau}$, and that $\tau_a(\tau_c)$ is increasing and convex over $\tau_c \in [0, \tau^N]$. It is interesting to observe that country A can sustain a tariff below τ^N even when $\tau_c = \tau^N$. Intuitively, co-operation between countries A and B is valuable even when C sets tariffs non-cooperatively and, under MFN, countries A and B can co-operate with one another only if they extend their low tariffs to exports from country C as well. The fact that a tariff below $\underline{\tau}$ can be sustained by A and B even if they face the tariff $\underline{\tau}$ from country

C reflects the relative patience of A and B compared with C. Finally, the positive slope exhibited by $\tau_a(\tau_c)$ reflects familiar reasoning: when country C co-operates with a lower import tariff, countries A and B recognize a higher cost of a trade war and are therefore able to sustain lower tariffs.

The properties of $\tau_c(\tau_a)$ and $\tau_a(\tau_c)$ imply that there are two cases to consider, depending on the value of δ_H. These two cases are distinguished by whether or not countries A and B can sustain free trade policies in a self-enforcing agreement (C cannot, given our assumption that $\delta_L < 4/7$). In particular, it can be shown that there exists a function $\delta_H = \delta_H(\delta_L)$ with $\delta_H(0) = 8/7 > \delta_H(4/7) = 4/7$ and $\partial\delta_H/\partial\delta_L < 0$ such that $(\tau_a = 0, \tau_b = 0, \tau_c = \tau_c(0))$ is sustainable as a self-enforcing agreement if and only if $\delta_H \geqslant \delta_H(\delta_L)$. Figures 7.2a and 7.2b illustrate.

Figure 7.2a illustrates Case 1, in which $\delta_H \in [\delta_L, \delta_H(\delta_L))$. Here, the point labelled H depicts the hegemonic equilibrium, in which A and B reduce their MFN tariffs below the symmetric most co-operative level $\underline{\tau}$. The hegemonic liberalization of A and B enhances the value of the agreement to C, thereby increasing the cost of a trade war, and also allowing C to undertake further liberalization. Note, however, that the 'multiplier' effect associated with the MFN liberalization of A and B cannot induce C to fully reciprocate with equal liberalization of its own, and so A and B act as 'hegemons', allowing C to 'free ride' to some extent on their MFN liberalization. The point H reflects the most co-operative MFN tariff combination sustainable: that is, the combination of MFN tariffs that maximizes the joint welfare of A, B and C, subject to

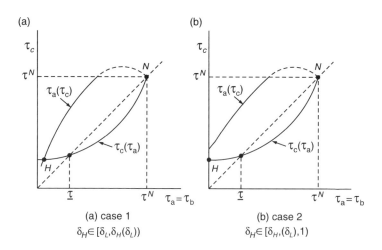

(a) case 1   (b) case 2
$\delta_H \in [\delta_L, \delta_H(\delta_L))$ $\delta_H \in [\delta_H, (\delta_L), 1)$

Figure 7.2   Tariff equilibria under hegemonic liberalization

their incentive constraints.[6] In Case 1, illustrated in Figure 7.2a, point H entails binding incentive constraints for all countries and all tariffs are strictly positive.

Figure 7.2b illustrates Case 2, in which $\delta_H \in [\delta_H(\delta_L), 1)]$. Here, the point labelled H again depicts the hegemonic equilibrium, in which A and B reduce their MFN tariffs below the symmetric most co-operative level $\underline{\tau}$. As in Case 1, the hegemonic liberalization of A and B enhances the value of the agreement to C, thereby increasing the cost of a trade war, and allowing C to undertake further liberalization. And again, as in Case 1, the point H reflects the most co-operative MFN tariff combination sustainable. However, in Case 2, illustrated in Figure 7.2b, point H entails free trade for countries A and B, with a binding incentive constraint only for country C, whose tariff is strictly positive.

In the next two sub-sections we assume $\delta_H \in [\delta_L, \delta_H(\delta_L))$, so that A and B cannot achieve free trade policies on an MFN basis, and ask how preferential agreements between them can affect the degree of multilateral tariff co-operation.

Free-trade Agreements

We first suppose that countries A and B negotiate a free-trade agreement. We abstract from enforcement issues associated with the free-trade agreement itself, and simply assume that it can be enforced. Moreover, we take the existence of the free-trade agreement between A and B to be immutable: that is, we assume that it would not break down in the event of a breakdown of the multilateral agreement. The ability of A and B to enforce their free-trade agreement when multilateral free trade cannot be enforced might be seen as reflecting the high discount factors shared by these two countries. Alternatively, cultural or political links between A and B might facilitate more explicit enforcement mechanisms than are possible in a multilateral agreement. In any event, our focus is on the impact of the free-trade agreement between A and B on the most co-operative tariffs sustainable in the multilateral agreement.

The free-trade agreement between A and B implies that $\tau_a^B = \tau_b^A \equiv 0$. The symmetry between A and B implies that they will impose a symmetric *multilateral* tariff on imports from their external trading partner (C), which we denote by $\tau^m \equiv \tau_a^C = \tau_b^C$. Under a reversion to the Nash equilibrium, the free trade agreement between A and B remains intact, and so the Nash punishment tariffs (and the best-defect tariffs) for A and B individually are given by (Equation 7.6) as $\tau^m = \tilde{\tau}_a^C(\tau_a^B = 0) = 3/22\beta \equiv \tilde{\tau} < \tau^N$. Hence, the free trade agreement between A and B will reduce the effectiveness with which these countries can punish C should C defect from the multilateral agreement. Finally, country C will continue to abide by the MFN principle under the multilateral agreement, and so we let $\tau_c \equiv \tau_c^A = \tau_c^B$. Under a reversion to the Nash equilibrium (or under a defection), country C's best-response tariff continues to be τ^N.

To derive the impact of the free trade agreement between A and B on the most co-operative multilateral tariffs sustainable under the multilateral agreement, we need to derive the new incentive constraints faced by each country as it sets its multilateral tariff policy. Now the one-time payoff in defecting from the multilateral agreement for each country is given by:

$$\tilde{\Omega}^A(\tau^m,\tau_c) \equiv W^A(0,\tilde{\tau};0,\tau^m;\tau_c,\tau_c) - W^A(0,\tau^m;0,\tau^m;\tau_c,\tau_c) = 11\frac{\beta}{18}(\tilde{\tau}-\tau^m)^2$$

$$\tilde{\Omega}^B(\tau^m,\tau_c) \equiv W^B(\tilde{\tau},0;\tau_c,\tau_c;0,\tau^m) - W^B(\tau^m,0;\tau_c,\tau_c;0,\tau^m) = 11\frac{\beta}{18}(\tilde{\tau}-\tau^m)^2$$

$$\tilde{\Omega}^C(\tau^m,\tau_c) \equiv W^C(\tau^N,\tau^N;\tau^m,0;\tau^m,0) - W^C(\tau_c,\tau_c;\tau^m,0;\tau^m,0) = 4\frac{\beta}{9}(\tau_c-\tau^N)^2$$

The per-period cost of a trade war that would follow a defection is now given by:

$$\tilde{\omega}^A(\tau^m,\tau_c) \equiv W^A(0,\tau^m;0,\tau^m;\tau_c,\tau_c) - W^A(0,\tilde{\tau};0,\tilde{\tau};\tau^N,\tau^N)$$
$$= \frac{2(\tau^m-\tilde{\tau})-(\tau_c-\tau^N)}{6} + \frac{\beta}{18}[(\tau_c)^2-(\tau^N)^2] - 5\frac{\beta}{9}[(\tau^m)^2-(\tilde{\tau})^2]$$

$$\tilde{\omega}^B(\tau^m,\tau_c) \equiv W^B(\tau^m,0;\tau_c,\tau_c;0,\tau^m) - W^B(\tilde{\tau},0;\tau^N,\tau^N;0,\tilde{\tau})$$
$$= \frac{2(\tau^m-\tilde{\tau})-(\tau_c-\tau^N)}{6} + \frac{\beta}{18}[(\tau_c)^2-(\tau^N)^2] - 5\frac{\beta}{9}[(\tau^m)^2-(\tilde{\tau})^2]$$

$$\tilde{\omega}^C(\tau^m,\tau_c) \equiv W^C(\tau_c,\tau_c;\tau^m,0;\tau^m,0) - W^C(\tau^N,\tau^N,\tilde{\tau},0;\tilde{\tau},0)$$
$$= \frac{(\tau_c-\tau^N)-2(\tau^m-\tilde{\tau})}{3} + 4\frac{\beta}{9}[(\tau^m)^2-(\tilde{\tau})^2] - 4\frac{\beta}{9}[(\tau_c)^2-(\tau^N)^2]$$

We can now present the incentive constraints that must be satisfied for any set of self-enforcing multilateral tariffs (τ^m,τ_c), given the presence of a free-trade agreement between A and B. As before, the one-time benefit in deviating from the multilateral agreement must be no greater than the discounted cost to that country of the ensuing trade war. Formally, we have:

$$ICA: \quad \tilde{\Omega}^A(\tau^m,\tau_c) \le \frac{\delta_H}{1-\delta_H}\tilde{\omega}^A(\tau^m,\tau_c)$$

$$ICB: \quad \tilde{\Omega}^B(\tau^m,\tau_c) \le \frac{\delta_H}{1-\delta_H}\tilde{\omega}^B(\tau^m,\tau_c) \qquad (7.12)$$

$$ICC: \quad \tilde{\Omega}^C(\tau^m,\tau_c) \le \frac{\delta_L}{1-\delta_L}\tilde{\omega}^C(\tau^m,\tau_c)$$

Any set of tariffs (τ^m, τ_c) satisfying (7.12) can be sustained as a self-enforcing multilateral trade agreement in the presence of a free-trade agreement between A and B.

In analogy with the approach taken above, we denote by $\tilde{\tau}_c(\tau^m)$ the lowest MFN tariff sustainable by country C when facing a multilateral tariff τ^m from each of the free-trade agreement partners A and B. From (7.12), $\tilde{\tau}_c(\tau^m)$ will be defined by the lower root of:

$$\tilde{\Omega}^C(\tau^m, \tau_c) = \frac{\delta_L}{1 - \delta_L} \tilde{\omega}^C(\tau^m, \tau_c) \qquad (7.13)$$

Solving (7.13) explicitly yields:

$$\tilde{\tau}_c(\tau^m) = \tau^N - \sqrt{(\tau^m - \tilde{\tau})\delta_L(\tau^m - 15/11\beta)}$$

We note that $\tilde{\tau}_c(\tau^m = \tilde{\tau}) = \tau^N$, $\partial \tilde{\tau}_c(\tau^m = \tilde{\tau})/\partial \tau^m = \infty$, and that $\tilde{\tau}_c(\tau^m)$ is increasing and convex over $\tau^m \in [0, \tilde{\tau}]$.

In fact, it can be shown that $\tilde{\tau}_c(\tau^m)$ lies everywhere above the analogous function derived under MFN, $\tau_c(\tau_a = \tau^m)$, over the range $\tau^m \in [0, \tilde{\tau}]$. This reflects the *punishment effect* of a free-trade agreement between A and B, in that the free-trade agreement has made these countries less effective punishers of C. Therefore C is less-effectively deterred from a defection by the threat of an ensuing trade war with A and B.[7] As a consequence of the punishment effect, it therefore follows that, facing a given multilateral tariff in countries A and B in the range $\tau^m \in [0, \tilde{\tau}]$, incentive compatibility requires country C to raise its tariff if a free-trade agreement between A and B is formed. Note also that the importance of this effect rises with δ_L, country C's discount factor, and vanishes when $\delta_L = 0$, as then $\tilde{\tau}_c(\tau^m) \equiv \tau_c(\tau_a = \tau^m) \equiv \tau^N$.

Similarly, exploiting the symmetry between A and B, we denote by $\tilde{\tau}^m(\tau_c)$ the lowest multilateral tariff sustainable by countries A and B given their free-trade agreement and facing an MFN tariff τ_c in country C. From (7.12), $\tilde{\tau}^m(\tau_c)$ will be defined by the lower root of:

$$\tilde{\Omega}^A(\tau^m, \tau_c) = \frac{\delta_H}{1 - \delta_H} \tilde{\omega}^A(\tau^m, \tau_c) \qquad (7.14)$$

Solving (7.14) explicitly yields:

$$\tilde{\tau}^m(\tau_c) = \frac{3(1 + \delta_H)}{2\beta(11 - \delta_H)}$$
$$- \frac{\sqrt{(36\delta_H/11)^2 - 4\beta(11 - \delta_H)\delta_H(\tau_c - \tau^N)[9/4 - \beta(\tau_c - \tau^N)]}}{2\beta(11 - \delta_H)}$$

We note that $\tilde{\tau}^m(\tau_c = \tau^N) = \tilde{\tau}$, and that $\tilde{\tau}^m(\tau_c)$ is increasing and convex over $\tau_c \in [0, \tau^N]$.

There are two important new features of $\tilde{\tau}^m(\tau_c)$. First, contrary to the analogous function derived under MFN, $\tau_a(\tau_c)$, multilateral co-operation from A and B ($\tau^m < \tilde{\tau}$) cannot be sustained without co-operation from C ($\tau_c < \tau^N$). This reflects the fact that, with an exception from MFN granted and their free-trade agreement in place, A and B no longer need to co-operate multilaterally in order to co-operate bilaterally. We shall refer to this as the *tariff discrimination effect* of a preferential agreement, since the ability to negotiate bilateral tariff preferences allows countries to discriminate in their external tariffs against outside countries. This effect by itself will cause a free-trade agreement between A and B to raise the lowest co-operative multilateral tariffs that A and B can sustain facing a given tariff from C in the multilateral agreement. Note also that the importance of this effect rises with δ_H, the discount factor for countries A and B. But a second new feature of $\tilde{\tau}^m(\tau_c)$ arises as a result of the *tariff complementarity effect*, and reflects the fact that the free-trade agreement between A and B makes these countries less enthusiastic about a high external tariff even in the absence of multilateral co-operation. This effect by itself will cause a free-trade agreement between A and B to reduce the lowest co-operative multilateral tariffs that A and B can sustain for a given tariff from C in the multilateral agreement. Note that the importance of this effect is independent of the size of the discount factors. As a consequence, whether or not the free trade agreement between A and B enhances or interferes with the ability of these countries to sustain low multilateral tariffs against imports from C for a given multilateral tariff choice of C, will depend on the relative strengths of these two effects, which depends in turn on the size of δ_H.

The general features of $\tilde{\tau}_c(\tau^m)$ and $\tilde{\tau}^m(\tau_c)$ are illustrated in Figure 7.3 for the case where A and B cannot sustain multilateral free trade.[8] The point labelled FTA in Figure 7.3 reflects the set of most co-operative multilateral tariffs sustainable in the presence of a free-trade agreement between A and B. These are the multilateral tariffs that maximize the joint welfare of countries A, B and C subject to their multilateral incentive constraints as contained in (7.12).[9]

As noted above, no general conclusion can be drawn about the impact of the free trade agreement between A and B on the most co-operative multilateral tariff levels. However, we can illustrate the possibilities in a useful special case. In particular, consider the case in which $\delta_L = 0$. As noted above, in this case, the punishment effect on C's ability to co-operate multilaterally is eliminated, leaving only two opposing effects of the free-trade agreement on the ability of countries A and B to co-operate multilaterally with C: a tariff discrimination effect that tends to make free-trade agreements bad for multilateral tariff co-operation and is stronger the higher is δ_H, and a tariff

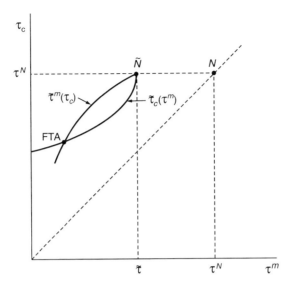

Figure 7.3 Most co-operative multilateral tariffs with free-trade agreements between A and B

complementarity effect that tends to make free-trade agreements good for multilateral tariff co-operation and whose strength is independent of δ_H. In this case, there exists a critical value of $\delta_H = 56/73 \equiv \tilde{\delta}$ such that free trade agreements are bad for multilateral tariff co-operation if and only if $\delta_H \in (\tilde{\delta}, 1)$.

Figure 7.4 illustrates by depicting the most co-operative multilateral tariffs under MFN (labelled MFN) and in the presence of a free-trade agreement between A and B (labelled FTA) in the case where $\delta_L = 0$ and $\delta_H \in (\tilde{\delta}, 1)$. As depicted, with $\delta_L = 0$, C must set its non-cooperative tariff τ^N regardless of the presence or absence of a free-trade agreement between A and B. Under MFN, countries A and B must offer the same liberalization to C that they achieve reciprocally, and the most co-operative MFN tariffs are depicted at point D. Countries A and B can sustain MFN tariffs below the Nash level even though country C offers nothing in return because A's liberalization is valuable to B and vice versa. Under a free trade agreement between A and B, however, these countries achieve the gains from co-operation bilaterally, and are therefore unwilling to liberalize their multilateral tariffs if their multilateral trading partners are unwilling to reciprocate. This is the tariff discrimination effect of the free-trade agreement, and it removes the ability to liberalize multilaterally away from the Nash point to point D. On the other

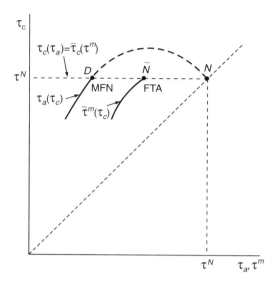

Figure 7.4 Most co-operative multilaterial tariffs under MFN and with a free-trade agreement between A and B

hand, the tariff complementarity effect of the free-trade agreement reduces the level of the multilateral tariffs desired by A and B in a Nash equilibrium, moving the Nash point from N in Figure 7.4 to the point labeled $\tilde{N}$. For $\delta_H \in (\bar{\delta}, 1)$, the tariff discrimination effect dominates the tariff complementarity effect and, as illustrated in Figure 7.4, the most co-operative multilateral tariffs rise with the arrival of the free trade agreement between A and B.

Customs Unions

We next suppose that countries A and B form a customs union. As with the free-trade agreement analyzed above, we abstract from enforcement issues associated with the customs union itself and simply assume that it can be enforced and is immutable. We consider the impact of this customs union on the most co-operative tariffs sustainable in the multilateral agreement.

As with the free-trade agreement, the customs union between A and B implies that $\tau_a^B = \tau_b^A \equiv 0$. And, as before, the symmetry between A and B implies that they will impose a symmetric *multilateral* tariff on imports from their external trading partner (C), which we denote by $\tau^m \equiv \tau_a^C = \tau_b^C$. However, under a reversion to the Nash equilibrium, the customs union between A and B remains intact, and so the Nash punishment tariffs (and the best-defect tariffs) for A and B, which will be chosen to maximize their *joint* welfare, are given by $\tau^m = \bar{\tau}_a^C (\tau_a^B = 0) = 3/10\beta \equiv \bar{\tau} \in (\tilde{\tau}, \tau^N)$. Hence, the customs union between A and B will reduce the effectiveness with which these countries can punish C with a high tariff, but the ability of A and B to punish C will not be diminished to the extent that it would be under a free-trade agreement between these two countries. This is because members of a customs union are concerned about the negative externality imposed on other customs union members when they lower their external tariff and thereby reduce the tariff advantage offered to their customs union partners. This concern leads customs union members to desire higher external tariffs than members of a free-trade agreement. Finally, as before, country C will continue to abide by the MFN principle under the multilateral agreement, and so we continue to let $\tau_c \equiv \tau_c^A = \tau_c^B$. Under a reversion to the Nash equilibrium (or under a defection), country C's best-response tariff continues to be τ^N.

To derive the impact of the customs union between A and B on the most co-operative multilateral tariffs sustainable under the multilateral agreement, we again need to derive the new incentive constraints faced by each country as it sets its multilateral tariff policy. Since A and B now choose their trade policies to maximize joint welfare, we shall have just two incentive constraints. In the presence of a customs union between A and B, the onetime payoff in defecting from the multilateral agreement for A and B jointly (expressed per country in A's notation) and for C is given, respectively, by:

$$\bar{\Omega}^A(\tau^m, \tau_c) \equiv W^A(0, \bar{\tau}; 0, \bar{\tau}; \tau_c, \tau_c) - W^A(0, \tau^m; 0, \tau^m; \tau_c, \tau_c) = 5\frac{\beta}{9}(\bar{\tau} - \tau^m)^2$$

$$\bar{\Omega}^C(\tau^m, \tau_c) \equiv W^C(\tau^N, \tau^N; \tau^m, 0; \tau^m, 0) - W^C(\tau_c, \tau_c; \tau^m, 0; \tau^m, 0) = 4\frac{\beta}{9}(\tau_c - \tau^N)^2$$

The corresponding per-period cost of a trade war that would follow a defection is now given by:

$$\bar{\omega}^A(\tau^m, \tau_c) \equiv W^A(0, \tau^m; 0, \tau^m; \tau_c, \tau_c) - W^A(0, \bar{\tau}; 0, \bar{\tau}; \tau^N, \tau^N)$$
$$= \frac{2(\tau^m - \bar{\tau}) - (\tau_c - \tau^N)}{6} + \frac{\beta}{18}[(\tau_c)^2 - (\tau^N)^2] - 5\frac{\beta}{9}[(\tau^m)^2 - (\bar{\tau})^2]$$

$$\bar{\omega}^C(\tau^M, \tau_c) \equiv W^C(\tau_c, \tau_c; \tau^m, 0; \tau^m, 0) - W^C(\tau^N, \tau^N; \bar{\tau}, 0; \bar{\tau}, 0)$$
$$= \frac{(\tau_c - \tau^N) - 2(\tau^m - \bar{\tau})}{3} + 4\frac{\beta}{9}[(\tau^m)^2 - (\bar{\tau})^2] - 4\frac{\beta}{9}[(\tau_c)^2 - (\tau^N)^2]$$

We can now present the incentive constraints (IC) that must be satisfied for any set of multilateral tariffs (τ^m, τ_c) that are self-enforcing under the multilateral agreement, given the presence of a customs union between A and B. As before, the one-time benefit in deviating from the multilateral agreement must be no greater than the discounted cost to that country of the ensuing trade war. Formally, we have:

$$ICAB: \quad \bar{\Omega}^A(\tau^m, \tau_c) \leq \frac{\delta_H}{1 - \delta_H} \bar{\omega}^A(\tau^m, \tau_c)$$

$$ICC: \quad \bar{\Omega}^C(\tau^m, \tau_c) \leq \frac{\delta_L}{1 - \delta_L} \bar{\omega}^C(\tau^m, \tau_c) \tag{7.15}$$

Any set of tariffs (τ^m, τ_c) satisfying (7.15) can be sustained as a self-enforcing multilateral trade agreement in the presence of a customs union between A and B.

In analogy with the approach taken in the previous subsections, we denote by $\bar{\tau}_c(\tau^m)$ the lowest MFN tariff sustainable by country C when facing a multilateral tariff τ^m from each of countries A and B, who together maintain a customs union between them. From (7.15), $\bar{\tau}_c(\tau^m)$ will be defined by the lower root of:

$$\bar{\Omega}^C(\tau^m, \tau_c) = \frac{\delta_L}{1 - \delta_L} \bar{\omega}^C(\tau^m, \tau_c) \tag{7.16}$$

Solving (7.16) explicitly yields:

$$\bar{\tau}_c(\tau^m) = \tau^N - \sqrt{(\tau^m - \bar{\tau})\delta_L(\tau^m - 6/5\beta)}$$

We note that $\bar{\tau}_c(\tau^m = \bar{\tau}) = \tau^N$, $\partial \bar{\tau}_c(\tau^m = \bar{\tau})/\partial \tau^m = \infty$, and that $\bar{\tau}_c(\tau^m)$ is increasing and convex over $\tau^m \in [0, \bar{\tau}]$.

Moreover, it can be shown that $\bar{\tau}_c(\tau^m)$ lies everywhere below the analogous function derived in the presence of a free-trade agreement, $\tilde{\tau}_c(\tau^m)$, over the range $\tau^m \in [0, \bar{\tau}]$. This reflects the fact that the punishment effect associated with a free-trade agreement between A and B is more pronounced than that associated with a customs union between these two countries. Consequently, country C is less effectively deterred from a defection by the threat of an ensuing trade war when A and B form a free-trade agreement than when they form a customs union. It therefore follows that, facing a given multilateral tariff from countries A and B in the range $\tau^m \in [0, \bar{\tau}]$, incentive compatibility requires country C to raise its tariff by a greater amount if a free-trade agreement between A and B is formed than if A and B form a customs union. Comparing $\bar{\tau}_c(\tau^m)$ to $\tau_c(\tau_a)$, the analogous function derived under the restriction of MFN, we note that $\bar{\tau}_c(\tau^m)$ lies above $\tau_c(\tau_a = \tau^m)$ for τ^m sufficiently close to $\bar{\tau}$ but below $\tau_c(\tau_a = \tau^m)$ for τ^m sufficiently close to zero. This reflects the fact that, for τ^m sufficiently close to zero, country C can be punished more severely by A and B when they join together in a customs union than when they select tariffs in a non-discriminatory fashion. Finally, note again that the importance of the punishment effect rises with δ_L, the discount factor for country C, and that, in particular, this effect vanishes when $\delta_L = 0$, as then $\bar{\tau}_c(\tau^m) \equiv \tilde{\tau}_c(\tau^m) \equiv \tau_c(\tau_a = \tau^m) \equiv \tau^N$.

Similarly, exploiting the symmetry between A and B, we denote by $\bar{\tau}^m(\tau_c)$ the lowest multilateral tariff sustainable by countries A and B, given their customs union and facing an MFN tariff τ_c from country C. From (7.15), $\bar{\tau}^m(\tau_c)$ will be defined by the lower root of:

$$\bar{\Omega}^A(\tau^m, \tau_c) = \frac{\delta_H}{1 - \delta_H} \bar{\omega}^A(\tau^m, \tau_c) \tag{7.17}$$

Solving (7.17) explicitly yields:

$$\bar{\tau}^m(\tau_c) = \bar{\tau} - \sqrt{\frac{(\tau^N - \tau_c)\delta_H\left(\frac{21}{8}\beta - \tau_c\right)}{10}}$$

We note that $\bar{\tau}^m(\tau_c = \tau^N) = \bar{\tau}$, and that $\bar{\tau}^m(\tau_c)$ is increasing and convex over $\tau_c \in [0, \tau^N]$. As with $\tilde{\tau}^m(\tau_c)$, the relative strengths of two opposing effects – the tariff discrimination effect (the strength of which increases in δ_H) and the tariff complementarity effect (which is independent of δ_H) – determine whether $\bar{\tau}^m(\tau_c)$ lies above or below $\tau_a(\tau_c)$ over the range $\tau_c \in [0, \tau^N]$, and therefore whether a customs union between A and B increases or reduces the lowest co-operative multilateral tariff that A and B can sustain for a given tariff from C in the multilateral agreement. However, as noted above, the tariff complementarity effect is weaker in the case of a customs union than in the case of a free-trade agreement (hence $\bar{\tau} > \tilde{\tau}$), and thus the critical value of δ_H above which a customs union between A and B increases the lowest co-operative multilateral tariff that A and B can sustain for a given tariff from C in the multilateral agreement will tend to be lower than the analogous critical value in the presence of a free-trade agreement.

The general features of $\bar{\tau}_c(\tau^m)$ and $\bar{\tau}^m(\tau_c)$ are illustrated in Figure 7.5 for the case where A and B cannot sustain multilateral free trade.[10] The point labelled CU in Figure 7.5 reflects the set of most co-operative multilateral tariffs sustainable in the presence of a customs union between A and B. These are the multilateral tariffs that maximize the joint welfare of countries A, B and C subject to their multilateral incentive constraints as contained in (7.15).[11]

As with a free-trade agreement, no general conclusion can be drawn about the impact of the customs union between A and B on the most co-operative multilateral tariff levels. Again, we illustrate the possibilities by turning to the useful special case where $\delta_L = 0$. As noted above, in this case, the punishment

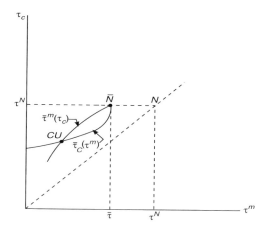

Figure 7.5   Most co-operative multilaterial tariffs with customs union of A and B

effect on C's ability to co-operate multilaterally is eliminated, leaving only two opposing effects of the customs union on the ability of countries A and B to co-operate multilaterally with C: a tariff discrimination effect, that tends to make customs unions bad for multilateral tariff co-operation and is stronger the higher is δ_H, and a tariff complementarity effect that tends to make customs unions good for multilateral tariff co-operation and whose strength is independent of δ_H but, as noted above, weaker than the corresponding effect associated with a free-trade agreement. Comparing the most co-operative tariffs under MFN with those in the presence of a customs union between A and B, we find that there exists a critical value of $\delta_H = 8/31 \equiv \bar{\delta}$ such that customs unions are bad for multilateral tariff co-operation if and only if $\delta_H \in (\bar{\delta}, 1)$. Moreover, note that $\bar{\delta} < \tilde{\delta}$: hence, for the intermediate range of $\delta_H \in (\bar{\delta}, \tilde{\delta}]$, customs unions are bad for multilateral tariff co-operation while free-trade agreements are good.

Figure 7.6 illustrates by depicting the most co-operative multilateral tariffs under MFN (labelled MFN) and in the presence of a free-trade agreement between A and B (labelled FTA) and in the presence of a customs union between A and B (labelled CU) in the case where $\delta_L = 0$. Figure 7.6a depicts the case in which $\delta_H \in (\delta_L, \bar{\delta})$, so that multilateral tariff co-operation under MFN is relatively ineffective. Here, the tariff complementarity effect outweighs the tariff discrimination effect for both free-trade agreements and customs unions, and each form of preferential agreement allows a lower level of multilateral tariffs to be negotiated than would exist under MFN. Figure 7.6b depicts the case where $\delta_H \in (\bar{\delta}, \tilde{\delta})$. Here, the tariff discrimination effect

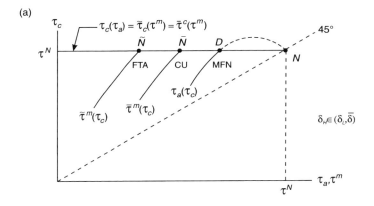

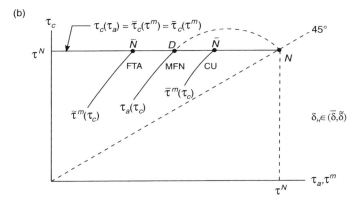

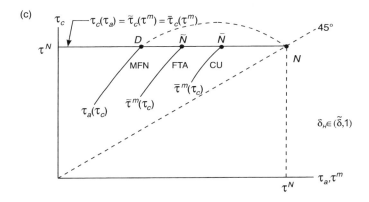

Figure 7.6 Most co-operative multilateral tariffs under MFN, with free-trade agreement of A and B, and customs union of A and B, $\delta_L = 0$

overwhelms the tariff complementarity effect for customs unions, but is out-weighed by the tariff complementarity effect for free-trade agreements, so that free-trade agreements continue to allow a lower level of multilateral tariffs but customs unions lead to a higher level of multilateral tariffs than would exist under MFN. Finally, Figure 7.6c depicts the case where $\delta_H \in (\bar{\delta}, 1)$. Here, the tariff discrimination effect overwhelms the tariff com-plementarity effect for both customs unions and free-trade agreements, so that both forms of preferential agreement lead to a higher level of multilateral tariffs than would exist under MFN.

4   CONCLUSION

We have considered a three-country world in which each country's import market is served by competing exporters in its two trading partners. We have assumed that weak multilateral enforcement mechanisms prevent govern-ments from implementing efficient trade policies through a multilateral agreement that requires tariffs to conform to the MFN principle. We then ask whether exceptions from MFN for the purpose of forming preferential agreements can lead to a more efficient tariff structure under the multilateral agreement.

We identify three opposing effects of preferential agreements on the multi-lateral tariff structure in this setting. A first effect of a preferential agreement, the *tariff complementarity effect*, derives from the complementary relationship across the tariffs a country selects on imports from different trading partners. We find that reducing a tariff on imports from one source makes tariff reductions on imports from all other sources more attractive. This effect works to reduce the desired external tariffs of countries that join together in a preferential agreement, and we find that it is stronger under a free-trade agreement than under a customs union.

Two additional effects of preferential agreements arise only when enforce-ment issues are considered. One of these, the *punishment effect*, is the flip-side of the tariff complementarity effect. This effect serves to weaken the ability of the member countries of a preferential agreement to punish devia-tions from the multilateral agreement, thereby interfering with the ability of countries to sustain low tariffs under the multilateral agreement. As with the tariff complementarity effect, this effect is more pronounced under a free-trade agreement than under a customs union. The other effect, the *tariff discrimination effect*, allows countries to discriminate against those who would 'free ride' under MFN, and thus works to increase the desired external tariffs of countries that join together in a preferential agreement. The strength of this effect is independent of the form of the preferential agreement.

The relative strengths of these three effects determine the impact of a preferential agreement on the tariff structure under the multilateral agreement, and we find that preferential agreements can be either good or bad for multilateral tariff co-operation, depending on parameters. In particular, we demonstrate that the three effects can be ranked when the non-member country is sufficiently impatient. In that event, the non-member country is focused on the present, and the punishment effect is eliminated. The tariff complementarity and discrimination effects remain, however, and the latter will dominate if and only if the two member countries are sufficiently patient. In this circumstance, the formation of a free-trade area leads to an overall deterioration in multilateral tariff co-operation. Furthermore, we find that customs union formation is more likely to harm multilateral tariff liberalization than is free-trade area formation, in the sense that the former leads to an increase in multilateral tariffs from member countries for a wider range of possible patience levels for the member countries.

Our results suggest a number of broader conclusions. First, it is important to keep in mind that since 1947 the formation of preferential agreements has occurred within the broader context of multilateral tariff co-operation under GATT (and now the WTO). Therefore, when assessing the impact of preferential agreements on external tariffs, it is critical that the analysis reflects the attempt to maintain multilateral tariff co-operation. The importance of this observation is manifested in our results above, where we find that the more ominous implications of preferential agreements for external tariffs arise only when attempts to maintain multilateral tariff co-operation and the associated enforcement difficulties are considered. Second, our results point to an intriguing possibility regarding the role of preferential agreements when the multilateral system is working poorly. The appeal of preferential agreements in such circumstances is sometimes viewed as signalling the demise of the multilateral system. Our results suggest that this conclusion is not necessarily warranted. Rather, our findings indicate that it is precisely when the multilateral system is working poorly (as when countries are sufficiently impatient) that preferential agreements can have their most desirable effects on the multilateral system.

Notes

1. For helpful comments, we thank Martin Richardson, an anonymous referee, John Piggott and Alan Woodland, Nita Watts, and the conference participants. This chapter was completed while Staiger was a Fellow at the Center for Advanced Study in the Behavioral Sciences. Staiger is also grateful for financial support provided by the National Science Foundation Grant no. SBR-9022192.

2. Thus, for tariffs, the superscript refers to the country to whom the tariff is applied, whereas the subscript identifies the import good and thereby the importing country.

3. We suppress country superscript on the import function $M_j(P_j^J)$ as only one country imports each good. We include country superscript on the export functions $X_{i(J)}^J(P_{i(J)}^J)$, $i = \{l, r\}$ as each good is exported by two countries.

4. This effect is reminiscent of an observation made by Richardson (1992), but occurs for different reasons and under different trading patterns. Richardson considers free-trade agreements between countries that are competing importers of a common good from third countries, and argues that in these circumstances each partner in the agreement will have an incentive to lower its external tariff to slightly below the external tariff of the other partners, to increase its share of tariff revenue collected on imports from outside the free-trade area. We focus, by contrast, on free-trade agreements between countries that are competing exporters of a common good to third countries, but that do not compete for imports of a common good from third counties.

5. This holds provided that country J's agreed-upon tariff is below the Nash level, and that the tariffs of other countries do not exceed $3/2\beta$ (so that trade is not prohibited). The effect of other countries' tariffs on country J's welfare may be understood in analogy with the reasoning developed above: when an importing country selects a lower MFN tariff, an exporting country experiences an overall increase in welfare, as the direct gain associated with the lower tariff on own exports exceeds the indirect loss associated with the lower tariff on competing exports.

6. It is straightforward to demonstrate that combinations of $\tau_a = \tau_b$ and τ_c along which $\hat{W}^A + \hat{W}^B + \hat{W}^C$ is held constant are represented over the positive-tariff quadrant as negatively-sloped curves, with joint welfare being higher on curves that are closer to the origin. Looking to Figures 7.2a and 7.2b, it is then straightforward to see that point H maximizes joint welfare. (Note that $\tau_a(\tau_c)$ is concave in these figures, since τ_c is on the y axis.)

7. At the same time, the free-trade agreement between A and B has no impact on their exported supplies to C, who therefore faces a onetime payoff from defection which is unchanged by the free-trade agreement.

8. As in the case of MFN tariffs, a function $\bar{\delta}_H(\delta_L)$ analogous to $\delta_H(\delta_L)$ can be defined such that $(\tau^m = 0, \tau_c = \tilde{\tau}_c(0))$ is sustainable as a self-enforcing multilateral agreement in the presence of a free-trade agreement between A and B if, and only if, $\delta_H \geqslant \bar{\delta}_H(\delta_L)$. We focus our discussion on the case where $\delta_H < \bar{\delta}_H(\delta_L)$.

9. In analogy with Note 6 for the MFN game, one can show that the iso-joint-welfare contour takes a negative slope through the positive-tariff quadrant, and this implies that the point labeled *FTA* in Figure 7.3 represents the most cooperative tariffs for the free-trade-area game.

10. As in the case of MFN tariffs, a function $\bar{\delta}_H(\delta_L)$ analogous to $\delta_H(\delta_L)$ can be defined such that $(\tau^m = 0, \tau_c = \bar{\tau}_c(0))$ is sustainable as a self-enforcing multilateral agreement in the presence of a customs union between A and B if, and only if, $\delta_H \geqslant \bar{\delta}_H(\delta_L)$. We focus our discussion on the case where $\delta_H < \bar{\delta}_H(\delta_L)$.

11. Comments characterizing the iso-joint-welfare contours analogous to those in Note 6 apply.

References

Bagwell, K. and R. W. Staiger (1996) 'Reciprocal Trade Liberalization', Cambridge, Mass: National Bureau of Economic Research Working Paper no. 5488, March.

Bagwell, K. and R. W. Staiger (1997a) 'Multilateral Tariff Cooperation During the Formation of Free Trade Areas', *International Economic Review*, vol. 38, no. 2, pp. 291–319.

Bagwell, K. and R. W. Staiger (1997b) 'Multilateral Tariff Cooperation During the Formation of Customs Unions', *Journal of International Economics*, vol. 42, nos 1/2, pp. 91–123.

Bhagwati, J. (1991) *The World Trading System at Risk* (Princeton, NJ.: Princeton University Press).

Bond, E. and C. Syropoulos, (1996) 'Trading Blocs and the Sustainability of Inter-Regional Cooperation', in M. Canzoneri, W. Ethier and V. Grilli (eds), *The New Transatlantic Economy* (Cambridge: Cambridge University Press).

Bond, E., C. Syropoulos, and L. A. Winters (1996) 'Deepening of Regional Integration and Multilateral Trade Agreements', CPER Discussion paper no. 131.

Dam, K. (1970) *The GATT: Law and International Economic Organization* (University of Chicago Press).

Kindleberger, C. P. (1981). 'Dominance and Leadership in the International Economy: Exploitation, Public Goods, and Free Rides', *International Studies Quarterly*, vol. 25, no. 2, pp. 242–54.

Richardson, M. (1992) 'On Equilibrium in a Free Trade Area with Internal Trade', mimeo, University of Otago, April.

Richardson, M. (1993) 'Endogenous Protection and Trade Diversion', *Journal of International Economics*, vol. 34, pp. 309–24.

Comment

Martin Richardson
UNIVERSITY OF OTAGO

The general issue considered in this chapter is how regional preferential trading areas (PTAs) affect the operation of a multilateral trade policy forum. The approach taken is a positive one, taking an agreement as given and looking at its consequences. The authors stress, quite correctly, that a key distinguishing element of their analysis is its dynamic setting in which trade agreements, by virtue of the sovereignty of their participants, cannot be enforced by external means and so must be 'self-enforcing' in the usual sense of repeated games. The thrust of the chapter is how the formation of a PTA amongst a sub-set of countries upsets the trade-offs involved in sustaining multilateral co-operation among all countries.

The authors examine this question in a three-country partial equilibrium model of tariff-setting with 'competing exporters' and find three general consequences of PTAs for multilateral tariff agreements. First, there is a *tariff complementarity* effect, in which reduction of a tariff on one source of imports leads a country to wish to lower its tariffs on other sources of imports of the same good. This suggests that a PTA has a liberalizing effect at the multilateral level. This effect leads to another, in a dynamic setting, as it means that PTA members are less able to punish non-members who cheat on a multilateral agreement as the members' optimal external tariffs are lower once the PTA is formed. The authors term this the *punishment effect* and note that it is harmful to multilateral co-operation, suggesting that PTAs raise the minimum tariff of non-members that such co-operation can sustain. Third, the chapter identifies a *tariff discrimination effect*, which is also harmful to multilateral co-operation and which arises, loosely, as PTA members realize gains from mutual liberalization and so no longer feel so great a need to co-operate multilaterally.

The authors describe these effects fairly generally, but show that definite conclusions can be drawn in one special case, in which member countries are not only more patient than the non-member country, but the latter also has a discount factor of zero. The punishment effect then disappears and the other two effects can be compared. However, when the non-member cares nothing for the future one would anticipate (correctly) that it will not co-operate in any multilateral agreement, and so we are left with an odd sort of exercise: one in which the non-member of the PTA is also a non-participant in the multilateral agreement! (This is not to suggest that the exercise is un-

186

enlightening; on the contrary, it illustrates some tendencies that might be quite general and it shows very clearly the discrimination effect of the FTA where a bilateral deal is made explicit.)

The identification of these effects is an important contribution of the chapter. An immediate question in the sort of linear model used is, of course, 'How general are the results likely to be?', and I suspect that these sorts of effects could be found in a variety of settings. For example, while the chapter identifies the tariff discrimination effect in a repeated game setting where multilateral co-operation can exist initially (through the threat of punishment) but is then less attractive when PTAs are available, this sounds like a phenomenon that might hold more widely – for example, in a situation in which the ability that a PTA provides to discriminate between sources of imports enables a government to increase the tariff it sets against non-members (Richardson, 1994).

Another question that is critical here, given the significance accorded to enforcement issues, is just how important these really are in the multilateral arena. There is a character in a Michael Frayn novel who takes on, quite sincerely, the opinions of the person he has spoken to most recently and I found myself in some sympathy with him as I read two of the chapters in this volume. Professor Ethier (Chapter 6) does not discuss enforcement issues and this did not seem to present problems in his analysis. Such issues have not been a serious consideration in practice, as retreat from liberal trade has generally not involved violating earlier tariff agreements but rather has been effected through the use of other, unrestricted, instruments. I find this argument quite convincing. Then I read Chapter 7 and found myself just as convinced that enforcement issues are *central* to the analysis of multilateral agreements! I am tempted to declare myself agnostic on the issue, but in fact I suspect that both approaches are right: it is probably true that 'cheating' on tariff agreements has been effected, in practice, by the use of alternative instruments but, nevertheless, if one wants to capture this dimension of behaviour in a simple model of trade policy the approach taken in the current chapter seems to be the right one.

I shall concentrate my remaining remarks on two aspects of the chapter; namely, the pattern of trade and the (absence of) political motivation of governments. I also have a number of other fairly minor remarks about certain aspects of the modelling.

First, the assumed trade pattern. The 'competing exporters' setting serves very nicely to capture popular concerns about PTAs which centre on trade diversion or 'fortress' effects: presumably this is exactly the fear that non-member exporters will be squeezed from markets by exporters in favoured partner countries. However, this 'reverse Meade pattern', in which each country exports a greater number of commodities than it imports is, as I understand it, empirically false (see Lloyd, 1982, p. 51). It is, however, a central element of the chapter as it gives rise to the tariff complementarity effect. This result runs counter to the general conclusion that PTAs lead to an *increase* in external tariffs against non-members by virtue of their internalizing the tariff externality stressed by, *inter alia*, Kennan and Riezman (1990). While the formation of a PTA leading to a reduction in external tariffs is not itself a new result (see Desruelle and Richardson (1997), Richardson (1995), and Cadot, de Melo and Olarreaga (1996), for example), its context in a welfare-maximizing setting *is* novel and important. However, if the trade pattern were the 'more normal' one of competing importers, the analysis of the present chapter would presumably lead to increasing external tariffs on the formation of a PTA and thus a punishment effect that enables PTA members to *more* effectively punish multilateral deviants. That is, the punishment effect would be *beneficial* for multilateral co-operation.

In this setting, a useful extension would be to consider the delegation issue identified by Gatsios and Karp (1991) in an asymmetric version of the current model. Presumably, the incentive to delegate tariff-setting authority to one member of a customs union (CU) is greater in the current setting than in a static context and one would suspect that delegating to the more 'aggressive' partner would have beneficial consequences for multilateral co-operation by making a trade war more harmful to the non-member.

The second modelling choice I wish to address is the lack of political economy considerations by national governments. The authors acknowledge this, referring to an earlier paper (Bagwell and Staiger, 1996). In that paper they had argued that such considerations do not help to explain why governments should *seek* regional agreements.

But the concern of the present chapter is *not* with the *formation* of PTAs but, rather, with the setting of trade policy *once such an agreement has been established*. Accordingly, political economy considerations might be thought to be of paramount importance. Of course, the question then arises of which of the myriad forms of political economy specifications of trade policy formation one might choose. I recall Ngo Van Long once citing, 'a theorem that any set of results can be generated by some set of assumptions', a dictum that is as true in political economy as elsewhere! Nevertheless, I think this would be a useful direction in which the authors might extend this work.

Certain features of the chapter are very appealing in the setting of the theme of 'international trade policy and the Pacific rim'. In particular, the complementarity effect seems significant in light of Professor Lloyd's comments that external tariffs in Australia and New Zealand declined as their FTA increasingly liberalized trade between them. (This is true at least in a correlation sense: policy-makers in New Zealand have argued that the FTA with Australia was an epiphenomenon of general liberalization, but it has been suggested that it was a cornerstone and that the causality runs the other way.)

A further issue in the Pacific setting is one which I think the authors' approach is very well suited to handle: the effects of regional deals on *other* regional deals. These are a distinguishing feature of the 'new' regionalism, as noted by Professor Greenaway in Chapter 1, above. As APEC becomes more important, what will be its consequences for CER? We are already seeing consequences of the EU for EFTA and it seems to me that the kinds of issues involved here are exactly those discussed in this chapter.

I found the argument that relatively patient countries might act as hegemons in multilateral agreements – lowering their own MFN tariffs to a degree not matched by others – very appealing. Coates and Ludema (1996) have a rather different explanation of the same sort of phenomenon, in which unilateral tariff reductions are intended to weaken foreign political opposition to trade liberalization, and I would like to see the relative merits of the two hypotheses discussed.

One final point: this chapter does not pretend to address the issue of *why* countries form PTAs, and so it does not address the question of how partners are chosen. Nevertheless, I think it would be interesting to see some numerical simulations of welfare *levels* in order to see if the analysis can shed some light on that question, particularly with the heterogeneity of time preferences across the countries, as modelled in the chapter. Furthermore, it would be interesting to know what the net consequences of PTAs are for members: under what conditions will a PTA that damages multilateral co-operation still be attractive for members to join? If these conditions are strenuous then it might be the case that the 'building blocks' version of PTAs still prevails.

In summary, my comments are largely suggestions for further work and, as such, they reflect a belief that the approach the authors have taken here is a valuable and promising one.

References

Bagwell, K. and R. Staiger (1996) 'Reciprocal Trade Liberalization', NBER Working Paper no. 5488, Cambridge, Mass.

Cadot, O., J. de Melo and M. Olarreaga (1996) 'Regional Integration and Lobbying for Tariffs against Non Members', mimeo (France: INSEAD)

Coates, D. and R. Ludema (1996) 'Unilateral Tariff Reduction as Leadership in Trade Negotiations', mimeo (Washington DC: Georgetown University).

Desruelle, D. and M. Richardson (1996) 'Fortress Europe: Jericho or Chateau d'If?', *Review of International Economics*, vol. 5, no. 1, February, pp. 32–46.

Gatsios, K. and L. Karp (1991) 'Delegation Games in Customs Unions', *Review of Economic Studies*, vol. 58, no. 2, pp. 391–7.

Kennan, J. and R. Riezman (1990) 'Optimal Tariff Equilibria with Customs Unions', *Canadian Journal of Economics*, vol. 23, pp. 70–83.

Lloyd, P. (1982) '3 × 3 Theory of Customs Unions', *Journal of International Economics*, vol. 12, no. 1/2, pp. 41–63.

Richardson, M. (1994) 'Customs Unions and Domestic Taxes', *Canadian Journal of Economics*, vol. 27, pp. 537–50.

Richardson, M. (1995) 'Tariff Revenue Competition in a Free Trade Area', *European Economic Review*, vol. 39, pp. 1429–37.

8 Do Two Wrongs Make a Right? Export Incentives and Bias in Trade Policy[1]

Richard G. Harris
SIMON FRASER UNIVERSITY AND CANADIAN INSTITUTE
FOR ADVANCED RESEARCH

and

Nicolas Schmitt
SIMON FRASER UNIVERSITY

1 INTRODUCTION

In the large literature on export promotion and South-East Asian trade policy, there is a tradition, going back at least to Corden (1971), of emphasizing the offsetting consequences of export promotion in the presence of protection of domestic industry. It is often claimed that the anti-export bias of protection is removed, or 'neutralized', by export incentives. Thus, the combined presence of fairly high levels of protection with equally large doses of export incentives results in an allocation of resources similar to that produced by a policy of unilateral free trade. On theoretical grounds, this proposition derives support from the familiar competitive production (supply-side) model of a small, open economy. In that model the relative output of exportables and importables is determined by the internal product price ratio. Given tariffs on imports, export subsidies can be used to restore the internal producer price ratio to the external world price ratio.[2] One could summarize by saying that this is an example in economic policy where 'two wrongs make a right'; that is, while each policy individually would reduce welfare, jointly they produce an outcome that is optimal.

The empirical relevance of this is quite obvious in a large number of countries. A good example is the summary of studies on Korean trade policy done by Nam (1990). He reports (p. 179, table 9.6) a survey of effective subsidy rates on export versus domestic sales for a wide range of industries during the 1970s. On average, the effective subsidy for export in manufacturing was about 16 per cent, but the effective rate for domestic sales was about 3.5 per cent, suggesting on balance a larger incentive to export than to sell in the domestic market. There is a general assessment in the literature on trade bias in East Asian economies that, in the more recent period, exports have been relatively favoured.[3]

Not surprisingly, a number of authors have wondered about the impact of such types of trade regime in East Asian economies where the export incentives appear to be at least as prominent as the import substitution aspect of the regime. Flatters and Harris (1995) noted that there are good reasons to suspect that many of these trade policies are in fact a form of what they label *export protectionism* – that is, they could result in a bias towards excessive exports at the expense of the rest of the economy. This chapter focuses on two models in which export incentives interact with tariff protection in non- offsetting ways.

The first model starts from the premise that one consequence of protection is to reduce competition. In small, open economies protection may lead to a high degree of seller concentration. It is possible under such circumstances that the traditional supply-side effects of protection are dominated by demand-side effects. In this model, it is shown that protection is export-promoting in the sense that increases in the degree of protection result in an increase in the size of the export sector, and this is welfare-reducing. Furthermore, it is shown that export incentives have no effect on the allocation of resources in the presence of protection; that is, they are completely neutral in terms of their impact on aggregate resource allocation. The source of these results derives from an important characteristic of general equilibrium in this economy. With a limit-pricing domestic monopoly, there is a strong 'no-import', or *market closure* effect of protection, which leads to the unusual importance of demand conditions for resource allocation.

The second model is a positive theory of the administrative structure of export incentive programmes that captures some important aspects of the process by which export incentives are determined in many of the East Asian economies.[4] The approach taken is similar to that in the political economy literature, as the determination of export incentives by the authorities administering the programmes is discretionary, subject to incomplete information, and contingent upon observed prices. The criterion upon which decisions to subsidize exports are arrived at is similar to that suggested in the normative literature on trade reform.[5] It is assumed that export authorities use linear and imperfect approximations to national welfare to evaluate export investment opportunities.[6] It is also assumed that the import protection regime is relatively permanent, and viewed by the export authorities as being independent of their actions – a feature of the trade policy regimes that Bliss (1987), among others, has emphasized. The main question addressed is how import protection interacts with the outcome of the discretionary export incentive regime. It is shown that, in some circumstances increases in import protection are export-promoting; the behaviour of the export authorities results in increased export incentives beyond those a complete welfare analysis would prescribe.

In each of these cases the model is highly stylized and we make no claim for the generality of these results. However, the influences identified clearly exist in countries characterized by the joint existence of both import substitution and export promotion schemes. They suggest that traditional views of protection, where export incentives neutralize the effects of protection, may be inappropriate in some circumstances.

The chapter proceeds as follows. In the second section, a model of monopoly-induced market closure is developed, and the role of import protection and export incentives is analyzed. Section 3 develops a positive model of administrative and discretionary export incentives, and the last section provides a summary and some concluding observations on the implications of these results.

2   IMPORT COMPETING MONOPOLY AND TRADE INTERVENTIONS WITH MARKET CLOSURE

In a large number of studies of protection in small, open economies, it has been shown that there is a tendency for protected industries to become heavily concentrated – that is, protection produces monopoly. We shall argue for the strong possibility that, with monopoly in the domestic market, no imports will occur in equilibrium – a result referred to as *market closure*. This is true even though tariffs are at less than conventionally calculated prohibitive levels. An equilibrium implication of this result is that increased import protection will be export-promoting. To make these points, a simple three-good Ricardian production model is used, in which the importable is an intermediate input – a case of obvious relevance to East Asia.

Market Structure in the Import Competing Sector

The market structure in the import competing sector is assumed to be a limit-pricing monopoly.[7] The monopolist sets a price just a shade below the world price plus tariff. The major feature of this assumption is that, as long as the monopolist's costs are below this price, she has the incentive to serve the entire domestic market since it is profitable to do so and has no incentive to export. This conclusion would still hold if the marginal revenue curve were to intersect the marginal cost curve at an output level where the price was below the limit price. This may conceivably occur if demand for the good in question is sufficiently elastic. But for a wide class of demand structures this will not be the case. With Cobb-Douglas preferences (unitary price elasticity of demand), for example, it always pays the monopolist to supply the entire domestic market and to limit price. We shall assume this to be the case throughout this section.[8] Partial equilibrium in this sector is illustrated in

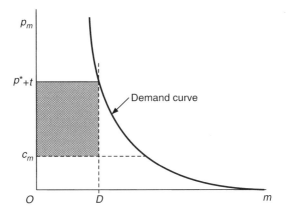

Figure 8.1 Partial equilibrium with a limit-pricing monopolist

Figure 8.1. Note that, in the partial equilibrium model and for a given demand curve, as tariff protection increases the monopolist's output, OD, decreases.[9] The shaded area indicates monopoly profit, which must be included in income and accounted for in the general equilibrium determination of demand conditions.

General Equilibrium

The rest of the model is a fairly conventional trade model for a small, open economy. There is a competitive export sector with a fixed coefficient production function that uses an import-competing, domestically-produced intermediate input, with price p_m, which is also a final consumption good. This good is available in perfectly elastic supply at the world price plus tariff $p_m^*(1+t)$. Exports are an intermediate good not consumed at home and sold at price p_x, fixed in world markets. There is a third good, not produced domestically but imported at price q. This can be thought of as a luxury consumer good and/or an imported capital good. Net government revenue is redistributed to consumers in a lump-sum fashion. All consumers have identical homothetic tastes. Technology is expressed by fixed coefficients with labour as the only input in the importable sector, while labour and the domestically produced good are inputs to the export sector. Labour input coefficients are denoted by a_i, the intermediate input coefficient by b_x, and the wage rate by w. Unit costs are thus given as $c_m = a_m w$ and $c_x = a_x w + b_x p_m$ in x. Labour is mobile between industries and in fixed inelastic supply to the economy in amount L. Output in each sector is denoted by Y_i.

In the absence of tariff revenue, domestic disposable income E, is the sum of labour income and monopoly profits, Π:

$$E = wL + \Pi \tag{8.1}$$

The share coefficient on the home-produced, import-competing good is denoted by $\beta(p_m, q)$. Final domestic consumption demand for the import-competing good is denoted by D, and intermediate input demand from the export sector by I. With limit-pricing monopoly and market closure, output of the import-competing sector, Y_m, equals total demand $D + I$. Factor demands are given by:

$$L_m = a_m(D + I), L_x = a_x Y_x, \ I = b_x Y_x \tag{8.2}$$

Profits in the monopoly sector, substituting for D and I, are given by:

$$\Pi = (p_m - c_m)(D + I) = (p_m - c_m)[\beta(wL + \Pi) + b_x Y_x] \tag{8.3}$$

The price–mark-up equation in the m sector is:[10]

$$\frac{p_m - c_m}{p_m} = \sigma \tag{8.4}$$

The mark-up factor σ is determined passively under limit-pricing monopoly as the limit price, and costs in that sector adjust. Since $p_x = c_x$ and labour is the only non-traded factor, input factor prices are determined in this model solely by the export sector. Note also that an important consequence of the market closure effect in the Ricardian model is that the economy is not specialized, producing positive quantities of both goods m and x.

Monopoly profit conditional on the mark-up and non-profit-related expenditures on the monopoly good is given by:[11]

$$\Pi = \frac{\sigma}{1 - \sigma\beta}(\beta wL + p_m b_x Y_x) \tag{8.5}$$

The leading coefficient in (8.5) can be thought of as the *profit multiplier*; this is a number greater than one which translates a dollar of expenditure by either labour or the export sector on the monopolist's good into dollars of profit to that sector. A multiplier effect exists by virtue of the fact that some of that profit is re-spent in the monopoly sector itself and thus generates additional profit.

Labour market clearing is given by:

$$L = a_m \beta \frac{W}{p_m} + a_m \beta \frac{\Pi}{p_m} + a_m I + a_x Y_x$$

Here we have expressed the two sources of domestic demand coming from profits and from wage income, $W = wL$. Equilibrium can be thought of as occurring in the following way. Wages are set by the 'export cost equals price' equation, and then export output adjusts to clear the labour market with equilibrium profits adjusting accordingly. Substituting in the expression for profit and collecting terms give an expression for the equilibrium relationship between wages, import prices and export output:

$$L\left\{1 - \left(\frac{\beta a_m}{1 - \sigma\beta}\right)\frac{w}{p_m}\right\} = a_m b_x\left\{\frac{1}{1 - \sigma\beta} + \frac{a_x}{a_m b_x}\right\}Y_x$$

Substituting for w/p_m from the mark-up equation and solving for the inverse export ratio, L/Y_x yields:

$$\frac{L}{Y_x}(1 - \beta) = a_m b_x + a_x(1 - \sigma\beta) \tag{8.6}$$

It is somewhat remarkable that *exports are uniquely determined by, and increasing in, the monopoly price–cost mark-up σ.* An increase in the mark-up raises exports. There are two factors at work. First, there is a strong real domestic demand effect due to the change in the product wage w/p_m. This can be seen most easily by assuming that the share in expenditure of profits on domestic goods is zero. In this case, the fall in the product wage w/p_m induced by a higher mark-up has a direct and immediate effect on domestic demand, leading to an expansion in the export sector. This would occur even were the domestic good m not used as intermediate input in the export sector, $b_x = 0$, in which case wages would not change as σ increase, but real demand from labour income would decline.

The second and offsetting effect is the change in profits that occurs as a result of the increase in the mark-up factor. Profits increase and demand derived from profits goes up.[12] The profitability effect of increased markups is, however, not sufficiently strong to offset the direct negative demand effect due to the change in the product wage. The net effect of the higher monopoly mark-up is negative on the import competing sector and positive on the export sector. At one level, the result is very intuitive; increased monopolization of the import-competing sector drives resources into the export sector.

Changes in Tariffs

A rise in t increases the limit price p_m, but since there are no imports there is no tariff revenue effect. Given the role of domestic intermediate inputs in the export sector, the cost-raising effect of higher input prices implies that tariffs lower wages. The comparative static result on mark-ups is:

$$\frac{d\sigma}{dp_m} = \frac{1}{p_m}\left[1 - \sigma - a_m\frac{dw}{dp_m}\right] > 0$$

As the mark-up is increasing with higher tariff rates, this implies that *protection has an export-promoting effect* from (8.6). Increases in the tariff lead to larger volumes of exports. Furthermore, since wages must fall as the price of the intermediate input increases, the real wage, measured either by w/p_m or w/p_x, falls.

Real profits in terms of the domestic good are given by:

$$\frac{\Pi}{p_m} = \frac{\sigma}{1-\sigma\beta}\frac{\beta wL}{p_m} + b_xY_x = \frac{\sigma\beta(1-\sigma)}{1-\sigma\beta}\frac{L}{a_m} + b_xY_x \tag{8.7}$$

There are two things to note about (8.7). One, a higher mark-up raises exports, Y_x, and the effect of this on real profits is positive. Two, the leading coefficient of (8.7) on the L-term is a function of σ. It is straightforward to show that a sufficient condition for this coefficient to increase with σ is that $\sigma < 1/2$, which is a plausible empirical restriction on the range of observed mark-ups.

Export Incentives

Is it possible that an export incentive policy will offset at least to some degree the effects of protection? Surprisingly, the answer is 'no'; export incentives in this model have no impact on the equilibrium. We first establish this basic result and then provide some intuitive explanation of why this occurs. Two types of incentive policies are considered: production subsidies to the export sector and import-duty drawbacks.

Consider an increase in a production subsidy rate s, applied to the cost of production in the export sector. Total export subsidies, S, which must be deducted from GDP to get aggregate household expenditure E, are given by $S = \tau p_xY_x$ with $\tau = s/(1-s)$. Substituting these into the definition for E and solving for profits gives:

$$\Pi = \frac{\sigma}{1-\sigma\beta}(\beta wL - \beta\tau p_xY_x + p_mb_xY_x) \tag{8.8}$$

Using the new definition for E and Π in the labour-market clearing condition, we solve for the inverse export ratio L/Y_x,

$$\frac{L}{Y_x}(1-\beta) = a_mb_x + (1-\beta)a_x + \beta a_m\Gamma \tag{8.9}$$

with Γ defined as:

$$\Gamma \equiv \frac{w}{p_m} a_x - \frac{s}{1-s} \frac{p_x}{p_m} = \frac{p_x}{p_m} - b_x \qquad (8.10)$$

which is independent of the subsidy rate s. The implication is that production subsidies to the export sector have *no effect* on output in the export sector provided that the relative price p_x/p_m remains constant. This is so even though the wage rate is increasing in the level of subsidy and therefore has an effect on labour income. One might think that the increase in the wage induced by the subsidy might offset the wage-reducing effect of protection on income. However, the effects of a change in s on profit income and government revenue *exactly* offset this.

A common form of export incentive is a duty-drawback scheme, in which producers using imported inputs are rebated the tariff portion of the input cost. This implies that the price paid for the import-competing input is equalised to the world price, but other domestic users must pay the tariff-inclusive price. The rationale for such a policy is that it offsets the cost-raising effect of a tariff on intermediate inputs to the export sector; a duty-drawback programme can restore a negative effective rate of protection on exports to zero. We model duty drawbacks by assuming that the import-competing monopoly sector gets the tariff inclusive price, but the government rebates the duty-equivalent costs to exporters using the intermediate input. In this case, total subsidies are given by

$$S = t p^* b_x Y_x \qquad (8.11)$$

It would be reasonable to suspect that some of the negative income effects of export incentives may not occur with this policy, as the wage rate is not affected by the level of the tariff, but this turns out not to be the case. The expression for equilibrium exports is *identical* to (8.9). We therefore draw the following conclusion:

Proposition 1:   The irrelevance of export subsidies
Export subsidies (either production-based or duty-drawback) have no effect on aggregate export volumes or on the allocation of resources in the presence of limit-pricing monopoly with market closure in the import-competing sector.

Increases in the level of protection from imports lead to increased exports, and the only mechanism for undoing this effect is to reduce protection. Tariffs do, however, affect income distribution, depending upon how they affect factor prices and monopoly profits.

The welfare implications of these results are fairly straightforward. Represent preferences by a linear homogeneous expenditure function $e(p,q)u$ where u is the aggregate level of utility. The labour-market clearing equation becomes:

$$L = a_m \frac{\partial e(p_m, q)}{\partial p_m} u + (a_m b_m + a_x) Y_x \qquad (8.12)$$

This is the relevant resource constraint on the welfare level u resulting from the market-closure effect. It is readily apparent from this equation that increases in p_m or Y_x reduce the welfare index, u. Thus changes in trade intervention which result in either increases in protection or increases in exports (or both) are necessarily welfare-reducing.

The very strong result that, under both general export subsidies and duty drawbacks, resource allocation is unaffected, for a given tariff rate, by the level of export subsidy leaves one wondering why this occurs and how general the result is. In this section an intuitive explanation is given that relies on a modified general equilibrium interpretation of the open-economy model. In this three-good model we can induce artificial preferences on the non-consumed export sector with Cobb–Douglas preferences for given prices (p_m, q) by the use of the trade-balance condition. This requires that spending on the third good equal export revenue, or $(1 - \beta)E = p_x Y_x$. We therefore induce Cobb–Douglas preferences over (m,x) space by using this identity. The aggregate representative consumer can be thought of as maximizing this utility function subject to the usual budget constraint. The economy's production possibility frontier (PPF) is given by AA' in Figure 8.2, with the slope determined by a_x/a_m. Given the monopoly distortion, the relative price line

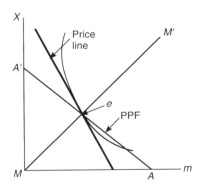

Figure 8.2   Equilibrium with market closure

facing the consumer is steeper than the slope of the PPF. Equilibrium is determined by the condition that the market in good m clears domestically. That is, income adjusts until the consumers' demand choices just lie on the *PPF* at point e.[13]

The effect of protection is to rotate clockwise the relative price-line facing the consumer (it is, in fact, trickier if true preferences are not Cobb–Douglas, since β also changes). This induces a shift of demand away from good m and toward good x. Equilibrium requires a reduction in the level of income for the market in good m to 'clear' domestically, and thus an expansion in the export sector. This is essentially why *import protection is export promotion*.[14]

Consider now export subsidies. Changes in export subsidies do not change internal relative prices p_m/p_x. Thus, the consumer's relative demands for the two goods do not change and therefore the market clearing condition is the same. Hence, export promotion has no effect in this economy. In the background, factor prices and government revenues are changing, but the level of aggregate consumer income, and thus demands in the economy, are invariant to these policy changes.[15]

3   DISCRETIONARY EXPORT INCENTIVE REGIMES

As noted in the introduction, many export incentives are set in an institutional and administrative framework with two characteristics. First, export incentives are determined via an administrative procedure, in which the *export authorities* have discretion as to the amount of the subsidy, but in which the information available to them is far from complete. Second, the level and instruments of protection are exogenous to, and outside the domain of the authority of the export programme administrators. This is implicitly an assumption about the institutional structure of trade policy, and it fits reasonably well with some accounts of trade policy formation in East Asia. In addition, it is assumed that the export authorities are motivated in their decisions by considerations of national welfare, albeit approximated by imperfect indicators, rather than by political objectives or more narrow self-interest objectives. For brevity, this type of trade policy regime will be referred to as an *administrative export regime*.

The Economy: Attracting Investment to the Export Sector

Consider a small open economy with two sectors of production: an exportable and an importable which is an intermediate input to the export sector. There is a single primary factor of production, labour, which can be employed in either sector. The export good is not consumed domestically and thus domestic welfare corresponds to domestic income evaluated at exogenous world prices. The importable sector is competitive and subject to tariff protection.

The export sector consists entirely of large-scale plants controlled by multi-national enterprises (MNEs). For simplicity, our unit of analysis is the 'representative' export plant. Countries compete for a share of global export capacity. Capacity once invested in a particular country results in proportional demands for labour and intermediate inputs. The international competition for export capacity is affected by international cost differences. Export incentives are set in light of the expected response of the allocation of capacity to changes in domestic costs, with export authorities focusing on a single investment decision at a time. The export authorities are motivated by trade-offs (made precise below) between national income objectives and the net revenue cost of any export programme. The country is not 'small' in the classic sense: the authorities know that changes in the cost structure of the export sector affect its share of global export capacity, and the factor incomes that capacity will generate. In this chapter we do not deal with the strategic aspects of interaction between countries competing for investment by a multinational enterprise.[16]

Let x denote the export capacity allocated to the country in question, and c the unit cost of export. A multinational makes its investment allocation decisions according to a profit-maximizing criterion which results in a capacity allocation rule denoted by:[17]

$$x = \phi(c)\phi'(c) < 0 \tag{8.13}$$

The importables sector, denoted with subscript a, produces with a diminishing-returns technology, $F(L_a)$. The product is sold in world markets at price p^* but imports are subject to a unit tariff, t; thus the domestic price is $p = p^* + t$. The demand for labour in this sector is determined by the condition 'wage equals value of marginal product', or $w = pMP(L_a)$, where MP is the marginal product of labour schedule in a. The economy has a fixed endowment of labour N, supplied inelastically. The export sector uses one unit of labour per unit of export capacity and b units of good a. The labour market is competitive with a market-clearing wage, w. Thus, unit cost in the export sector is $c = w + bp$ in the absence of export incentives. Export incentives are treated as a subsidy s per unit of intermediate input purchased. With subsidy, the unit cost in the export sector becomes $c = w + bp - bs = w + bp^* + bt - bs$.

Factor market-clearing requires that the wage adjusts such that $L_a + x = N$. General equilibrium can be defined for a given subsidy tariff pair (s, t) as a wage and capacity (w, x) such that:

$$
\begin{aligned}
w &= (p^* + t)MP(N - x) \\
x &= \phi(w + bp^* + bt - bs)
\end{aligned}
\tag{8.14}
$$

Objectives of the Export Authorities

Export authorities are presumed to understand the allocation rule (8.13) for capacity and that, to increase or decrease investment in export capacity, they must change the cost structure facing the MNE. At the same time they are assumed to evaluate the benefits from changes in export subsidies by using an *approximate* indicator of national welfare.

The true welfare function in this model is simply national income evaluated at some outside consumption price,

$$W^* = wx + p^*F(N - x) + (t - s)bx^{18} \qquad (8.15)$$

Differentiating W^*, treating p^* and t as constants, gives the expression:

$$dW^* = xdw + (w - w^*)dx + (tb - sb)dx - bxds \qquad (8.16)$$

This expression is the basis for justifying a particular objective function for the export authorities in an administrative export regime. In particular, assume that they know that the income generated in export plants is w per unit of employment and that the opportunity cost of a unit of labour is $w^* = p^*MP$. Given the presence of the tariff on the import-competing sector, they use the standard world price methodology in calculating shadow prices for inputs. The export authorities take w and w^* as being exogenous and constant at their observed values, thus ignoring the wage-change term (dw) in their approximation to (8.16). The objective function of the export authorities is thus assumed to be given by the following linear function of x, an approximate cost–benefit index,

$$W(x, s) = (w - w^*)x - sbx + tbx \qquad (8.17)$$

The export subsidy is determined by the authorities as a solution to the problem:

$$\max_s W(x, s) \quad \text{subject to} \quad x = \phi(c) \qquad (8.18)$$

Note that the authorities are assumed to calculate the non-linear response of changes in investment by the MNE to changes in domestic cost conditions. This assumption can be justified by assuming they have past experience of the export sector's response to cost changes. They are not, however, good general equilibrium theorists, or at least do not have that type of information; this implies that their (discretionary) export incentives change as new information comes in, as reflected in the linear coefficients in the 'approximated' net benefit function, W.

The objective function of the export authorities corresponds closely to that used in conventional cost–benefit analysis of export incentive programmes. Warr (1990) summarizes a number of studies on export incentive programmes for Indonesia, Korea, Malaysia and the Philippines, which provide estimates of the ratio of shadow prices to market prices. Warr describes a net benefit function[19] equivalent to (8.17). A major incentive that exists for subsidization is the difference between the market price and the shadow price of domestically-produced inputs. These differences are considerable, as he discusses. For example, in the case of labour, he reports a ratio of shadow price to market wage of 0.75 for Indonesia, 0.91 for Korea, 0.83 for Malaysia, and 0.64 for the Philippines.

Equilibrium with an Administered Export Regime

The first-order condition to the problem (8.18) is:

$$\{(w - w^*) - (s - t)b\}(-b\phi_c) - bx = 0 \qquad (8.19)$$

Evaluating the left-hand side of (8.19) at the *cost-neutralising* level of export incentives (that is, $s = t$), it is clear that its sign depends on the level of exports, x. Suppose that for $s = t$, costs are such that the economy is barely attracting any export capacity, or $x \approx 0$. In that case, the left-hand side of (8.19) is positive and the authorities will be inclined to subsidize beyond the cost-neutralizing level. To repeat, a key point in this process of the determination of the export subsidy is that it depends on the level of the incentives to the export authorities which are, in turn, positively related to the difference between the market wage and shadow wage, $w - w^*$.

The subsidy offered to the MNE by the export authorities is characterized as the solution to (8.18). This problem can be rewritten usefully in the following way, using the fact that $w - b(s - t) = c - bp^*$, and defining $c^* \equiv w^* + bp^*$, where c^* is the cost of inputs per unit of export output evaluated at the shadow prices of those inputs. The equivalent problem to (8.18) is to choose a cost level c such as to solve:

$$\max_{c} (c - c^*)\phi(c) \qquad (8.20)$$

The choice of export incentives in an administered export regime can be viewed as being equivalent to the problem of setting a *cost structure* in the export sector, such as to maximize the 'rents' accruing to domestic factors, taking the opportunity cost per unit of export capacity as constant and equal to c^*. Let $c_0 = w_0 + bp^*$ be the cost that would just occur were the cost raising effect of the tariff exactly offset at current market wages, or $s = t$. If $\phi(c_0) = 0$ then the desired cost level will be above c^* but below c_0. The choice of

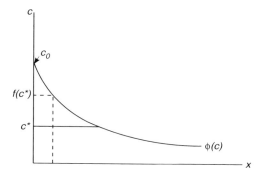

Figure 8.3   Export authorities' determination of the cost level in the export sector

subsidy, and hence cost, is depicted in Figure 8.3. It will necessarily imply a
positive export subsidy such that $s > t$. The desired cost level will satisfy a
conventional mark-up rule:

$$\frac{c - c^*}{c} = \frac{1}{\lambda}$$

(8.21)

where λ is the (absolute) elasticity of the capacity allocation rule with respect
to cost.[20] The higher this elasticity, the lower the mark-up. Denote the costs
level in the solution to (8.18) by the solution function $c = f(c^*)$. The decision
rule in $f(\cdot)$ depends *only* on the properties of the ϕ function and on the
shadow cost c^*. It is possible, depending upon the position of the ϕ curve,
that the export authorities levy export taxes on MNE investment. If the level
of investment in the export sector by foreign firms is sufficiently large at
$c = c_0(s = t)$, the solution to (8.18) could be an export tax with $c > c_0$. From
now on, we restrict our attention to the case in which s is greater than t, so that
a net export investment subsidy is offered in equilibrium.

Changes in protection have an impact on the economy via the conventional
channels, but in this model they also induce an endogenous (discretionary)
response by the export authorities. Hence, a higher tariff, at a given allocation, would lead, on impact, to increased subsidies to the export sector, since
this would leave c^* unchanged, and export subsidies should be raised to leave
c constant. However, the ultimate effect is not known, since wages must adjust
to clear factor markets. As wages adjust, the chosen subsidy will change. Note
that, as $w - w^* = tMP(N - x)$, the $w - w^*$ coefficient in W will increase as the
size of the a sector gets smaller for a given tariff. Thus, there is a natural
feedback mechanism as the incentives to subsidize exports increase as the
export sector gets larger. The full equilibrium of an administrated export
regime is described by equations:

$$w^* = p^*MP(N - x)$$
$$x = \phi[f(c^*)] \tag{8.22}$$
$$c^* = w^* + bp^*$$

Let (w_e, c_e, x_e) denote a solution to this system. By inspection of (8.22) this system gives an equilibrium which is *independent of the tariff rate*. The endogenous response of the export authorities is such as to eliminate the effect on the economy of changes in tariff protection. The major reason is that the shadow wage does not depend on the tariff rate even though the market wage does. Increasing the tariff raises the market wage and thus increases the required export subsidy, but the mark-up of c over c^* remains the same, and thus the original shadow wage effectively clears the labour market.

An Optimality Result

How does this equilibrium compare with one in which trade policy instruments are chosen optimally and with full information? Let $V(x) \equiv p^*F(N - x) - p^*bx$. It is useful to rewrite the true welfare function in the form:

$$W^* = cx + V(x) \tag{8.23}$$

With both tariffs and subsidies as instruments, for given x, any target cost level $\hat{c}$ can be realized by appropriately choosing tariffs and subsidies. An *optimal trade policy* is therefore equivalent to choosing a domestic cost level c such as to solve:

$$\max_c cx + V(x) \quad s.t. \quad x = \phi(c) \tag{8.24}$$

The first-order conditions for this problem are:

$$(c - c^*)\phi_c = -x$$
$$c^* \equiv -V'(x) \tag{8.25}$$

As $-V'(x) = p^*MP(N - x) + p^*b$, the solution to (8.24) is equivalent to the equilibrium of the system in (8.22). Hence, the outcome of the administrative trade regime is *equivalent* to an optimal trade policy and, furthermore, it is independent of the level of the tariff. Any change in tariffs is offset appropriately by a change in the export subsidy.

A social planner does not take c^* as given, as do the export authorities. But the actions of the export authorities, together with market-equilibrium conditions, produce an outcome that is equivalent to a trade policy optimum.

One can think of this result as rationalizing the decentralization of policy decisions. The general equilibrium aspects of the domestic economy are summarized in the cost signal c^*. The export authorities take c^* as given, and are given the task of exploiting the external monopoly power in the export capacity market by setting a mark-up of domestic costs in the export sector over c^*. It is straightforward to generalize this model to one with many export sectors, each sector with an independent export authority. If all sectors draw their labour from the same economy-wide pool, all relevant general equilibrium information is summarized in the cost statistic c^*, and each export authority sets its own mark-up. What is noteworthy is that the conventional *small project* type of cost–benefit objective as embodied in (8.17) provides the correct set of incentives for the export authorities even though they have market power in the external market for foreign direct investment.

Estimating Wage Effects: Sophisticated Export Authorities

That outcomes under an administered export regime are independent of the level of the tariff could be viewed as a possible rationalization for the use of export subsidies in 'small open economies' that compete for investment by multinationals. We now demonstrate, however, that this result is sensitive to the manner in which the export authorities estimate the net benefits of the subsidy. An example is given of a procedure by which the export authorities estimate the response of the economy to their actions, which results in a discrepancy between the optimal trade policy and the equilibrium of an administered export-incentive regime. Furthermore, the magnitude of the discrepancy is sensitive to the level of protection.

It has been assumed that the authorities maximize the cost–benefit criterion (8.17), treating wages, both market and shadow, as being exogenous to their actions. But increased subsidies to export industries drive up the demand for labour in those industries, raising the market wage, and hence labour income. For this reason, in the evaluation of export subsidies, the authorities, in an attempt to be sophisticated in their analysis, may choose to estimate the response of market and shadow wage rates to changes in the level of the subsidy, and to incorporate this effect in their evaluation of net benefits. The authorities may have reasons of self-interest for doing so; either their compensation or bureaucratic budgets may depend on the outcome of export projects evaluated. If (8.17) is the stated objective the authorities are instructed to target by their superiors, they may be rewarded in the light of outcomes as measured by this numerical indicator.

Suppose, therefore that the authorities treat both w and w^* as functions of x because of the labour market effect of export expansion. The decision rule of an administered trade regime on the level of subsidy is then derived from the first-order condition:

$$\{(w - w^*) - (s - t)b\}(-b\phi_c) - bx + \frac{\partial(w - w^*)}{\partial s}x = 0 \qquad (8.26)$$

Since $w - w^* = tMP(N - x)$ is now treated as a function of x in the setting of s, the existence of the tariff provides an additional reason to subsidize exports at the margin, which is not present in (8.19). If (8.26) is evaluated as a trade policy optimum, it is clear that the last term is positive – by increasing export capacity, the gap between the market wage and the shadow wage increases, giving rise to an additional perceived benefit at the margin from subsidy. The first-order condition (8.26) can be rewritten as:

$$\frac{c - c^*}{c} + \frac{\theta}{\delta}\frac{tMP(N - x)}{c} = \frac{1}{\lambda} \qquad (8.27)$$

where δ is the absolute value of the elasticity of demand for labour in the importables sector, and θ is the ratio of labour in the export sector to labour in the a sector; $\theta = L_x/L_a$. It is clear from this rule that it tends to lead to larger export subsidies and a domestic cost level closer to c^* than would be the case under an optimal trade policy. What is also important is that the subsidy rule (8.27) is now a function of the tariff rate. An increase in the tariff, raising for any given x the term $tMP(N - x)$, increases the perceived marginal return to the authorities of an additional dollar of subsidy. The export authorities are now attempting to manipulate the market and shadow prices of labour. In the presence of a tariff on intermediate inputs to the export sector, raising wages also implies increasing the gap between the market and the shadow wage.

There is now a clear general equilibrium link between changes in tariff protection, export subsidies and an additional feedback effect not present in (8.22). The effect of changes in the tariff rate on costs in the export sector net of subsidy is dependent upon how the elasticities of labour demand and capacity allocation change with changes in x. However, assuming these to be constant, one can get some additional comparative static results. The complete system can be written as a two-equation system in c and x. The first equation is the capacity allocation function $x = \phi(c)$, and the second the subsidy rule (8.27) with $c^* = p^*MP(N - x) + p^*b$. These become, after substitution.

$$x = \phi(c)$$
$$c\left(1 - \frac{1}{\lambda}\right) = p^*b + \left(p^* - \frac{t\theta}{\delta}\right)MP(N - x) \qquad (8.28)$$

If the elasticities δ and λ are treated as constants, sufficient conditions for the export sector to expand in response to a tariff *increase* is that the elasticity λ be greater than one, and that tariff rates not be too large. Inspection of the subsidy–cost mark-up rule reveals that an increase in t for any given x will lead to a *decrease* in the tariff-net-of-subsidy cost level c. In this case, changes in tariffs cause changes in the export subsidy which more than compensate for the input-cost-raising effect of the tariff. Since ϕ is downward-sloping, this gives rise to an *increase* in the size of the export sector.[21] This example illustrates how the level of import protection can structure incentives for export authorities which are not cost neutral. High tariffs create large gaps between shadow and market wages, which influence the magnitude of the bureaucratic incentive to subsidize. From a welfare perspective, this structure of objectives and actions on the part of the export authorities leads to sub-optimal welfare results. The export sector is over-subsidized relative to a trade policy optimum and this effect is exacerbated the higher the tariff rate.

The reason for the divergence between the trade policy outcome and the welfare optimum is the inappropriate nature of the objective function (8.17) if the export authorities attempt to introduce general equilibrium wage effects into their analysis. The correct or true objective function W^* is not (8.17), when the latter is viewed as a non-linear function of x, correcting for the dependence of the wage rate on the allocation of resources between the export and non-export sectors. If the true objective function were used and full global general equilibrium information were available to the authorities, this would simply be equivalent to doing a full-information welfare-optimal calculation. While logically correct, most programme evaluation by trade policy bureaucrats ultimately boils down to the exercise of fairly simple rules on shadow prices under less than full information on the underlying preferences and technology. The use of an approximate cost–benefit criterion such as (8.17) may lead to abuse of the intended procedure. Export authorities are led to subsidize in an attempt to boost the gap between market and shadow wages. This gap, in turn, is one reason for the existence of the subsidy programme, and thus the existence of the export authorities. Protection leads to a set of *administrative incentives* in the conduct of trade policy, which may bias the policy outcome towards excessive exports. Moreover, this incentive is stronger the higher the level of protection in the economy.

4   CONCLUSION

An implication of the small open economy competitive production model is that it is possible to achieve a free-trade equivalent outcome by offsetting the distortions induced by import substitution with the correct set of export incentives. This is one of those relatively rare examples in economics where 'two wrongs make a right'. These policies, while individually sub-optimal, are jointly optimal. In this chapter two important exceptions to the spirit of this argument are provided, by departing in each case from the classical assumptions of the small open economy model. This analysis may be particularly relevant for East Asian and other small open economies in which both export promotion and import substitution are prominent features of the trade policy regimes.

The first exception is based on the observation that protection in small open economies produces increased concentration, including possible monopolization of, the domestic market. The general equilibrium impact of a monopoly market structure under tariff protection is shown, in quite general circumstances, to result in market closure. The domestic producer chooses to supply all of the domestic market. There are two important general equilibrium implications of this. First, import substitution produces export promotion. The demand side of the market dominates, and increased rates of tariff protection can result in a reduction of resources allocated to the protected sector. In a model with a two-sector supply side this results in an increase in the size of the export sector. Second, export incentives will not succeed in reversing the effects of this policy. The basic reason is that relative producer costs do not determine resource allocation in this type of model. Export incentives change factor prices and monopoly sector profitability, but do not affect relative demand prices; it is the latter which determine the allocation of resources in the economy with market closure. In general, ignoring the demand side when domestic markets become closed because of protectionist policies can lead to erroneous assessments of the net impact of export incentives.

The second qualification stems from the discretionary and contingent nature of the administration of many export incentive schemes. Export 'policy' is modelled as a regime in which incentives provided for investment in export capacity by foreign multinationals are set endogenously by export authorities with less than full general equilibrium knowledge. They are, however, motivated by domestic welfare considerations, and provide export incentives according to an approximate cost–benefit test. The net outcome of this type of administered export incentive regime is quite interesting. In one particular case it results in a strong optimality result – a national trade policy optimum is achieved. However, in other plausible scenarios, the use of inappropriate cost–benefit indicators, with weights which depend on the degree of protection in the economy, produces export incentive policies which tend to over-compensate for tariff protection and to induce an excessive allocation of resources to exports.

Both sets of results suggest caution in assessing the bias of trade regimes, in which both protection and export promotion are quantitatively important. One implication is that the use of traditional policy evaluation indicators, such as effective rates of protection, when the instruments being evaluated are in fact endogenously determined, may be misleading. Another implication is that trade reform needs to be done carefully, taking into proper account all general equilibrium effects, including changes in the way in which policy is administered.

Notes

1. The authors are grateful for the helpful comments of conference participants Rod Falvey, Don White and an anonymous referee. Remaining errors are the responsibility of the authors.
2. Falvey and Gemmell (1990a, 1990b) both survey and provide an excellent evaluation of the traditional normative literature on compensating export incentives.
3. See Flatters and Harris (1995) for a review of the evidence.
4. Wade (1990) reviews and discusses East Asian trade policy which is suggestive of this interpretation of interventionist export incentive schemes in these economies.
5. See Diewert, Turunen-Red and Woodland (1991), and Turunen-Red and Woodland (1991) for derivation of rules on Pareto improving local trade policy reform based on full information general equilibrium comparative statics.
6. An alternative positive theory of export promotion is found in the political economy literature on trade policy – see Hillman (1989) for a survey. It is possible that one could construct a model in which both protection and export incentives are determined endogenously in response to interest-group pressures.
7. Eastman and Stykolt (1960) were the first to develop this model of oligopolistic behaviour by import-competing producers in small, open economies.
8. With sufficiently elastic demand, the monopolist will price below the limit price. It is possible in this case that as the tariff increases it will eventually cease to bind, and thereafter have no effect. We shall not consider this case here. A similar situation occurs as competition increases in the industry; for example, with domestic Cournot oligopoly competition subject to a limit price. These issues are taken up further in Harris and Schmitt (1996a).
9. The popular alternative model of imperfect competition in import competing sectors assumes that foreign and domestic goods are imperfect substitutes. In these models an increase in tariffs leads to a *shift* in the demand curve for the import competing good, due to the substitution effect between foreign and domestic varieties. Home suppliers of the domestic good respond by increasing output. In the model considered here, the two goods are *perfect* substitutes and the solution reached is a corner solution – no consumption of the foreign good. Increases in the tariff result in matching foreign and domestic price increases, inducing movement along the demand curve, requiring a reduction in domestic output.
10. Solving equation (8.4) for wages, it can be seen that positive wages restricts σ to less than unity.
11. Note that it is necessary that $\sigma\beta < 1$ for profits to be positive in equilibrium. As we assume $\sigma < 1$ this is satisfied.
12. In a model with no spending on the domestic good by labour, it can be shown that a rise in p_m in fact raises spending on the domestic good and thus exports contract because of the induced effect of higher profits on spending on the domestic good. Results are thus sensitive to strong asymmetries in income elasticities of demand between labour and profit-income recipients.

13. The similarity between this model and the familiar Salter model of non-traded goods should be apparent to the reader.

14. This model also illustrates the difference between trade reform versus a move to complete free trade. Under free trade, specialization in the export good would occur. The market closure effect results in a discrete change in the equilibrium. The welfare losses relative to free trade are larger in this model than in the conventional small open economy model.

15. This argument does not hinge on the Ricardian production structure of this model. A multi-factor Heckscher–Ohlin model will give essentially the same irrelevance result on export incentives and the conclusion that protection is export-promoting. Conclusions as to the distributive effects are more complicated in a Heckscher–Ohlin version of the model, since they involve a mixture of Stolper–Samuelson effects and real profit creation effects. See Harris and Schmitt (1996a).

16. Strategic interaction among countries with these types of trade regime is taken up in Harris and Schmitt (1996b).

17. Markusen (1984) and Horstmann and Markusen (1987) provide detailed models of MNE plant location which are consistent with a rule such as (8.13).

18. Alternatively, $W^* = wx + G + pF(L_a) - wL_a$; that is, the wage bill, plus net government revenue, plus specific factor rents in sector a. Government revenue depends on tariffs, imports, exports and export subsidies. Let M denote imports of a. Then, $G = tM - sbx$ and $M = bx - F(L_a)$. Substituting yields an expression equivalent to (8.15).

19. See Warr (1990), p. 151, equ. 8.4.

20. This system has a reasonable economic solution if the capacity elasticity has an absolute value greater than one in equilibrium for obvious reasons analogous to the monopoly problem. From now on, we assume λ is greater than one.

21. The result hinges on the fact that the capacity allocation function ϕ is decreasing in c. In (c, x) space, the subsidy rule schedule can be upward- or downward-sloping, but a tariff increase shifts the chosen c down for any given x.

References

Bliss, C. (1987) 'Taxation, Cost Benefit Analysis and Effective Protection', in D. Newberry and N. Stern (eds), *The Theory of Taxation for Developing Countries* (Oxford: Oxford University Press / World Bank), pp. 141–62.

Corden, M. (1971) *The Theory of Protection* (Oxford: Oxford University Press).

Diewert, W. E., A. H. Turunen-Red and A. D. Woodland (1991) 'Tariff Reform in a Small Open, Multi-Household Economy with Domestic Distortions and Nontraded Goods', *International Economic Review*, vol. 32, no. 4, pp. 937–58.

Eastman, H. and S. Stykolt (1960) 'A Model for the Study of Protected Oligopolies', *Economic Journal*, vol. 70, pp. 336–47.

Falvey, R. E. and N. Gemmell (1990a) 'Compensatory Financial and Fiscal Incentives to Export', in C. R. Milner (ed.), *Export Promotion Strategies: Theory and Evidence* (Brighton: Harvester Wheatsheaf), pp. 109–29.

Falvey, R. E. and N. Gemmell (1990b) 'Trade Taxes and Welfare: The Case of Export Incentives in South-East Asian Countries', *Australian Economic Review*, 4th quarter, pp. 61–73.

Flatters, F. and R. G. Harris (1995) 'Trade and Investment: Patterns and Policy Issues in the Asia-Pacific Rim', in W. Dobson and F. Flatters (eds), *Pacific Trade and Investment: Options for the 90's* (Kingston: John Deutsch Institute for the Study of Economic Policy).

Harris, R. and N. Schmitt (1996a) 'Protection and Market Closure', mimeo, Department of Economics, Simon Fraser University, Canada.

Harris, R. and N. Schmitt (1996b) 'Export–Investment Subsidies in the Presence of Import Protection', mimeo, Department of Economics, Simon Fraser University, Canada.

Hillman, A. (1989) *The Political Economy of Protection* (Chur: Harwood).

Horstmann, I. and J. Markusen (1987) 'Strategic Investment and the Development of Multinationals', *International Economic Review*, vol. 16, pp. 205–26.

Markusen, J. (1984) 'Multinationals, Multiplant Economies and the Gains from Trade', *Journal of International Economics*, vol. 32, pp. 103–29.

Melvin, J. M. and J. D. Warne (1973) 'Monopoly and the Theory of International Trade', *Journal of International Economics*, vol. 3, pp. 117–34.

Nam, C. H. (1990) 'Export Promotion Strategy and Economic Development in Korea', in Milner (ed.), *Export Promotion Strategies: Theory and Evidence* (Brighton: Harvester Wheatsheaf), pp. 165–83.

Turunen-Red, A. and A. D. Woodland (1991) 'Strict Pareto-Improving Multilateral Reforms of Tariffs', *Econometrica*, vol. 59, no. 4, pp. 1127–52.

Wade, R. (1990) *Governing the Market* (Princeton, NJ: Princeton University Press).

Warr, P. (1990) 'Export Processing Zones', in C. R. Milner (ed.), *Export Promotion Strategies: Theory and Evidence* (Brighton: Harvester Wheatsheaf), pp. 130–62.

Comment

Rod Falvey

UNIVERSITY OF NOTTINGHAM

In this chapter the authors take issue with the proposition that export-promotion policies can always be used to neutralize the negative impacts of protection on export industries. They suggest that there may be many circumstances under which an allocation of resources similar to that under free trade will not be attainable in this way. The two aspects they focus on in particular are imperfect competition in the import-competing sector, and the inevitable 'rules of thumb' used by export authorities in setting the levels of export incentives. The authors' approach is to develop stylized models that illustrate as starkly as possible the points they wish to make, while being careful 'to make no claim for the generality of the results'. But inevitably the generality of the results is an issue. While both parts of the chapter examine the links between protection and export promotion, the two models developed and the issues addressed are sufficiently different that it is useful to consider them separately.

Section 2 examines a small economy consuming two goods (a final import and an importable that is both an intermediate and a final good) and (potentially) producing two goods – the importable and an exportable whose production requires the importable as an intermediate. Production takes place under Ricardian assumptions. In free trade only the exportable is produced domestically. Importable production is then induced by a tariff. By virtue of the Ricardian assumption, once the tariff is high enough that importable production becomes profitable, imports of that good are eliminated, an outcome the authors refer to as 'market closure'. A key assumption of the model is that domestic production of the importable is then monopolized.

The authors use this structure to derive three main results: (i) that protection is export-promoting – that is, that increases in the tariff lead to increases in exports; (ii) that export subsidies have no effect on export volumes or the allocation of resources; and (iii) as a consequence, given the existence of protection, a neutral trade regime cannot exist in this model. These interesting and strong results are obtained using quite restrictive assumptions, making it important to identify which assumptions are driving the results and which can be generalized. From this perspective several comments are in order with respect to (i) above, in addition to those provided in the chapter. First, it is a 'local' rather than a 'global' result. Once the tariff is high enough to establish the domestic industry, then it is true that further tariff increases lead to increases in exports. But exports always remain below their free trade levels. Second, it depends on an imperfectly competitive import-competing sector. In a competitive sector, increases in the tariff above that necessary to establish the domestic industry would be redundant, and have no effects. Finally, for protection to raise exports requires that domestic demand for the importable falls as its price rises, thereby releasing resources for exportable production. However, expanding exports demand more importables as intermediates. What is required then is a more than offsetting fall in final demand for the importable. The assumptions of Section 2 guarantee this, but note that we would not get this outcome under the assumptions of the third section. Similarly, result (ii) above, on the irrelevance of export incentives, would disappear if exportables happened to be consumed domestically.

Section 3 employs a similar model, except that domestic production of the importable is now competitive, and occurs under diminishing returns (so that there is domestic production under free trade). Most significantly, the home country is now 'large' in the exportable market. The major objective in this part seems to be to examine different 'rules of thumb' for determining the optimal export subsidy.

My first comment is that the focus on export *subsidies* in this part seems to be somewhat misplaced. While it is not motivated this way in the chapter, one can interpret $\phi(c)$ as foreign demand for home exports (x) expressed as a function of their price (c). In the free-trade equilibrium, the competitive export producers equate the marginal cost of exportables with their price. However, this is not the outcome that maximizes home welfare. Under the assumptions of the model, home welfare is highest when the value of home output at world prices is maximized; and this requires that the marginal revenue from exports be equated to their marginal cost. In order to exercise its monopoly power in the exportable market, the home country must *reduce* its exports below their free-trade level. A tariff on imports of the intermediate good will raise the cost of exportable production, and if set appropriately can move the competitive equilibrium to where the optimal outputs are produced. Were the tariff set above (below) this level, the optimum could be achieved through an export subsidy (tax), which moves the average revenue curve in the appropriate direction, as discussed in this chapter. Only if the tariff is set too high will an export subsidy be called for, and then only if the tariff itself cannot be adjusted.

Indeed, despite the rather innovative interpretation here, this is really a fairly standard two-sector general equilibrium production structure. Setting a subsidy on the intermediate use of importables equal to the tariff will neutralize the tariff's direct effect on exportable costs, but will still leave its indirect protective effect via the labour market. When interpreting the discussion in the sub-section of section 3, 'Equilibrium with an Administered Export Regime', one should recall that this is the only exportable produced in this economy *and* that this exportable is not consumed domestically. If the importable is only used as an intermediate in exportable production, then a prohibitive tariff will be reached long before exports are eliminated, given that net exports from the production sector are required to finance imported consumer goods. In fact, this prohibitive tariff may be reached while exports are still above the optimum. Any further expansion of 'importable' production would then need to be sold on the world market, requiring an export subsidy – but on *this good* not the 'traditional' export. If the importable is consumed domestically, then the case where $x \approx 0$ involves a tariff that has driven this economy almost to autarky and is therefore far greater than the optimal tariff.

Viewing the model in this way also assists in interpreting the issue of formulating rules for export incentives. There would be no need for intervention if, under free trade, exports were monopolised *and* the profits were retained in the home country. But, as modelled, the exporting decision is made by foreigners (MNEs), which makes the home retention of the profits problematic. Hence the indirect monopolization through an export authority which sets the relevant export tax/subsidy. If this authority knows the marginal revenue function (as is assumed in the chapter), then it is a matter of determining the output at which marginal revenue is equated with marginal cost at world prices (MC^*), and setting an appropriate export tax to achieve this output. Perhaps the simplest approach requires the export authority to adjust the export tax (t) according to: $dt = k \cdot [MC^* - MR]$, where k is a (small) positive scalar. This approach will eventually achieve the optimum, although perhaps after some small oscillations. Attempts to move more rapidly to the optimum will involve estimation of the MC^* function, requiring more detailed and complex calculations involving estimated shadow prices of inputs. As the chapter notes in the sub-section of section 3 headed 'Estimating Wage Effects: Sophisticated Export Authorities', mis-estimation of this relationship and the application of inappropriate adjustment rules can lead to an outcome that is sub-optimal. This is clearly an important topic and one worthy of research beyond the stylized model of this chapter.

Finally, two general comments. First, the chapter assumes that duty drawbacks are paid as a subsidy on exports equal to the notional duty on their intermediate input even when the intermediate used is produced domestically. In practice, governments are often reluctant to go beyond reimbursement of duty actually paid. If the drawback scheme is restricted to intermediates actually imported, its introduction will have an impact on domestic output. Indeed, where importables are not consumed domestically, the tariff in Section 3 will be completely ineffective. Finally, one limitation of working with full employment models involving only two production sectors is that trade policy can either promote 'all' importables, 'all' exportables, or be neutral. In reality, explicit protection will be limited to some importables, and export incentives will be limited to some exportables (typically new or 'non-traditional' exports), implying that 'neutrality' may have more limited objectives than returning us to something approximating free trade.

9 Trade Reform with a Government Budget Constraint

James E. Anderson
BOSTON COLLEGE AND NATIONAL BUREAU OF ECONOMIC RESEARCH

1   INTRODUCTION

Practical trade policy advice must usually recognize that trade taxes help to raise government revenue required for other fiscal purposes. In contrast, the theory of trade policy analysis typically uses the simplifying assumption that tariff revenue is 'passively' redistributed, so that a fall in revenue is offset by a fall in the lump sum transfer from the government to the private sector. The passive transfer assumption was perhaps an appropriate simplification in the economies of the Organisation for Economic Cooperation and Development (OECD) in the era of rapid growth, but it is clearly inappropriate to the present concern over public debt along with resistance to tax increases or cuts in the provision of public-sector goods.[1] The passive transfer assumption was never appropriate for the governments of developing nations, which are typically dependent on tariff revenue.

The standard case against taxing trade assumes a passive budget constraint. This chapter shows that cuts in trade taxes may often be inefficient in the standard convex competitive model with an active government budget constraint, along which changes in distortionary fiscal instruments must be made. Thus the case for trade reform is probably better argued from the benefits of the international division of labour, the stimulation of competition, and the reduction of rent-seeking behaviour.

The analysis in this chapter offers simple and useful sufficient conditions under which trade reform matched by revenue-neutral spending cuts or tax increases will raise welfare. The elements of the analysis differ fundamentally from those assuming a passive budget constraint, in ways not previously appreciated in the trade literature or in the related public finance literature. The key concept is the (compensated) marginal cost of funds (MCF) of a given class of taxes. The MCF is compared to the marginal benefit of the funds in terms of goods and services so financed, or in terms of the marginal benefit of reductions in other taxes, equal to *their* MCFs.

The analysis also points to operationality, as the MCF is a very useful summary index number of the properties of tariff and tax systems. As a demonstration, the chapter concludes with calculations of the MCF for tariffs and for consumption taxes from a computable general equilibrium (CGE) model of Korea in 1963. With more experience on reasonable values of MCF for tariffs and for domestic taxation from simulations of other CGE models, it may be possible to make trade reform recommendations with confidence, and perhaps even to extrapolate to countries where no CGE model is available.

The theoretical analysis and its application in this chapter both cast doubt on the general desirability of tariff cuts matched by consumption-tax rises within the class of convex competitive models. The theoretical conditions that guarantee welfare improvement are implausibly stringent, and the simulation results show that, even with higher initial tariffs than indirect taxes, welfare falls with a cut in tariffs combined with a revenue-neutral rise in consumption taxes.

The analysis ties the theory of protection together with the theory of public finance. The two literatures have developed somewhat separate terminologies, and integration based on a dual approach proves useful. The standard theory of protection assumes that a benevolent, welfare-maximizing government seeks a welfare-improving tariff reform, subject to unspecified constraints which make impossible the move all the way to free trade (Bertrand and Vanek, 1971; Bruno, 1972; Lloyd, 1974; Hatta, 1977). The government budget constraint is passive, as the fall in distortionary tax revenue is offset in the budget by a fall in the lump sum transfer from the government to the private sector. The theory of public finance, in contrast, uses the active budget constraint, in which the provision of goods and services by the government sector (hereafter termed 'public goods', for convenience)[2] is paid for by distortionary taxation. In the marginal analysis of this problem, the MCF plays a key role. The MCF is usually developed in an uncompensated (real income variable) form, often in the context of a rather opaque primal analysis. In contrast, the compensated version developed here with dual methods is necessary for a clean analysis of the MCF of trade taxes versus the MCF of consumption or other taxes.[3]

Previous treatment of the gradual reform of tariffs in the presence of an active government budget constraint includes two papers by Abe (1992 and 1995).[4] This chapter generalizes and simplifies Abe's results, considers some additional structures and cleans up his (1992) treatment of marginal changes in public-goods supply. Related work by Diewert, Turunen-Red and Woodland (1989 and 1991) analyzes sufficient conditions for tariff reform to improve productivity and Pareto efficiency when commodity tax changes replace transfers as a means of compensating households. In their papers, as well as in Abe (1995), the set of commodity tax instruments is complete. In contrast, here there is a limited set of commodity tax changes, in the second-best tradition of the gradual reform and public finance literatures. Significantly, the two most famous results in second-best public finance literature are extended here to the gradual reform context. The Ramsey (1927) inverse elasticity optimal tax principle is to tax every taxable good in inverse proportion to its elasticity of demand. This suggests that trade should be taxed. The Diamond and Mirrlees (1971) optimal commodity tax principle is to preserve productive efficiency. This implies that a small (price-taking) country should not discriminate between foreign and domestic supply of identical products.[5] The gradual reform extension of the Ramsey principle is the 'wider base' intuition that it is efficient at least to begin taxing differentiated trade a bit. The gradual reform extension of the Diamond and Mirrlees principle (that it pays to cut trade taxes and raise consumption taxes) applies only under quite stringent conditions which restrict substitution.

The political reasons for gradualism, as opposed to a move all the way to constrained optimal taxes, are left outside the analysis, in common with all the gradual reform literature. Endogenous choice of gradualism is easy to derive by embedding the present analysis in a *political support function* analysis (Hillman, 1989). In planning its trade reform and fiscal policy, the government trades off general welfare (representing the interests of informed but unorganized interests) against the interests of informed and organized factions (the source of funds usable for winning the support of uninformed and unorganized interests which lose from increases in taxes or cuts in government spending). Whether the welfare increase from a reform package analyzed in this paper is large enough to offset the loss of the special interests depends on the weights of the political support function. A more complete analysis requires a development along the lines of Grossman and Helpman (1994), which endogenizes that portion of the political support function that relates policies offered to contributions given.

This chapter focuses on efficiency while ignoring distributive issues by using the representative agent model. (Grossman and Helpman submerge distributive issues by using the special case in which utilities are directly transferable.) For analysis of trade reform in a model where the benevolent government engages in redistribution, including redistribution via the provision of public goods, see Diewert, Turunen-Red and Woodland (1989 and 1991).

Section 2 develops the intuition of the analysis. The third section sets out the basic structure of the model and relates it to the classic analysis of trade reform with redistribution. Section 4 considers tariff reform matched by cuts in supply of public goods. Trade reform is welfare-improving if public goods are over-supplied in an intuitive and useful sense. The fifth section shows that with substitutability, marginal replacement of trade taxes by consumption taxes on traded goods is welfare-improving – the marginal reform version of the Diamond and Mirrlees theorem. Section 6 considers the relative efficiency of the taxation of non-traded goods, showing that some taxation of both traded and non-traded goods is efficient. From given interior positions of taxes and tariffs, it is not generally possible to rank the MCFs. The seventh section illustrates the estimation of the MCF for trade taxes and for consumption taxes on non-traded goods.

2   INTUITIVE SKETCH OF THE ANALYSIS

The general method of analysis of trade or tax reform is founded on the concept of the marginal cost of funds. The MCF of a tax (say, tariffs) is compared to the marginal benefit of the funds raised by the tax. The marginal benefit is equal either to the marginal value of the goods and services financed by the tax (tariff) or to the MCF of the taxes that are reduced as a response to the rise in tariff revenue. MCF is often not cleanly developed and may be unfamiliar to trade theorists, so this section discusses its intuition in detail.

In contrast, all readers will be familiar with the concept of marginal dead-weight loss and may have the impression that this is the key concept for understanding the desirability of trade reform. This indeed is the focus of all textbook analysis of trade reform and all the classic papers on gradual reform are based on it. If trade reform takes place along an active government budget constraint, however, the concept of marginal dead-weight loss is generally irrelevant. It characterizes only the special case, in which the only role of government is to levy trade taxes and redistribute them in a lump sum. The graphical analysis here will drive this point home.

MCF for any tax is defined here as the ratio of the marginal compensation required to maintain real income as the tax rises to the compensated marginal tax revenue raised by the tax increase. In other words, it gives, at the margin, the compensation required per dollar of revenue raised. The public finance literature also (more often) presents an uncompensated, or money metric utility version of MCF, and this version is the usual one reported in computations. See Anderson and Martin (1995) for an argument as to why this is not an appropriate definition.

The general method of this chapter is to compare the MCF for a given tax with the marginal benefit of the revenue raised – either of the government spending or of the reduction in other taxes (valued at their MCF) that it permits. If the marginal benefit exceeds the MCF of the tax that must be raised, the prospective change is welfare-improving. The marginal benefit is also defined at constant real income. The MCF has a clear and intuitive structure and readily extends to aggregation in the many-tax case and to incorporate other fixed distortions.

MCF Illustrated

To illustrate the concepts in the scalar case, consider an imported good with quantity denoted m selling at price p, wedged above its international price p^* by a tariff. A small change in the tariff results in the following key elements:

$$mdp, \text{ the external compensating transfer at the margin,}$$

and

$$[m + (p - p^*)m_p]dp, \text{ the revenue change at the margin}$$

The ratio of these defines the MCF:

$$MCF^p = \frac{mdp}{[m + (p - p^*)m_p]dp} = \frac{m}{MR'}$$

the compensation cost per dollar of revenue raised at the margin via dp.

The earlier tradition of trade reform analysis (and public finance tax incidence analysis) relied on the concept of marginal dead-weight loss, equal to $(p - p^*)m_p dp$. Marginal dead-weight loss applies only in the case of a lump sum redistribution of the revenue (in which case, the MCF of the lump sum tax is equal to one and the marginal gain of a switch from distortionary tax to lump sum tax is equal to the marginal dead-weight loss). The analysis below shows that the marginal dead-weight loss and the MCF have no tight relationship to each other. An example is provided in which the marginal dead-weight loss and the MCF are negatively correlated, both as the tax rises and as the strength of the substitution effect (the responsiveness of demand to price) increases.

Figure 9.1 illustrates the concepts of MCF and dead weight loss. MR is the marginal revenue schedule based on the import demand schedule. The tax is set at level t. The areas of rectangles a and b, and of triangle d are the basic building blocks for the standard welfare analysis. $a + b$ is the revenue raised, while $a + b + d$ is the consumer surplus lost. The net welfare effect of a tariff t with revenue redistributed in a lump sum is the dead-weight loss of triangle d. The 'average' version of the MCF idea, the compensation cost per dollar raised, is equal to $(a + b + d)/(a + b)$. In this form, dead-weight loss d appears to be the central concept. In contrast,

$$MCF = tB/tA = (a + b)/a$$
$$\neq (a + b + d)/(a + b)$$

The marginal version of MCF is the central concept of tax analysis, as the formal analysis below shows. Only in the special case of a lump sum

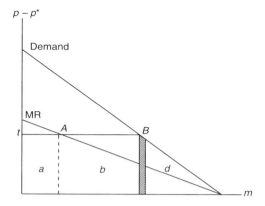

Figure 9.1   The marginal cost of funds and dead-weight loss

redistribution does a further cancellation of terms permit reducing the problem so that marginal dead weight loss, $(p - p^*)m_p dp$ (the area of the narrow, shaded trapezoidal section of the triangle d) is relevant.

MCF versus Marginal Dead-weight Loss

It is clear both from the diagram and the algebra that, while MCF has some relationship to marginal dead-weight loss, the relationship is highly non-linear and the two concepts are fundamentally different. They share a property in that MCF differs from 1 and marginal dead-weight loss differs from zero because of the existence of the substitution effect.[6] However, varying the strength of the substitution effect or the size of the tax can affect the two concepts in opposite directions. To see this, note that MCF in the scalar case can be reduced to:

$$MCF = \frac{1}{1 + (p - p^*)m_p/m} = \frac{1}{1 - \frac{\tau}{1+\tau}\varepsilon}$$

where ε is the elasticity of demand and τ is the *ad valorem* tax rate. In contrast, the negative of the marginal dead weight loss formula is:

$$-MDWL = -(p - p^*)m_p = \frac{\tau}{1 + \tau}\varepsilon m$$

For the constant elasticity case, $m = \mu(1 + \tau)^{-\varepsilon}$, MCF is everywhere increasing in τ, while the negative of MDWL is first increasing and then decreasing in τ. Moreover, MCF is everywhere increasing in ε, while the negative of MDWL is first increasing and then decreasing in ε.

The difference in the two concepts means that the general analysis of distortionary tax trade-offs based on MCF is *fundamentally* different from the classic special-case analysis of distortionary versus non-distortionary trade-offs based on the marginal dead-weight loss concept. MCF is the basic concept, while the marginal dead-weight loss only applies to a special case.

3 FORMAL ELEMENTS OF THE ANALYSIS

The key relationships of the model are the private-sector and public-sector budget constraints. For any exogenous fiscal policy change there must be an endogenous fiscal policy change to balance the government budget. The two fiscal changes then imply a change in welfare along the private-sector budget constraint. To demonstrate the method of this chapter and its relationship to the earlier literature, this section reviews the standard analysis of a tariff cut offset by a rise in lump sum taxes.

The model throughout is of a competitive economy with no distortions other than fiscal distortions. All tradable goods face fixed international prices. Non-tradable goods play an important role. Where necessary for clarity and sharp results, further restrictions on tastes and technology will be employed, especially with regard to non-traded goods. Substitutability assumptions will be introduced as needed. Finally, for simplicity, the model is static. This assumption is appropriate for a credit-constrained government and economy, and is also rationalized by political agreements which constrain the government budget deficit. For a treatment of the complexities of intertemporal tax structure issues, see Anderson and Young (1992).

The basic building blocks of the model are the representative consumers' expenditure function and the gross domestic product (GDP) function. The consumers' expenditure function $e(p, \pi, u)$ gives the minimum value of expenditure on private goods at price vector p, and public goods at marginal valuation π required to support utility level u. The GDP function $g(p, \pi^*, v)$ gives the maximum value of production of private goods at price p and public goods at price π^*, using the vector of primary inputs v in a convex technology. The value g also measures the total payments to factors. (If necessary, a diminishing-returns technology can be augmented by dummy factors to receive the residual returns.) There are also some untaxed tradable goods with unit price that are suppressed as active arguments, so that p is a relative price vector. Untaxed non-traded goods introduce no essential element and so are suppressed for simplicity.

The level of public-good production G is set by the government, so it is convenient to work with quantity-restricted private behavioural functions. Thus, define the private-goods expenditure and private-goods GDP functions as:

$$\bar{e}(p, G, u) = \max_{\pi}\{e(p, \pi, u) - \pi G\} \qquad (9.1)$$

$$\bar{g}(p, G, v) = \min_{\pi^*}\{g(p, \pi^*, v) - \pi^* G\} \qquad (9.2)$$

See Anderson and Neary (1992) for a similar development and further details.

The net expenditure on private goods at domestic prices is defined as

$$E(p, G, u, v) = \bar{e}(p, G, u) - \bar{g}(p, G, v) \qquad (9.3)$$

Conventionally, subscripted variable labels denote partial differentiation. Then from the properties of equations (9.1) to (9.3), $-E_G = -\bar{e}_G + \bar{g}_G = \pi - \pi^*$, the gap between the virtual price of the public goods π and the marginal resource cost of public goods π^*. E_p is the vector of excess demands.

The next step is to build the private and government budget constraints. The private budget constraint is:

$$E(p, G, u, v) + G\bar{g}_G G(p, G, v) - \rho = 0 \qquad (9.4)$$

The second (negative) term is needed because private consumption is covered by factor payments received from public as well as private production. The third term, ρ, the lump sum transfer from the government to the private agent, is to connect with the earlier literature. The government budget constraint is:

$$(p - p^*)'E_p(p, G, u, v) + G\bar{g}_G G(p, G, v) - \rho = 0 \qquad (9.5)$$

The first term is the government (distortionary tax) revenue, the second term is minus the government expenditure on the public good, and the third term is the transfer to the private sector. (If lump sum taxation is allowed, ρ can be negative.)

A tariff reform is equivalent to a change in the domestic price vector, p. It is convenient to incorporate various classes of tariff reforms in the convention:

$$dp^i = W^i p dt$$

where dt is a scalar and W^i is a diagonal matrix and the superscript i denotes a further restriction on W, i being a member of an index set. For example, the *uniform radial cut* rule implies that the elements of the principal diagonal of W are equal to the initial tariff rates on the domestic base, so that $dp = (p - p^*)dt$.

The classic treatment of tariff reform (Hatta, 1977 and others) considers the effect on the differential of system (9.4) and (9.5) of an *exogenous* change in dp solved for the *endogenous* change in the redistribution $d\rho$ and the welfare change du. Illustrating the method, analyze a uniform radial change dt. Differentiate the government budget constraint and solve for $d\rho/dt$:

$$\frac{d\rho}{dt} = E_p'(p - p^*) + (p - p^*)'E_{pp}(p - p^*) + G\bar{g}_{Gp}(p - p^*) + (p - p^*)'E_{pu}\frac{du}{dt}$$

Substitute into the differential of the private budget constraint, isolating terms in du on the left-hand side:

$$\left(1 - (p - p^*)'E_{pu}/E_u\right)E_u\frac{du}{dt} = -\left(E_p'(p - p^*) + G\bar{g}_{Gp}(p - p^*)\right) + \frac{d\rho}{dt}\bigg|_u$$

$$= \left(E_p'(p - p^*) + G\bar{g}_{Gp}(p - p^*)\right)\left[-1 + \frac{1}{MCF^t}\right]$$

$$(9.6)$$

On the left-hand side, the change in money-metric utility is multiplied by a term which is positive in the normal goods case (Hatta, 1977). On the right-hand side, the first bracketed term is a scale effect, the lump sum compensation required to offset a 1 per cent rise in taxes on the representative agent. The second, square-bracketed term on the right-hand side of (9.6) contains the essential welfare analysis. MCF is defined by:

$$MCF^t = \frac{E_p'(p - p^*) + G\bar{g}_{Gp}(p - p^*)}{E_p'(p - p^*) + (p - p^*)'E_{pp}(p - p^*) + G\bar{g}_{Gp}(p - p^*)} \qquad (9.7)$$

Note that (9.7) properly generalizes the ratio $(a + b)/a$ in Figure 9.1. The -1 term under the square bracket represents the direct effect of the rise in tax on welfare; a one-dollar increase in tax payments requires a one-dollar increase in compensation. The second, ratio term represents the offsetting effect of endogenous fiscal policy coming through the government budget constraint. For each dollar raised and redistributed, the benefit is one dollar, the numerator, but each dollar raised through distortionary tax comes at a marginal cost of MCF, the denominator. According to this analysis, the problem with raising tariffs in order to redistribute the resulting funds is that the MCF for tariffs is greater than 1, which is the marginal benefit of the cut in lump sum taxes.

The structure of the right-hand-side expression allows a further simplification:

$$\left(E_p'(p - p^*) + G\bar{g}_{Gp}(p - p^*)\right)\left[-1 + \frac{1}{MCF^t}\right] = (p - p^*)'E_{pp}(p - p^*)$$

where the right-hand side is the familiar marginal dead-weight loss term. Here, it appears that the problem with distortionary taxation versus non-distortionary taxation is the existence of the substitution effect, as agents avoid distortionary tax. The existence of the substitution effect is the essential reason that MCF also lies above 1. However, the argument above in the linear case shows that there is no necessary relationship between MCF and marginal dead-weight loss; the magnitude of the substitution effect directly affects marginal dead weight loss, while it has no unambiguous effect on MCF.

The usual treatment of this case first solves (9.5) for the government expenditure, then substitutes into Equation (9.4) to obtain the social budget constraint

$$E(p, G, u, v) - (p - p^*)'E_p(p, G, u, v) = 0 \tag{9.8}$$

and then analyzes the link between dp and du at constant G. Redistributive fiscal policy thus makes the government budget constraint passive.

4 TARIFF REFORM WITH SPENDING CUTS

A simple story with practical importance is the analysis of trade reform where government budgetary balance implies that spending cuts must offset cuts in tariff revenue. Formally, G must change endogenously as a result of the change in p. What rules can deliver welfare improvements along the path to the optimal tariffs?

The analysis proceeds in three steps. First, totally differentiate the government budget constraint (9.5) with respect to p, G and u, and solve for dG/dt under the restriction W^i.[7] This yields:

$$\frac{dG}{dt} = \frac{1}{\gamma}\left([E_p' + (p - p^*)'E_{pp} + G\bar{g}_{Gp}]W^i p + (p - p^*)'E_{pu}\frac{du}{dt}\right) \tag{9.9}$$

where γ is the marginal fiscal cost of the public good:

$$\gamma = -(\bar{g}_G + G\bar{g}_{GG} + (p - p^*)'E_{pG}) = \left(\pi^* + G\pi_G^* - (p - p^*)'E_{pG}\right) \tag{9.10}$$

The first two terms give the marginal cost of G to a monopsonistic buyer. The third term, $(p - p^*)'E_{pG}$, is the tax revenue change induced by the change in G.[8]

Second, totally differentiate the private budget constraint (9.4) with respect to exogenous dp, and endogenous dG and du using previously established properties of E and $\bar{g}$:

$$E_u du = -(E_p' + G\bar{g}_{Gp})dp + (\pi + G\pi_G^*)dG \qquad (9.11)$$
$$= -(E_p' + G\bar{g}_{Gp})dp + \tilde{\pi}dG.$$

The second term on the right-hand side, $\tilde{\pi}$, the marginal net benefit of the public good, is equal to the virtual price plus the net factoral income effect of the change in public-goods production.[9] Note that $\tilde{\pi} \geq \pi$.

Third, substitute the expression for dG/dt from the differential of the government budget constraint into (9.11), then isolate terms in du on the left-hand side of the equation:

$$\mu^{-1}E_u \frac{du}{dt} = -(E_p' + G\bar{g}_{Gp})W^i p + \frac{\tilde{\pi}}{\gamma}\left(E_p' + (p - p^*)'E_{pp} + G\bar{g}_{Gp}\right)W^i p \qquad (9.12)$$
$$= \left(-1 + \frac{\tilde{\pi}}{\gamma MCF^p}\right)E_p' W^i p$$

where

$$\mu^{-1} = \left(1 - \frac{1}{\gamma}(p - p^*)'E_{pu}/E_u\right) \qquad (9.13)$$

and

$$MCF^p = \frac{(E_p' + G\bar{g}_{Gp})W^i p}{\left(E_p' + (p - p^*)'E_{pp} + G\bar{g}_{Gp}\right)W^i p} \qquad (9.14)$$

Here, (9.14) generalizes (9.7) to the case where tax changes are not constrained to uniform radial changes.

On the left-hand side of equation (9.11), the rate of change of money metric utility $E_u du/dt$ is multiplied by a coefficient, given by (9.13), usually assumed to be positive, the *normal economy assumption*. The inverse of this coefficient, μ, is often called the shadow price of foreign exchange in the international trade literature, while for fiscal policy Anderson and Martin (1995) suggest calling it the 'fiscal multiplier'. Comparing (9.13) with the left-hand side of (9.6), the coefficient will differ in form for each fiscal experiment while remaining positive with the normal economy assumption.

On the right-hand side of (9.12) are the compensated terms which sign the rate of change of utility. The term outside the brackets is a positive scalar, by construction. The term in brackets signs the welfare change and is positive if the ratio of the marginal benefit $\tilde{\pi}$ to marginal social cost γMCF^p is greater than 1. The term γMCF^p is the marginal social cost of a unit of the public good financed through distorting p.

The intuition of (9.12) is simple. Assuming a normal economy, (9.12) implies that welfare rises with tariffs if the marginal benefit of public goods $\tilde{\pi}$ exceeds the marginal social cost of obtaining the public good. Thus:

Proposition 1: The public goods supply proposition Tariff reductions financed by cuts in government service are welfare-decreasing (increasing) in a normal economy with underprovision (overprovision) of public goods relative to their cost, or as

$$\left(-1 + \frac{\tilde{\pi}}{\gamma MCF^p}\right) > (<)0$$

More intuition about Proposition 1 follows by relating it to the optimal provision of public goods. With lump sum taxation available and distortionary taxes equal to zero, the differential of the government budget constraint implies: $dG/d\rho = -1/(\pi^* + G\pi_G^*)$.

Public-goods provision will fall with a rise in lump sum transfers ρ. The differential of the private budget constraint implies:

$$\begin{aligned} E_u du/d\rho &= 1 + (\pi + G\pi_G^*)dG/d\rho = 1 - (\pi + G\pi_G^*)/(\pi^* + G\pi_G^*) \\ &= 1 - \tilde{\pi}/\gamma \\ &= -(\pi - \pi^*)/(\pi^* + G\pi_G^*) \end{aligned}$$

Utility is increasing in lump sum tax reductions with no distortions when the ratio of the net benefit $\tilde{\pi} = \pi + G\pi_G^*$ to the marginal fiscal cost $\gamma = \pi^* + G\pi_G^*$ is less than 1. This condition implies $\pi < \pi^*$ because of the cancelling of terms, as is intuitively acceptable. But the fiscal policy logic of the marginal net benefit to marginal fiscal cost ratio is general. In the lump sum tax experiment, the MCF for lump sum taxation is implicitly present multiplying γ, but is identically equal to 1. Recognizing this, Proposition 1 properly generalizes the logic of the first best case by using the appropriate MCF times the appropriate marginal fiscal cost formula in the cost portion of the social benefit–cost ratio.

Proposition 1 relates to Proposition 2 of Abe (1992), but is a good deal more intuitive; in contrast to Abe, Proposition 1 does not require any added conditions on cross effects. Because Abe defines marginal cost and marginal benefit of public production in a highly eccentric way,[10] his condition of underprovision of public goods is not the same, and he therefore needs auxiliary conditions to sign the welfare change. Moreover, his oversupply condition produces the anomaly that tariff increases may raise welfare even with public goods oversupplied under his definition.

Proposition 1 also relates to the extensive literature on project evaluation based on the concept of the shadow price of public goods (see, for example, Squire, 1989). The shadow price of G is the net marginal social benefit to the economy of a gift of the foreign exchange needed to buy one unit of $G : \sigma = [\tilde{\pi} + MCF^p(p - p^*)'E_{pG}]$. Welfare falls with a tariff reduction if, manipulating equation (9.12):

$$\sigma - MCF^p(\pi^* + G\pi_G^*) > 0$$

That is, tariff cuts hurt welfare if public goods are undersupplied, where the undersupply condition, alternatively to Proposition 1, is that the shadow price of public production exceeds the product of the direct marginal outlay needed times the marginal cost of funds raised through distortionary trade taxation.

The bracketed 'underprovision of public goods' term in Proposition 1 is neat and intuitive, but in practice assessing its sign is complicated. Possibly the marginal fiscal cost γ and, more probably, MCF^p will be high in developing nations where the marginal benefit of public goods is also high. Empirical work must provide the assessment, and indeed there exist a number of estimates of MCF for various fiscal policies in a number of countries. While data are lacking for many developing nations, there is now available a set of CGE models which can be tweaked to provide some simulated values of γ and MCF. The most problematic variable is the marginal benefit of public goods. In some plausible models, such as the *dependent economy* model, in which external prices entirely determine internal (non-traded good and factor) prices, the factoral income effect of public goods is equal to zero, so the marginal benefit reduces to the unobservable virtual price of public goods π. Even here, for some important kinds of public goods such as education there are at least useful lower bounds available from observable data.

5 TARIFF REFORM WITH CONSUMPTION TAXES

A basic principle of public finance is that *optimal* revenue taxation should preserve production efficiency (Diamond and Mirrlees, 1971), which, among other things, means that it should not discriminate between foreign and domestic sources of production for the same good. In this sense, trade should not be taxed (Anderson, 1994). In starting from a *suboptimal* tax structure, under what conditions is it possible to state a like result, that it pays to reduce trade taxation and replace it with consumption taxation? This section shows that the policy of uniform radial reductions in tariffs matched by uniform radial increases in consumption taxation, or uniform radial replacement, cannot be guaranteed to be welfare-improving without further substitutability restrictions between private and public goods, along with non-subsidization conditions. One sufficient condition is the *non-subsidized dependent economy case*, where there are at least as many traded goods and factors as there are non-traded goods and factors in a constant returns technology. This case implies a powerful general equilibrium zero substitutability restriction in the excess demand system.

Let q denote consumer prices and p denote producer prices of tradable goods, both taxed or subsidized away from international prices p^*. No traded inputs are taxed in this section, for simplicity. Non-tradable private goods are untaxed, with market clearing prices, h. It is convenient now to drop the notation for lump sum transfers, ρ.

The net expenditure function is now derived as:

$$E(p,q,G,u) = \max_h \{\bar{e}(q,h,G,u) - \bar{g}(p,h,G)\} \tag{9.15}$$

where the restricted expenditure and GDP functions are obtained by extending (9.1) and (9.2) in the obvious way to incorporate private nontraded goods. Then $E_q = x$, the vector of final goods subject to tax or subsidy, and $E_p = -y$, minus the vector of supply subject to tax or subsidy.

The public-sector budget constraint is:

$$(p - p^*)'E_p + (q - q^*)'E_q + \bar{g}_G G = 0 \tag{9.16}$$

The private-sector budget constraint is:

$$E(p,q,G,u) + \bar{g}_G G = 0 \tag{9.17}$$

The exogenous fiscal policy is a change in trade taxes, offset for revenue neutrality by an endogenous change in consumption taxes, now with constant public-good supply.

To specialize the fiscal policy to the uniform radial replacement case, it is assumed that:

$$dp = (p - p^*)d\tau \tag{9.18}$$
$$dq = dp + (q - p^*)d\theta$$

The meaning of (9.18) is simplest in the case of initial pure trade taxation, $p = q$. With $d\theta = 0, d\tau$ is a standard uniform radial change in trade taxes. The change in θ modifies this with an additional uniform radial change in the consumer tax vector.

As a preliminary step in what follows, denote the (utility and public good constant) private marginal cost of the tax changes as:

$$R^q = E'_q(q - p^*) + G\bar{g}_{Gq}(q - p^*)$$

for the consumption tax, and

$$R = R^q + E'_p(p - p^*) + G\bar{g}_{Gp}(p - p^*)$$

for the trade tax. These expressions are obtained from differentiating (9.17) and using (9.18). R^q and R give the lump sum transfer needed to maintain u at constant G under the consumption and trade tax changes respectively. They combine the direct marginal cost with the indirect marginal cost through changing factoral income from public-goods production.

The fiscal policy change must meet the government budget constraint, implying by totally differentiating (9.16) and using (9.18) that:

$$d\theta/d\tau = -MCF^\theta/R^q\{R/MCF^\tau + [(p - p^*)'E_{pu} + (q - p^*)'E_{qu}]du\} \quad (9.19)$$

where

$$MCF^\theta = \frac{R^q}{R^q + l^q} \quad MCF^\tau = \frac{R}{R + l^q + l^p}$$
$$l^q = (q - p^*)'E_{qq}(q - p^*) + (p - p^*)'E_{pq}(q - p^*)$$
$$l^p = (q - p^*)'E_{qp}(p - p^*) + (p - p^*)'E_{pp}(p - p^*)$$

Here, l^q and l^p are familiar dead-weight loss terms, while MCF^j stands for the marginal cost of funds raised by a small change in the superscript variable, j.

Substituting (9.19) into the differential of the private-budget constraint (9.17) and isolating terms in du on the left-hand side of the equation:

$$\mu^{-1}E_u\frac{du}{d\tau} = \left(\frac{MCF^\theta}{MCF^\tau} - 1\right)R \quad (9.20)$$

where

$$\mu^{-1} = 1 - MCF^\theta[(p - p^*)'E_{pu} + (q - p^*)'E_{qu}]/E_u$$

As always, μ is assumed to be positive. If trade is not subsidized, and if trade is a substitute for public-goods production, R is positive. Then the sign of the welfare change from a uniform radial replacement of tariffs with consumption taxes ($d\tau < 0$) is positive if the bracket term is positive, or $MCF^\theta < MCF^\tau$, the marginal cost of funds raised through consumption taxation is less than the marginal cost of funds raised through trade taxation. Condition (9.20) is entirely intuitive, and easy to apply, based on simulations of MCF from CGE models.

What theoretical restrictions are able to guarantee the condition? Note that if $R^q \geq R > 0$, and l^q and l^p are both negative, MCF^θ is indeed smaller than MCF^τ. As for $R^q \geq R > 0$, this holds if:

(i)   public and private goods are substitutes in production, meaning that $\bar{g}_{Gp} = -\pi_p^* > 0$ and $\bar{g}_{Gh} = -\pi_h^* > 0$;
(ii) traded goods and home goods are substitutes, meaning that $h_q > 0$;
(iii) trade is not subsidized, $E_p'(p - p^*) + E_q'(q - p^*) > 0$; and
(iv) consumption is not subsidized, $E_q'(q - p^*) > 0$.

The restriction on l^q and l^p is far more problematical. The sum of l^q and l^p is necessarily negative. However, as for l^q and l^p separately, a cross-effect arising through the non-traded good prevents signing them from theory, even under strong assumptions such as substitutability.

Sharp results come with the *dependent economy* production and trade structure. Technology is subject to constant returns to scale and there are at least as many homogeneous (perfect substitutes with domestic products) traded goods and factors as there are non-traded goods and factors. In these circumstances the producer prices of non-traded goods are determined by the producer prices of traded goods and factors independently of the consumer prices. Thus $E_{pq} = E_{qp} = 0$ and $\bar{g}_{Gq} = \bar{g}_{Gp} = 0$. Then $MCF^\theta < MCF^\tau$ if $R^q \geqslant R > 0$.

Proposition 2:   The marginal Diamond–Mirrlees proposition A uniform radial marginal replacement of trade taxes with consumption taxes is welfare-improving in a normal dependent economy, provided trade and consumption are not initially subsidized.

These are, of course, oversufficient conditions. Nevertheless, a part of the significance of Proposition 2 is negative: even quite restrictive conditions do not suffice to guarantee that a replacement of trade taxation with consumption taxation at the margin will be welfare-improving.

Proposition 2 contrasts with Abe (1995), who considers welfare-improving tariff and consumption tax changes in a dependent economy when both tariffs and taxes change *exogenously* according to a derived rule, and the supply of public goods changes endogenously along with the level of utility. Abe sets the rule such that the net welfare effect of the change in p and q is equal to zero, with the welfare effect of the change coming through the increase in public-goods production, which is enabled by the revenue increase. In contrast to Proposition 2, Abe's proposition requires a great deal of information to form the weights in the linear tax rule. Diewert, Turunen-Red and Woodland (1989), in their Theorem 7 and Corollary 7.1, provide conditions under which uniform tariff cuts combined with *unspecified* commodity tax changes will suffice for Pareto improvement. In contrast, the present analysis uses a uniform radial increase to balance the government budget. Also, it allows taxation of only the non-numeraire goods, so the restriction on the set of instruments places it in the second-best world of the optimal tax literature.

As in section 4, a simple and useful condition signing the welfare effect of the revenue neutral tariff reform is presented. However, part of the significance of Proposition 2 is negative: fairly strong qualifications are needed to guarantee that uniform radial replacement is beneficial.

6 TAXATION OF NON-TRADED VERSUS TRADED GOODS

The first great result of public finance analysis is the Ramsey inverse elasticity principle. It implies that domestic and imported goods should generally be taxed differently, and if import taxes should be higher due to elasticities of demand being lower, then liberal trade obligations conflict with fiscal efficiency. Moreover, optimal tax rates will differ across broad product categories, hence there are fiscal inefficiencies in the uniform tariff structure advocated by the World Bank and in trade negotiations. In contrast, the logic of the preceding section applies when domestic and imported goods are perfect substitutes: foreign and domestic suppliers of the same good should face the same tax – that is, trade should be untaxed.

This section attempts to provide some theoretical insight into how costly is the decision to bind tariff levels in a World Trade Organization (WTO) deal, or a regional trade agreement, when imports and home goods are imperfect substitutes. A general formula for evaluating the replacement of trade taxes with taxes on home goods is offered. Intuitively, as in equation (9.20), it comes down to the MCF of home goods taxation versus the MCF of trade taxation. These are complex expressions, so only very special cases can be ranked from theory alone.

When trade taxes are high and home good taxes are very low it usually (save for a limiting counter-example in which some good is inelastically demanded)[11] pays to switch at the margin. Symmetrically, with low trade taxes and high home good taxes it pays to switch at the margin. The intuition is that a uniform radial replacement policy lowers the tax needed on each initially taxed good while raising it on each initially untaxed good. Since MCF is quadratic, rising more than in proportion to the tax, the replacement policy marginally tends to reduce loss. Cross-effects qualify the insight with non-zero initial taxation of both sets of goods.

The home good consumption price vector is h and the home good producer price vector is h^*. The specific tax $t = h - h^*$ is an instrument. The numeraire (including at least one export good) price is constant. For simplicity, restricted imports are confined to final goods only. Under these restrictions, the expenditure function is $e(p, h, G, u)$ and the GDP function is $g(h^*, G)$. Equilibrium in the home good markets determines $h^*(t, p, G, u)$ as a function of t, p, G, u implicitly in:

$$e_h(p, h^* + t, G, u) - \bar{g}_h(h^*, G) = 0 \tag{9.21}$$

The private and government budget constraints are:

$$e(p, h, G, u) - \bar{g}(h^*, G) + G\bar{g}_G = 0 \tag{9.22}$$

$$[p - p^*]'e_p + [h - h^*]'e_h + \bar{g}_G(h^*, G)G = 0 \tag{9.23}$$

Now consider uniform radial replacement of parametric trade taxes with revenue neutral endogenous home good taxes:

$$dp = (p - p^*)d\alpha \tag{9.24}$$

$$dt = (h - h^*)d\eta$$

In the non-traded good market, dt implies h^* changes by h_t^* while h changes by $I + h_t^*$, both obtained by implicit differentiation of (9.21).
Using the same methods as before,

$$\mu^{-1}E_u \frac{du}{d\alpha} = \left(\frac{MCF^\eta}{MCF^\alpha} - 1\right)R^p \tag{9.25}$$

where

$$MCF^\alpha = \frac{R^p}{R^p + l^p} \quad MCF^\eta = \frac{R^h}{R^h + l^h},$$

$$R^p = e_p'(p - p^*) + G\bar{g}_{Gh}'.h_p^*(p - p^*), \quad R^h = e_h'(h - h^*) + G\bar{g}_{Gh}'.h_t(h - h^*)$$

$$l^p = (p - p^*)'(e_{pp} + e_{ph}h_p^*)(p - p^*) + (h - h^*)'(e_{hp} + e_{hh}h_p^*)(p - p^*)$$

$$l^h = (h - h^*)'e_{hh}[I + h_t^*](h - h^*) + (p - p^*)'e_{ph}[I + h_t^*](h - h^*)$$

When might MCF^η be less than MCF^α in (9.25)?

Proposition 3:   The wider base proposition With consumption taxes initially equal to zero, a uniform proportional rise in consumption taxes combined with a uniform radial reduction in trade taxes is welfare improving provided traded goods are not perfectly inelastically demanded.

For this case, MCF^η is equal to 1, while MCF^α is greater than 1. By continuity, welfare should continue to rise with small home-goods taxation. The reasoning is symmetrical: a regime with no taxation of imperfectly substitutable imports can always improve welfare with at least a bit of trade taxation. Proposition 3 is the formal counterpart to the intuitive notion that at the margin it always pays to add new goods to the tax base.

General results for switching between trade and home-good taxation from interior positions are not possible, as the MCF expressions depend on the entire substitution effects matrix interacted with the tax structure.

7   TOWARDS OPERATIONALITY

This chapter stresses the importance of the MCF of trade taxes relative to that of domestic taxes. Thus it concludes with illustrative estimates of MCF^θ and MCF^τ for a stylized small-scale CGE model of the Korean economy in 1963, found in the public domain GAMS (general algebraic modelling system) software library. For more details, see Chenery, Lewis, de Melo and Robinson (1986).

There are three sectors, agriculture, manufacturing and services. Each sector has an import available at a fixed international price competing with a domestic product which is an imperfect substitute in demand via a CES preference structure. The CES aggregate consumption bundles substitute with each other according to a Cobb–Douglas preference structure. Each sector exports at a fixed international price a product which is an imperfect substitute in supply for the domestic product according to a CET joint-output technology. Each sector produces its output with intermediate goods with fixed coefficients, while the value-added technology has a CES form. Agricultural labour is not mobile, and sectoral capital is fixed in the short run. There is, in effect, a representative consumer who receives all sources of income.[12] Government consumption is modelled as absorbing revenue but not supplying a public good. Imports are subject to tariffs, and indirect taxes apply to all domestic transactions. Income taxes in the model are equivalent to lump sum taxes, as labour supply is inelastic. The model is fully Walrasian.

The MCF is a compensated implicit derivative. It is built up from two separate simulations of the change in money metric utility with respect to a small *external* transfer. In the first, the government budget is balanced by a uniform radial tax change, while in the second it is balanced by a lump sum transfer. The results are not very sensitive to the size of the perturbation, nor to variation in the size of elasticities of substitution, so the sensitivity analysis is not reported. The computational methods are described in an Appendix available from the author.

The simulation of the model at the base values of the substitution parameters yields an MCF for tariffs of around 1.57, while the MCF for indirect taxes is around 1.74. (The MCFs are calculated based on a uniform radial change in tariffs and in indirect taxes, respectively.) These values appear reasonable, based on two sorts of check. First, Devarajan, Squire and Suthiwart-Narueput (1995) report estimates of MCF for income and commodity taxes combined ranging from 1.32 to 1.47 for the USA, while an estimate for Sweden is recorded at 2.2, Ballard, Shoven and Whalley (1985) report MCF estimates for the USA ranging from 1.17 to 1.57. Second, the values of both MCFs for Korea are consistent with the tax rates and simulated values of the general equilibrium (uncompensated) elasticities in the model. This observation is based on a crude use of the general formula for MCF, in which diagonal terms only are used.

Significantly, the MCF for tariffs is lower than that for indirect taxes. This is a surprise, because indirect taxes are relatively low – less than or equal to 5 per cent, in contrast to tariffs ranging from 8 per cent to 22 per cent. The finding illustrates the practical importance of the theoretical ambiguity: replacing trade taxes with domestic taxes is not necessarily beneficial.[13]

The results should probably not be taken too seriously as a description of the pay-off to marginal trade reform in the Korean economy of 1963. Instead, they illustrate the principles of the chapter and their applicability to the calculation of the key MCF variables under the discipline of using real world tariffs, domestic taxes, public expenditure and production/consumption shares. In future work, it would be very useful to calculate MCF for distortionary income taxation, and to extend the set of countries for which MCF calculations exist.

This chapter casts doubt on the general desirability of trade reform with an active government budget constraint. No theoretical or empirical presumption in favour of liberalization can be established in the highly plausible case where foreign and domestic goods are imperfect substitutes.

Notes

1. For example, the current US government budget process requires that revenue cuts be matched by spending cuts or other revenue increases. This requirement temporarily threatened the NAFTA obligations.
2. There is no difference between public goods and government-provided goods in a representative consumer economy.

3. Anderson and Martin (1995) argue that the compensated version of the MCF is a much cleaner concept and avoids the potential errors that have often cropped up with use of the uncompensated MCF.
4. Panagariya (1992) treats a revenue-neutral switch among tariffs in a 'three final good, one imported input' model. Falvey (1994) considers conditions under which tariff cuts may raise both welfare and revenue.
5. A large country achieves productive efficiency with a tariff structure which equates the domestic marginal rates of transformation with the marginal rates of transformation in trade.
6. For an inelastic demand curve, MR and the demand curve coincide, MCF is equal to 1 and the dead weight loss is equal to 0.
7. If G is a vector, the analysis proceeds under some auxiliary rule $dG = H^j G d\alpha$, where H^j is a spending change rule and $d\alpha$ is a marginal change in the expenditure.
8. A common theoretical convenience is to assume this term is equal to zero, a practice that is likely to be seriously wrong empirically and may be misleading in understating the marginal fiscal cost of the public good. $E_{pG} = 0$ requires 'additive separability' in both preferences and technology.
9. One unit of public goods production reduces private production by $-\pi^*$, and raises the factoral income received from public goods production by $\pi^* + G\pi_G^*$.
10. In my notation, Abe defines the 'marginal cost' as $p^{*'}\bar{g}_{pG}$ and the 'marginal benefit' as $p^{*'}\bar{e}_{pG}$. These expressions bear no particular relation to the marginal cost and virtual price which are the natural ones used here.
11. Imported inputs may be a good candidate to tax, as they are thought to have low elasticity of demand; see Panagariya (1992). The first version of this chapter provided a graphical example of an inelastically demanded imported input which received all the tax at the optimum.
12. For the intertemporal aspect of the model, there are different marginal propensities to save out of different sources of income. This divergence from the representative consumer story does not affect the static properties of the model.
13. Regrettably, in the CGE model used, there is no labour supply decision; hence income taxes are equivalent to lump sum taxes and it is not possible to evaluate trade reform paid for with realistic distortionary income taxation.

References

Abe, K. (1992) 'Tariff Reform in a Small Open Economy with Public Production', *International Economic Review*, vol. 33, pp. 209–22.

Abe, K. (1995) 'The Target Rates of Tariff and Tax Reform', *International Economic Review*, vol. 36, pp. 875–86.

Anderson, J. E. (1994) 'The Theory of Protection', in D. Greenaway and L. A. Winters (eds), *Surveys of International Trade* (Oxford: Basil Blackwell).

Anderson, J. E. and W. Martin (1995) 'The Welfare Analysis of Fiscal Policy: A Simple Unified Accounting', mimeo, Boston College.

Anderson, J. E. and J. P. Neary (1992) 'Trade Reform with Quotas, Partial Rent Retention and Tariffs', *Econometrica*, vol. 60, pp. 57–76.

Anderson, J. E. and L. Young (1992) 'Optimal Taxation and Debt in an Open Economy', *Journal of Public Economics*, no. 47, pp. 27–57.

Ballard, C., J. Shoven and J. Whalley (1985) 'General Equilibrium Computations of the Marginal Welfare Cost of Taxes in the United States', *American Economic Review*, vol. 75, pp. 128–38.

Bertrand, T. J. and J. Vanek (1971) 'The theory of Tariffs, Taxes and Subsidies: Some Aspects of the Second Best', *American Economic Review*, vol. 61, pp. 925–31.

Bruno, M. (1972) 'Market Distortions and Gradual Reform', *Review of Economic Studies*, vol. 39, pp. 373–83.

Chenery, H. B., J. Lewis, J. de Melo and S. Robinson (1986) 'Alternative Routes to Development', in H. B. Chenery, S. Robinson and M. Syrquin (eds), *Industrialization and Growth: a Comparative Study* (London: Oxford University Press).

Devarajan, S., L. Squire and S. Suthiwart-Narueput (1995) 'Reviving Project Appraisal at the World Bank', World Bank Policy Research Working Paper, no. 1496.

Diamond, P. A. and J. Mirrlees (1971) 'Optimal Taxation and Public Production', *American Economic Review*, vol. 61, pp. 8–27 and 261–78.

Diewert, W. E., A. H. Turunen-Red and A. D. Woodland (1989) 'Productivity- and Pareto-Improving Changes in Taxes and Tariffs', *Review of Economic Studies*, vol. 56, pp. 199–216.

Diewert, W. E., A. H. Turunen-Red and A. D. Woodland (1991) 'Tariff Reform in a Small Open Economy with Domestic Distortions and Nontraded Goods', *International Economic Review*, vol. 32, pp. 937–57.

Ethier, W. J. (1995) *Modern International Economics*, 3rd edn (New York: Norton).

Falvey, R. (1994) 'Revenue Enhancing Tariff Reform', CREDIT Paper 94/5, University of Nottingham.

Foster, E. and H. Sonnenschein (1970) 'Price Distortion and Economic Welfare', *Econometrica*, vol. 38, pp. 281–97.

Grossman, G. and E. Helpman (1994) 'Protection for Sale', *American Economic Review*, vol. 84, pp. 833–50.

Hatta, T. (1977) 'A Theory of Piecemeal Policy Recommendations', *Review of Economic Studies*, vol. 44, pp. 1–21.

Hillman, A. (1989) *The Political Economy of Protection* (New York: Harwood Academic Press).

Lloyd, P. (1974) 'A More General Theory of Price Distortions in Open Economies', *Journal of International Economics*, vol. 4, pp. 365–86.

Lopez, R. and A. Panagariya (1992) 'On the Theory of Piecemeal Tariff Reform: The Case of Pure Imported Intermediate Inputs', *American Economic Review*, vol. 82, pp. 615–25.

Panagariya, A. (1992) 'Input Tariffs, Duty Drawbacks and Tariff Reform', *Journal of International Economics*, vol. 32, pp. 131–48.

Ramsey, F. (1927) 'A Contribution to the Theory of Taxation', *Economic Journal*, vol. 37, pp. 47–61.

Squire, L. (1989) 'Project Evaluation in Theory and Practice', in H. Chenery and T. N. Srinivasan (eds), *Handbook of Development Economics*, vol. II (Amsterdam: Elsevier).

Comment

Arja Turunen-Red
UNIVERSITY OF NEW ORLEANS

This chapter brings together ideas from international trade theory and public economics in an interesting and useful way. In my comments, I discuss the connection of this chapter with the existing literature and interpret Proposition 1 of Anderson in the light of Abe (1992).

Literature Background

The (unilateral) tariff reform problem concerns the design of changes in a country's tariff structure that will in some sense improve the initial situation, given that a movement to the first-best optimum is not permitted. As tariff reforms usually cause some to gain while others lose, the traditional approach has emphasized the attainment of Pareto improvements via compensating changes in other policy variables. The early literature (for example, Hatta, 1977) accompanied tariff reforms by compensatory lump sum transfers and thus it was sufficient, in this literature, to consider tariff reforms that yield welfare improvements in a single-household economy. A more recent approach (Dixit and Norman, 1980; Diewert, Turunen-Red and Woodland 1989) is to use commodity taxes to attain the redistribution of gains necessary for a Pareto improvement to become feasible.[1] Other government policy instruments may also be applied. As suggested by Woodland (1985), one such alternative is the income tax schedule while another is the provision of public goods.[2] Anderson's Proposition 1 which matches a tariff reform with changes in the supply of public goods is therefore, in a sense, an anticipated extension of the tariff reform literature. The difference is that Anderson (like Abe) is not concerned with Pareto improvements but considers only aggregate efficiency gains which may be attained via reductions of tariffs.

Anderson makes a distinction between the earlier tariff reform literature in which the government budget constraint has been treated, according to him, as 'passive', while in the present chapter and in the work of Abe – and only in them – the government budget constraint is deemed 'active'. Anderson defines an 'active' government budget constraint as the case in which the government budget balance forces an endogenous change in some *distortionary* policy instrument as another distortionary instrument is altered exogenously. From this point of view, the tariff reform literature that employed lump sum transfers to guarantee Pareto improvements admittedly

239

dealt with a 'passive' government budget constraint. However, the more recent literature, in which perturbations of commodity taxes are used as the compensating mechanism to accompany tariff reform, would seem to qualify as including an 'active' government budget constraint. The difference between the various papers seems to lie, first, in the choice of the policy instruments that are considered variable (the government budget constraint has never been ignored in any of the literature), and, secondly, in the specificity of the compensating policy changes that accompany tariff reform. In the earlier literature, the direction of these accompanying policy changes was usually not specified, whereas Anderson considers combinations of policy reforms in which all changes in the government policy variables have a definite direction.

Anderson's results are expressed using marginal concepts that are not necessarily familiar. This departure from the tradition of the tariff reform literature seems inspired by the theory of tax reform, and especially by the empirically-orientated approach of Ahmad and Stern (1984 and 1991). In the Ahmad and Stern approach, one computes the marginal social (utility) cost of extra revenue arising from different taxes, and chooses, between any two possibilities, the one with the lower social cost. The Anderson approach to policy reform is analogous to that of Ahmad and Stern in that the *marginal cost of funds* and the *marginal economic cost* and *marginal benefit* of public-good production yield the monetary (compensated) equivalents of the Ahmad and Stern social (utility) cost.

Tariff Reform and the Provision of Public Goods

Anderson's Proposition 1 states a condition which guarantees that a tariff reduction, financed by cuts in public services, is welfare-improving. The result is derived within a competitive model of a small open economy which is structurally identical to that of Abe (1992), with one expository difference: following the tariff reform literature, Abe replaces the individual budget constraint with the country's trade balance. However, as we may drop either the country's trade balance (as Anderson), or the aggregate individual's budget constraint (as Abe), or the government budget constraint, the results obtained by Abe and Anderson ought to be analogous. Intuitive understanding of why this is not so is the goal of the remainder of this section.

Consider, for example, a theorem of Abe on reducing a country's maximal (*ad valorem*) tariff rate, balanced by an endogenous change in the supply of the public good. Abe shows that this direction of policy reform is welfare improving if (i) tariffs are non-negative; (ii) there are no inferior private goods; (iii) the private goods with the highest tariff are net substitutes for all private goods and net complements to the public good in production; and

(iv) the public good is initially 'oversupplied', that is, using Anderson's notation, $p^{*T}E_{pG} < 0$. Excluding the first two assumptions, which require no explanation, these conditions are natural in the light of the earlier tariff reform literature. We expect a reduction of a given tariff to be welfare-improving if the product in question is a net substitute (complement) for goods with lower (higher) tariff rates; Abe's net substitutability condition on private goods agrees with this intuition. Assumption (iii) on the public-good provision, on the other hand, implies that the endogenous change in G accompanying the tariff reform ought to be a reduction. Finally, the 'oversupply' criterion (iv) balances the direct and indirect consequences of the change in G; by the homogeneity properties of the E-function, we obtain:[3]

$$p^{*T}E_{pG} = \tau^T E_{pG} + \bar{g}_G - \bar{e}_G \equiv \Delta \text{ tariff revenue} - MC^G + MB^G \qquad (1)$$

Thus, if Abe's 'oversupply' criterion holds, the marginal cost of public-goods provision exceeds the sum of the marginal benefit of G and the marginal effect of G on the country's tariff revenue. In these circumstances, a small perturbation of G cannot alter the country's tariff revenue to such a degree and yield such a welfare loss that a reduction of G would not be welfare-enhancing, given the efficiency gains arising from the reduction of the highest (*ad valorem*) tariff.

Using the Anderson's definitions, we may rewrite equation (1) as follows:

$$p^{*T}E_{pG} = \Delta \text{ tariff revenue} - \pi^* + \pi \equiv \pi - \gamma \qquad (2)$$

where γ is Anderson's '*marginal fiscal cost*' of the public good and π is its '*virtual price*'. Abe's criterion for a public good to be overprovided can therefore be expressed as

$$\pi < \gamma \qquad (3)$$

Anderson's Proposition 1, in turn, demonstrates that cuts in tariffs and public services are welfare-improving in a normal economy if the public good is oversupplied according to the criterion:

$$\frac{\tilde{\pi} - \gamma MCF}{\gamma MCF} < 0 \qquad (4)$$

In (4), the marginal benefit of G is defined as:

$$\tilde{\pi} \equiv \pi - (\Delta \text{ income from } G - \text{production}) \qquad (5)$$

and its marginal cost equals the product of the marginal economic cost of a change in G, denoted by γ, and the marginal cost of funds obtained from a tariff reform, denoted by MCF.

Formula 4 generalizes Abe's definition of public overproduction in two ways. First, Anderson's definitions of $\tilde{\pi}$ and the MCF include the effects of changes in G and the country's tariff structure on the factor income arising from the public production. Abe assumes these effects away (Condition F of Abe) and thus for him, $\tilde{\pi} \equiv \pi$. Furthermore, for Abe, the MCF is equal to unity as Abe's characterization of public overproduction in (3) corresponds to lump sum financing of public services;[4] Anderson, on the other hand, gives condition (4), which deals directly with the distortionary, tariff-based financing of the public-good production. Once these differences are taken into account, however, conditions (3) and (4) of Abe and Anderson are analogous. The appearance of differences between the results of Abe and Anderson is made sharper by Abe's definitions of the marginal cost and marginal benefit of public goods which are not based on the decomposition in equation (1) but simply divide Abe's oversupply criterion into consumption ('marginal benefit') and production ('marginal cost') components.

Anderson utilizes no net substitutability conditions in his Proposition 1, whereas such conditions were used by Abe to supplement his overprovision criterion. We have seen, however, that Abe's net substitutability conditions are natural in light of the earlier tariff reform literature, and arose in the context of a specific tariff cut. In contrast, Anderson's theorem is general and allows for an arbitrary direction of tariff reform. This additional generality comes at a price: the expressions for $\gamma, \tilde{\pi}$, and the MCF are complex, with many net substitutability terms, and it is not clear which specific assumptions are needed to guarantee that Anderson's oversupply condition (4) holds for any particular direction of tariff reform.

Concluding Comments

The tariff reform literature has identified conditions under which particular directions of tariff perturbations are Pareto-improving. To make these results operational one must check the derived conditions empirically, which typically involves the country's net substitution matrix and income derivatives of consumption. Furthermore, one must identify the compensating transfers or changes in commodity taxes, the directions of which have been left unspecified in the literature.

Anderson, in contrast, is interested in policy packages in which reforms of tariffs are combined with *specific* changes in other policy variables (for example, public goods). The emphasis on this problem setting of *tied policy reform* is one of Anderson's contributions.[5] Anderson's results are derived using the concept of the MCF, which allows Anderson to state some of his propositions without explicit reference to net substitutability of goods. While these results are worthwhile, the marginal concepts employed by Anderson are complex expressions which include terms from the country's net substitution matrix and other variables. It is not clear whether the theoretical neatness of Anderson's results corresponds to less bothersome empirical calculations than the earlier literature.

Notes

1. In Diewert, Turunen-Red and Woodland (1989), the set of commodity tax instruments was complete, and adjustment of all taxes was implicitly allowed. However, because of the homogeneity of the model, this modelling choice represents no loss of generality in comparison to Anderson, who chooses the consumer tax rate on the numeraire equal to zero.
2. Konishi (1995) has analyzed commodity tax reforms which are accompanied by changes in a non-linear income tax in a closed economy model.
3. The decomposition (1) was not used by Abe (1992). The symbol Δ in (1) denotes a change in the ensuing expression.
4. This can be seen by considering the effect of a change in G in equation $E(p, G, u, v) = \tau^T E_p$.
5. Tied policy reform has been considered by, for example, Lahiri and Raimondos-Moller (1996) in the context of tied aid, and by Turunen-Red and Woodland (1993) in the context of tied tariff reform.

References

Abe, K. (1992) 'Tariff Reform in a Small Open Economy with Public Production', *International Economic Review*, vol. 33, no. 1, pp. 209–22.

Ahmad, E. and N. Stern (1984) 'The Theory of Reform and Indian Indirect Taxes', *Journal of Public Economics*, vol. 25, no. 3, pp. 259–95.

Ahmad, E. and N. Stern (1991) *The Theory and Practice of Tax Reform in Developing Countries* (Cambridge: Cambridge University Press).

Diewert, W. E., A. Turunen-Red and A. Woodland (1989) 'Productivity and Pareto Improving Changes in Taxes and Tariffs', *Review of Economic Studies*, vol. 56, pp. 199–216.

Dixit, A. and V. Norman (1980) *Theory of International Trade* (Cambridge: Cambridge University Press).

Hatta, T. (1977) 'A Recommendation for a Better Tariff Structure', *Econometrica*, vol. 45, pp. 1859–69.

Konishi, H. (1995) 'A Pareto-Improving Commodity Tax Reform under a Smooth Nonlinear Income Tax', *Journal of Public Economics*, vol. 56, pp. 413–46.

Lahiri, S. and P. Raimondos-Moller (1997) 'On the Tying of Aid to Tariff Reform', *Journal of Development Economics*, vol. 54, no. 2.

Turunen-Red, A. and A. Woodland (1993) 'Partial Tariff and Quota Reform in a Small Open Economy', mimeo, Department of Economics, University of Texas at Austin.

Woodland, A. (1985) 'Recent Developments in the Theory of Tariff Reform', mimeo, University of Sydney, Department of Econometrics.

10 The Political Economy of Administering Trade Laws[1]

Wolfgang Mayer
UNIVERSITY OF CINCINNATI

1 INTRODUCTION

Domestic industries can be protected from foreign competition through a vast array of policy measures. Some measures – such as import tariffs, quantitative restrictions, and anti-dumping and countervailing duties – are aimed explicitly at strengthening the competitive position of domestic firms, while others – such as product standards, testing and labelling requirements, and even certain types of sales taxes[2] – have differently stated aims but the same ultimate effects of industry protection. Students of the political economy of international trade assert that both explicit and implicit measures of protection are the result of governments' attempts to maximize their political power. In a democracy, this generally means that a government legislates and administers laws with the objective of maximizing its chances of being re-elected.

A common feature of most countries' current trade restrictions is that they are anchored in laws that are revised infrequently, while implementation of these laws through administrative practices is adjusted on a daily basis.[3] Passage of legislation is the final step of a time-consuming political process that requires formal initiation, debate among politicians and public, testimony from expert witnesses, compromising amendments, and drafting of the final text. The administering of laws, on the other hand, is conducted with little or no public debate by administrators, who work on behalf of elected officials.[4] Trade laws spell out which products are subject to tariffs, what tariff rates are imposed, and how imported products are to be valued. They also state the conditions under which anti-dumping and countervailing duty actions can be taken; and they may specify products that are subject to quality or safety standards, and how they are to be inspected. Trade laws set the rules for protection, but how much protection is actually provided depends on the implementation of trade laws. In particular, trade laws set limits to the discretionary power of administrators but, within these limits, administrators have a great deal of leeway. Administered protection can therefore be viewed

245

as a short-run phenomenon conducted within the guidelines set by legislation which, in turn, is adjusted only over the long run.

The general objective of this chapter is to shed light on the relationship between legislated and administered protection when governments write and implement trade laws with the goal of staying in power. We are going to lay out a model in which governments write or revise tariff laws quite infrequently, whereas administrative measures may be adopted or adjusted at any time. We address three, more specific, questions in this context: first, how will a government adjust its administrative measures of protection, consisting of non-tariff trade barriers and an enforcement budget, when the competitiveness of an industry changes temporarily? Second, why does a government employ both tariffs and non-tariff trade barriers, and why does it restrict its ability to administer non-tariff barriers when it writes its trade laws? Third, how are trade laws revised when a government becomes aware of fundamental changes in the competitive strength of one of its industries? In setting up the model and answering these questions, short-run administrative actions are considered to be of two types: actions that are capable of affecting the tariff-equivalence rate of the whole set of non-tariff measures, and actions that influence the rigour with which legislated and administered measures of protection are enforced. Concerning the former, we do not distinguish explicitly among the many alternative instruments different countries employ;[5] instead, we consider their tariff equivalence value only.[6] Concerning the latter we allow for the fact that enforcement of nominal trade restrictions depends on both the budget allocated to enforcement and the incentives for importers to circumvent trade restrictions. Long-run trade laws, in contrast, permit a government to legislate nominal tariff rates and to set limits on the use of administrative actions.

The relative ease with which administrative measures can be adjusted in response to changing competitive pressures is of great value in a government's struggle to retain power. In fact, one wonders why governments pass tariff laws at all if they can accomplish the same degree of protection, with much greater speed and tailored to the specific needs of an individual industry, through administrative actions. The reason for governments to rely on both legislative and administrative measures of protection is that, at least in democracies, the former receive direct or indirect approval from the voting public, while the latter are adopted without endorsement from the public. In the terminology of Buchanan and Tullock (1962), there are *external costs* that individuals expect to experience when any agent, such as the government in power, is authorized to take action on behalf of an entire group, such as the country's citizenry. The greater the scope of authorization – or, as one might say, the wider the limits on discretionary power – the higher are these external costs to the public, and the lower is the public's approval of the way policies are chosen. The government, when deciding on the employment of administrative measures of protection, has to weigh the benefits from quick and flexible responses to changing conditions of international competitiveness against the political costs of choosing the degree of trade protection without explicit approval from the public.

Trade laws specify nominal tariff rates and set limits on the use of administrative measures. When trade laws are adopted, government, public and industry interest groups do not know how competitive different industries will be in the future. Most important, the government can only guess as to what world prices will be at the critical time of the next election. Given its beliefs about world prices at election time, the government passes laws that set the general direction for trade policy while, at the same time, leaving room for quick policy adjustments in response to temporary world price changes. Accordingly, trade laws are not altered unless fundamental shifts in an industry's competitiveness occur. When the government's expectations about the competitiveness of one of its industries change in a very fundamental way – such as when it becomes increasingly likely that currently low world prices will persist for a long time – political pressure to revise current trade laws builds up; the government must then assess how to change the legislated rate of tariff protection, as well as the limits on discretionary power to take administrative measures.

The model of this chapter is based on the political support function approach initiated by Stigler (1971), formally developed by Peltzman (1976), and adapted to the examination of international trade issues by Hillman (1982 and 1989). The government's objective is to maximize political support for its trade policy actions, with support being sought from both the public and industry interest groups. At election time, the competitiveness of domestic industries is known, but legislated nominal tariff rates and the government's authority to manipulate actual rates of protection are given. When trade laws are written, on the other hand, the government can choose tariff rates and limits on its discretionary power, but the future competitiveness of its industries is not yet known. Whatever laws were legislated in the past, and whatever administrative actions are taken in the present, a government can never be certain of securing the political support required for re-election. The inability of a government to protect its industries, the excessive acquisition of discretionary power, or a combination of the two, may become the reason for its demise.

This paper distinguishes between nominal rates of protection, consisting of legislated nominal tariff rates and the tariff-equivalent rates of non-tariff barriers, and actual rates of protection. The latter are the nominal rates when adjusted for the degree of enforcement. Enforcement of trade policies is costly, as it requires checking of import shipments, verification of claims made by importers, testing of products, prevention of smuggling, and many other activities. Furthermore, enforcement becomes increasingly difficult the greater the incentive for importers to evade import restrictions. Importers have the greater incentives to get around import restrictions the greater is the difference between domestic and world-market prices. Hence, stronger nominal protective measures do not automatically assure more protection; they may have to be backed up by a higher enforcement budget in order to assure increased actual protection of an industry. However, a larger enforcement budget, just like larger discretionary authority, entails political costs; political support declines with the size of the budget. In spite of the political costs of spending on law enforcement, the government will adopt an enforcement budget to provide industries with the level of actual protection that maximizes political support. Enforcement budgets may also become a substitute for administrative actions of protection; when a government's limits on using non-tariff barriers have been reached, stricter enforcement of nominal rates may be the only way to raise political support.

2 THE POLITICAL SUPPORT FUNCTION WITH ADMINISTRATIVE CHOICES

Political Support in the Absence of Administrative Costs

The political support function approach, pioneered by Peltzman (1976) to explain industry regulation, was introduced to the international trade literature by Hillman (1982). His formulation stipulates that a government's political support from voters declines when the domestic price rises relative to the world price, whereas its political support from firms rises as their profits under a protectionist regime increase relative to what they would be under free trade. This chapter retains the first part of this formulation but amends the second part by stipulating that political support from firms is positively related to protection-induced gains in product *prices* rather than in profits. This change in specification is justified by invoking the *informativeness principle*, as it pertains to the design of compensation formulas. Political support by an industry is viewed as compensation for the government's efforts in designing industry-friendly trade policies, since changes in prices provide a more appropriate indicator of the government's efforts on behalf of producers.[7]

The political support functions of Peltzman and Hillman, while intuitively appealing, are not based on explicit microfoundations. Such microfoundations can, however, be established by borrowing from the work of Grossman and Helpman (1994). Their incumbent politician maximizes the weighted sum of political contributions from industry lobbies and of the public's aggregate welfare. Each industry lobby presents a schedule that states its contributions at different domestic prices as they are associated with different trade policies. The lobby makes its political support, in the form of contributions, dependent on commodity prices rather than profits. One can argue that commodity prices are a better indicator of the government's efforts than profits, since profits, while they depend on prices, are also affected by other influences and therefore convey less information about the government's efforts on behalf of the industry. Accordingly, the political support function in the absence of administrative costs is stated as:

$$V(p - \pi) = M[(p - \pi), g(p - \pi)] \tag{10.1}$$

where $g(\cdot)$ is positively related to the difference between the price under government intervention p and under free trade π, and political support M declines with the first argument, as the increased price hurts consumers, and rises with the second argument, as the higher price results in stronger political support from industry. $V(\cdot)$ is assumed to be strictly concave, with a unique maximum at a finite price difference.

The gap between domestic and world price is assumed to be generated by an *ad valorem* tariff, t. The price difference is measured by T, where $T = (p - \pi) = \pi t$. The political-support maximizing price difference, T^*, being unique, any fluctuation in world price results in tariff adjustments; the import tariff changes at the same rate as the world price but in the opposite direction; and the domestic price moves in the same direction as the world price, but at a smaller rate. That is,

$$dt^*/t^* = -d\pi/\pi \quad \text{and} \quad dp/p = [1/(1+t^*)]d\pi/\pi^8 \tag{10.2}$$

When the competitiveness of a domestic industry declines, as the world price of its product falls, the industry will receive protection; but this protection merely cushions the impact of the deteriorating price development; it does not reverse it.

Political Support from Legislated and Administered Protection

When the government contemplates protection for one of its industries, it has legislative and administrative measures at its disposal. Legislation sets the nominal *ad valorem* tariff rate, t, and thereby drives a wedge between domestic and world prices. Administrative actions – in the form of countervailing and anti-dumping actions, escape clause procedures, various quantitative restrictions, technical standards, customs valuations, inspection rules, licensing requirements, and a host of other grey-area measures – segment domestic from world markets and create differences between domestic and world prices that can be measured by the tariff-equivalent rate of administered protection, α. Consequently, the nominal rate of protection, provided by both legislated tariff and administered non-tariff measures, is given by $(t + \alpha)$.

Administrative measures possess the desirable features of speed and flexibility; the response time to changing world market conditions is short and the ability to tailor protection to the specific needs of an industry is high. This power of quick and flexible response is, however, confined to a certain range of tariff-equivalent rates. Trade laws spell out which administrative measures are available and how they can be employed; they set upper and lower limits to tariff-equivalence rates. We denote the maximum rate of administered protection by $\bar{\alpha}$ and, since there is no subsidization of imports through administrative actions, the range of attainable nominal rates of administered protection is:

$$0 \le \alpha \le \bar{\alpha} \tag{10.3}$$

Extending the upper limits of administered protection through revisions of trade laws is possible, but politically costly. Once the law has set the limits, the government has complete control over its actions within those limits and the public loses influence over specific policy choices. The wider the limits, the greater is the public's loss of influence and the more distrustful it becomes of the government. Consequently, we assume that legislating for discretionary power over policy entails political support costs, denoted by C.

Enhancement of discretionary power is one source of political liability for the government. Another is expansion of the government's budget. A larger budget, denoted by b, implies greater potential for control by the government, and therefore added political costs. A budget, however, is necessary to enforce the nominal tariff rates and non-tariff barriers that have been established by the trade laws. We must distinguish between a country's *nominal* rate of protection, as it would be if legislated tariff rates and contemplated administrative measures were fully enforced, and *actual* rates of protection, as they are experienced by consumers and producers. The *nominal* rate of protection was defined by $(t + \alpha)$; the *actual* rate of protection is given by $(t + \alpha)e$, where $0 \le e \le 1$ is a coefficient of enforcement. The value of e is assumed to be positively affected by the enforcement budget and negatively related to the gap between the domestic and the world price, T; the larger is T, the greater the incentive for importers to evade import barriers and the less the effectiveness of any nominal import control measures. The enforcement function is written as:

$$e(b/T), \quad \text{where } e(0) = 0, \ e(\infty) = 1, \text{ and } e'(\cdot) > 0, e''(\cdot) < 0 \text{ for all } b/T > 0 \tag{10.4}$$

The government's political costs, based on the use of discretionary power and the size of the enforcement budget, is expressed by:

$$C(\bar{\alpha}, b) \tag{10.5}$$

where $C_{\bar{\alpha}}(0, b) = 0$ and $C_{\bar{\alpha}}(\cdot) > 0$, $C_{\bar{\alpha}\bar{\alpha}}(\cdot) > 0$, $C_b(\cdot) > 0$, $C_{bb}(\cdot) > 0$, and $C_{\bar{\alpha}b}(\cdot) = 0$ for all $\bar{\alpha} > 0$.[9] The marginal cost of using discretionary power is insignificant when the scale of discretionary power in use is very small; but it, as well as the marginal cost of a higher budget, is positive and rising when discretionary power in use is not negligible. The marginal cost of discretionary power is independent of the size of the budget.

The introduction of administrative activities, in the form of imposing non-tariff barriers and enforcing nominal rates of protection, modifies the political support function to:

$$m(\alpha, b; t, \bar{\alpha}; \pi) = V[Te(b/T)] - C(\bar{\alpha}, b) \tag{10.6}$$

where $T = \pi(t + \alpha)$ measures the gap between domestic and world price if both legislative and administrative measures of protection are completely enforced. In the short run, such as at election time, the government can choose only the tariff-equivalent rate of administered protection, α, and the enforcement budget, b; but its choices are constrained by the existing trade laws' setting of nominal tariff rates and the upper limits on the use of administrative measures of protection $\bar{\alpha}$. The prevailing world price, π, is known and exogenously given. In the long run, the content of trade laws with respect to nominal tariff rates and the government's authority to take administrative action can be revised, and the government will revise them with an eye on the next election.

3 CHOOSING ADMINISTRATIVE MEASURES OF PROTECTION

When a government implements its trade laws, it chooses the tariff-equivalent rate of administered protection, α, and the enforcement budget, b, that maximize its political support, as given by equation (10.6). For the choices, marked by an asterisk, to be optimal, the Kuhn–Tucker first-order conditions are:

$$m_\alpha(\alpha^*, b^*; t, \bar{\alpha}; \pi) \quad \begin{cases} \leq 0 & \text{if } \alpha^* = 0 \\ = 0 & \text{if } 0 < \alpha^* < \bar{\alpha} \\ \geq 0 & \text{if } \alpha^* = \bar{\alpha} \end{cases} \tag{10.7}$$

$$m_b(\alpha^*, b^*; t, \bar{\alpha}; \pi) \quad \begin{cases} \leq 0 & \text{if } b^* = 0 \\ = 0 & \text{if } b^* > 0 \end{cases} \tag{10.8}$$

where $m_\alpha(\cdot) = V'[T^*e(b^*/T^*)]\pi[e(b^*/T^*) - (b^*/T^*)e'(b^*/T^*)]$, $T^* = \pi(t + \alpha^*)$, and $m_b(\cdot) = V'[T^*e(b^*/T^*)]e'(b^*/T^*) - C_b(\bar{\alpha}, b^*)$. Unless the government determines that free trade maximizes its political support, some enforcement of trade-restricting laws is required, implying that $b^* > 0$ and that (10.8) holds as an equality. Assuming this to be the case for the remainder of the analysis, it must be that $V'[T^*e(b^*/T^*)] > 0$ and that the sign of (10.7) is the same as the sign of $[e(b^*/T^*) - (b^*/T^*)e'(b^*/T^*)]$.

When the government's optimal choice of administrative measures of protection falls within the legislated range, (10.7) holds as an equality and $[e(b^*/T^*) - (b^*/T^*)e'(b^*/T^*)] = 0$; the *actual* rate of protection, $Te(b/T)/\pi$, is maximized by adjusting the nominal rate such that the gains from a higher nominal rate are just offset by losses from the importers' heightened attempts to evade the rising barriers of protection. When the upper limit on administered protection is strictly binding, *then,* $\alpha^* = \bar{\alpha} < \alpha^N$, where α^N is the value of α that would maximize the *actual* rate of protection in the absence of such limits; in this case, $m_\alpha(\cdot) > 0$ in (10.7). If the lower constraint on administrative actions becomes strictly binding, meaning that the government would like to employ administrative import subsidies to maximize political support when such subsidies are not available, then $\alpha^* = 0 > \alpha^N$, and $m_\alpha(\cdot) < 0$ in (10.7).

Administered protection enables a government to react quickly to changes in the competitiveness of one of its industries. When the government is in a position to adjust both the enforcement budget and non-tariff barriers, such that (10.7) and (10.8) hold as equalities, differentiation of these equations with respect to π yields:

$$(\partial \alpha^*/\partial \pi) = -(m_{\alpha\pi}m_{bb} - m_{b\pi}m_{\alpha b})/(m_{\alpha\alpha}m_{bb} - m_{\alpha b}m_{b\alpha}) = -(t + \alpha^*)/\pi$$
$$(10.9)$$

$$(\partial b^*/\partial \pi) = (m_{\alpha\pi}m_{b\alpha} - m_{b\pi}m_{\alpha\alpha})/(m_{\alpha\alpha}m_{bb} - m_{\alpha b}m_{b\alpha}) = 0 \qquad (10.10)$$

where $m_{\alpha\pi} = [(t + \alpha)/\pi]\,m_{\alpha\alpha}$, $m_{b\pi} = [(t + \alpha)/\pi]\,m_{\alpha b}$, $m_{\alpha\alpha} = V''\pi^2$ $[e - e'b/T]^2 + V'\pi^2 b^2 e''/T^3 < 0$, $m_{\alpha b} = m_{b\alpha} = V''\pi(e - e'b/T)e' - V'\pi b e''/T^2$ and $m_{bb} = V''e' + v'e''/T - C_{bb} < 0$. As long as the government has recourse to measures of administered protection, it relies exclusively on them; a decline in the world price – weakening the competitive position of a domestic industry – results in a higher tariff-equivalent rate of administered protection, whereby the rate of protection adjusts in such a way that $T^* = \pi(t + \alpha^*)$, the optimally-chosen wedge between nominal domestic and world price, remains unchanged. As long as the desired adjustments in non-tariff protective barriers are feasible, there is no need to change the enforcement budget. This rule of not relying on the enforcement budget in fact holds more generally: for any exogenous change affecting political support in the short run, the government will not alter its enforcement budget as long as non-tariff trade policy adjustments are possible. This can also be seen from:

$$(\partial \alpha^*/\partial t) = -1, \quad (\partial \alpha^*/\partial \bar{\alpha}) = 0, \quad (\partial b^*/\partial t) = 0, \text{ and } (\partial b^*/\partial \bar{\alpha}) = 0 \quad (10.11)$$

When there is a change in legislated tariffs, the administered tariff-equivalence rate is employed as a perfect substitute for legislated tariffs. When there is a change in the upper limit of non-tariff barriers, it affects neither the chosen rate of administered protection nor the enforcement budget so long as the optimal α^* is still available.

When non-tariff measures of protection are at their upper limit and the government, in the absence of this limit, would like to raise them further – that is, $\bar{\alpha} < \alpha^N$ – then α^* can no longer be adjusted and the government must rely entirely on the enforcement budget when reacting to world price increases. Differentiating (10.8), which holds with strict equality, with respect to π yields:

$$(\partial b^*/\partial \pi) = -(m_{b\pi}/m_{bb}) \qquad (10.12)$$

where m_{bb} is always negative, while the sign of $m_{b\pi}$, as stated after (10.10), is determined by two influences. The first influence – reflected by the first term of m_{ab}, in which $(e - e'b/T) > 0$ at $\alpha^* = \bar{\alpha}$ – has a negative effect on the budget. When the world price increases at the upper limit of administered protection – where the wedge between actual domestic and world price, $Te(b/T)$, falls short of what it would be if α could be freely adjusted to α^N and where $(e - e'b/T) > 0$ means that this wedge widens with a rise in the world price – the enforcement budget can be cut, since this price wedge has moved closer to the ideal price wedge, namely the one at α^N, and less budget is required to substitute for the inability to raise α above $\bar{\alpha}$. The second influence – measured by the second term of m_{ab} – has a positive impact on the budget. As the world price rises, the gap between nominal domestic and world price, T, widens, and the importers' incentives to evade protective barriers grow. Accordingly, the government will raise its enforcement budget in response to the increase in world price. Which of the two influences is stronger cannot be determined without further information; however, as the difference between $\bar{\alpha}$ and α^N becomes larger, it becomes more likely that the enforcement budget will shrink when the world price rises.

For later reference, we now state the following comparative statics results for the case when the upper limit on the use of administered protection is strictly binding:

$$(\partial b^*/\partial t) = (\partial b^*/\partial \bar{\alpha}) = -(m_{bt}/m_{bb}) = -[\pi/(t + \alpha^*)][m_{b\pi}/m_{bb}]$$
$$= [\pi/(t + \alpha^*)][\partial b^*/\partial \pi] \qquad (10.13)$$

$$(\partial \alpha^*/\partial \pi) = (\partial \alpha^*/\partial t) = 0; (\partial \alpha^*/\partial \bar{\alpha}) = 1 \qquad (10.14)$$

A small increase in the world price or legislated tariff has no effect on the degree of administered protection, since the latter remains at the predetermined upper limit, but a higher tariff rate does affect the enforcement budget, moving it in the same direction as in the case of a world price increase discussed above. When the government could vary the value of α in any direction, an increase in the limits on administered protection, $\bar{\alpha}$, had no effect on either the rate of protection or the budget, as was stated in (10.11). When the limits on administered protection are binding, on the other hand, both rate of protection and budget will adjust; the new upper limit becomes the chosen rate of protection and the budget adjusts in the same direction as in the case of a world price increase.

Lack of competitiveness of domestic industries is not the only serious concern for the political-support-maximizing government. Excessive protection of firms that are already highly competitive also lowers the government's political support, because the public is hurt by unnecessarily high domestic prices. This situation arises when, for given positive tariff rates, world prices have risen so high that maximum political support calls for administrative import subsidies but these subsidies are not available; that is, the optimal rate of administered protection in the absence of constraints would be $\alpha^N < 0$, but α^* is restricted to being non-negative. In this case, the government's budget response to a further rise in world price is again expressed by (10.12), but its interpretation is now different as both terms in the $m_{\alpha b}$ expression are positive. At $a^* = 0 > \alpha^N$, the wedge between domestic and world price is again below the optimum but, since $[e - e'b/T] < 0$ now, this wedge becomes smaller when the world price rises, moving it further away from the ideal wedge that prevails at $\alpha^N < 0$. Consequently, the first influence now calls for an increase in the enforcement budget to move this wedge closer to the optimum. Second, as before, the higher world price increase raises the incentive to evade trade barriers. Accordingly, if the world price rises at $\alpha^* = 0$, the government will always respond with a larger enforcement budget.

The comparative statics results for the case of $\alpha^* = 0 > \alpha^N$ can be summarized as follows:

$$(\partial b*/\partial t) = -m_{bt}/m_{bb} = -[\pi/(t + \alpha^*)][m_{b\pi}/m_{bb}] = (\partial b*/\partial \pi) > 0 \quad (10.15)$$

$$(\partial b*/\partial \bar{\alpha}) = (\partial \alpha*/\partial t) = (\partial \alpha*/\partial \pi) = (\partial \alpha*/\partial \bar{\alpha}) = 0 \qquad (10.16)$$

The government's goal is to gain the kind of political support that maximizes its chances of re-election. Unexpected changes in an industry's competitiveness relative to the rest of the world may or may not be cause for concern about re-election. Specifically, fluctuations in world price will not affect the level of political support for the government as long as the optimal degree of administered protection falls between the upper and lower limits established by law. Any world price change is countered by an equal-value, opposite-direction adjustment of the administered rate of protection. The wedge between nominal domestic and world prices, measured by T, remains unchanged. When the constraints on administrative measures become binding, on the other hand, world price changes always alter political support. A fall (increase) in world price erodes (strengthens) political support for the government if administrative protection is constrained at the upper level and strengthens (erodes) political support if protection is constrained at the lower level. This can be seen from differentiating (10.6) with respect to π and taking account of optimal responses in α^* and b^*:

$$dm/d\pi = m_\alpha(\partial\alpha^*/\partial\pi) + m_b(\partial b^*/\partial\pi) + m_\pi = \begin{cases} m_\pi < 0 & \text{if} \quad \alpha^* = 0 \\ 0 & \text{if} \quad 0 < \alpha^* < \bar{\alpha} \\ m_\pi > 0 & \text{if} \quad \alpha^* = \bar{\alpha} \end{cases}$$

$$(10.17)$$

where $m_\pi = [(t+\alpha)/\pi]m_\alpha$ and all terms are evaluated at the optimal choices, as expressed by (10.7) and (10.8). The fact that a decline in the domestic industry's competitiveness cuts into the government's political support when the upper limit of administered protection has been reached suggests that the government is interested in having this limit expanded. There is, however, a political cost to this expansion of discretionary power, as was mentioned earlier. Consequently, in deciding what the limits on discretionary power should be – a decision that has to be made when trade laws are written – the government has to weigh the benefits from greater policy flexibility against the costs of alienating the political sensitivities of its people.

4 THE MAKING OF TRADE LAWS

A country's trade laws set the nominal tariff rates and define the limits of administered protection. A government evaluates these laws at all times, but revises them only when they no longer provide a basis for strong and sustained political support. At the time that trade laws are written or revised, a government can only guess what an industry's competitive position will be in the future. Its beliefs about the world price at a future election date are described by the distribution $F(\pi, \sigma)$ on the closed interval $[\underline{\pi}, \bar{\pi}]$, where σ is a parameter that determines the shape of the distribution.

The government's goal, in writing or revising its trade laws, is to legislate a nominal tariff rate, t, and an upper limit on the tariff-equivalent rate of non-tariff measures, $\bar{\alpha} \geq 0$, that maximize expected political support; that is:

$$\max_{t,\bar{\alpha}} \int_{\underline{\pi}}^{\bar{\pi}} \mu(t, \bar{\alpha}; \pi) dF(\pi, \sigma) \tag{10.18}$$

where $\mu(\cdot) = m[\alpha^*(t, \bar{\alpha}, \pi), b^*(t, \bar{\alpha}, \pi), t, \bar{\alpha}; \pi]$ becomes the political support function when the government's ability to adjust α and b optimally is taken into account. The first-order conditions for maximizing expected political support require that:

$$\int_{\underline{\pi}}^{\bar{\pi}} [m_\alpha(\partial\alpha^*/\partial t) + m_b(\partial b^*/\partial t) + m_t] dF(\pi, \sigma) = 0 \tag{10.19}$$

$$\int_{\underline{\pi}}^{\bar{\pi}} [m_\alpha(\partial\alpha^*/\partial\bar{\alpha}) + m_b(\partial b^*/\partial\bar{\alpha}) + m_{\bar{\alpha}}] dF(\pi, \sigma) \leq 0 \tag{10.20}$$

where m_α and m_b have been defined in (10.7) and (10.8), $m_t = m_\alpha$, $m_{\bar{\alpha}} = -C_{\bar{\alpha}}$, and (10.20) holds as a strict equality for $\bar{\alpha} > 0$. We also note that the effects of the legislative choices of t and $\bar{\alpha}$ on the optimal administrative choices of α^* and b^* have been described by (10.11), (10.14) and (10.16).

In interpreting (10.19) and (10.20), the terms inside the brackets take on different values depending on α^* falling within the legislated range of administrative policy options or being at either the upper or the lower limit of these options. If α^* falls strictly within these limits, then $m_\alpha = 0$; but if $\alpha^* = 0$ or $\alpha^* = \bar{\alpha}$, and the constraints are strictly binding, then $m_\alpha < 0$ or $m_\alpha > 0$. Whether these constraints are binding depends, in turn, on the world price, π, for given values of tariffs and upper limits on α, as one can see from equation (10.9). In particular, there exists a world price π^0 that, for given values of t and $\bar{\alpha}$, is sufficiently low that $\alpha^* = \alpha^N = \bar{\alpha}$; and there exists a world price π' that is sufficiently high that $\alpha^* = \alpha^N = 0$. Accordingly, the distribution of world prices, as perceived by the government at the time of writing the trade laws, can be segmented into three ranges: a low price range, $\underline{\pi} \leq \pi < \pi^0$, for which the upper limit on the use of administrative measures is strictly binding; a middle price range, $\pi^0 < \pi < \pi'$, for which there are no constraints on administrative actions; and a high price range, $\pi' < \pi \leq \bar{\pi}$, for which the lower constraint on administrative measures is binding. The value of π^0 declines with both t and $\bar{\alpha}$, whereas π' decreases with t but is independent of $\bar{\alpha}$.

Segmenting world prices into the ranges discussed above, we rewrite (10.19) and (10.20) as:

$$\int_{\underline{\pi}}^{\pi^0(t,\bar{\alpha})} m_t(\cdot) dF(\pi, \sigma) = -\int_{\pi'(t,\bar{\alpha})}^{\bar{\pi}} m_t(\cdot) dF(\pi, \sigma) \qquad (10.21)$$

$$\int_{\underline{\pi}}^{\pi^0(t,\bar{\alpha})} m_\alpha(\cdot) dF(\pi, \sigma) \leq C_{\bar{\alpha}}(\cdot) \qquad (10.22)$$

with strict equality of (10.22) for $\bar{\alpha} > 0$, and where $m_t > 0$ for $\pi < \pi^0; m_t < 0$ for $\pi > \pi'; m_\alpha = m_t$; and $C(\cdot)$ is independent of the world price. The left-hand side of (10.21) expresses the gain in expected political support from a legislated tariff increase if future world prices are so low that available administrative measures have reached their upper limit; the higher the tariff, the closer the government can come to the rate of protection that would be optimal in the absence of any constraints. The right-hand side of (10.21), on the other hand, measures the additional costs of such a tariff increase; they come into play if future world prices turn out to be so high that the government would like to use administrative subsidies, but these are not available. The legislated tariff is raised to a level such that the gain from alleviating possible underprotection is exactly equal to the loss from aggravating possible overprotection. The left-hand side of (10.22) also refers to a gain in expected political support as the damage from underprotection is reduced; but this time the gain is the result of expanding the upper limit on administrative measures rather than raising the tariff rate. When the government decides how to set this legislated upper limit, it weighs this gain in political support in case of future underprotection against the increase in political cost from expanding its discretionary power. The more sensitive the public is to a government that enacts specific trade policy measures without receiving its full consent, the lower the upper limit on the tariff-equivalent rate of administered protection.

When a government writes its trade laws, it complements the setting of nominal tariff rates with the granting of authority to employ administrative measures of protection as long as there is some price uncertainty. While the choice of nominal tariff rates is not restricted, the upper limit on the tariff-equivalent rate of administered protection must be non-negative. One can show that the optimal choice of this upper limit is not merely non-negative; it must be positive. To see this, consider what would happen if $\bar{\alpha}^*$ were zero; then $\pi^0 = \pi'$ and for any choice of t^* that satisfies (10.21), the left-hand side must be positive while there is any price uncertainty. This implies that the left-hand side of (10.22), evaluated at a zero upper limit on non-tariff barriers, must also be positive; since $C_{\bar{\alpha}}(0,b) = 0$, (10.22) cannot be satisfied at $\bar{\alpha} = 0$, and $\bar{\alpha}^*$ must be positive.

5   REVISIONS OF TRADE LAWS

A country's trade laws are revised quite infrequently. Once passed, they remain in force as long as there is no significant, permanent shift in the competitive strength of the country's main industries. Temporary periods of declining competitiveness of domestic industries are countered through various measures of administered protection. A revision of trade laws is called for when administered protection becomes ineffective; that is, when the industry's competitiveness has changed to such an extent that non-tariff measures of protection are repeatedly employed at their limits and are expected to remain employed at these limits in future periods. The present section examines how the content of trade laws, with respect to both nominal tariff rates and limits on administered protection, are adjusted by a political-support maximizing government if the latter perceives a fundamental change in the competitiveness of one of the country's industries.

A change in the government's beliefs about an industry's competitiveness is described by a change in the parameter value σ of the world price distribution function $F(\pi, \sigma)$. Differentiating (10.19) and (10.20) with respect to σ yields:[10]

$$\frac{\partial t^*}{\partial \sigma} = \frac{A}{D} < 0 \qquad (10.23)$$

$$\frac{\partial \bar{\alpha}}{\partial \sigma} = \frac{B}{D} \qquad (10.24)$$

where

$$A = \left(\int_{\underline{\pi}}^{\pi^0} \theta(\pi) dF(\pi, \sigma) \right) \left(\int_{\pi'}^{\bar{\pi}} \gamma(\pi) F_\sigma(\pi, \sigma) d\pi \right) - C_{\bar{\alpha}\bar{\alpha}} \left(\int_{\underline{\pi}}^{\pi^0} \gamma(\pi) F_\sigma(\pi, \sigma) d\pi + \int_{\pi'}^{\bar{\pi}} \gamma(\pi) F_\sigma(\pi, \sigma) d\pi \right)$$

$$B = -\left(\int_{\underline{\pi}}^{\pi^0} \theta(\pi) dF(\pi, \sigma) \right) \left(\int_{\pi'}^{\bar{\pi}} \gamma(\pi) F_\sigma(\pi, \sigma) d\pi \right) + \left(\int_{\underline{\pi}}^{\bar{\pi}} \theta(\pi) dF(\pi, \sigma) \right) \left(\int_{\underline{\pi}}^{\pi^0} \gamma(\pi) F_\sigma(\pi, \sigma) d\pi \right)$$

$$D = \left(\int_{\underline{\pi}}^{\pi^0} \theta(\pi) dF(\pi, \sigma) \right) \left(\int_{\pi'}^{\bar{\pi}} \theta(\pi) dF(\pi, \sigma) \right) - C_{\bar{\alpha}\bar{\alpha}} \left(\int_{\underline{\pi}}^{\pi^0} \theta(\pi) dF(\pi, \sigma) + \int_{\pi'}^{\bar{\pi}} \theta(\pi) dF(\pi, \sigma) \right)$$

where $\quad \theta(\pi) = m_{\alpha\alpha} - (m_{\alpha b})^2 m_{bb} = -(C_{bb} m_{\alpha\alpha} - \pi^2 V' V''(e)^2 e^{\alpha}/T]/m_{bb} < 0,$ $\gamma(\pi) = [m_\alpha + (t + \alpha)\theta]/\pi$, and it is assumed that the new distribution dominates the old distribution in a first-order stochastic sense, such that $F_\sigma(\pi, \sigma) \leq 0$ with strict inequality holding over some interval of π. We also assume that the government's coefficient of relative risk aversion with respect to the protective measure $(t + \alpha)$, expressed by $-(t + \alpha)\mu_{tt}/\mu_t$, is less than (plus) one, where $\mu(.)$ was defined in equation (10.18). Since $\mu_{tt} < 0$ for all world prices, $\mu_t < 0$ for $\pi \in (\pi^1, \bar{\pi})$ and $\mu_t > 0$ for $\pi \in [\underline{\pi}, \pi^0)$, the coefficient of relative risk aversion is always negative within the range of high world prices and positive within the range of low world prices. The restriction that its value is less than plus one implies that $\gamma(\pi) < 0$ for all relevant world prices. Finally, we note that the denominator of both equations is always positive.

When the government believes that its industry will be more competitive in the future than it has been so far, it adjusts both the legislated nominal tariff rate and the limit on using non-tariff trade barriers. Its change in beliefs is expressed by a first-order stochastic dominance of the new world-price distribution; that is, the government considers the probability that the actual price at election time will be equal to or lower than a given value, to have become smaller for at least some prices and not larger for all other prices. The government legislates a lower tariff rate, as the need for protection has declined. This is expressed by (10.23).

The expectation of a more competitive industry also affects the government's legislation of limits on administered protection; but, as (10.24) reveals, we need some additional information about the range of world prices over which the probability declines that the actual price will be lower than a given value. Specifically, we need information about the range of world prices for which $F_\sigma(\pi, \sigma) < 0$. One possible scenario is that $F_\sigma(\pi, \sigma) < 0$ for the range of low world prices $\underline{\pi} \leq \pi < \pi^0$, while $F_\sigma(\pi, \sigma) = 0$ for the range of high world prices $\pi' < \pi \leq \bar{\pi}$; (what happens to the distribution of world prices over the intermediate price range, for which administrative measures are fully effective in maximizing political support, is irrelevant in this context). Under this scenario, the likelihood is reduced that the domestic industry will be threatened by stiff foreign competition in the range of prices where it hurts. The government's response will be to diminish its reliance on discretionary power by lowering the upper limits on non-tariff trade barriers. Combined with cuts in the nominal tariff rate, expressed by (10.23), the revision of trade laws takes the form of a general liberalization of trade.

A second scenario for a change in the distribution of world prices is that $F_\sigma(\pi, \sigma) = 0$ for the range of low world prices but $F_\sigma(\pi, \sigma) < 0$ for the range of high world prices. There is a belief that world prices, on average, will rise, and that this rise is the result of higher prices becoming more likely than before. In this case, (10.23) and (10.24) reveal that the government still lowers nominal tariffs while at the same time raising the upper limits on the use of administered protection. Legislated tariff rates decline without regard to the price range in which world price increases are expected to occur. The tariff decline, however, reduces the government's ability to protect its domestic industry in times of low world prices. Since, under this second scenario, low world prices are just as likely as before to occur, the government substitutes greater discretionary power in the use of administered protection for the decline in legislated protection.

When the government's beliefs about the future competitiveness of an industry change, its expectations about future political support will also change. The range within which world prices are expected to change is again critical, as can be seen by differentiating the objective function of (10.18) with respect to σ. When the belief is that world prices will rise in the low range, there is a gain in expected political support; when the belief is that prices will rise in the high range, there is an erosion of expected political support. In the first case, there is a decline in the threat to a domestic industry accompanied by a decline in the use of discretionary power; in the second, there is no change in the threat to a domestic industry, but the government must bear the extra political costs of enlarging its discretionary power. Consequently, governments running for re-election feel most secure when they perceive a decline in low-price competition from world markets.

6 CONCLUSION

The answer to the first of the three questions posed above – namely, how a political-support maximizing government adjusts its trade policy when there is a temporary decline in the competitiveness of one of its industries – depends critically on whether the government faces binding restrictions on the use of non-tariff measures of protection. When these restrictions are not binding, temporary declines in world prices are countered by raising non-tariff barriers, without any changes in the enforcement budget. When the upper limit on non-tariff measures of protection is binding, however, the enforcement budget becomes an imperfect substitute for the primary instrument of protection; it may be necessary to expand the budget to raise the degree of actual protection. But a temporary world price change does not result in a revision of trade laws.

Our second question inquired why governments employ both tariff and non-tariff measures of protection and why limits are imposed on the latter. Uncertainty about future world prices, combined with the inability to change legislation from day to day, is shown to be the reason for governments to employ both tariffs and administrative measures of protection. Furthermore, limits on administrative measures are imposed because the benefits from increased reliance on administrative measures in case of low future world prices must be weighed against the increased political costs when more discretionary power is appropriated. The less sensitive a country's citizenry is to the expansion of discretionary power, the more its government depends on administrative measures of protection.

The third question concerned the need for revising trade laws. Governments revise laws when they perceive a fundamental shift in the competitiveness of one of their industries. The belief that low world prices are going to be permanent, and that the industry's competitiveness is severely threatened, results in higher tariff rates, as well as expanded limits on administrative action. Consequently, a permanent, severe decline in competitiveness is met by legislation of a more protectionist trade policy, whereas a temporary, or less permanent but modest, decline in competitiveness is met by more protectionist administrative action.

This model has assumed that the legislating government is free to choose tariff rates and limits on measures of administrative protection. International agreements might impose limits on tariff rates through tariff bindings and on the availability of certain specific non-tariff measures of protection. This model suggests that governments may accept lower tariff rates, and possibly even the removal of some non-tariff barriers, if they believe that they have sufficient recourse to other non-tariff barriers to maintain the desired level of political support. An overall liberalization of trade through negotiations is possible, however, when the negotiated outcome itself convinces governments that, by imposing restrictions on what other trading partners can do, their own industries' competitiveness is less likely to be threatened.

Notes

1. Part of this research was supported by a grant from the C. P. Taft Memorial Fund of the University of Cincinnati. I also enjoyed the hospitality of the Center for Economic Studies at the University of Munich in preparing the original conference draft.

2. Numerous illustrations of hidden protective devices in Pacific Rim countries have been pointed out by the United States Trade Representative (1995). For example, Korea has been accused of applying 'regulations supposedly intended to protect health and safety [that] often deviate substantially from international practices in both substance and method' and Korea's 'changes to regulations are rarely notified in a timely manner to importers or exporters' (p. 213). Malaysia's sales tax on fruits and other agricultural products is an example of a protective device, since the tax is fully collected on imports but domestic production conditions make it virtually impossible to collect the tax from domestic producers (p. 224).

3. Frey's (1984, p. 34) contention that 'Trade restrictions are seldom voted on directly..., the commonly used instrument for international protection is the administrative regulation of imports' is shared by others, such as Leidy (1994, p. 264), who remarks that 'the directive legislative path to protection has become a measure of last resort' while 'administrative means of protection...have become substantially more accessible'.

4. Baldwin and Moore (1991, p. 264) are quite explicit on this relationship when they state that 'Protection-seeking industries can complain to their representatives and senators, who will subsequently communicate their constituents' concerns to administrators'. The view that government agencies, without direct monitoring by Congress, produce policies desired by Congress is fully developed in Weingast (1984).

5. Governments employ a wide variety of instruments to protect industries, as can be discerned from a reading of United States Trade Representative (1995). Somewhat unusual illustrations from Pacific Rim countries are the following: in the past, Australia has been accused not only of employing restrictive standards requirements and design rules but also of limiting imports through state-specific packaging regulations (p. 15). China is said to keep imports out through a myriad of licensing requirements, where 'the ministry that oversees the manufacture of the

same product is involved in the approval process' (p. 51). Korea subjects imported fruit to lengthy tests and treatment, frequently leading to decay of the product; it also employs government-mandated shelf-life dates for food products rather than manufacturer's use-by or sell-by dates as in almost all other countries (p. 213). Thailand has been accused of having arbitrary customs valuation procedures, in which 'The Thai Customs Department may use as a check price the highest previously-invoiced price of a product imported from any given country' (p. 303).

6. Such tariff-equivalent measures are quite frequently employed in empirical analysis as well. For example, in a study of Japanese trade protection, Sazanami *et al.* (1995, pp. 6–7) estimate that Japan's implied tariff barrier rate is 272.5 per cent for food and beverages, 91.5 per cent for textiles and light industry products, 126.9 per cent for chemical products, and 660 per cent for cosmetics.

7. See Milgrom and Roberts (1992, p. 219) for an insightful discussion of the choice of performance measures.

8. From now on, all variables with an asterisk denote political-support-maximizing choices.

9. Here and later in the text, subscripts of functions denote derivatives with respect to the indicated argument.

10. The derivations resulting in the stated equations are available on request.

References

Baldwin, R. E. and M. O. Moore (1991) 'Political Aspects of the Administration of the Trade Remedy Laws', in R. Boltuck and R. E. Litan (eds), *Down in the Dumps* (Washington, DC: The Brookings Institution).

Buchanan, J. M. and G. Tullock (1962) *The Calculus of Consent* (Ann Arbor, Mich: University of Michigan Press).

Frey, B. S. (1984) *International Political Economics* (Oxford: Basil Blackwell).

Grossman, G. M. and E. Helpman (1994) 'Protection for Sale', *American Economic Review*, vol. 84, no. 4, pp. 833–50.

Hillman, A. L. (1982) 'Declining Industries and Political-Support Protectionist Motives', *American Economic Review*, vol. 72, no. 5, pp. 1180–7.

Hillman, A. L. (1989) *The Political Economy of Protection* (Chur: Harwood Academic Publishers).

Leidy, M. P. (1994) 'Quid Pro Quo Restraints and Spurious Injury: Subsidies and the Prospect of CVDs', in A. V. Deardorff and R. M. Stern (eds), *Analytical and Negotiating Issues in the Global Trading System* (Ann Arbor, Mich.: University of Michigan Press).

Milgrom, P. and J. Roberts (1992) *Economics, Organization and Management* (Englewood Cliffs, NJ: Prentice Hall).

Peltzman, S. (1976) 'Toward a More General Theory of Regulation', *Journal of Law and Economics*, vol. 19, no. 2, pp. 211–40.

Sazanami, Y., S. Urata and H. Kawai (1995) *Measuring the Costs of Protection in Japan* (Washington, DC: Institute for International Economics).

Stigler, G. J. (1971) 'The Theory of Economic Regulation', *Bell Journal of Economics and Management Science*, vol. 2, no. 1, pp. 3–21.

United States Trade Representative (1995) *1995 National Trade Estimate Report on Foreign Trade Barriers* (Washington, DC: US Government Printing Office).

Weingast, B. R. (1984) 'The Congressional-Bureaucratic System: A Principal Agent Perspective (with Applications to the SEC)', *Public Choice*, vol. 44, no. 1, pp. 147–91.

Comment

Elhanan Helpman
TEL AVIV UNIVERSITY

Administrative protection has grown in importance in recent years, following decades during which it has been replaced gradually by tariffs. Mayer's paper is not concerned directly with explaining this shift, but it does provide, indirectly, some possible explanations, by examining the political economy considerations that determine the extent to which a government chooses to engage in legislative as opposed to administrative protection.

In Mayer's view, legislative protection is very costly to the executive because it requires a legislative process that is both lengthy and hard to enact. Administrative protection, on the other hand, can be changed rapidly, using the degree of discretion provided by the legal framework. For these reasons legislative protection is changed infrequently, while administrative protection is adjusted frequently to changing circumstances.

I like these distinctions between the two forms of protection. They suggest a view of policy formation as a two-stage process. The first stage consists of institutional design, whereby a legislative process prepares the legal framework for protectionist policies. At this stage, tariffs are set and so are the boundaries of discretionary policy changes via administrative protection. These measures build on expectations about possible future values of the relevant variables, such as world prices; and as a result, the choice of measures is made in the face of substantial uncertainty about the circumstances in which they will apply. In the second stage, which may consist of a lengthy time period, the government adjusts the rate of protection to changing circumstances, as permitted by the prevailing legal framework. In principle, the two stages can alternate indefinitely, although the chapter does not engage in an analysis of such dynamics. This framework is appealing for this sort of analysis.

To deal with these issues, Mayer adopts a political support function approach to the process of policy formation. In the analysis of the second stage (that is, the choice of administrative protection), the reduced form of the political support function depends on the overall level of *nominal* protection (which results from the existing level of legislative protection and the chosen level of administrative protection), on the range of permissible discretion, and on the size of an enforcement budget. The level of legislated tariffs and the enforcement budget are taken as given at this point in time; they were determined earlier by the legislative process. The enforcement budget is brought in to bridge the distinction between the *nominal* rate of protection and the *actual* rate. The actual rate of protection depends on the nominal rate of protection and the enforcement budget; the larger the enforcement budget, the closer the actual rate of protection to the nominal rate, with the former being smaller than the latter.

In this setup, the political support function is modified from the usual formulation to net out the costs of administrative activities, which are a rising function of the enforcement budget and the degree of allowable discretionary power. It is not clear to me why these costs should depend on the degree of discretionary power allowed by the institutional framework. One may think that it is at least as plausible that these costs depend on the *exercised* degree of discretion. It would be interesting to have a better discussion of these costs and perhaps derive them from a more detailed theoretical framework. My feeling is that this sort of elaboration is important, particularly in view of the fact that no explicit costs are attached to the legislative process. But if the legislative process is costless, while the administrative process is not, why not rely on the legislative process only? The reason is, of course, that it is implicitly assumed that the legislative process is not only *not* costless, but rather that it is very costly relative to the administrative process. For these reasons, a clearer specification of the nature of these costs is most desirable. For example, an extension of the analysis to a dynamic framework cannot be performed without it, and it will be an important ingredient in any attempt to understand the frequency with which laws are changed in order to accommodate shifts in circumstances.

Despite these remarks, the analysis of the administrative stage yields interesting insights, which make sense in the postulated framework. The analysis of the legislative stage, which incorporates the administrative stage in a natural way, is less revealing; however, it is in a sense more speculative because the costs of this process are not stated explicitly.

My feeling is that the specification of the model may overstate the importance of the discretionary policy option, because there are important costs of discretion that were not incorporated into the model. Take, for example, the activities of special interest groups. With policy discretion in place, such groups will actively seek protection, taking advantage of changing circumstances. These pressures for short-term variations in discretionary action can be avoided if the institutional framework does not leave room for much discretion. There exist many examples of trade liberalization programmes that were not carved in stone being hampered by special interest groups, and either postponed or modified to their advantage. In such circumstances, it is preferable to leave little room for discretion. On the other hand, special interest groups are also active at the legislative stage. It may, therefore, be difficult to design a system immune to political pressure that will pass the legislative stage. Nevertheless, it may well be the case that the relative costs of a legislative process as compared to an administrative process are higher for special interests just as for the policy-maker. In this event it is not clear how their influence of special interests will change the balance between administrative and legislative protection.

My last point, as illustrated by the role of special interest groups, is that the choice of administrative versus legislative measures can be viewed as a trade-off between flexibility and credibility. In order to deal adequately with this tradeoff it is necessary to introduce some strategic considerations into this framework. This avenue carries much potential for future explorations.

Part III
APEC

11 The History and Structure of APEC[1]

1 INTRODUCTION

Steadily expanding economic activity in the Asia-Pacific region over the past 20 years or so has led to increasing economic interdependence. This, in turn, generated a need for a forum to bring decision-makers at government level together. In January 1989, the then Australian Prime Minister, Mr Bob Hawke, proposed in a speech in Seoul, Korea, a meeting of senior ministers from economies in the region with high levels of common trade to establish a framework for regional economic co-operation. The process came to be known as Asia Pacific Economic Co-operation (APEC).

The first ministerial-level meeting was held in Canberra in November 1989. Since then, ministerial meetings have been held in Singapore (November 1990), Seoul (November 1991), Bangkok (November 1992), Seattle (November 1993), Jakarta (November 1994), Osaka (November 1995), the Philippines (December 1996). The ninth meeting is to be held in Canada in 1997.

The first informal meeting of economic leaders was held at Blake Island, USA in November 1993, immediately following the ministerial meeting. This was followed by leaders' meetings in Bogor, Indonesia in November 1994, and in Osaka in November 1995.

APEC comprises Australia, Brunei, Canada, Chile, China, Hong Kong, Indonesia, Japan, Korea, Malaysia, Mexico, New Zealand, Papua New Guinea, the Philippines, Singapore, Chinese Taipei, Thailand and the USA. Table 11.1 presents summary statistics for these nations.

2 HISTORY AND RATIONALE[2]

The APEC proposal was the natural response to the prevailing circumstances of the time: the Canada–USA free trade agreement (FTA) had just been concluded successfully, the European Community was fast moving towards the Single Market initiative and, at the December 1988 GATT ministerial 'mid-term review' in Montreal, prospects for an agreement on the Uruguay Round looked dim.[3] There was a need for a forum that could bring Asia-Pacific economies together to mobilize support for multilateral liberalization, from which they had benefited so much in the past, and to respond to growing regionalism in Europe and North America.

269

Table 11.1   APEC member statistics, 1994

APEC member	Population (millions)	GDP (US$ billions)	Percentage of exports to APEC[a]
Australia	17.8	323.8	75.1
Brunei[a]	0.3	4.0	78.5
Canada	29.2	548.4	90.5
Chile	13.9	52.2	48.9
China	1200.0	611.4	72.7
Hong Kong	6.1	132.8	74.6
Indonesia	193.1	158.0	76.8
Japan	125.0	4651.1	71.3
Korea	44.5	379.6	68.2
Malaysia	19.5	70.6	78.0
Mexico	91.8	373.6	88.1
New Zealand	3.5	50.9	69.0
Papua New Guinea	4.0	5.3	86.6
Philippines	67.0	63.9	76.3
Singapore	2.9	68.9	74.4
Thailand	59.6	138.2	67.5
USA	261.0	6738.4	60.2
Chinese Taipei	21.1	241.2	76.7

Notes:
[a] 1993 data. Financial measure of exports reflects trade in merchandise goods. Figures are rounded to first decimal place. GDP is in current prices.

Sources: Australian Department of Foreign Affairs and Trade (1995), based upon *IMF Direction of Trade Statistics*, 1994 and *International Financial Statistics*, June 1995; UN, *Monthly Bulletin of Statistics*, July 1995.
The Central Bank of China (Taiwan) *Financial Statistics*, June 1995;
The Economist Intelligence Unit, various publications.

Not surprisingly, two main objectives of APEC in Prime Minister Hawke's January 1989 proposal, put forward after a meeting with President Roh Tae-Woo of Korea but without consultation with the USA, were to bring the Uruguay Round to a successful conclusion and to promote liberalization of trade and investment policies at the regional level. A third objective, with a distinct Asian flavour, was to promote projects of common economic interest. The Bush Administration in the USA, which took office in January 1989, understood the importance of APEC for North America and quickly moved to ensure a seat for the USA and its FTA partner, Canada, at APEC's first ministerial meeting. This meeting, held in Canberra in November 1989, was attended by twelve member countries: five developed countries including the USA, Japan, Canada, Australia and New Zealand; six members of the Association of South-East Asian Nations (ASEAN): namely, Brunei, Indonesia, Malaysia, the Philippines, Singapore and Thailand; and Korea.[4] In

1991, Korea negotiated the inclusion of China, Hong Kong and Taiwan, while in 1993–4, Mexico, Chile and Papua New Guinea were admitted. Since the Canberra meeting, APEC ministerial meetings have been held annually.

Because of its diverse membership, APEC proceeded cautiously, aiming to develop closer ties through consultation, co-operation and consensus rather than formal negotiations. Indeed, it was not until its fourth meeting that APEC decided to establish a formal secretariat. At that same meeting, it also decided to create an Eminent Persons Group (EPG) 'to develop a vision of trade in the Asia Pacific region'.[5] The USA, which inherited the chairmanship of APEC from Thailand at this point, appointed C. Fred Bergsten of the Institute for International Economics, Washington, DC as the chairman of the EPG. The EPG produced two reports (APEC 1993 and 1994) attempting to articulate a vision for APEC. Their term having expired in 1995, they were recently allowed to disband. As Barfield (1996) points out correctly, 'it was the Clinton administration that moved to change the focus of APEC from an informal consultative mechanism to a more formal organization promoting trade liberalization – and ultimately preferential trade arrangements – within the Pacific region'. At the Seattle meeting in November 1993, US President Bill Clinton called for the creation of a Committee on Trade and Investment that would 'create a coherent APEC perspective and voice on global trade and investment issues'. The present structure of APEC, depicting the links between the leaders' meetings, the EPG, and the other groups that have been established, is presented in Figure 11.1.

Perhaps the most significant of the APEC ministerial meetings was the one held in Bogor, Indonesia, in November 1994. At that meeting, backed by US support, President Suharto provided the lead for an agreement to establish free trade by the year 2010 in the developed member countries, and by 2020 in the developing member countries. Though the meaning of 'free trade' in this context has remained unclear and no strategy for achieving the goal has been articulated, the agreement was undoubtedly a departure from APEC's past practice of limiting itself to a low-key, consultative approach.

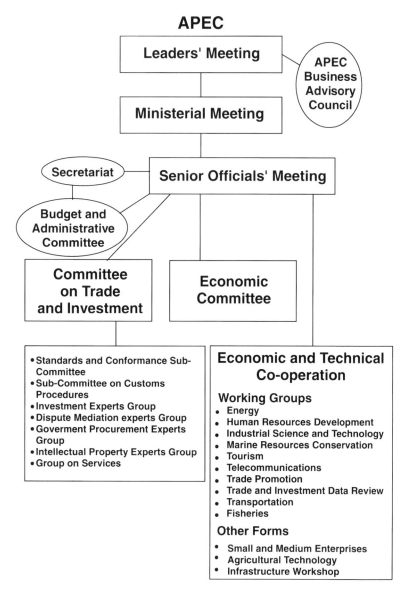

Figure 11.1   Structure of APEC
Source: Australian Department of Foreign Affairs and Trade.

Notes

1. This chapter has been compiled by the editors of the conference volume. It reproduces parts of an Australian Department of Foreign Affairs and Trade (DFAT) publication, *Asia Pacific Economic Cooperation Briefing Notes* (September 1995), along with a slightly edited revision of the Annex to Arvind Panagariya's conference paper on APEC, which appears as the second section of the chapter.
2. In writing this historical note, Panagariya acknowledges heavy reliance on Corbet (1995), who, having been responsible for organizing some key conferences leading to the founding of APEC, provides an excellent discussion of its evolution.
3. At that time, the Congressional authority to the US president to negotiate the round was due to expire in December 1990. The authority was subsequently renewed and the expiration date extended to December 1993.
4. The origins of APEC lay in the Gotemba Group which met once or twice a year between 1984 and 1989; however, this group did not include the USA or Canada. Japan pushed for the entry of these countries, while Indonesia and Malaysia resisted it. For details, see Corbet (1995), who played an important role in the creation of the Gotemba Group.
5. APEC (1993) p. 70.

References

APEC (1993) *A Vision for APEC*, Report of the Eminent Persons Group to APEC Ministers (Singapore: Asia Pacific Co-operation).

APEC (1994) *Achieving the APEC Vision*, Second Report of the Eminent Persons Group to APEC Ministers (Singapore: Asia Pacific Co-operation).

Barfield, C. E. (1996), 'Regionalism and U.S. Trade Policy', in J. Bhagwati and A. Panagariya, (eds), *The Economics of Preferential Trade Agreements* (Washington, DC: AEI Press).

Corbet, H. (1995) 'Progress of the APEC Process up to the Bogor Declaration', Paper presented at the Conference on Economic Co-operation in the Asia-Pacific Region organized by the Sigur Center for East Asian Studies, Washington, DC, June 22–23.

Australian Department of Foreign Affairs and Trade (1995) *Asia Pacific Economic Cooperation: Briefing Notes*, APEC Branch, Canberra, September.

12 APEC Leadership in Liberalization: An Untested Experiment

Mari Pangestu

CENTRE FOR STRATEGIC AND INTERNATIONAL STUDIES, JAKARTA

1 INTRODUCTION

The year 1996 is an important year in trade policy history as it marks the beginnings of two key institutions which will lead us on the road towards an open and rules-based trading system. In November 1996, cynics and optimists alike await the announcement of the action plans for trade liberalization and facilitation by economies from the Asia Pacific Economic Co-operation (APEC) group. The action plans will provide the first glimpse of the track towards the long-term goals set out by APEC's Bogor Declaration in 1994: to achieve free and open trade and investment in the region no later than 2010 for industrialized economies, and 2020 for developing economies. Meanwhile, at the end of the year, ministers from members of the World Trade Organization (WTO) meet for the first time since it was set up in early 1995. The agenda calls for evaluation of the implementation of Uruguay Round commitments, and discussion of unfinished business such as negotiation on services.

The two institutional developments are not unrelated, since APEC is not a free trade area, but a unique experiment in 'open regionalism', intended to contribute to strengthening the global trading system. We are at the beginning of the APEC process and announcements of the members' action plans in November, to be followed by the WTO Ministerial meeting, provide a *real* opportunity to show APEC's collective leadership. The main question now appears to be whether and how we expect the APEC experiment of voluntary liberalization based on peer pressure and confidence building to work? Will the process result in significant liberalization? Will there be bold moves in the breadth, speed and depth of liberalization and facilitation beyond the WTO commitments? How will 'peer pressure' work? The important point is that APEC 'cannot fail because for the foreseeable future there is no alternative to this approach' (Soesastro, 1996). The aim of this chapter is to address such questions, in the context of an analysis of the APEC process and progress to date.

2 FRAMEWORK FOR APEC LIBERALIZATION

It is important at the outset to have an understanding of the APEC process as it has evolved in the last few years, and the nine principles and action plan framework agreed upon in Osaka.

APEC: Principles of Liberalization

From the outset, APEC was not intended to become a negotiating body. The process of liberalization was stressed to be voluntary and based on concerted unilateral actions to be undertaken by each country in accordance with its own plans and priorities, and taking into account the different levels of development. Agreement is reached through a consultative process and is based on consensus. The latter principle is adopted from ASEAN and has been criticized as meaning that progress in APEC is as fast as the slowest member.

In the beginning, this led to a distinction being drawn between the Asian consensus approach and the Western negotiation and legal commitment approach. Evidence of the progress achieved in APEC to date has temporarily quieted discussion of this issue. In reality, even though APEC agreements are not binding and have no legal force, much has been achieved through a process of consultations and consensus building that has been pushed along by the political will of the leaders. It is also true that both sides have learnt about each other's approach to arriving at a decision. The developed economies have learnt that this evolutionary process has its merits and that the only way to achieve progress in APEC is by getting everyone on board. The developing and Asian economies have also appreciated the need to have principles, targets and agreements (albeit non-binding) underlying their liberalization.

One important component of the debate leading up to Osaka was whether liberalization under APEC should be undertaken on an unconditional MFN basis or otherwise. Initially, in fact, there were proponents for creating APEC as a free-trade area, in which case liberalization offers would be given only to members and reciprocal concessions would be required even from members. This idea was not acceptable to most APEC members and the focus of discussion has shifted to the understanding and realization of the concept of 'open regionalism'. The concept means different things to different people, but in essence it is taken to mean liberalization undertaken by a member in the region which does not disadvantage non-members.

The Osaka meeting resulted in nine general principles which will underlie liberalization and facilitation (see Box 12.1). APEC has achieved remarkable progress in arriving at these principles to realize the Bogor goals. Even though the principles are often thought to be inconsistent and weak, because

Box 12.1   Nine principles of APEC liberalization and facilitation

1. Comprehensiveness
The APEC liberalization and facilitation process will be comprehensive, addressing all impediments to achieving the long-term goal of free and open trade and investment.

2. WTO-consistency
The liberalization and facilitation measures undertaken in the context of the APEC Action Agenda will be WTO-consistent.

3. Comparability
APEC economies will endeavour to ensure the overall comparability of their trade and investment liberalization and facilitation, taking into account the general level of liberalization and facilitation already achieved by each APEC economy.

4. Non-discrimination
APEC economies will apply, or endeavour to apply, the principle of non-discrimination between and among them in the process of liberalization and facilitation of trade and investment. The outcome of trade and investment liberalization in the Asia-Pacific region will be the actual reduction of barriers, not only among APEC economies but also between APEC economies and non-APEC economies.

5. Transparency
Each APEC economy will ensure transparency of its respective laws, regulations and administrative procedures which affect the flow of goods, services and capital among APEC economies in order to create and maintain an open and predictable trade and investment environment in the Asia-Pacific region.

6. Standstill
Each APEC economy will endeavour to refrain from using measures that would have the effect of increasing levels of protection, thereby ensuring a steady and progressive trade and investment liberalization and facilitation process.

7. Simultaneous start, continuous process and differentiated time tables
APEC economies will begin simultaneously and without delay the process of liberalization, facilitation and co-operation with each member economy contributing continuously and significantly to achieve the long-term goal of free and open trade and investment.

8. Flexibility
Considering the different levels of economic development among the APEC economies and the diverse circumstances in each economy, flexibility will be available in dealing with issues arising from such circumstances in the liberalization and facilitation process.

9. Co-operation
Economic and technical co-operation contributing to liberalization and facilitation will be actively pursued.

Source: APEC (1995), *The Osaka Action Agenda: Implementation of the Bogor Declaration*, 19 November.

they include elements to appease all members they for the most part dispelled concerns about the emergence of a closed APEC regional co-operation and fears that APEC would become a free-trade area. The principles of WTO consistency and non-discrimination reaffirm the open regionalism concept of liberalization. The non-discrimination principle does not, of course, go as far as saying that unilateral liberalization must be on an unconditional MFN basis applying to all WTO members, which would create a problem because some APEC members, particularly China, are not yet members of the WTO.

Another key principle reaffirming the wide scope of APEC liberalization is the comprehensiveness principle, which was accepted after protracted deliberation, during which some economies, notably Japan, wanted to exclude 'sensitive' sectors such as agriculture from the liberalization programme. The fact that they ultimately conceded the comprehensive principle is partially offset by the inclusion of the flexibility principle, which makes it possible to wait until the last possible moment to liberalize a particular sector. More importantly, the principle allows for different paths to liberalization and facilitation, taking into account the diversity of the APEC economies.

The principles of 'standstill' and 'simultaneous start and substantial progress' lend credibility to the APEC process. This means that, theoretically, economies are 'locked in' to their commitments, cannot raise other barriers as they reduce traditional barriers, and are under pressure for continued progress. If the standstill principle is fully implemented, it amounts essentially to a soft, 'binding' process. This principle can assist governments in countering protectionist pressures from domestic vested interests.

The principle of comparability captures the essence of 'peer pressure' and 'confidence building' to undertake liberalization and facilitation collectively. The former will come about as APEC governments are 'forced' to compare their offers and implementation thereof with those of other economies. If this principle is combined with the presence of 'champions', then peer pressure could be effective. Individual APEC governments will feel more confident in continuing the liberalization and facilitation process if other economies are undertaking similar efforts and may be able to use 'peer pressure' to counter domestic vested interests. Of course, for this principle to work, an acceptable criterion of comparability needs to be established and protracted debate about how to compare individual action plans has to be avoided. At the time of writing, we wait to see the beginnings of the application of this important principle at the November 1996 APEC meetings when the individual action plans of the APEC members are announced.

APEC: Action Plans

As well as the principles, the Osaka action plan also lays out the general guidelines on the contents of the action plans for liberalization and facilitation by each APEC economy. There are three types of action plan: individual; collective plans by APEC forums; and APEC actions related to multilateral forums. The action plans are further elaborated with issue-specific guidelines. Fifteen issues were identified and the proposed objective, scope and nature of the concerted trade and investment liberalisation and facilitation (TILF) are spelled out in considerable detail (see Box 12.2 for a summary) to guide both the individual (IAP) and collective action plans (CAP). As for the framework for TILF under multilateral actions, echoing the Leaders' Statement on the issue, it was stated that:

> APEC economies will take the lead in strengthening the open multilateral trading system and enhancing global liberalization momentum by participating actively and positively in multilateral negotiations and exploring the possibility of taking joint initiatives under the WTO, including initiatives for the WTO Ministerial Meeting in Singapore.

The coverage indicates that a progressive approach to impediments has been adopted. Thus achieving free trade and investment in the region does not just involve reducing traditional cross-border impediments to trade in goods, such as tariffs and non-tariff measures, but includes liberalization in the new fields covered under the Uruguay Round of trade negotiations

---

Box 12.2   Fifteen specific areas of the Osaka action plan

1. Tariffs
2. Non-tariff measures
3. Trade in services with detailed programme of reform in telecommunications, transport, energy and tourism
4. International investment
5. Standards and conformance
6. Customs procedures
7. Intellectual property rights
8. Competition policy
9. Government procurement
10. Deregulation
11. Rules of origin
12. Dispute mediation
13. Mobility of business people
14. Implementation of the Uruguay Round
15. Information gathering and analysis

Source: APEC (1995) *The Osaka Action Agenda: Implementation of the Bogor Declaration*, 19 November.

(services, investment, and intellectual property rights) as well as facilitation measures such as standards and conformance, customs procedures, rules of origin and mediation of disputes. In addition, areas not yet covered fully in the WTO, such as competition policy and government procurement, have also been included. In line with the idea of the role of APEC in multilateral action, the implementation of the Uruguay Round is included as a specific action plan with the objectives of faithful implementation and possible deepening, broadening and acceleration. Conceptually at least, the APEC vision of liberalization is much more comprehensive and forward-looking than the multilateral agenda.

Translating these guidelines into an acceptable operational format will be the main challenge for the immediate future. This process is unlikely to be completed quickly, but a credible start has to be made. It is also true that the progress achieved means that the bulk of APEC work will now be done by the senior officials and experts specializing in the various areas in the Osaka Action Agenda (OAA). However, the political will of leaders is still needed to push the process along and ensure that the momentum built up thus far will be maintained.

Resistance and arguments about the negative effects of TILF also need to be anticipated, and the balancing role of economic technical co-operation given serious attention so that it becomes meaningful.

A difficult, not totally intractable, problem is defining the scope of these issues. What should be included? How do we ensure that economies provide the same information set and a common format? How should progress be measured? These are only some of the complex issues that face APEC governments. The APEC experiment of open trade and investment based on a combination of the implementation of CAP and IAP is still untested and sceptics abound. For example, some have described the OAA as 'no action, no agenda' (*The Economist*, 25 November 1995).

3 PROGRESS IN APEC LIBERALIZATION: BENCHMARK AND REMAINING IMPEDIMENTS

What does APEC have to achieve in terms of liberalization? Recent studies undertaken by APEC (1995a and 1995b) attempted to assess the progress in liberalization to date and the remaining impediments or the miles that have to be travelled to reach the Bogor goal of free trade and investment in the region.[1] The two studies take a broad approach to trade and investment issues, recognizing that international economic transactions involve traditional flows of goods as well as other new, and growing, cross-border transactions in services, investment and finance, information and people. The main findings are as follows.

Market Access in Goods

The studies looked mainly at the traditional impediments to cross-border flows, tariffs, and non-tariff barriers (NTBs). The results based on available comparable data on tariffs and NTBs for the APEC members from UNCTAD, Uruguay Round (UR), commitments and individual country information indicate that while substantial progress in liberalization has been achieved, impediments do remain, even for developed APEC members.

In summary, the good news is that unilateral liberalization began prior to, and has gone beyond, the UR commitments of APEC members of WTO (see Figure 12.1), and the main driving force for such liberalization has been competition and the recognition of the need to adjust and restructure their economies. The general trends are that NTBs are being removed and replaced by tariffs and, on average, tariffs and NTBs are falling for all APEC

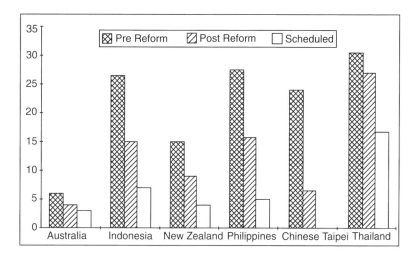

Figure 12.1 Average tariff reduction and available scheduled reductions for some APEC economies

Notes: Australia—1988, 1993 and 1996; weighted average tariffs for manufacturing (in 1996, estimated at 3 per cent).
Indonesia—1986, 1995 and 2003; unweighted average tariffs.
New Zealand—1988, 1993 and 2000; unweighted average tariffs (in 2000, estimated at 4 per cent).
Philippines—1985, 1995 and 2004; unweighted average tariffs.
Chinese Taipei—1998 and 1994; unweighted average tariffs for manufacturing.
Thailand—1987, 1994 and 1997; unweighted average tariffs (1997 number is estimated).

Source: APEC, Individual notifications and other sources.

economies – and more rapidly for some of the developing members which initially had the much higher average tariffs. Another positive trend is towards greater transparency, with pre-announced schedules of tariff reductions becoming more prevalent. While protection by most members remains high for sensitive sectors, there is an encouraging trend of a separate, usually slower and smaller reduction schedule to remove the protection. There were also significant achievements with respect to the level of tariff bindings and reduction of tariffs under their Uruguay Round commitments for most APEC economies that are WTO members.

However, significant variations in tariffs still exist between sectors, and tariffs tend to be high in sectors where domestic producers are often not competitive, such as textiles (see Figure 12.2). All economies retain some tariffs, including the developed economies. NTBs are used frequently in some sectors, such as agriculture, labour-intensive manufactures, steel and automobiles (see Figure 12.3). Fewer schedules for reduction of NTBs have been announced than for tariffs and there is as yet no commonly accepted measure of the incidence of NTBs. However, the variation in protection by sector is evident from a combined measure capturing the incidence of tariffs and NTBs, by using import tax equivalents which estimate differences between cross-border (CIF) and domestic prices (see Figure 12.4).

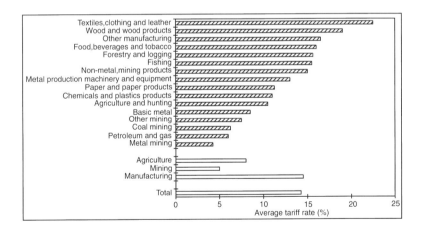

Figure 12.2   Unweighted tariff averages for APEC, 1993

Notes: Sectoral classifications are 2-digit ISIC (Rev. 2). Data are for 1993 for all APEC economies, except Singapore (1989); Indonesia and the Philippines (1990); Chile, Malaysia, Mexico and Thailand (1991); and Korea and Chinese Taipei (1992). No data are available for Papua New Guinea or Brunei.

Source: APEC (1995a), Section 4.

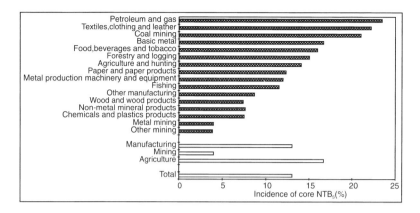

Figure 12.3 Incidence of 'core' non-tariff barriers for APEC, 1993

Notes: Sectoral classifications are 2-digit ISIC (Rev. 2). Data are for 1993 for all APEC economies, except Singapore (1989); Indonesia and the Philippines (1990); Chile, Malaysia, Mexico and Thailand (1991); and Korea and Chinese Taipei (1992). No data are available for or Papua New Guinea Brunei.

Source: APEC (1995a), Section 4.

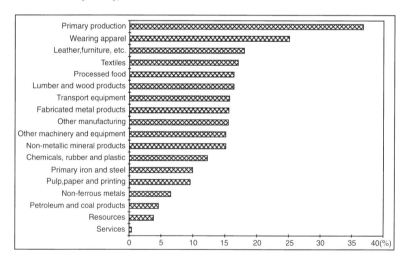

Figure 12.4 Average import tax equivalents for all APEC economies, 1992

Note: Import tax equivalents are the differences between domestic and border (CIF) prices expressed as a percentage of the border price.

Source: Bureau of Industry Economics (1995), calculated from the 1992 GTAP data base.

The real increase in market access achieved through Uruguay Round commitments could be marred by tariff bindings that are above the rates actually applied; by potential back loading or by having many (49 per cent) of the bilateral quotas on textiles and clothing being removed only in the tenth year; and by the actual level of protection in agriculture remaining high after tariffication of NTBs under the Uruguay Round, as a result of a less-than-objective calculation of tariff equivalents.

There is thus a great deal of scope for continuing to enhance market access for goods, for example by implementing the standstill agreement on tariffs and NTBs (as stated in the Bogor declaration) to prevent increases in other barriers as the traditional barriers fall. Progress can also be made through a programme of tariff and NTB reduction that might include the following elements: reduce the bound rate to match the applied rate; increase the percentage of tariff lines that are bound; reduce maximum and peak tariffs; eliminate all surcharges; make all NTBs transparent and have a schedule of reduction; make exceptions transparent, with the objective of minimizing the exceptions. Such moves would not only reduce the level of, but also the variation in, effective protection.

Market Access in Services

APEC members have consistently been deregulating their services unilaterally both prior to and following the conclusion of the UR. Some market-opening measures and easing of requirements on foreign ownership in the services sector have been undertaken unilaterally by some APEC economies. However, the most prevalent liberalization of trade in services is in the form of changes in regulation and procedures over a wide range of service activities. Careful interpretation is warranted, since liberalization of the regulation does not necessarily mean greater market access.

On the multilateral front, the General Agreement on Trade in Services (GATS) negotiated under the UR represents the first time that services have been brought under the multilateral trading rules. Although the GATS provisions are incomplete, very little by way of liberalization has been achieved. At least a definition of basic principles guiding liberalization in services, namely most favoured nation (MFN) treatment, national treatment, and transparency, was agreed upon, so that progress has been made in defining the framework for future liberalization in this field.

Nevertheless, the services market remains highly regulated throughout the sector and closed in some parts, despite the opportunity APEC members had in their GATS negotiations to make 'commitments' to adhere to the principles of free-market access and national treatment. Clarification of current policies on market access and national treatment in services, could facilitate trade significantly by reducing the uncertainty due to gaps in information. But there remains considerable scope for future liberalization by, for example, extending commitments to currently unbound service sectors and undertaking a transparency exercise listing existing impediments in the services sector, with the objective of putting a 'cap' on the existing level of impediments. Further work will also be needed to refine the framework under which liberalization should occur, especially taking into account the links between services and foreign direct investment (FDI) and technology.

Liberalization of Investment

FDI has played a major role in the growth and dynamism of the Asia-Pacific region and in integrating the economies in the region through trade–investment linkages. Impediments to investment can be classified under administrative procedures; market access; national treatment standards (for example, restricting FDI in some sectors); and incentives and operational restrictions (for example, trade balancing requirements).

APEC members have progressed in liberalizing their investment regimes in response to the changing structure of FDI flows. All the economies recognize the importance of creating an open investment regime and encouraging foreign investment in a neutral manner or without undue dependence on incentives. Liberalization efforts in the APEC economies have focused primarily on the removal and simplification of administrative impediments, such as screening and notification procedures. Developing APEC members have been active in encouraging investment by reducing restrictions in non-sensitive areas and developed economies have pushed liberalization even into previously sensitive areas.

However, there continues to be a lack of wide application of market access and national treatment and APEC members have been slow to commit themselves to a discipline on the use of incentives and operational restrictions (see Figure 12.5).

Under the Agreement on Trade Related Investment Measures (TRIMs) in the Uruguay Round, a narrow range of operational restrictions were brought under the discipline of the multilateral trading system for the first time. Only four trade-related investment measures are covered: local content, trade balancing, foreign exchange, and domestic sales requirements. To date, five APEC economies have notified their TRIMs and all are related to local content measures, especially in the automotive, agriculture and chemical sectors. The fact that only a few APEC members have submitted notification reflects, in part, the limited performance or operational requirements that have been included in TRIMs. There is clearly scope for expanding the list of TRIMs.

The question arises how APEC member economies can further progress in investment liberalization. A positive way forward, given current achievement,

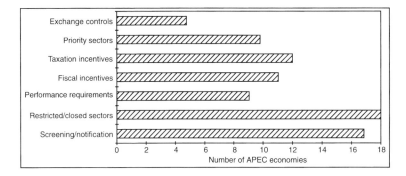

Figure 12.5 Major foreign direct investment impediments within APEC (number of economies)

Notes: The figure indicates the number of APEC economies applying any of the identified impediments to foreign direct investment. Impediments identified in each category are only those that violate market access and national treatment. Thus the figure excludes measures that apply consistently across domestic and foreign investment, such as investment incentives and performance requirements. Such measures, although satisfying national treatment, are nevertheless market-distorting and economically inefficient.

Source: APEC (1995a), Section 4.

is to monitor and implement the already agreed upon APEC non-binding investment principles, which include the application of the national treatment principle to investment flows and the controlled use of performance requirements. Further work improving the framework for investment liberalization, could include strengthening the investment principles underlying liberalization, and ensuring that the transparency principle, already agreed upon, is met through accessible, timely and regularly updated information on members' investment regimes.

Presence of Other Impediments

The two studies mentioned above (p. 279) focused on border barriers to trade and investment. However, it was recognized that more work will be needed to include other impediments and that improvements are needed in the existing information, measurement and framework to be able to capture the 'real' impediments affecting trade and investment flows in the region. In particular, the private sector stressed that attention needs to be given to policy-based obstacles to international trade and investment arising from divergence in approaches to domestic economic and commercial policy. Differences in, or lack of transparency of, domestic regulatory and administrative systems or product standards add greatly to the costs of international commerce. The issues raised should clearly be incorporated in APEC's priorities in considering liberalization as well as facilitation measures in trade and investment.

4 CONCLUSIONS: TESTING THE EXPERIMENT

What would be the measure of success in the untested APEC experiment? A number of possibilities arise, some tangible and others not so tangible. But, first, one should not expect too much from the APEC meeting in Manila in 1996 but should see it as the beginning of the process of implementing the action plans, which must necessarily be an ongoing process. At the minimum, Manila should be seen as the first step towards the design of a template for enacting trade and investment liberalization and facilitation. Given the degree of complexity of many of these issues in the fifteen areas in Box 12.2, lack of data, of a well-defined framework to enable comparisons of the action plans, and of identifiable benchmarks, it will be impossible to expect that the exercise of producing a template will be completed quickly. However, individual action plans should contain specific liberalization and facilitation actions which go beyond their current commitments and have clear time-frames.

Other than through the content of action plans, how best to bring peer pressure to bear on members is not self-evident. Making the peer pressure model work will require APEC to answer some basic issues: what should be done about the identifiable gaps in members' individual actions as well as in the collective action plans, and how highlighting these gaps can and should be used to push these members on track to Bogor, will be precisely the test of APEC peer pressure. Will the observation of gaps and the fact that an economy is 'behind' compared with other economies, push it to improve its action plan in subsequent years? Will observation of the liberalization efforts of others provide an economy with more confidence to embark on a similar path?

The above discussion provides indications as to certain areas where liberalization and facilitation can take place, given a thorough analysis of their current status. One of the main issues faced by APEC is how best to formulate action plans and fulfil the objectives and goals it has set out. Some of the main issues to consider are:

(i)   The need for targets and target dates: should leaders further specify targets or should it be left to each individual economy?

(ii) WTO-related: a new negotiating round and inclusion of present non-members in WTO.

(iii) Testing the principles, especially standstill, comprehensiveness and comparability:

(a) standstill – the need to have an accurate reflection of current status to act as a benchmark;

(b) comprehensiveness – something in each area; and

(c) comparability – structure of IAP is important; should comparability be based on evaluating all commitments or more productive if review and evaluation are focused on actions already taken rather than on intended statement of future TILF (Elek, 1996, p. 7).

(iv) Dispute mediation in APEC.

Much of this chapter has dealt with the tangible objectives and results that could arise from APEC. However, the analysis would not be complete if we did not also consider achievement in the non-tangible areas where APEC has been seen to be important. It has been clear from the outset that many view APEC as being focused too much on trade liberalization; but US support of APEC has been motivated by its interest in opening up markets in the region. This and increased use of bilateral or unilateral actions, rather than the multilateral system, will put a divide between APEC members; and these issues will continue to be contentious, especially in light of US domestic policy. Thus, APEC must adopt a balanced approach and the true test of the success of the APEC experiment cannot be merely progress in trade liberalization. This means that the facilitation and development co-operation aspects have to be highlighted more, and not remain subordinate to trade liberalization. Importantly, the OAA has addressed the facilitation issue comprehensively; but the development co-operation issue is still nebulous, though there are guidelines on technical co-operation.

The broad view of APEC also advocates APEC as a vehicle for community building around the Pacific, including the structuring of trans-Pacific relations and avoiding the natural divide down the Pacific ocean. The strategic value of APEC is that it could increase US economic engagement in the Asia-Pacific region as a way of strengthening the basis for its presence in the region. But APEC also serves as a forum for engaging China constructively in the regional and international arenas. The USA and China are two big countries, and nations for whom multilateralism is not a natural instinct (Soesastro, 1996).

5 POSTSCRIPT

Since this chapter was written, the Manila Action Plan for APEC was announced in November 1996. The assessment of the action plans is a mixed one. While some economies announced some measures for reduction of tariffs, including the Philippines, and specified their Bogor goals of free trade specifically in terms of tariffs, many economies just reiterated their Uruguay Round commitments. The problems in assessing the action plans are: comparability in terms of both format and content; transparency; and independent assessment and monitoring of progress. The comparability issue is especially fraught with complexities caused by major measurement problems, lack of appropriate benchmarks and criteria for measuring progress, different starting points, and whether progress should be measured by each area of activity or as net progress when looking at all areas. However, this is at the heart of the peer pressure model, and continuous improvements within APEC, as well as by outside and independent bodies, will be needed to ensure the success of the exercise.

Note

1. The two studies were prepared for the APEC Committee on Trade and Investment (CTI) in 1995 and were intended to gather information in a systematic and comprehensive way about measures that affect international transactions in the APEC region.

References

APEC (1995(a)) *Survey of Impediments to Trade and Investment in the APEC Region*, Report prepared by the Pacific Economic Co-operation Council (PECC) for APEC (APEC 95-CT-01.2).

APEC (1995(b)) *A Map of Market Opening Measures by APEC Economies*, Report prepared by PECC for APEC (APEC 95-CT-01.2).

Bureau of Industry Economics (1995) 'Potential Gains to Australia from APEC Open Regionalism and the Bogor Declaration', *Occasional Paper No. 29* (Canberra: AGPS).

Elek, A. (1966) 'From the Saga of Osaka to the Music of Subic: APEC's challenges for 1996', Paper presented at seminar on Philippine Approaches to APEC in Manila, 28 November; revised February 1996.

Martin W. and A. Winters (1996) 'The Uruguay Round: A Milestone for the Developing Economies', in B. Bora and M. Pangestu (eds), *Priority Issues in Trade and Investment Liberalization: Implications for the Asia Pacific Region* (Singapore: PECC Secretariat).

PECC (1996) *APEC Leadership in Strengthening the Multilateral Trading System*, Memorandum presented at the World Trade Congress, Singapore, April 24–26.

Soesastro, H. (1996) *APEC Post Osaka*, (Jakarta: Centre for Strategic and International Studies).

13 APEC as Seen Through the Eyes of a Japanese Economist[1]

Ryutaro Komiya

AOYAMA-GAKUIN UNIVERSITY, TOKYO

THE IMPORTANCE OF ASIA PACIFIC ECONOMIC CO-OPERATION (APEC) TO JAPAN

The trade policy authorities in Japan were profoundly interested in the formation of APEC, and has been enthusiastic about APEC's development.

For Japan, it is very important that the multilateral world trade system should grow and function smoothly. After the Second World War, Japan benefited greatly from the trade regime established by the General Agreement on Tariffs and Trade (GATT) and the International Monetary Fund (IMF). Without the GATT–IMF regime, the remarkable post-war growth of the Japanese economy would have been impossible. Thus, informed opinion in Japan hopes strongly that the global system of multilateral free trade will be maintained and further developed.[2]

The development of regionalism since the 1980s, which contains elements running counter to the development of the global free-trade system, has been of concern to many in Japan. This regionalism has taken the form of regional preferential trade agreements (hereafter, regional agreements) based on GATT Article XXIV (and some other provisions), including customs unions and free-trade areas. Of course, it cannot be said that all such regional agreements are undesirable. When a preferential trading region is formed, the so-called trade creation effect could become much greater than the trade diversion effect, and regional agreements may also benefit countries not parties to them. But there are also instances in which countries outside the agreement suffer substantial disadvantages, especially those previously having close trade relations with one or more countries in the agreement.

From the second half of the 1980s, a number of trends emerged in the world trade system that may well greatly concern Japan and several other countries in situations similar to Japan's:

(i)   The tendencies toward 'closedness' seen in two giant regional agree-
        ments, the European Union (EU) and the North American Free Trade
        Association (NAFTA), manifested in high tariff and non-tariff barriers
        erected toward countries outside the region. The latter include rules of
        origin, anti-dumping measures and hub-and-spoke policies.
(ii)   The continuing proliferation of regional agreements. According to the
        World Trade Organization (WTO), 109 regional agreements were noti-
        fied to the GATT Secretariat between 1947 and 1994, of which thirty-
        three came into effect in the nine years between 1986 and 1994 (see
        WTO, 1995).
(iii)   Many of the regional agreements do not follow the requirement of
        GATT Article XXIV, in that they do not cover 'substantially all trade'.
(iv)   Similarly, many of the regional agreements do not follow, or cannot be
        expected to follow, the further requirement of Article XXIV, that the
        customs union or free-trade area will be completed within a reasonable
        length of time.
(v)   The hub-and-spoke approach, in which a large trade area or large
        country (hub), such as the EU, the European Free Trade Association
        (EFTA), the USA, or NAFTA, conclude separate free-trade area
        agreements with many small countries (spokes), also contravening
        GATT rules, as in (iii) and (iv) above.[3]

The world trading system, based on the principle of general most favoured
nation (MFN) treatment of GATT Article I, has thus gradually been eroded
by these developments. If this erosion continues, the effectiveness of GATT's
basic principles of non-discrimination and multilateralism will be weakened,
and world trade will become inefficient and unfair because of arbitrary
distortions.

Among the present members of GATT, only Hong Kong and Japan do not
belong to any regional agreement under GATT Article XXIV (WTO, 1995,
p. 1), and there is little possibility that Japan will participate in any such
regional agreement in the near future.

After many years of effort, Japan's application for accession to GATT was
eventually accepted in 1955. But for many years since then the UK, France,
many other European countries, and former British and French colonies,
applied GATT Article XXXV to Japan, and withheld MFN treatment. The
number of countries applying that Article to Japan reached forty-seven in
total, and much of Japan's commercial diplomacy for many years was devoted
to negotiations to have its application withdrawn. Today, this is almost entirely
a matter of the past, but if the tendencies for the huge trade areas or countries
– such as the EU, the USA and NAFTA – to form trade blocs and/or to
operate hub-and-spoke policies proceed unchecked, GATT Article I will
begin to lose its substance. There is thus a fear that the position of Japan in

the world trade system may then once again come to resemble the situation when many countries applied GATT Article XXXV to Japan. Such a situation is obviously undesirable, not only for Japan, but also for many smaller countries (including the 'spoke' countries) as well as being detrimental to the overall efficiency and equity of the world economy.

To halt the reckless establishment of regional agreements and the hub-and-spoke policies of large trade areas and countries, and to prevent a loss of the substance of the general principle of MFN treatment, the conditions for regional agreements established under Article XXIV should be clarified and made sufficiently strict. At the Uruguay Round (UR) of trade negotiations under GATT, agreement was reached to make the 'reasonable length of time' condition (to be observed when establishing regional agreements according to Article XXIV) a period of ten years in principle. But there was no clarification of the 'substantially all trade' requirement. The meaning of the requirement should be made clear by establishing a target percentage of the intraregional trade of a free-trade area or a customs union to be subject to complete free trade; and if, after a ten-year period, such a 'substantially all trade' requirement is not fulfilled, the regional agreement should become null and void.

During the late 1980s and early 1990s a number of developments caused the Japanese authorities anxiety about the future of the world trade system, and sometimes even a sense of crisis:

(i) The UR negotiations that began in 1986 did not proceed smoothly, and at times even seemed to become deadlocked.

(ii) The fear that the EC would become more closed with a move towards 'Fortress Europe' in 1992.

(iii) The free-trade area agreement in 1989 between Canada and the USA and the move toward Mexico's participation in it.

(iv) The regional trade agreement between the USA and Israel in 1985, and the hub-and-spoke policy moves thereafter by the USA to conclude similar agreements on an individual basis with some Latin-American countries, Singapore, South Korea, and others.

(v) The establishment of NAFTA in 1992.

Among these developments, the news that the USA was beginning to move to conclude bilateral free-trade area agreements with Singapore and South Korea must have been a great shock to the Japanese authorities, since such US hub-and-spoke policies could potentially give rise to enormous distortions of Pacific trade, including that of Japan.[4]

In this situation, the members of the Association of South East Asian Countries (ASEAN) (Australia, Hong Kong, Japan, New Zealand, South Korea and Taiwan) have important common interests in maintaining and developing a world trade system that is free and open and, in particular, in keeping the EU and North America as open as possible. Moreover, given the noticeably high rates of economic and trade growth in recent years in these countries and in some other East Asian countries, they thought that they could gain in negotiating capabilities *vis-à-vis* the EU and the USA, if they joined together.[5]

It may be supposed that such thinking influenced the Japanese trade policy authorities' initiation in 1987 of discussions on an economic co-operative group in Asia and the Pacific, which was later to develop into APEC. The establishment and development of APEC was considered to be valuable to Japan at the time, and its successes to date have enhanced its importance to Japan substantially.[6]

In addition to the issues outlined above, Japan's bilateral trade relationship with the USA has been another important factor in the Japanese authorities' enthusiasm for APEC. In recent years, trade friction between Japan and the USA has accounted for a large proportion of Japan's trade problems.

A number of East Asian nations, starting with Japan, have had continuous difficulties in their economic and trade relations with the USA. These have included at times persistent demands by the US government for liberalization by the trade partner or some other unilateral concessions. It was probably felt that such problems would be eased to some extent if some kind of multilateral organization could be established in the East Asia-Pacific area, whether or not the USA was included, though the Japanese authorities did not even remotely consider a multilateral organization in the East Asia-Pacific area that would not include the USA. The issue of rice imports into Japan, for example, was probably easier to resolve because it was handled at the UR rather than bilaterally between Japan and the USA.[7]

Australia, meanwhile, one of the countries that moved most enthusiastically in the early stages of negotiations for forming and promoting APEC, harboured dissatisfaction with decisions reached in past bilateral trade negotiations between Japan and the USA, as these did not pay enough attention to the interests of third countries with which the two parties had close trade relationships. South Korea and other East Asian countries, as well as the EU, have also expressed dissatisfaction on occasion, and Australia and South Korea probably expected the formation of APEC to reduce the number of situations producing unsatisfactory outcomes for them.

WHAT IS APEC?

No other organization like APEC exists, and it may be difficult for people other than those directly concerned to understand what it is. In its formative stages, it was sometimes said that APEC was a deliberative council, something like the Organization for Economic Co-operation and Development (OECD). However, the OECD is a group of developed nations which pursue broadly similar economic policies, and all are members of GATT and Article VIII members of the IMF.[8] In contrast, the members of APEC are countries and areas at widely differing stages of economic development, and include those with fundamentally different ways of thinking about economic policy. The OECD facilitates inter-governmental exchanges of information, and prepares and publicizes various statistics and study reports on particular issues. Its members exchange opinions concerning macroeconomic and other policies, and undertake (and submit to) a degree of mutual persuasion. The OECD also formulates codes that serve as guidelines to policies in areas such as international capital movements and service trade, and the members must basically observe these codes. It is generally clear what the OECD is, what obligations a country assumes when it becomes a member and what benefits accrue to it as a member.

In contrast to the OECD, it is difficult for outsiders to understand what APEC is, partly because it has only a short history. Existing official documents of APEC are the joint declarations of the seven ministerial meetings and three unofficial summit meetings held so far. There are no conventions or rules fundamental to the organization, and most of the members are so far opposed to the institutionalization of APEC, though they have agreed to establish a modest secretariat. Without a rigid legal structure, the members agree in areas where they are able to agree, which allows the wheels of the deliberative body to move little by little. Such an approach gives APEC an Asian touch to its operation that differs somewhat from the Western approach. Concerning the results of the recent Osaka Conference of APEC, it was reported that there was no use of words such as 'negotiation', 'binding' or 'reciprocity', and, instead, the words 'voluntary', 'non-binding' and 'unilateral' were frequently heard; and it was said that this difference of style made the meeting more comfortable and congenial for Asians.

The three main pillars of APEC at present are: (i) the liberalization of trade and investment; (ii) the facilitation of trade and investment; and (iii) economic and technical co-operation. Some of the specific items included in (ii) and (iii) may be truly valuable in terms of the region's growth of trade, investment and economic development, and their importance should not be slighted when compared with the liberalization of trade and investment. Liberalization will involve questions of collaboration with the World Trade Organization (WTO), or division of responsibility between APEC and other international institutions. Similarly, work on economic and technical co-operation involves the problem of sharing the responsibility and the burden of assistance with the World Bank, the Asia Development Bank, and other aid institutions.

APEC

Perhaps the issue of greatest interest to many, including newspapers and other media, is (i) above and particularly the liberalization of trade. But for outsiders there are some difficulties in understanding what is meant by liberalization of trade and investment within APEC.

In the statement made after the APEC Summit Conference in Bogor, it was said that the objective of 'free and open trade and investment' would be achieved by the developed nations of APEC by the year 2010 and by the developing nations by 2020.

Concerning the liberalization of investment, only limited agreement was reached on trade-related investment at the UR and, so far, almost no multilateral rules relating to international investment exist, apart from those within the EU and the OECD's code on international capital movements. Although it is significant that APEC has adopted liberalization of investment as a basic policy objective, there is a long way to go before agreement is reached on specific and effective rules, and longer before those rules are implemented.

The terms 'free trade' and 'liberalization of trade' have been given different meanings in different countries and at different periods. Taken in its narrowest sense, the liberalization of trade meant, in the past, in Japan and in a number of other countries, the removal of quantitative restrictions (QR) on imports. In other instances, it has referred to the removal of QR on imports *plus* removal or the substantial reduction of other non-tariff barriers *and* of tariffs. Free trade within a free-trade area consistent with GATT Article XXIV means the complete removal of tariff and non-tariff barriers to intra-area trade; and, under the original meaning of Article XXIV, even anti-dumping duties may not be used within a free-trade area.

If discussions had been held at the APEC conferences in Jakarta and Bogor in 1994, or at Osaka in 1995, about the meaning of free and open trade, which was taken as the goal to be reached by the member nations in either 2010 or 2020, the conferences would probably have ended without any agreement being reached. It is exactly because the meaning of the words 'free and open trade' is left unclear that APEC is able to move forward.

The meaning of the words 'open regionalism' that are used at times in APEC is also unclear. 'Open' probably does not mean that any country that wants to can enter.

In common-sense terms, if free and open trade means the removal of QR on imports as well as a substantial reduction of import tariffs, plus the removal or alleviation of non-tariff barriers (such as anti-dumping and countervailing duties), which are major trade impediments and cannot be rationalized in economic (or social) terms, the distances APEC member nations will have to travel before they are in a position to realize that objectives vary considerably from country to country. Members such as Hong Kong and Singapore are already quite near to that objective, and others that are members of the OECD are relatively close to achieving it. On the other hand, among the developing-country members, there are some IMF Article VIII members, and some countries that still have not advanced beyond IMF Article XIV status,[9] although they are WTO members, and some countries that are still not members of WTO. Countries like China still have a very long way to go, and it is difficult to imagine when they will be able to achieve 'free and open trade and investment'.

Although the OECD countries mentioned above appear to be close to achieving free and open trade, most of the remaining barriers may be seen as hard-core, making the distance still to go difficult, even though short.

A review of the initial action offered by each APEC member at the Osaka Conference shows that the liberalization measures offered by countries that played major roles at the UR, such as the USA, Japan, and a few others, were either limited in their actual effects or merely advance implementation of the UR tariff rates: the USA offered no tariff measures at all. One may note, however, that the principal negotiating nations at the UR made substantial tariff concessions there (or even before the UR), and are now busy absorbing their domestic impact. It was thus difficult for them, given their domestic politics, to propose new tariff reductions in Osaka. In contrast, there were a number of other countries that offered tariff reductions across a wide area that appear to carry with them quite substantial effects. This was a welcome development in terms of APEC's growth, but their offers suggest that those countries had not been very serious in mutual tariff reductions at the UR.

A second difficult point to understand regarding APEC is the confrontation between (i) the MFN approach and (ii) the reciprocity approach in moving forward with liberalization of trade and investment. Under (i), the liberalization measures decided by the APEC members will be applied unconditionally to countries outside the region. Under (ii), when liberalization measures decided on by the APEC members are applied to countries outside the region (with the EU principally in mind), the condition is set that the countries outside APEC will carry out liberalization measures equivalent in value to those of APEC. The underlying tone in APEC is said to be that the Asian members support the MFN approach, the USA insists on the reciprocity approach, and Australia is in between. But either approach will involve difficulties.

First, if the reciprocity approach is to be pushed forward legally under GATT, APEC will have to become a free-trade area under GATT Article XXIV, and APEC members must remove tariffs and other trade regulations for 'substantially all trade' among the members within a reasonable length of time. As pointed out earlier, however, APEC comprises countries and areas that are at different stages of economic development and that currently have different levels of trade liberalization. Thus, many members of APEC would feel it difficult to meet the GATT conditions for a free-trade area even though they have agreed to realize free and open trade and investment in its present unclear format.

As mentioned above, Japan and some other APEC members view regional agreements which do not satisfy (or seem unlikely to satisfy) GATT Article XXIV conditions as harmful, producing distortions in the world-wide system of multilateral free trade. For them, participation in a regional agreement with a dubious final outcome would be unwise as it would weaken their position as opponents of the types of agreement of which they disapprove.

Next, the MFN approach, whereby APEC members would apply their liberalization measures unconditionally to WTO members outside APEC, would present no special problems for countries that are small in scale in the world trade system, or for countries whose tariff and non-tariff barriers are now quite high. For these two categories of countries, unilateral trade liberalization would promote their national interests.

Larger countries, however, are likely to benefit more if they and their trading partners reduce trade barriers simultaneously, and such countries will wish to use reduction or removal of their trade barriers as levers in negotiation with their trading partners.

Moreover, although trade liberalization measures are generally beneficial for a country as a whole, they usually involve some disadvantages for particular groups within the country and, realistically, it is next to impossible to compensate fully for such disadvantages. For this reason, trade liberalization is accompanied domestically by political pain. If most countries carried out liberalization simultaneously and shared the political pain involved, liberalization would be politically easier to accomplish.

Countries such as Australia, Canada, Japan and the USA have participated in a number of GATT multilateral trade negotiations on a full scale in the past, and have experienced the associated political pain. Their trade barriers have become relatively low, and those that remain are 'hard core'. It would be politically difficult for these countries to carry out trade liberalization unilaterally and to offer the results unconditionally to other countries and the EU.

In particular, the USA is conducting aggressive trade negotiations with many of its trade partners, including the EU, and applying trade policies that are thought to fit its national interests. The US government plays trade policy games all the time and it may be thought that the US relationship with APEC is little more than another of these. With future trade negotiations with the EU in mind, the USA will probably not show enthusiasm for unilateral (non-reciprocal) trade liberalization within APEC based on what is called 'concerted unilateral action'.

In the early stages of the formation of APEC, the US government did not show much enthusiasm, other than indicating that it would participate. After President Clinton assumed office, however, the USA began to emphasize trade liberalization at APEC venues (beginning with the Seattle Conference in 1993), recognizing the importance of the high rate of economic growth of East Asia. But the US government has not so far put in order the domestic preconditions for an extensive reduction of US tariff and non-tariff barriers, and seems to lack the willingness to do so, at least for the present. When the US representative talks about trade liberalization at APEC, therefore, it appears that what is meant does not include trade liberalization *by* the USA but seems to mean trade liberalization by other APEC members along the lines of US wishes.

It thus appears that basic problems remain unresolved in pushing forward APEC's further trade liberalization.

AGRICULTURAL IMPORTS INTO JAPAN

The agricultural sector is one of the few areas where, although Japanese import tariffs are still quite high, the Japanese government feels it difficult to lower them. Needless to say, there has been strong pressure on Japan for further liberalization of agricultural imports, and it is often asked whether the Japanese government would include agricultural products as targets of free trade by the year 2010. But it is not easy to foresee what changes will occur by 2010 in Japanese agriculture or agricultural policy. Concerning the next five (or perhaps seven or eight) years, I would guess roughly as follows:

(i) The agricultural labour force in Japan consists of small farmers and their families, who cultivate the small pieces of land they own; there are very few employed workers in Japanese agriculture; and farmers and their families now form only a small portion of the total Japanese labour force. Perhaps 60 per cent or more of those who now work in agriculture are 55 years of age or older, and thus have virtually no possibility of moving into other industries; some workers in their forties and fifties move to agriculture from other sectors of the economy, but very few who are thirty or younger do so; and this trend of a decreasing and ageing agricultural labour force is set to continue.[10] Japanese agricultural output is expected to stagnate or decline from now on, and may decline fairly rapidly beyond a certain time in the future. Japanese agriculture now mainly concentrates on food production, with very few non-food items being produced other than flowering and foliage plants.

(ii) In Japan, the Tokyo, Osaka and Fukuoka axis (the centre, with Sendai now being added) are industrialized, relatively rich and well developed, but prefectures distant from the centre (the periphery) have been stagnant and relatively poor. They are mostly agricultural prefectures. From the second half of the 1960s to the early 1980s, many industrial factories were built in the periphery because of the abundant labour force there. Recently, however, Japanese enterprises have begun shifting production offshore to South-East Asia and China, causing concern about industrial employment in the agricultural prefectures. Light-industry manufactures and agricultural and fishery speciality products, which have been produced by the periphery, are now also facing keen competition from imports, especially those from East Asia. Hence, maintenance of agricultural income is a matter of great concern for the economies of these prefectures.

(iii)   The agricultural sector has a powerful influence on Japanese domestic politics. The non-agricultural population has so far been sympathetic to farmers and has not shown much opposition to agricultural protection. Such policies can therefore be expected to continue, with no major changes in the near future. Since the majority of the Japanese populace supports the maintenance of free trade, however, the strengthening of barriers against agricultural imports is unlikely.

(iv)   If the Japanese economy recovers from the current recession and then continues to grow, agricultural imports will increase steadily. Japan is now the world's largest food-importing country, and the value of its food imports in US dollar terms doubled from $23.7 billion to $47.6 billion during the seven years from 1987 to 1994. No other major trading country has increased its food imports so rapidly.

If the APEC objective of free and open trade is interpreted as the complete removal of quantitative restrictions on imports as well as tariffs, Japan's chances of achieving that objective with respect to agricultural products in the near future are slim. Future Japanese trade policy, however, will be directed toward freer and more open trade including trade in agricultural products, and agricultural imports into Japan are likely to increase steadily in the future.

THE SUCCESS OF APEC

Even if APEC itself may not have contributed to achieving substantial increases in trade volumes or direct investment in the seven or so years since its inception, it can be claimed to have achieved substantial successes in ways that cannot readily be measured.

As a multilateral deliberative forum, targeting co-operation for development and the liberalization of trade and investment in the Asia-Pacific area, APEC has also become a powerful group in promoting multilateral free trade throughout the entire world. The countries that played a key role in establishing this deliberative council are the countries of the Western Pacific rim – the ASEAN countries, Australia, Japan and South Korea. These countries form the core of APEC.

The USA, though hesitant at first, has come to participate actively in APEC. The high rate of economic growth in East Asia, and the fact that US Pacific trade now exceeds its Atlantic trade made it impossible for the USA not to join such an economic deliberative body as APEC; and almost the same can be said of Canada. Meanwhile, China, whose participation in the WTO has not yet been accepted and has had little chance to play a positive role in important multilateral conferences, has requested enthusiastically to join APEC. The 'three Chinas' – China, Taiwan, and Hong Kong – joined APEC from the Third Ministerial meeting in Seoul, the first time that all three participated together in an international conference. This was a remarkable achievement for Korean diplomacy, South Korea then being the host country.

APEC has taken several years to assume its current form, and its organization and functions are still undergoing change. Its development has been the product of participation by many statesmen and senior officials in several countries. Its success can be measured by the fact that many countries in the Asia-Pacific region eagerly participate in it, and that many more wish to become members, as it provides an important opportunity to exchange information and to discuss problems of common interest. The Asia and Europe Summit Meeting held in Bangkok in March 1996 may be taken to reflect the rising negotiating power of East Asian countries which has been promoted through APEC.

The above evaluation of the successes of APEC applies to its development so far. But if it remains simply a forum in the coming years, it will not be evaluated as a success. The future evaluation of APEC will depend crucially on the progress made over the next few years in liberalization, facilitation of beneficial actions, and economic co-operation among its members.

Notes

1. The views expressed in this chapter are the personal views of the author, and should not be taken as being those of the Japanese government. The author is an academic economist and, while also Director General of the Research Institute of International Trade and Industry of the Japanese Ministry of International Trade and Industry (MITI), has little specialist knowledge of APEC. He wishes to express his thanks to a number of colleagues at MITI and Aoyama Gakuin University, who provided information and made comments on an earlier draft.

2. Even after the end of the Second World War, free trade was not universally favoured in Japan, and even now, the agricultural sector, some politicians, and some of those in citizens' movements are opposed to trade liberalization.

3. For the negative effects on world trade caused by the 'hub-and-spoke' approach, see Anderson and Snape (1994).

4. The Japanese trade policy authorities seem to have paid little attention until recently to the negative effects on the world trade system of the hub-and-spoke policies of the USA and EU. When NAFTA was formed, it might have been felt that the new organization would promote the Uruguay Round, but the welcome given to it by the Japanese authorities was surprising. Under the Canada–US Free Trade Area Agreement reached before NAFTA, passenger cars produced at Honda's plant in Canada with engines made in the USA, and then exported to the USA were treated by US customs as passenger cars produced outside the free-trade area because of a particular interpretation of the 'country of origin' rule. This decision was very unpleasant news to Japan. When NAFTA was created, the Japanese government should not have welcomed it but should rather have requested that NAFTA be kept as open as possible to countries outside it, and said that Japan would be watching NAFTA's future development closely.

   Although existing as regional agreements within APEC, the Australia and New Zealand Closer Economic Relationship Agreement (ANZCER) and ASEAN Free Trade Area Agreement (AFTA) perhaps differ from NAFTA, in that they do not appear to have significant trade diversion effects, although it is difficult to predict how AFTA will develop in the future.

5. The Japanese government thought from the beginning that an Asia-Pacific economic deliberative body without the USA was out of the question, and that a gain in negotiating capabilities would be produced even with the USA included in the organization. On the other hand, during the earliest period of APEC's establishment, there was the possibility, quite undesirable for Australia, that Japan and the USA would agree on a free-trade area.

6. My knowledge about the process of APEC's formation and its later development is mainly from Funabashi (1995) and Kikuchu (1995).

7. The tension of 'trade friction' between Japan and USA has substantially decreased recently, in my view, and this is likely to continue, even if there are some ups and downs along the way.

8. Article VIII members of the IMF are, roughly speaking, those who abolished all exchange controls on current account transactions (quantitative import restrictions) for balance of payments reasons, and Article XIV members are those who still maintain such controls and restrictions.

9. As note 8.

10. There are difficulties in measuring the ratio of the agricultural labour force to the total labour force in Japan, because an overwhelming majority of those who work in agriculture are engaged in other jobs also. Similar difficulties exist in defining a concept of (or measuring the extent of) the mobility of labour between agriculture and other industries.

References

Anderson, K. and R. Snape (1994) 'European and American Regionalism: Effects and Options for Asia', *Journal of the Japanese and International Economies*, vol. 8.

Funabashi, Y. (1995) *Asia Pacific Fusion: Japan's Role in APEC* (Washington, DC: Institute for International Economics).

Kikuchi Tsumotu, (1995) *APEC: Groping for a New Asia Pacific Order* (in Japanese) (Tokyo: Japanese Institute for International Affairs).

WTO (1995) *Regionalism and the World Trading System* (Geneva: World Trade Organisation).

14 APEC and the United States of America

Arvind Panagariya
UNIVERSITY OF MARYLAND

1 THE EVOLUTION OF US TRADE POLICY

I have been assigned the task in this volume of articulating the North American view on the Asia-Pacific Economic Co-operation forum (APEC). Of course, just as there is no single Asian view on APEC, there is no single North American view on it; but to minimize the confusion that can result from this multiplicity of views, I shall organize my discussion around the US government's strategy towards APEC. In examining this strategy critically, I hope also to cover alternative views on the subject.

The major objective that has guided US trade policy in recent years, particularly under President Clinton, is export expansion. Though many instruments, including aggressive unilateralism, manifest in Super 301 and Special 301 of the 1988 Trade Practices Act[1], have been used to achieve this objective, the instrument that has assumed the central role recently is preferential trading arrangements (PTAs). In the western hemisphere, with the North American Free Trade Area (NAFTA) already established, the USA is promoting the Free Trade Area (FTA) of the Americas, an arrangement expected to give US firms preferential access to the entire western hemisphere. In Europe, the USA has encouraged the idea of a Transatlantic Free Trade Area (TAFTA), proposed originally by Klaus Kinkel of Germany. In Asia, at the APEC ministerial meetings and through the American-led Eminent Persons Group (EPG), the USA has resisted liberalization based on the most favoured nation (MFN) principle and insisted on reciprocity for large countries such as the USA.[2]

It must be acknowledged that the USA is not unique in promoting PTAs. The European Union (EU) has done the same on a larger scale and for much longer. What is different about the USA, however, is its history. Until recently, the USA, unlike Europe, had been a staunch opponent of regional arrangements and the prime force behind multilateralism. Having witnessed the pernicious effects of discriminatory trade and payments regimes during the Great Depression, the USA emerged at the end of the Second World War as the champion of a non-discriminatory world trade regime firmly grounded in the MFN principle. Speaking for the US policy-makers, Howard Ellis (1945) denounced bilateral arrangements in the strongest terms: 'There are good reasons for believing that no device portends more restrictions of international trade in the postwar setting than bilateral arrangements'. The US commitment to multilateralism manifested itself in efforts to create the International Trade Organization (ITO), an institution intended to establish a rules-based trade regime throughout the world. But because the US Congress failed to ratify it, the ITO was stillborn. Undeterred, the US government supported the establishment of the General Agreement on Tariffs and Trade (GATT) in 1947, and led the world into a series of highly successful rounds of multilateral trade negotiations, of which seven were completed with the Tokyo Round in 1979. Throughout, the USA had stood firmly behind the multilateral approach and rejected all calls for participation in regional arrangements, including a North Atlantic Free Trade Area proposed by the UK. The only regional arrangement the USA did support was the European Economic Community (EEC), which was seen as a necessary counter-weight to Soviet power.

The turning point in this history came in 1982 when, at the GATT ministerial meeting in Geneva, the USA tried to get the eighth GATT round of negotiations started but was frustrated by the EEC, which was then suffering from economic difficulties described as 'Euro-sclerosis'. At that point, a disappointed William Brock, the United States Trade Representative saw the regional approach as the only alternative left to keep trade liberalization moving ahead. In the absence of multilateral progress, he saw open-ended, ever-expanding FTAs as an alternative instrument for achieving world-wide free trade.[3] Negotiations were opened with Israel and Canada, and FTA agreements were concluded with them in 1985 and 1988, respectively.

In the meantime, the Uruguay Round of negotiations under GATT (UR) was launched in 1986. But the European Community (EC), preoccupied now by its Single Market initiative, remained a reluctant player in the ensuing negotiations. This gave the USA a reason as well as an excuse to continue pursuing PTAs.[4] In 1989, negotiations were opened with Mexico which, in 1992, culminated in the signing of the agreement establishing NAFTA.

Happily, despite Lester Thurow's famous pronouncement that 'GATT is dead', GATT did not die, and the UR was concluded successfully in December 1993. The US threat to pursue regional arrangements of its own had the desirable impact of bringing a reluctant EC to the negotiating table. The GATT has been revived, revitalized and, at last, transformed from a treaty into a proper international institution, the World Trade Organization (WTO).

Today, with the original objective behind the switch in US policy towards preferential trading having been achieved, it might seem that there is no further need to promote PTAs. But a taste for bilateral negotiations and the preferential access they bring have changed the dynamics of the trade-liberalization process. The USA has decided to 'walk on both legs'. From being a staunch opponent of bilateralism, the US government has turned into an aggressive proponent of it. The original US vision of promoting liberalization on the MFN principle has been replaced by demands for reciprocity and the simple-minded view that *any* reduction in trade barriers is a good thing. This switch in US thinking is best summarized in the following assertion by Lawrence Summers (1991), the Deputy Secretary of Treasury in the Clinton Administration: 'economists should maintain a strong, but rebuttable, pre-sumption in favor of all lateral reductions in trade barriers, whether they be multi, uni, bi, tri, plurilateral. Global liberalization may be best, but regional liberalization is very likely to be good'.

Jagdish Bhagwati and I have argued elsewhere (Bhagwati 1995; Panagariya 1996a; Bhagwati and Panagariya 1996a) that this is a flawed vision, if it can be called a vision. Writing in 1950, Jacob Viner, who pioneered the theory of preferential trading, was himself puzzled by the general support of PTAs by pro-free-trade economists of his time: 'The major explanation seems to lie in an unreflecting association on their part of any removal or reduction of trade barriers with movement in the direction of free trade.' He then went on to explain that clever politicians had always known that a reduction in trade barriers can, in fact, be used to *increase* protection and, in so doing, provided the essential idea behind the later development of the concept of effective protection.

In addition to the possibility that PTAs can slow multilateral progress, there are at least four reasons for scepticism towards PTAs as an instrument of trade liberalization.[5] First, being discriminatory in nature, they can, and do, lead to trade diversion.[6] Because weaker, uncompetitive industries are often those that succeed in lobbying against foreign competition, PTAs may often be voted in when trade diversion is either an unstated objective or a major result. This is a point made forcefully in the recent theoretical work by Grossman and Helpman (1995) and Krishna (1995). Similarly, the careful empirical work of Kowalczyk and Davis (1996) shows that, in NAFTA, the sectors allowed the longest phase-out periods for implementing the accord were those in which US lobbies were most powerful. Most importantly, the recent study by Yeats (1996) provides systematic evidence of wholesale trade diversion in the Southern Cone Common Market or MERCOSUR. The view that a PTA between countries that either trade a lot with each other or share a common border does not lead to serious trade diversion (the so-called 'natural trading partners' hypothesis) has been promoted by Krugman (1991) and Summers (1991), but has been shown to have no foundation in theory by Bhagwati and Panagariya (1996), and to be inconsistent with reality by Yeats's study just mentioned.

The second problem with PTAs is that they can lead to increased protection against outside countries. In bad times, pressures for protection grow and when a PTA member is unable to raise trade barriers against a partner, the burden of any increased trade barriers falls disproportionately on the outside countries. Such increases in trade barriers can turn even an initial trade creation into trade diversion.[7] This is not idle speculation. After Israel concluded FTAs with both the EU and the USA, tariffs against the outside world were raised;[8] and, in the aftermath of the peso crisis, Mexico raised tariffs against non-NAFTA countries on 503 items from less than 20 per cent to 35 per cent.[9] Another way in which the burden can be transferred to outside countries is through increased anti-dumping duties and other safeguard actions against them.

Third, in FTAs, which seem to be the dominant form of PTAs today, rules of origin are creating a spaghetti bowl. This problem is bound to be compounded as overlapping FTAs proliferate. As it is, the rules of origin in NAFTA are complicated; but suppose that Chile, already with a free trade agreement with MERCOSUR, joins NAFTA. Because MERCOSUR does not have a free-trade agreement with NAFTA, the rules of origin attached to Chile's entry into NAFTA are likely to be more complicated than those for NAFTA. The new rules of origin would open a further avenue for trade diversion. Thus, a manufacturer in Chile would have to decide whether to buy his components in the MERCOSUR area or in North America, depending on whether the final product is to be sold in MERCOSUR or in NAFTA. If the manufacturer relies on a single source of supply, he will be able to satisfy the rules of origin for one of the two destinations. Moreover, if the most efficient supplier happens to be in Asia, trade diversion will be inevitable.

Finally, measures that are inconsistent with WTO rules have begun to sneak back into PTAs. One such example is the trade-balancing requirement within MERCOSUR. The WTO has just outlawed this trade-related investment measure. Yet it has been introduced by the members of MERCOSUR to affect firms operating within the union. Thus an Argentine company operating in Brazil must export as much of Brazilian goods to Argentina as it imports from that country. Similarly, voluntary export restraints (VERs) have been outlawed by the UR agreement. Yet, within NAFTA such VERs were resurrected on tomato imports into the USA from Mexico. At the time of writing, we do not have evidence of such WTO-inconsistent measures being widespread, but they certainly have the potential to subvert the multilateral process.

2 APEC AND THE USA

To ensure open access for US firms in Asian markets, the USA has actively opposed the formation of an exclusively Asian trading bloc, despite US adherence to NAFTA. Thus, when in December 1990, Prime Minister Mahathir Mohamed of Malaysia proposed the establishment of an East Asian Economic Group (EAEG), the US Secretary of State, James Baker, vehemently opposed it. Baker's efforts at the ASEAN post-ministerial conference held in

July 1991 led to the downgrading of the group to an East Asian Economic Caucus (EEAC) and prevented Japan and Korea from joining it.

APEC had been proposed by the Australian Prime Minister, Mr Bob Hawke, in January 1989 without consulting the USA. Seeing its importance, the Bush Administration quickly moved to ensure a seat for the USA and its FTA partner, Canada, at the first formal meeting of the organization, held in Canberra in November 1989.[10] Because of its diverse membership, APEC proceeded cautiously, aiming to develop closer ties through consultation, cooperation and consensus rather than through formal negotiations. Indeed, during its first four years, it operated without a formal secretariat.

As Barfield (1996) points out correctly, 'it was the Clinton administration that moved to change the focus of APEC from an informal consultative mechanism to a more formal organization promoting trade liberalization – and ultimately preferential trade arrangements – within the Pacific region'. This impetus, provided at the Seattle meeting in November 1993, culminated the following year in the Bogor declaration. Led by President Suharto of Indonesia, APEC members agreed to establish free trade by the year 2010 in the developed member countries and by 2020 in the developing member countries. Though the meaning of 'free trade' in this context has remained unclear, and no strategy for achieving the goal has been articulated, the agreement was a departure from APEC's past practice of limiting itself to a low-key, consultative approach.

Since the Bogor meeting, the US approach has been to encourage unilateral liberalization by developing Asian members, but to resist any reductions in its own trade barriers on an MFN basis. The groundwork for this approach had been laid down by the American-led EPG in its second report (APEC, 1994); the EPG noted:

> considerations suggest that, while APEC members should implement unilateral liberalization to the maximum extent possible, it will be expedient to pursue a strategy of negotiated liberalization as well. The largest members, including the United States, are unlikely to liberalize unilaterally when they can use the high value of access to their markets to obtain reciprocal liberalization from others. The same view applies to other economies in the region.
>
> The closely related consideration is that APEC as a whole is the world's largest trading region, considerably larger than even the EU . . . the region would give away an enormous amount of leverage if its members . . . especially its large members – were to liberalize unilaterally to any significant degree.

Thus, the EPG essentially ruled out liberalization by the USA within the APEC framework unless it be discriminatory, though the same was welcome if undertaken by smaller economies of the region, mainly developing Asian countries.

It may be argued that, because the EPG did not represent the USA but served the APEC, its views cannot be taken as representing the US position. But the Economic Report of the President's Council of Economic Advisers (1995) echoes the EPG by focusing on liberalization by Asian members of APEC while saying little about corresponding liberalization by the USA. To quote from the report:

> Although the opportunities for U.S. businesses are tremendous, the obstacles are often very large. Between 1989 and 1992, automobile sales in Malaysia, the Philippines, and Thailand doubled, but tariffs on automobile imports into those countries remain high at between 17 and 57 percent... Market-opening initiatives through APEC will help reduce these barriers, creating tremendous opportunities for U.S. companies and workers.

There is little mention in the report of the high tariffs on textiles, apparel and footwear in the USA, or the gains from removing them. Nor is there any mention of a speedier phase-out of the Multi-fibre Arrangement (MFA) affecting products of interest to Asian exporters.

Finally, it may be noted that at the Osaka ministerial meeting in 1995, whatever liberalization was announced came from developing Asian countries, such as China and Indonesia. The only liberalization announced by the USA was that of *exports* of certain goods with possible military use.[11] Mickey Kantor, the United States Trade Representative at the time, and now the Commerce Secretary, insisted that future trade liberalization will allow 'no free riders'. (Barfield, 1996).

It is unlikely that the US objective of improved market access in Asia without a corresponding liberalization of its own markets within the APEC framework will in fact be attained. At the time of writing (mid-November 1996), preparation for the 1996 APEC summit, to be held in the Philippines, is under way. At this summit, the USA plans to use APEC as one of the forums for developing a consensus on liberalization in the area of information technology, a subject that was expected to be discussed more fully at the WTO ministerial meeting in Singapore. Developing Asian countries, for their part, plan to announce modest liberalization on an MFN basis. Prospects for more substantial liberalization by Asian countries within the APEC framework, without the USA undertaking similar liberalization, appear dim.

3 LIBERALIZATION WITHIN THE APEC FRAMEWORK

Let me now address more directly the possible ways of liberalizing trade within the APEC framework in the future. There is a consensus among APEC members that whatever liberalization takes place should be

GATT-consistent. Indeed, given the recent tightening of multilateral rules as a result of the UR, it is difficult to imagine that any significant liberalization can be pursued in a manner inconsistent with GATT. Short of initiating another round of multilateral negotiations, this narrows down APEC's options to four modes of liberalization: one-way trade preferences by developed to developing member countries under the Generalized System of Preferences (GSP); reciprocal trade preferences between developing member countries under the Enabling Clause of GATT; FTAs and customs unions (CUs) under GATT Article xxiv; and unilateral liberalization on an MFN basis.

Of these four modes, the first two are unlikely to play any significant role in APEC. Developed-country members are in no mood to offer trade preferences on a non-reciprocal basis. Nor are developing member countries in East Asia keen to trade preferences with each other on a discriminatory basis. The ASEAN Preferential Trading Arrangement (APTA), negotiated in 1977 and superseded by the ASEAN Free Trade Area (AFTA) in 1992, falls into this category, but the consequent exchange of trade preferences has been minimal (Panagariya, 1993 and 1994). Even if this mode were to be employed, since it cannot include developed countries, it would be done outside APEC. Instead, the member countries have chosen to lower trade barriers on a non-discriminatory basis.

The main mode of trade liberalization in Asia has been either unilateral liberalization by developing countries as a part of their trade reforms, or negotiated liberalization on an MFN basis under the auspices of GATT. Though APEC and AFTA may have helped to speed up the commitments to liberalization under these modes (as Bergsten (1996) likes to claim to be the case) they have not been the primary force.

For its part, the US government is not in the least interested in offering reductions in its trade barriers without reciprocity. In other words, the USA does not plan to lower trade barriers on a non-discriminatory basis, since such a move would give the EU additional access to the US market without having to offer any reciprocal liberalization. Therefore, if trade liberalization within the APEC framework is to incorporate all members without violating GATT, the logical outcome is an APEC free trade area or customs union. Though neither the US administration nor the EPG has explicitly advocated such a bloc, it is the only possible implication of the demand for reciprocity while preserving consistency with GATT. An FTA does, infact, sit well with the Clinton Administration's new-found wisdom on trade policy, which has elevated PTAs to more or less the same status as multilateral liberalization. Thus, echoing Lawrence Summers, quoted earlier, the Report of the President's Council of Economic Advisers (1995, pp. 214–15) notes.[12]

Possibly the most distinctive legacy of this Administration in international trade is the foundation it has laid for the development of open, overlapping plurilateral trade agreements as stepping stones to global free trade. The Administration's plurilateral initiatives in North America, the rest of the Western Hemisphere, and Asia embody principles of openness and inclusion consistent with GATT. They will serve as vehicles for improving access to foreign markets.

Of course, the Asian member countries do not share US enthusiasm for either reciprocity or 'negotiated liberalization'. Instead, they have shown a clear preference for adherence to the MFN principle. At Osaka, the Asian view of 'concerted unilateralism' prevailed, with each member being offered the opportunity to adopt voluntarily its separate path to liberalization. In pursuit of the Bogor goal of free trade by 2010 or 2020, the member countries were asked to provide a first 'down payment' for free trade at the following annual meeting in the Philippines in December 1996.

Thus, on the face of it, Asian members of APEC may have countered the US insistence on reciprocity successfully. (As an aside, it may be noted that the EPG, which had advocated the US position forcefully, their term having expired, were allowed to disband rather than be given another term.) Saxonhouse (1996) certainly takes this view. But I must agree with Barfield (1996), that in any future liberalization, the 'United States . . . is likely to demand reciprocity'. At Osaka, the Clinton Administration chose to adopt a low profile, perhaps as a part of its overall strategy of avoiding any new trade policy initiatives until after the next election. This stance was consistent with the Administration's decision to put all other trade policy issues (accession of Chile to NAFTA, China's entry into WTO, and acquisition of 'fast track' negotiating authority) on to the back burner. But after the election, regardless of who wins it, there is likely to be a return of the US demands for reciprocity at APEC ministerial meetings.

4   AN APEC FTA?

I have made the point that unless negotiations take place on a multilateral basis, reciprocity necessarily amounts to an FTA or CU under GATT Article XXIV. Because a CU requires the surrender of the authority to choose the external tariff, the bigger members of APEC, in particular the USA, are not interested in it. This limits the choice to an APEC-wide FTA.

In Panagariya (1993 and 1994), I have discussed at length why a discriminatory arrangement such as NAFTA is neither feasible nor desirable among countries in East Asia. In a modified form, most of those arguments extend to the larger set of countries included in APEC. Rather than repeat the arguments put forward there, let me venture to discuss a different argument, made originally in Panagariya (1995 and 1996a) and developed fully in

Bhagwati and Panagariya (1996b).[13] According to this argument, because negotiable barriers to trade such as tariffs are high in some APEC members and low in others (see Appendix Table 1 on pp. 312–15), an FTA among them will result in large redistributive effects, with some countries actually losing. In particular, the countries which have high tariffs are likely to lose from an FTA with countries with low tariffs.

To make the point more simply, suppose Indonesia and Singapore were to form an FTA. Because Singapore already has free trade, the FTA will result in Indonesia offering Singapore tariff-free access to its market without reducing the tariff on goods from outside countries. As long as the FTA does not eliminate imports of any products from outside countries, there will be little change in Indonesia's internal price structure, and hence no improvement in its internal efficiency.[14] Yet, it will lose the tariff revenue collected on imports from Singapore. The revenue will be transferred to exporters from Singapore, who now have access to the internal price of Indonesia. Indonesia's preferential liberalization will hurt itself and benefit Singapore.

If Indonesia were to liberalize on an MFN basis, however, its internal price structure would come to correspond to the border price structure. Therefore, the usual efficiency gains would accrue. With the internal price of imports declining, the tariff revenue lost on imports from all sources would be passed on to Indonesian consumers. There is a fundamental difference between preferential and non-discriminatory liberalization in that the former largely benefits the union partner, while the latter benefits the country which liberalizes.[15]

As argued originally in Panagariya (1996a), this analysis undermines the popular view that NAFTA benefited Mexico. I will argue that, having extended a large margin of preference to the USA without receiving the same in return, on balance Mexico lost from entering NAFTA. The analysis also explains why the exchange of trade preferences within the ASEAN framework has been minimal. The distributional conflict I have highlighted is reflected well in the following statement by a former foreign minister of Indonesia at the 25th Anniversary celebration of the ASEAN:

> Singapore and Malaysia are always telling us to lower tariffs and duties and let their goods into the country. But, in return, how about the free movement of labour? We will take your goods if you take our surplus labour supply. When they hear this and think about all those Indonesians coming to work in their countries, then they say, 'wait a minute, may be it's not such a good idea'.

As Appendix Table 1 shows, except in textiles, apparel and leather, tariffs on industrial products in the USA and Japan are low. Tariffs on all industrial products in Singapore are virtually non-existent. In other countries, particularly China, Indonesia and Thailand, tariffs are high. Clearly, the scope for redistributional effects in the event of preferential liberalization is large.

5 BACK TO MULTILATERALISM

At the present time, a discriminatory APEC bloc is neither desirable nor feasible, which naturally raises the question what role APEC can play in pushing for further trade liberalization?

On the Asian side, particularly among smaller members, there appears to be some enthusiasm for concerted unilateral liberalization. However, the scope is limited for additional liberalization over and above what countries have committed themselves to under the UR, or plan to undertake as a part of their own national reforms as, for example, Indonesia, Thailand and China have done. APEC may be able to speed up the implementation of the UR or national reforms, but any progress beyond that is difficult to envisage. As regards the bigger member countries, they are aware that while unilateral liberalization may bring triangular efficiency gains, it will also bring rectangular terms-of-trade losses. Therefore, they are unlikely to undertake any significant unilateral liberalization. This conclusion leaves in doubt the fate of the Bogor declaration that free trade will be attained by 2010 and 2020.

But maybe not. Representing as they do more than half of world income and trade, APEC members could not only achieve that goal for themselves but also for the rest of the world. But that would require abandoning the pursuit of the illusory 'open regionalism', which is nothing but 'Maya' (or, as Srinivasan (1995) calls it, an oxymoron) and using APEC's clout to nudge the world towards the sure, one fold path to nirvana: multilateralism. In particular, APEC could urge the adoption by the WTO of the free trade goal by 2010 for developed countries, and 2020 for developing countries.[16] Wolf (1996) has noted that an important ingredient missing from the WTO agenda is a deadline for the achievements of global free trade. APEC's deadlines for free trade could thus become the missing deadline of the WTO.

In addition, since investment liberalization has been an integral part of the APEC agenda, it could also lead in this area. Recently, the development of an investment code has become a priority for the WTO; and this item of the WTO agenda is currently being focused on the Multilateral Agreement on Investment (MAI) of the Organization of Economic Co-operation and Development (OECD). APEC could consider developing an alternative agreement on investment which would better serve its membership. The developing Asian countries are not members of OECD, and an OECD-driven investment code may not best serve their interests.

Appendix Table 1   Unweighted average percentage tariff rates pre- and post-Uruguay Round

	Australia 1 pre-UR	Australia 2 post-UR	Canada 1 pre-UR	Canada 2 post-UR	Indonesia 1 pre-UR	Indonesia 2 post-UR	Japan 1 pre-UR	Japan 2 post-UR	Korea 1 pre-UR	Korea 2 post-UR	Mexico 1 pre-UR	Mexico 2 post-UR	Malaysia 1 pre-UR	Malaysia 2 post-UR
Paddy rice	11.0	1.0	70.0	0.0	9.0	9.0	500.0	444.0	49.0	49.0	8.0	8.0	49.0	49.0
Wheat	1.0	0.0	26.0	26.0	0.0	0.0	308.0	193.0	272.0	13.0	0.0	0.0	272.0	13.0
Grains	0.0	0.0	24.0	24.0	6.0	6.0	336.0	180.0	327.0	95.0	0.0	0.0	327.0	95.0
Non-grain crops	3.3	3.3	3.0	3.0	54.7	38.3	42.0	38.7	51.7	47.7	3.0	3.0	51.7	47.7
Wool	0.0	0.0	0.0	0.0	0.0	0.0	0.0	0.0	0.0	0.0	0.0	0.0	0.0	0.0
Livestock	0.0	0.0	0.0	0.0	0.0	0.0	0.0	0.0	118.0	83.0	0.0	0.0	118.0	83.0
Forestry	0.0	0.0	0.7	0.0	4.7	4.7	0.4	0.2	4.2	2.4	1.3	1.3	6.4	6.3
Fishing	0.0	0.0	0.1	0.5	13.4	13.4	4.1	2.7	14.8	10.3	5.5	5.5	7.5	4.8
Coal	0.0	0.0	0.0	0.0	2.6	2.6	0.4	0.3	2.2	0.6	0.6	0.6	1.8	1.8
Oil	0.0	0.0	0.0	0.0	0.7	0.7	0.0	0.0	2.4	2.4	0.0	0.0	0.9	0.9
Gas	1.7	0.7	1.6	1.6	0.7	0.7	1.7	0.0	1.8	1.6	0.9	0.9	1.5	1.5
Other minerals	0.7	0.5	0.0	0.0	2.4	2.4	0.6	0.0	4.4	2.7	4.8	4.8	3.5	3.5
Processed rice	1.0	0.0	7.0	7.0	0.0	0.0	36.5	36.5	78.0	41.0	0.0	0.0	78.0	41.0
Meat	4.5	0.5	26.0	26.0	12.7	10.7	308.0	193.0	114.0	32.5	19.5	19.5	272.0	13.0
Milk	19.0	7.0	157.0	157.0	0.0	0.0	207.0	207.0	111.0	111.0	4.0	4.0	111.0	111.0
Other food	0.0	0.0	0.0	0.0	0.0	0.0	0.0	0.0	0.0	0.0	0.0	0.0	0.0	0.0
Beverages and tobacco	0.0	0.0	0.0	0.0	0.0	0.0	0.0	0.0	29.5	20.8	0.0	0.0	29.5	20.8
Textiles	23.6	14.1	15.9	10.4	31.6	24.2	6.1	4.0	16.1	10.7	12.6	12.6	23.3	16.1
Wearing apparel	58.9	37.2	22.6	16.4	38.8	29.8	13.5	9.1	20.5	13.8	14.6	14.6	24.3	17.6
Leather	22.8	14.9	15.4	10.2	14.5	12.9	15.1	12.9	18.4	9.4	9.7	9.7	22.3	18.2
Lumber	15.7	7.4	9.2	4.0	27.5	24.6	4.4	1.6	16.8	12.0	12.6	12.6	24.5	17.9
Pulp paper	11.3	6.3	7.3	0.0	10.6	10.6	2.5	0.0	7.5	0.0	4.5	4.5	5.9	5.3
Oil and coal	1.6	0.9	0.8	0.5	3.7	3.7	1.6	1.4	7.7	4.2	2.5	2.5	8.2	7.1
Chemicals	11.2	7.3	10.9	6.0	5.6	5.6	5.4	2.5	15.3	6.7	8.9	8.9	7.7	6.7
Non-metallic mineral products	12.5	8.4	10.3	4.8	17.1	15.1	3.2	1.4	18.0	12.3	12.0	12.0	22.7	19.3

Primary ferrous metals	8.8	1.6	7.7	1.4	5.5	5.5	4.3	0.9	8.4	1.9	6.0	6.0	4.9	4.9
Non-ferrous metals	10.3	4.8	4.0	1.9	10.8	10.4	1.8	0.6	14.4	6.5	4.7	4.7	6.0	5.2
Fabricated metals	15.8	10.9	8.3	4.9	20.4	20.2	4.6	0.9	18.3	11.8	12.6	12.6	16.7	13.6
Transport	13.2	9.8	6.5	4.3	15.8	15.0	2.4	0.0	13.8	11.4	8.8	8.8	14.5	14.2
Machinery	12.6	7.8	5.1	2.3	14.6	14.2	3.8	0.1	18.1	7.1	11.7	11.7	8.4	5.4
Other manu-facturing	15.5	11.6	10.4	4.2	32.2	28.6	4.1	2.3	18.6	8.8	15.4	15.4	14.4	12.6
Electricity, water and gas	0.0	0.0	0.0	0.0	0.0	0.0	0.0	0.0	0.0	0.0	0.4	0.4	0.0	0.0

	New Zealand 1 pre-UR	New Zealand 2 post-UR	Philippines 1 pre-UR	Philippines 2 post-UR	Singapore 1 pre-UR	Singapore 2 post-UR	Thailand 1 pre-UR	Thailand 2 post-UR	USA 1 pre-UR	USA 2 post UR	China 1 pre-UR	China 2 post-UR
Paddy rice	11.0	1.0	49.0	49.0	5.9	2.2	49.0	49.0	0.0	0.0	0.0	0.0
Wheat	1.0	0.0	272.0	13.0	7.0	2.69	272.0	13.0	13.0	4.0	0.0	0.0
Grains	0.0	0.0	327.0	95.0	14.1	5.29	327.0	95.0	0.0	0.0	3.0	3.0
Non-grain crops	3.3	3.3	51.7	47.7	22.2	7.49	51.7	47.7	42.0	42.0	13.9	11.8
Wool	0.0	0.0	0.0	0.0	2.3	0.9	0.0	0.0	8.0	5.0	15.0	15.0
Livestock	0.0	0.0	118.0	83.0	25.8	9.6	118.0	83.0	0.0	0.0	71.7	39.6
Forestry	0.0	0.0	3.0	3.0	0.0	0.0	6.2	4.9	0.0	0.0	7.3	7.1
Fishing	1.6	0.7	11.0	7.1	1.9	0.7	36.8	12.7	0.3	0.2	23.0	17.1
Coal	0.0	0.0	7.8	7.8	0.0	0.0	8.7	8.7	0.0	0.0	15.0	13.5
Oil	0.0	0.0	3.0	3.0	0.0	0.0	4.3	4.39	0.4	0.4	2.0	2.0
Gas	0.0	0.0	5.2	5.2	0.0	0.0	0.0	0.09	0.0	0.0	3.5	27.5
Other minerals	2.7	1.3	10.2	9.9	0.0	0.0	10.9	7.29	0.7	0.2	18.7	18.5
Processed rice	1.0	0.0	78.0	41.0	10.6	3.9	78.0	41.09	2.0	2.0	47.4	0.0
Meat	4.5	0.5	272.0	13.0	15.2	3.1	272.0	13.09	13.0	4.0	28.0	37.6
Milk	19.0	7.0	111.0	111.0	22.3	4.2	111.0	111.09	92.0	92.0	28.0	25.3
Other food	0.0	0.0	0.0	0.0	16.5	6.1	0.0	0.09	0.0	0.0	28.7	26.0
Beverages and tobacco	0.0	0.0	29.5	20.8	25.0	9.3	29.5	20.89	0.0	0.0	65.0	62.5
Textiles	10.9	8.2	33.6	23.3	1.2	0.4	56.6	26.59	9.6	7.4	55.0	38.9
Wearing apparel	40.5	31.3	39.7	26.3	3.9	3.9	56.7	22.9	17.9	15.9	83.3	39.9
Leather	34.3	25.6	25.4	25.4	0.5	0.5	43.2	28.5	7.4	6.6	64.8	43.4
Lumber	23.3	11.8	24.9	24.9	1.3	0.2	34.3	16.1	3.5	1.1	51.0	32.1
Pulp paper	20.3	0.0	25.1	24.1	0.0	0.0	24.3	20.3	1.7	0.0	31.3	27.2
Oil and coal	3.8	3.0	12.7	12.7	10.7	10.7	21.4	21.1	1.7	0.8	15.5	15.5
Chemicals	13.7	7.7	19.5	17.4	1.1	0.4	34.0	30.1	4.7	3.1	31.8	28.3
Non-metalic mineral products	13.3	9.5	26.6	26.4	0.0	0.0	31.9	25.8	7.6	5.2	45.9	35.2
Primary ferrous metals	10.8	8.5	12.8	12.8	0.0	0.0	14.2	13.8	3.7	1.0	22.3	18.9
Non-ferrous metals	15.3	9.5	20.8	19.0	0.0	0.0	16.2	11.7	1.7	1.0	11.9	10.9
Fabricated metals	16.6	13.2	30.7	30.6	0.0	0.0	33.6	31.8	4.1	2.2	44.4	34.5

Transport	14.4	12.3	22.4	22.2	0.9	0.9	50.6	41.1	2.9	2.5	69.3	69.3
Machinery	19.5	9.9	23.3	20.4	0.1	0.0	35.7	25.4	3.4	1.5	31.5	28.4
Other manu-facturing	26.5	18.1	31.1	31.1	0.4	0.3	41.6	26.8	5.5	2.7	70.9	44.4
Electricity, water and gas	0.0	0.0	0.0	0.0	0.1	0.0	0.0	0.0	0.0	0.0	3.0	3.0

Source: The Pacific Economic Cooperation Council for APEC, 1995, Survey of Impediments to Trade and Investment in the APEC Region.

Notes

1. Section 301 of the US Trade Act of 1974 introduced a provision for retaliation against foreign practices that 'unreasonably' restrict US exports. The Omnibus Trade Practices Act of 1988 strengthened Section 301 of the 1974 Act by introducing what are called Super 301 and Special 301 provisions. Accordingly, the United States Trade Representative is required to identify foreign practices which, if eliminated, will have the greatest benefit for US commerce and to seek removal of those practices under the threat of retaliation. Investigation of policies of foreign countries which restrict US exports of goods and services is done under Super 301, and of policies that deny American residents the protection of intellectual property rights (for example, patents, trademarks and copyright) under Special 301. It is expected that with the strengthened dispute-settlement machinery of the WTO and expected implementation of the Trade-Related Intellectual Property Rights Agreement of the Uruguay Round Agreement, the scope for unilateral actions under Super 301 and Special 301 will be reduced considerably.
2. The EPG were appointed to advise APEC in 1992 for a term of three years, which expired in 1995. The USA, being the incoming chair of APEC at the time, was able to have C. Fred Bergsten of the Institute for International Economics appointed to chair the group.
3. As Bhagwati (1993) notes, Brock's approach was not circumscribed geographically and he had offered FTAs even to Egypt and the Association of South East Asian Nations (ASEAN).
4. Reason because the EC needed the extra push to start negotiating seriously; excuse because the USA had by then discovered a taste for negotiations in a regional context and would have wanted to pursue NAFTA irrespective of the EC's willingness to negotiate seriously under GATT.
5. Whether PTAs are a building block or a stumbling block on the way to multilateral free trade is a controversial issue. The rapidly growing theoretical literature on this subject is reviewed in Bhagwati and Panagariya (1996a). For contributions favourable to PTAs, see Krugman (1991), Summers (1991), Frankel and Wei (1997), and Goto and Hamada (1996). The last of these contributions favours unequivocally an APEC FTA.
6. Trade diversion is said to have occurred when, as a result of the tariff preference, a member country expands its exports to another member by displacing more efficient suppliers located outside the union. Trade creation occurs when such expansion is at the expense of the less efficient suppliers in the importing member country. Trade diversion is likely to reduce welfare, and trade creation likely to increase it.
7. This point was made forcefully by Bhagwati (1993).
8. For details, see Halevi and Kleiman (1994).
9. I have frequently encountered the argument that, in comparison with the increases in trade barriers in the wake of the macroeconomic crisis in Mexico in the early 1980s, the recent tariff increases were minuscule. There are two problems with this argument. First, since the early 1980s, there has been a complete reversal in the conventional wisdom on how countries should respond to balance-of-payments crises. In the past, the uniform advice, including that given by the IMF, to countries facing balance-of-payments crises was to raise trade barriers. Today, the advice is to take the opportunity to carry out trade reforms that are difficult in times of stability. As a result, even India, the last major bastion of

protectionism, ended up liberalizing its trade regime after a balance-of-payments crisis, even though the country had no PTA with the USA or the EU. Second, Mexico was given a massive $40 billion debt-relief package to deal with the recent peso crisis, which was not available at the time of the previous crisis.

10. In a recent paper, Bergsten (1996), whose views mirror that of the Clinton Administration on US trade policy in Asia, puts the following positive spin on the US success in blocking an exclusively Asian trade bloc: 'By joining East Asia and North America, APEC has eliminated any possibility of the three-block world that was widely feared a few years ago'.

11. See *The Economist*, 25 November 1995, pp. 75–6.

12. One may also note in passing that in early 1994, the Administration had also discussed the possibility of extending NAFTA to Korea. See Saxonhouse (1996) for details.

13. See also Panagariya (1996b).

14. Strictly speaking, this assumes that Indonesia and Singapore are small relative to the rest of the world.

15. As shown in Panagariya (1995), this analysis remains valid in a modified form if the FTA is formed when import quotas exist.

16. This suggestion essentially follows Bhagwati's (1995) suggestion that APEC should transform its goal of open and free trade and investment in the region, from an APEC-alone liberalization, into an APEC initiative in conjunction with the G7 to launch the next round of *multilateral trade negotiations* to reduce trade barriers on a non-discriminatory MFN basis.

References

APEC (1993) *A Vision for APEC*, Report of the Eminent Persons Group to APEC Ministers (Singapore: Asia-Pacific Co-operation).

APEC (1994) *Achieving the APEC Vision*, Second Report of the Eminent Persons Group to APEC Ministers (Singapore: Asia-Pacific Co-operation).

Barfield, C. E. (1996) 'Regionalism and U.S. Trade Policy', in J. Bhagwati and A. Panagariya (eds) *The Economics of Preferential Trade Agreements* (Washington, DC: AEI Press).

Bergsten, C. F. (1996) 'Globalizing Free Trade', *Foreign Affairs*, May/June, pp. 105–20.

Bhagwati, J. (1993) 'Regionalism and Multilateralism: An Overview', in J. de Melo and A. Panagariya (eds) *New Dimensions in Regional Integration* (Cambridge: Cambridge University Press).

Bhagwati, J. (1995) 'U.S. Trade Policy: The Infatuation with Free Trade Areas', in J. Bhagwati and A. O. Krueger (eds), *The Dangerous Drift to Preferential Trade Agreements* (Washington, DC: American Enterprise Institute for Public Policy Research).

Bhagwati, J. and A. Panagariya (1996a) 'Preferential Trading Areas and Multilateralism: Strangers, Friends or Foes?' in Jagdish Bhagwati and A. Panagariya (eds), *The Economics of Preferential Trade Agreements* (Washington, DC: AEI Press).

Bhagwati, J. and A. Panagariya (eds) (1996b) *The Economics of Preferential Trade Agreements* (Washington, DC: AEI Press).

Council of Economic Advisors (1995) *Economic Report of the President, 1995* (Washington, DC: Council of Economic Advisers).

Ellis, H. (1945) 'Bilateralism and the Future of International Trade', *Essays in International Finance*, no. 5, Summer (Princeton, NJ: Princeton University).

Frankel, J. and S. J. Wei (1997) 'The New Regionalism and Asia: Impact and Options', in A. Panagariya, M. G. Quibria and N. Rao (eds), *The Global Trading System and Developing Asia* (Hong Kong: Oxford University Press).

Goto, J. and K. Hamada (1996) 'Regional Economic Integration and Article XXIV of the GATT', Discussion paper, Economic Growth Center (New Haven, Conn.: Yale University).

Grossman, G. and E. Helpman (1995) 'The Politics of Free Trade Agreements', *American Economic Review*, September, pp. 667–90.

Halevi, N. and E. Kleiman (1994) 'Israel's Trade and Payments Regime', Paper prepared for the Regional Trade Group, Institute for Social and Economic Policy in the Middle East, Kennedy School of Government, Cambridge, Mass.

Kowalczyk, C. and D. Davis (1996) 'Tariff Phase Outs: Theory and Evidence from GATT and NAFTA', in Jeffrey Frankel (ed.), *Regionalization of the World Economy* (Chicago: University of Chicago Press).

Krishna, P. (1995) 'Regionalism and Multilateralism: A Political Economy Approach', mimeo, Economics Department, Columbia University.

Krugman, P. (1991) 'The Move to Free Trade Zones', Symposium on *Policy Implications of Trade and Currency Zones*, sponsored by the Federal Reserve Bank of Kansas City.

Melo, J. de and A. Panagariya (eds) (1993) *New Dimensions in Regional Integration* (Cambridge: Cambridge University Press).

Panagariya, A. (1993) 'Should East Asia Go Regional? No, No and Maybe', WPS 1209 (Washington, DC: World Bank).

Panagariya, A. (1994) 'East Asia and the New Regionalism', *World Economy*, vol. 17, no. 6, November, pp. 817–39.

Panagariya, A. (1995) 'Rethinking the New Regionalism', Paper presented at the Trade Expansion Program Conference of the UNDP and World Bank, January.

Panagariya, A. (1996a) 'The Free Trade Area of the Americas: Good for Latin America?', *World Economy*, vol. 19, no. 5.

Panagariya, A. (1996b) 'Preferential Trading and the Myth of Natural Trading Partners', Working Paper no. 200, Center for Japan–US Business and Economic Studies, Stern School of Business, New York University.

Saxonhouse, G. R. (1996) 'Regionalism and U.S. trade Policy in Asia', in J. Bhagwati, and A. Panagariya (eds), *The Economics of Preferential Trade Agreements* (Washington, DC: AEI Press).

Srinivasan, T. N. (1995) 'APEC and Open Regionalism', mimeo.

Summers, L. (1991) 'Regionalism and the World Trading System', Symposium, on *Policy Implications of Trade and Currency Zones*, sponsored by the Federal Reserve Bank of Kansas City.

Viner, J. (1950) *The Customs Union Issue* (New York: Carnegie Endowment for International Peace).

Wolf, M. (1996) 'A Vision for World Trade', *Financial Times*, 27 February, p. 12.

Yeats, A. J. (1996) 'Does Mercosur's Trade Performance Justify Concerns About the Effects of Regional Trade Arrangements? Yes!', mimeo, World Bank.

Part IV
Trade and Endogenous Growth

15 Trade and Trade Policy in Endogenous Growth Models

M. Scott Taylor
UNIVERSITY OF BRITISH COLUMBIA

1 INTRODUCTION

Since the late 1980s, trade theorists have been aware that trading opportunities and trade policy can have important, and lasting, effects on a nation's rate of economic growth. Conversely, since the time of Edgeworth, Mill and Ricardo trade economists have been studying the consequences of ongoing improvements in technology and growth of factor endowments for trading opportunities and trade policy. I follow this division of labour by specializing this review in a similar, and, I hope, complementary manner. The first goal of this chapter is to synthesize the major theoretical results from *the new growth theory* linking international trade and trade policy to permanent and lasting effects on growth rates. The second goal is to study how the consequences of ongoing endogenous growth may affect the incentives governments have to restrict trade at a point in time, and how endogenous growth can shape and limit the form of self-enforcing trade liberalizations that are supportable over time.

As with any review, this one must be selective and hence, by design, incomplete. There are now well over a hundred papers on endogenous growth and trade, and some criteria must be adopted to limit the scope of the analysis and to set its focus. In an attempt to provide an analytical review of the literature I have chosen to review in detail only a relatively small subset of it. This sub-set was chosen to illustrate as clearly as possible the four major channels through which trade and trade policy can affect growth, and it undoubtedly reflects my own reading and predispositions. I can only apologize at the outset to those whose work I have left out, by either ignorance or oversight.

Given the limitations of space, I am deliberately excluding any examination of the effects of industrial policy – such as research and development (R&D) and production subsidies – of competition policy, and of policies affecting intellectual property rights. I will have relatively little to say about North–South models with innovation and imitation, and will primarily discuss

R&D-based models where growth occurs via the purposeful action of economic agents seeking profits.[1] And, not surprisingly, I will have nothing definitive to report on the normative implications of trade policy in an endogenous growth context. Apart from some limited and somewhat artificial exercises, there is nothing to compare with the scale or scope of conventional trade policy discussions in this regard. This is certainly an area worthy of further research, but normative analysis within an endogenous growth framework is not at all easy going.[2] We can add to the usual difficulties introduced by a dynamic environment the further contributions of both intratemporal and intertemporal distortions, and issues of time-consistency. Grossman and Helpman (1993a) contain a cogent review of the issues involved and I have little to add here. I will, however, report on the welfare results that are known as they relate to my discussion of the literature.

The chapter proceeds as follows. In Section 2 I first define and then examine within the context of the literature the scale, allocation, spillover and redundancy effects. These are the four channels through which 'openness' to international markets in goods, knowledge and factors can affect a country's growth rate. After identifying and explaining each effect, I turn to at least one illustrative trade policy example drawn from published work, the examples having been selected to allow me to draw a direct link between the dominance of one or another channel of influence and the effect of a trade-policy experiment. My reading of the endogenous growth literature suggests that the details of model structure often have an undue impact on the outcome of any trade-policy experiment. Therefore, I have chosen to focus on the mechanisms that translate trade and trade policy to growth, rather than report exhaustively on the outcomes of many different policy experiments in many different contexts.

In Section 3 I turn to a relatively neglected role for endogenous growth theory – explaining the pattern of protection over time. Because growth alters a nation's production structure over time, it also alters the incentives and motivations for governments to restrict international trade. Here I review recent work by Michael Devereux to illustrate that within an endogenous growth framework, the incentive to restrict trade is importantly affected by the interplay of knowledge spillovers and the rate of endogenous growth. The concluding Section 4 sums up the review and makes some suggestions for future research.

2   THE THEORY

The literature on endogenous growth and trade has experienced an explosion of sorts since the seminal work of Romer (1987) and Grossman and Helpman (1990). While there are many different approaches to modelling endogenous growth and trade, there are also some strong similarities across models. As a consequence, it is useful to begin with a taxonomy that describes the effects that mobility of goods, knowledge and factors can have on growth. By examining how these various forms of openness can affect growth, we can then move to examine the growth implications of trade restrictions.

It is perhaps wise to remind the reader at the outset that the connection between growth rates and welfare levels is rarely direct, even in a closed economy. Therefore, focusing on growth alone can in some cases be misleading. It must be granted, however, that if trade policy creates changes in growth rates, these effects are likely to have welfare consequences of an order of magnitude more important than the usual static consumption and production distortions created by trade restrictions. Therefore, I take it as fundamental that we distinguish and clarify what is a level effect from what is a growth effect. Complicating the analysis, however, is the fact that almost any change in tastes, technologies or endowments can, in principle, affect growth rates in an endogenous growth framework. As a result, if we are not careful, an 'almost anything goes' flavour can creep into the analysis, and this would be both inaccurate and a disservice to those who have contributed to this field.

By employing an analytical taxonomy I hope to impose a discipline on this review that will help to give the reader a flavour of the key channels through which trade can affect growth, and at the same time help us to glean some important lessons for trade policy. The taxonomy I employ is borrowed from Rivera-Batiz and Romer (1991a), and Grossman and Helpman (1993a, ch. 9). Rivera-Batiz and Romer employed this taxonomy to explain their own results, but here I use it as an organizing principle for a much larger set of results. Take for the starting point of our analysis a two-country trading world where each country is engaged in both production and R&D. Then a tariff, a subsidy, or a quantitative restriction, if it is to affect growth, must have an intermediate effect on one or all of the following: (i) the scale of R&D or production activities – *the scale effect*; (ii) the allocation of primary factors across activities – *the allocation effect*; (iii) the flow of knowledge across countries – *the spillover effect*; and, finally, (iv) the originality of the R&D conducted in each country – *the redundancy effect*. In what follows I will explain and explore each of these effects in turn.

The Scale Effect

Much has been made of the fact that a common feature of endogenous growth models is that the size of the market or scale of factor endowments directly affects the growth rate of per capita output. This feature has been both ridiculed and embraced by those commenting on the research.[3] In a closed economy, scale can be related unambiguously to the magnitude of primary factor endowments, but in an open economy we must be careful to distinguish between three very different scale effects. In an open economy, scale effects are created both by an increase in the world's primary factor base and by the integration of markets across countries. For example, in an open economy there are scale effects created by integrating the world market for primary factors of production (that is, labour or capital mobility), by integrating the flows of intangible and non-rival 'knowledge capital' (that is, effects created by the international transmission of ideas), and by the integration of goods markets (that is, effects created by expanding international trade). As a result, it is useful to discuss each source of scale effects separately; moreover, to reinforce the point that scale effects in a trading world are conceptually distinct from those in a closed economy, I will often refer to these as 'integration effects'.

Integration via Trade in Goods

It should come as no surprise to trade theorists that integration in goods or factor markets can often substitute for each other, and that integrating the flows of useful technical information around the world could also have a decisive impact on goods trade and growth. To start, however, I employ two models of endogenous growth where the flow of goods is very difficult to separate from the flow of knowledge. These models are introduced first because they capture the core intuition that larger markets can mean faster growth, and because they set the stage for me to disentangle the separate impacts of flows of goods and of knowledge in subsequent sections.

A useful formal specification that demonstrates integration effects is the 'lab equipment' model developed by Rivera-Batiz and Romer (1991b). They assume that labour and human capital are the only primary factors used in production, and that there is only one final good in existence. Production incorporates constant returns to scale (CRS) in labour, human capital and intermediate inputs, and an important simplifying assumption is that all production activities share the same production function. For example, one unit of any intermediate can be produced by forgoing one unit of final goods production, and B units of new product designs per unit time can be produced by forgoing one unit of final goods production. Hence, not only do final goods and intermediates share the same production function, but designs are produced by a production function that differs at most by a scalar. More formally, we have:

$$X_l = L_m^\alpha H_m^\beta \int_0^n x_{im}^{1-\alpha-\beta} di$$

$$\frac{dn}{dt} = BL_r^\alpha H_r^\beta \int_0^n x_{ir}^{1-\alpha-\beta} di$$

where x_{ij} is the employment of intermediate i in sector j, dn/dt is the rate of new product introduction, and X_l measures manufactured output of both final goods and intermediates. L refers to labour, H to human capital, and subscript r refers to the research sector and subscript m to manufacturing. Even though there are three conceptually distinct activities: R&D; manufacturing intermediate products; and manufacturing final output, I will follow Rivera-Batiz and Romer (hereafter designated R&R), and refer to this as a one-sector model because all activities share the same factor intensities.

To examine international trade, R&R assume that there are two identical countries in the world. Since there is only one final output, all trade in this model is intra-industry trade in intermediate products. Perhaps the most important feature of this set up is that, given the one-sector structure, the relative prices of all outputs (the final good, the intermediates, and the designs) are fixed by technology alone. For example, taking the final good as numeraire we know that the resource cost of a new patentable design is just $1/B$ units of the final good. Not surprisingly, this one factor structure in concert with R&R's assumption of identical countries, leaves 'quantities' to do all the adjusting in the movement to trade.

Consider the effects of trade. With international trade the market for each intermediate product doubles, each country engages in intra-industry trade, and the profitability of R&D rises. This rise in the profitability of R&D must now be eliminated by some process. Since the price of final output relative to the price of a new design is fixed by the one-sector structure, the relative price of patent ownership cannot rise to capitalize the greater profits. Since the value of holding a design for a new product must also equal the present discounted value of operating profits *ad infinitum*, operating profits per variety must somehow be reduced to restore a zero profit equilibrium in the R&D sector.

The vehicle for the elimination of excess profits is a faster rate of introduction of competing products. To see this effect, note that the R&D equation can be written (given symmetric intermediates) as:

$$\frac{dn}{dt} = BL_r^\alpha H_r^\beta n x^{1-\alpha-\beta}$$

Given the constant elasticity of substitution (CES) formulation the number of available varieties rises to $n + n^* = 2n$ in trade, but each variety is now employed at only half its previous level or $x/2$. If we assume a constant intersectoral allocation of resources to isolate a pure scale effect we have:

$$\left[\frac{dn}{dt}/n\right]^T = 2^{\alpha+\beta}\left[\frac{dn}{dt}/n\right]^A$$

where superscript *T* refers to trade and *A* to autarky. Therefore, the rate of product development rises with trade. Given this faster rate of introduction of competing products, there is a greater number of new products at each point in time, a reduced market share for each product, and hence lower operating profits. From the final output production function we can also note that a faster rate of product introduction also means that final output also grows faster. We have a pure scale effect created by the integration of goods markets.

It is important to note that the rate of growth does not rise because the market for any intermediate is larger with trade than in autarky. In fact, although the overall size of the market for intermediates doubles with trade, the quantity of any intermediate produced remains unchanged with each country employing $x/2$ units. Growth accelerates because the productivity of R&D rises with the now greater slate of intermediate products available in trade. This level effect on the productivity of R&D, translates into a growth effect on final output.

In the 'lab equipment' model, technology ties down the cost of inventing a new product relative to other potential economic activities. When market size is enlarged and profits rise, R&D is left to carry all the burden of adjustment and create a scale effect. A similar result can be found in the Quality Ladders model of Grossman and Helpman (1991b), although the specifics are quite different.

In the Quality Ladders model Grossman and Helpman (henceforth designated G&H) assume that entrepreneurs conduct R&D to improve on the existing quality of a fixed set of vertically differentiated producer (or consumer) goods. Each innovation represents a move up the quality ladder for that product, and subsequent innovations build on the work of predecessors. Profits are reaped on each product improvement until another innovator displaces the industry leader by moving another step up the quality ladder. The flow of profit from any innovation is proportional to current expenditure on goods, and current expenditure is increasing in the size of the labour force *L*. G&H develop a two-sector trade model using this framework, but here I use the one-sector model to illustrate a slightly different mechanism that implements a scale effect.

In this framework it is most natural to think of technical knowledge flowing with the good because only by observing and inspecting a product can a prospective innovator improve on it and thereby move up the quality ladder. As a result, in this specification it is again difficult to separate the flow of non-appropriable knowledge capital embodied *within* the good from the good itself. In this sense, this model is similar to the earlier R&R specification. Moreover, in the one-factor Quality Ladders model the expected present discounted value of owning a patent on a new product is given entirely by technology. That is, we find that relative prices are again fixed by technology, and with an expansion in market size all the adjustment must occur through quantities.

Suppose the labour force doubled then, in contrast with R&R, this market expansion raises the profitability of conducting R&D because the market for new products is now twice as big. Because the relative price of a patent on a new design cannot increase, R&D must adjust to drive excess profits to zero. Greater R&D now lowers the expected duration of monopoly power for any quality leader. By lowering the expected duration of monopoly power, larger profits are earned for a shorter time period and the value of a patent relative to all other activities is maintained. As a consequence of the increase in R&D, we again find that growth is hastened via a scale effect.

The approaches of R&R and G&H both yield similar predictions concerning market expansion and growth. They differ significantly, however, in the means by which the profitability of R&D is enhanced, and the exact mechanism through which rents are dissipated. Despite these differences, a robust feature of models where it is difficult to distinguish between the flow of goods and the flow of knowledge is that a scalar increase in market size will increase R&D. As a result, growth can be enhanced as a result of trade in goods alone. An almost inescapable consequence of this form of integration effect is that if trade restrictions limit the extent of the market by shutting out foreign products, or lower the profitability of entering foreign markets, then economic growth should be correspondingly lower. Before turning to two trade policy experiments which find just this, I should qualify my remark by noting that in some situations where trade increases market size, it may not raise the profitability of R&D.

For example, G&H (1993b) present a small, open-economy model where openness to trade in goods does not have a direct effect on the profitability of R&D. In their model, the small, open economy produces two final goods that are produced with non-tradable intermediates and industry-specific primary factors. R&D efforts increase the number (measure) of intermediate products produced domestically. To generate diversified production in a steady state, the share of intermediate goods in final goods production is fixed and identical across sectors. A consequence of this assumption is that when this small, open economy is exposed to international trade there is no direct increase in the profitability of R&D, and hence no direct scale effect from the integration of goods markets. Not surprisingly, in this situation trade policy does not have any direct scale effects either. As G&H show, the implications of trade policy for growth hinge entirely on how policy reallocates factors of production across the manufacturing and R&D sectors (that is, on allocation effects) and not on how trade policy affects the extent of the market.

In contrast, when scale effects are operative they can have important consequences for any trade policy experiment. For example, R&R (1991a) examine the growth consequences of symmetrical tariffs being imposed by two identical countries. There is only one final output good, and all trade is intra-industry trade in intermediate producer goods. Intermediates are used along with labour and human capital in final goods production, and one unit of any intermediate can be produced from one unit of final output. Importantly, the R&D sector in this model differs from the 'lab equipment' specification described for R&R (1991b) and relies only on the input of human capital and the current stock of freely available knowledge capital. This two-sector structure plays an important role in determining the impact of trade policy, as discussed below.

R&R show that the imposition of symmetrical tariffs reduces growth rates in both economies. However, the reduction in growth rates is not monotonic in the tariffs chosen. As a result, if both governments were to start from non-zero tariffs a further increase might well lead to higher growth rates. The reason why tariffs have a non-monotonic effect on growth is that they create both inter-industry resource reallocations and reductions in the effective market size for intermediate products. When the Foreign country imposes tariffs on Home exports of intermediate products the profitability of R&D falls at Home. The tariff acts like a tax on the rents of Home innovators and this, all else equal, would reduce the amount of human capital allocated to R&D and lower growth via a scale effect. Moreover, since larger tariffs squeeze the effective market size for any innovative product we would expect this effect to be monotonic. However (for analytical reasons), R&R are wedded to a symmetrical structure where Home simultaneously imposes a tariff on Foreign intermediates. This tariff on imports of Foreign varieties reduces their use in final goods production at Home and similarly reduces the marginal product of human capital in this sector. Even though there are now two opposing effects, R&R show that growth is always lower with the symmetrical tariffs, but the two partially counteracting effects have varying strengths and this gives rise to non-monotonicity.

A final trade policy experiment that relies heavily on integration effects via goods trade is conducted in Taylor (1994). There I employ a one-factor continuum Ricardian model where continual process innovation drives growth in the long run. There I show that opening up an economy to trade creates what I call 'market expansion effects' that raise R&D and increase the rate of growth. Market expansion created by trade in goods raises the profitability of R&D, leads to an increase in growth rates, and supplies dynamic gains from trade. Since this model is a variant of the one-factor Quality Ladders model, the intuition here is very similar to that discussed earlier. Given the Ricardian structure, the price of any good relative to the value of a design is fixed by technology. With an expansion of market size brought about by trade, R&D increases to dissipate extra-normal returns, the pace of process improvements in the continuum of industries increases, and the growth rate rises.

I would summarize as follows. In models where 'knowledge' is in part embodied in the goods that are traded, and the continual accumulation of knowledge capital drives long-run growth, then access to larger markets will enhance growth. Moreover, trade policy that restricts such access will lower growth. There are at least two important caveats to this statement. First, we have seen that in some cases there may be no direct link between market size and the profits to innovation, and in this case the general equilibrium implications of trade policy will carry the day. I explore this possibility more fully in the section on allocation effects (pp. 332–4). Second, in many situations, knowledge capital may in fact be disembodied, and if this is the case restrictions on trade in goods may have no direct effect on the productivity of research efforts. Accordingly, I now turn to examine the independent effects of integration of knowledge flows and integration of goods flows.

Integration via Flows of Knowledge

To investigate the separate effects that integration of goods and knowledge flows may have on economic growth we need a specification that allows for such a separation. Moreover, once we separate these two influences it becomes critically important to identify the geographic extent of knowledge flows. The 'knowledge-driven' specifications of R&R (1991a) and G&H (1993a, ch. 9) allow for such a separation because they adopt a two-sector structure, where productivity in the R&D sector rises with the extent of knowledge spillovers, whereas productivity in the goods sector is affected by the availability of traded intermediates. In 'knowledge-driven' specifications the R&D sector produces designs according to:

$$\frac{dn}{dt} = \delta R K$$

where K is the current knowledge capital that innovators can draw on, δ is a productivity parameter, and R is the input of primary resources into R&D. If we assume that K is proportional to the total number of products already discovered in the world $(n + n^*)$ then we would say that spillovers are perfect and as a result the flows of knowledge are perfectly integrated around the world. If we take K to be proportional to a specific country's cumulative success in innovating (that is, proportional to either n or n^*), then we would say that spillovers are imperfect and that the flows of knowledge around the world are not integrated. In this case, knowledge is country-specific. Let me delay for the moment any discussion of how these different specifications affect the motives for and implications of trade policy, and consider the growth consequences of integrating knowledge flows around the world.

To start, assume that integration of knowledge flows occurs prior to integration of goods markets. Then G&H (1993a, ch. 9) show that if we take two identical countries in isolation and integrate the flows of knowledge, growth necessarily accelerates. To understand why this result obtains, note that with no integration K is taken to be proportional to the number of products in existence in the domestic (Home) economy and we may as well replace K with n. With integration in the flow of ideas across countries, K now equals $n + \sigma n^*$, where σn^* is a measure of the novel products discovered in the Foreign country. For a given allocation of resources across manufacturing and research the increment of σn^* to the knowledge stock at Home raises the productivity of research and increases the flow of new products. This direct scale or integration effect raises the growth rate of final output. A second effect is also possible because the marginal product of resources used in the research sector rises and this may in turn attract further resources into R&D. Hence the growth rate may also rise from an induced allocation effect. Consequently the integration of knowledge flows, even in the absence of goods trade, can stimulate growth.

From the above it should be clear that the extent to which the growth rate rises depends on the extent of redundancy or duplication in world-wide research efforts. If there is nothing new in the Foreign country, then $\sigma = 0$, all Foreign's efforts are redundant, and growth at Home is unaffected by the integration of knowledge flows. Conversely, if $\sigma = 1$, then all Foreign's efforts are novel and growth is considerably accelerated. In fact, if $\sigma = 1$, G&H go on to show that if we now integrate goods markets, by opening trade in intermediate products, goods trade has only a level effect and no growth effect. Trade doubles the total market size for intermediate products in relation to autarky, but the share of this market for any individual intermediate product falls by half. As a result, there is no increase in the flow of profits from innovation. In addition, although productivity in final goods production rises with the now greater availability of intermediate products, the availability of more varieties of intermediate products does not create a corresponding productivity boost in the R&D sector in knowledge-based specifications. As a result, goods trade alone does not create an additional scale effect, and growth rates are unaffected.

To summarize, then, it may appear that if the flows of knowledge and goods can be separated, and if we start from a position of integrated knowledge flows, trade restrictions that lower goods trade may have only level and not growth effects. This statement is, however, misleading, on two counts. First, the experiment conducted by G&H showing that goods trade had no consequences for growth was one of a move from complete isolation of goods markets to complete free trade in goods. While their result is suggestive of the impact tariffs may have, it is not conclusive. For example, recall that in R&R (1991a) tariffs depress growth rates below their free-trade level; but R&R

also show that for high enough tariffs growth rates once again approach their free-trade level. Hence the total elimination of goods trade may have no effect on growth but a partial elimination will have an effect. Second, in the discussion above, the extent of redundancy was taken as exogenous, but trade in goods may help to eliminate redundancy and thereby spur growth. As a result, if trade policy creates redundancy by sheltering domestic markets and domestic innovators, it may still have important consequences for growth.

Integration via Factor Markets

In many of the existing models, complete integration via factor markets will have no effect on growth rates if either or both goods markets are integrated or knowledge spillovers are international. For example, in the R&R (1991b) 'lab equipment' specification, trade in goods alone creates the same increase in growth rates as does full integration. In the R&R (1991b) and G&H (1993a) 'knowledge-driven' specifications, factor mobility will typically have no effect on growth rates if production is diversified, trade in goods is already achieved, and knowledge spillovers are complete.

Complete integration is equivalent to a scaling-up of market size that will, in most closed economy models, raise growth rates. For some combination of the integration effects via goods trade or knowledge flows to 'work' in open economy settings we are going to have to start with a model with scale effects in autarky. Two recent papers in this area show how scale effects can be removed in models where R&D and new product introduction are still a feature of long-run growth. Jones (1995) eliminates scale effects by altering the knowledge-based accumulation equation to:

$$\frac{dn}{dt} = \delta R^\gamma K^\rho, \quad \text{where} \quad \rho < 1, \gamma < 1$$

where K is again proportional to the cumulative number of innovations already discovered, and R is a measure of resources allocated to R&D. The assumption of $\gamma < 1$ is meant to capture the potential for duplication and overlap that can occur when unorganized and independent researchers conduct R&D contemporaneously. $\rho < 1$ allows for accumulated knowledge to raise research productivity but does not allow for the proportional spillovers assumption ($\rho = 1$) used elsewhere in the literature.

Jones shows that this specification eliminates scale effects so that the size of a country's factor-endowment base has no effect on its rate of growth of per capita output. Instead, he finds that per capita output growth g_y is driven entirely by the rate of population growth, n, with $g_y = \gamma n / [1 - \rho]$. With zero population growth, per capita output is constant. In Jones's specification, long-run growth is driven entirely by parameters that are usually taken to be exogenous to the economic system.

In Young (1995) scale effects are eliminated in a more subtle manner and as a result Young finds that even with zero population growth per capita output grows. He assumes that innovation can occur on two dimensions. Innovators can improve on the quality of the existing products as in the quality ladders formulation, and they can increase the spectrum of differentiated products available. Young shows that in his simplest specification the rate of growth of final output is unaffected by scalar increases in the factor-endowment base. As discussed earlier, an expansion of market size enlarges the rents to any innovation and this must be dissipated through some process. In Young's model the rents are dissipated through largely duplicative research conducted to differentiate products, and hence the growth rate does not rise as a consequence. In a more complicated scenario, Young also shows that scale effects can be negative, with an increase in the scale of factor endowments actually reducing the rate of economic growth.

As yet, neither the work of Young nor of Jones has been translated to a trading context, although many of the results seem clear enough. Young notes that trade between two similar economies in his scenario would bring only level effects on utility but not an increase in growth rates. Growth may still increase as a result of other general equilibrium effects, but the direct effect of scale will be absent. But as I show below, it is difficult to determine a priori the direction of these these general equilibrium allocation effects on the rate of growth.

The Allocation Effect

The presence of integration effects in goods, knowledge or factors is just one channel through which international trade and trade policy can affect growth. A potentially equally important channel is created when trade changes the composition of national output and thereby alters relative factor prices and the allocation of resources to manufacturing and R&D. Here we should be careful to distinguish between within-country and across-country allocation effects. If the proximate cause of growth is located nationally, then within-country allocation effects are critical, as for example, when growth occurs via the introduction of new non-tradable intermediates, as in G&H (1993b). If the proximate cause driving growth is international, perhaps because intermediate inputs are tradable, then both within-country and across-country allocation effects are relevant.

To make these ideas more precise, consider the small, open-economy model of G&H (1993b) that was discussed earlier. In this framework, intermediates are not traded, one final good uses human capital as a specific factor, the other final good uses labour as a specific factor, and R&D uses only human capital. G&H show that an import tariff or export subsidy that protects the human capital-intensive final good must slow growth. Protection here raises the return to human capital and drives up the cost of conducting R&D. Recall that in this framework there are no direct-scale effects, and hence these allocation effects fully determine the consequences of trade policy for growth. Alternatively, a tariff or export subsidy that protects the labour intensive good raises the growth rate. Here again, the result follows entirely from simple allocation effects.

If the proximate cause of growth is determined internationally, then things are a little different. The simplest model in which to examine the interplay of within-country and across-country allocation effects is in Grossman and Helpman (1990). G&H (1990) adopt a Ricardian framework to derive the first rigorous link between trade policy and economic growth. In their formulation, two final consumption goods enter period utility, but each country is (by assumption) the monopoly provider of just one. Each of the final goods is produced by labour alone, together with a list of tradable intermediate inputs. Given this Ricardian specification, we can identify the unit labour requirements of intermediates and of R&D. G&H quite naturally associate a higher relative productivity in R&D as a comparative advantage in R&D versus manufacturing. Trade takes place at both the final-goods level (inter-industry trade), and most importantly for our discussion here, also at the intermediate goods level (intra-industry trade).

G&H consider a series of policy interventions, but here I want to focus on just two. To begin, suppose that the countries share identical technologies and hence no country has a comparative advantage in R&D. G&H show that when there is no comparative advantage in R&D, small tariffs on final good imports (imposed from a starting position of free trade) have no effect on growth rates. A tariff on final-good imports does move resources in the policy-active country towards final-goods production and away from R&D and manufacturing, but this within-country allocation effect has no impact on growth rates at the margin. Growth rates are not affected, because a reverse within-country allocation occurs in the foreign country. The world allocation of resources to R&D stays the same, but its allocation across countries changes. Since no country has a comparative advantage in R&D, a small intervention has no effect on growth.

In a world with non-identical countries and comparative advantage, tariffs and other trade interventions do have growth effects via the allocation effect. For example, when the two countries differ in their ability to conduct R&D versus manufacturing, G&H find that small tariffs on final-good imports will lower growth rates if they are undertaken in the country with a comparative advantage in R&D, and will raise growth rates if protection is undertaken in the country with a comparative disadvantage in R&D. In both cases, the within-country allocation effects do not cancel at the aggregate level because of differences across countries. Similar, and even stronger, results occur in multi-factor models with non-identical countries.

The conclusion to draw from this work is that allocation effects can be very strong, and in fact so strong that what appears to be a growth-enhancing policy may, in fact, lower the growth rate instead.[4] Moreover, the strength of the allocation effect depends on both the production and trade structure and on the similarity across countries. Most trade policies will reallocate resources across sectors of the economy, both at home and abroad. It is tempting to think that small interventions between similar countries may be offsetting and that, as a consequence, trade policies will have little effect on growth. Conversely, if the countries are very dissimilar, then allocation effects may be strong and growth rates can fall. There is some truth to this argument, but it should not be overstated. By reallocating R&D activities across countries, trade interventions can lead to a magnification of differences across countries over time if spillovers are less than perfect.

The Spillover Effect

In the previous sections I have shown that the geographical extent of knowledge spillovers is a critical factor in assessing the impact of trade policy. It is then not surprising that a variety of approaches have been taken to investigate the sensitivity of these models to changes in assumptions regarding knowledge spillovers. Contributors to the existing literature have relaxed the assumption of perfect and instantaneous international spillovers in four ways, and each makes varying assumptions about the diffusion process. We could assume that, in the long run, technical knowledge is freely available everywhere in the world, but that technical information diffuses slowly over time. This approach is taken by G&H (1990). Another approach is to assume that the diffusion lag across countries is infinite, but that diffusion within countries is instantaneous. This approach is taken by Feenstra (1990). Third, we could link the diffusion rate to an endogenous variable of the system (such as trade flows) but assume that the diffusion process itself is not a purposeful activity. This approach is taken in G&H (1991a). Finally, we could link the diffusion process to the purposeful activities of economic agents seeking a profit (that is, to the imitative efforts of entrepreneurs) and this is the approach taken in the innovation-imitation models of endogenous growth (for example, see Segerstrom, Anant and Dinopoulos (1990)). Each of these approaches has some strong points and I will investigate the first three, leaving the reader to investigate the large and still-growing literature on North–South models concerned with imitation and innovation.

G&H (1990) were the first to consider the consequences of diffusion lags in the flow of knowledge. To focus on the effects of a slow diffusion rate, it is useful to take an extreme version of their model, where countries are identical except for scale. As a result, no country has what G&H call a conventional comparative advantage in either R&D or manufacturing. Recall that, in this context, and with instantaneous spillovers, G&H find that a small tariff on the imported final good, or a small export subsidy on final-goods exports has no effect on either country's growth rate. G&H also show, however, that if knowledge spillovers diffuse slowly across countries, then the larger country has an 'acquired' comparative advantage in R&D. As a result, any trade policy that moves resources in the larger country towards final goods production and away from R&D will lower the growth rate. For example, if the larger country imposes a tariff on final-good imports, then R&D in the country falls, and so too does the rate of growth. If an export subsidy is applied by the large country, then again growth slackens. As a result, we have a strong trade policy result that relies on the scope of knowledge spillovers.

A more extreme assumption is that knowledge spillovers are purely national in scope and not international. This case was first examined by Feenstra (1990). Feenstra shows that, in the case of national spillovers, the rates of innovation can be different in the two countries in the long run, and a country that starts behind can fall further behind with trade. What happens is that the smaller country innovates less rapidly in the trade equilibrium than it does in autarky; and that the difference between the two growth rates is proportional to the size of the two economies. In this case, the wages in the smaller country fall over time, although they now have access to a greater number of varieties and the rate of introduction of new varieties is also faster. As a result, the smaller country can lose from trade, but does not necessarily do so. A set of similar results is obtained in G&H (1993a, ch. 8), and Devereux and Lapham (1994).

The second approach linking diffusion to an endogenous variable is examined in G&H (1991a). Here, the knowledge stock is taken to depend not only on the number of varieties that have been invented, but also on the cumulative volume of trade up to time T. They assume that the useable knowledge stock $K = nF(T/n)$, where F is increasing. They then show that the effect on growth, and hence on welfare, of a small tariff on the import good depends quite critically on the functional form of F, and the technology parameters in final goods and intermediate goods production. They also show, however, that when tariff reduction raises the volume of trade in relation to the number of products, then R&D increases and the economy grows faster. Moreover, growth in this economy is already too slow, so that this increase in the growth rate raises welfare.

The conclusion I draw from these studies is that it is hard to overestimate the importance of our assumption regarding the scope of knowledge spillovers. The positive properties of models with and without integrated knowledge flows differ dramatically, and so too can the normative consequences. Without integrated knowledge flows, small differences, history and temporary protection can all matter in the long run, because these models exhibit path dependence. As a result, small doses of appropriately placed and appropriately timed interventions can have large and lasting consequences.

The Redundancy Effect

Trade policy can lower the originality of research conducted in trade partner countries, and since information is a non-rival good, this is an unnecessary waste of resources from a global point of view. From an analytical perspective, if part of the world is conducting redundant research then the knowledge spillovers that flow to the rest of the world are thereby reduced; and this has consequences for growth that are similar to those created by a fall in the stock of available knowledge capital. Certain trade policies, by eliminating competition in intermediate goods, can create redundancy and hence lower growth. For example, take the extreme case of a restrictive trade policy by considering autarky. G&H (1993a, pp. 239–45) show that free trade in goods can eliminate redundant research across countries, and as a result provide an extra boost to growth over and above that provided by the international transmission of knowledge spillovers. In their experiment, trade in goods provides an economic incentive to eliminate duplication and the market pushes σ to zero (see p. 330). Alternatively, their result also indicates that if trade policy moves these two economies from a situation with completely free trade in goods to one with no goods trade, then redundancy in research should result and growth will be slower.

A similar but less stark experiment is conducted in Rivera-Batiz and Romer (1991a). They consider the case where each country selectively prohibits the import of some intermediate good; and this is meant to capture the effects of quotas or other quantitative restrictions. They assume that it is easier to reinvent a product than to invent a new one, and hence innovators in each country necessarily copy the product designs that are prohibited entry to their home market from abroad. By assumption, this imitative activity is legal, given lax protection of intellectual property rights. With this form of selective protection, domestic researchers reinvent the wheel via redundant research. As a result, moving away from free trade in goods enlarges the scope for redundant research and lowers growth rates.

3   A MISSED OPPORTUNITY

An important feature of the preceding review is that none of the literature cited has asked how growth *per se* may affect a nation's ability or willingness to restrict trade over time. Even though models of endogenous growth predict important changes in the production structure of the economy over time, no published work to date examines how these changes in turn may affect the incentive to restrict trade. This section translates the recent results of Devereux (1997) to conventional offer curve analysis as a means for suggesting further work along these lines. Devereux examines how ongoing endogenous growth may affect the ability and willingness of nations to impose tariffs over time. His most important result is that the gradual process of endogenous growth can drive gradual trade liberalization over time, leading to free trade as an endogenous outcome. A striking result of his analysis is the prediction that high growth rates of income should be associated with high and rising trade ratios and falling tariffs over time: low growth rates of income should be associated with diminishing trade ratios and rising tariffs over time. Here I wish to focus on an aspect of Devereux's analysis that is not highlighted in his paper – the importance of knowledge spillovers for the determination of optimal trade policy. Earlier sections of this chapter have shown that the extent of knowledge spillovers is an important determinant of the effects of a given trade policy; here I wish to show that the extent of knowledge spillovers can also determine in an important way the motives for trade policy.

Devereux adopts a relatively simple, two-good Ricardian model, where growth occurs via (unbounded) learning-by-doing that is external to firms. There are only two countries – Home and Foreign, all markets are competitive and, for tractability, Devereux imposes a series of symmetry assumptions to make the two countries mirror images of each other. Consumers spend identical shares of their incomes on each good, countries are of identical size, and production technologies differ across countries but are otherwise symmetrical. In his notation we have for tastes, technologies and endowments in the Home country:

$$W = \sum_{t=0}^{\infty} U_t \delta^t, \quad \text{where} \quad U_t = c_{1t}c_{2t} \quad \text{and} \quad 0 < \delta < 1$$

$$y_{1t} = a_{1t} \quad y_{2t} = bl_{2t} \quad l_{1t} + l_{2t} = 1$$

$$((a_t - a_{t-1})/a_{t-1}) = \sigma(l_{1t-1} + \lambda l^*_{1t-1})$$

$$((b_t - b_{t-1})/b_{t-1}) = \sigma(l_{2t-1} + \lambda l^*_{2t-1})$$

where a^* indicates Foreign-country variables, λ measures the geographical extent of spillovers, U_t is period t utility, c_{1t} and c_{2t} are period t consumption of goods one and two, W is overall welfare, δ is the discount factor, l_{1t} and l_{2t} represent labour allocated to industries 1 and 2 respectively, a_t and b_t represent productivity parameters, and y_{1t} and y_{2t} represent period t production levels of goods one and two; $\lambda = 1$ represents perfect international spillovers across countries (that is, integrated knowledge flows) and $\lambda = 0$ represents purely national spillovers. Similarly, σ measures degree of increasing returns (the common across goods and countries) in the learning-by-doing technology. Foreign has an identical set-up, except that Foreign's 'a' industry is good 2 rather than good 1.

By choice of labels and initial conditions, Devereux ensures that each country has an initial comparative advantage in its 'a' good: Home has a comparative advantage in good 1, and Foreign has a comparative advantage in good 2. Given the symmetry of the set-up, each country allocates half of its labour force to each good in autarky. If free trade with zero tariffs could be assured, both country's would specialize in their export good and the world terms of trade would settle at 1. Because free trade increases specialization and accelerates learning-by-doing, growth rates rise with trade. Governments do, however, have an incentive to restrict trade, and it is assumed that while workers can choose to allocate across sectors at the start of every period, they are fixed in place when the government sets its tariff rate. A very important consequence of this assumption is that today's tariff choice has no impact on tomorrow's growth rate, since labour is (at least temporarily) locked in place. At the start of each period workers disperse between sectors as they anticipate wage rates, and Devereux shows that workers expecting a tariff war never specialize, but that they do reallocate across industries over time in response to changing industry productivities.

Balanced Growth via International Spillovers

To make the connection between conventional static tariff theory and Devereux's results it may be useful to recast his analysis in terms of offer curves. Note that for *a given labour* allocation across industries, which is what governments face when they choose tariffs, the model has fixed 'endowments'. A typical international equilibrium can then be described with our usual offer curve diagram, and I show three such potential equilibria in Figure 15.1.

Home's offer curves are labelled, O_1, O_2 and O_3 and the corresponding Foreign offer curves are starred. Ignore, for the moment, the dashed lines. Choosing good 2 as the numeraire, and assuming that Home imposes an *ad valorem* tariff at rate $S - 1$ we have in any period t, because of equal spending shares, that: $P_t c_{1t} = S_t c_{2t}$ where P_t and S_t are the domestic prices at Home for good 1 and good 2, respectively. Budget balance at a point in time requires $P_t X_t = M_t$, where M_t is Home imports of good 2, and X_t is Home exports of good 1. By eliminating P_t, denoting (momentarily fixed) production levels by y_{it} for $i = 1, 2$, and making use of the definitions $c_{1t} = y_{1t} - X_t$ and $c_{2t} = y_{2t} + M_t$ we have the offer curve for Home during period t: $y_{1t}/X_t = S_t y_{2t}/M_t + S_t + 1$. By similar methods, if Foreign imposes an *ad valorem* tariff at rate $T - 1$ on Home exports of good 1 we have the Foreign offer curve given by: $y_{2t}^*/X_t^* = y_{1t}^* T/M_t^* + T_t + 1$. These offer curves are upward-sloping, as shown in Figure 15.1.[5] This diagram has three different interpretations.

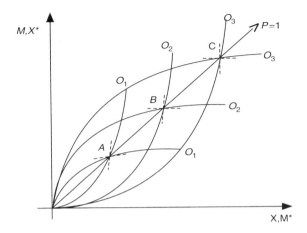

Figure 15.1   Three potential equilibria (Devereux, 1997)

To begin, we can view the diagram as depicting the effect of balanced growth across countries starting from an initial equilibrium at *A*. By balanced growth, I mean growth that leaves both the ratio of outputs in each country unchanged and the share of output across countries the same. As a result of balanced growth, the offer curves shift out uniformly and reach equilibria at points *B* and *C* over time. Moreover, whatever the initial endowments, we could choose units of measurement such that the original equilibria at *A* has a world terms-of-trade equal to 1 and hence, given my assumptions on balanced growth, this terms-of-trade would remain constant over time. It is worth noting at this point that the trade ratio – the sum of exports and imports divided by gross domestic product (GDP) – is constant across these three equilibria. Now introduce trade policy and reinterpret the three sets of offer curves as follows. Suppose that originally with free trade in goods, the international equilibrium is at point *B*. At *B*, both countries have an incentive to restrict trade, and a Nash equilibrium in tariff levels will result in both countries applying positive tariffs. Moreover, with symmetric countries and goods, tariffs will be identical across countries, the world terms of trade will remain at 1, but trade flows must fall, as must welfare in both countries. Hence the equilibrium at *A* could be interpreted as a Nash equilibrium in tariffs, given a potential free trade equilibrium at *B*.

Consider the effect of balanced growth on this trade-war equilibrium. We know that, if balanced growth occurs, this shifts the free-trade offer curves of both Home and Foreign from their potential free-trade intersection at *B* to one depicted by *C*. Moreover, we know that at *C* each country has an incentive to restrict trade and, given symmetry, each will impose an identical tariff on imports. Given the symmetry across countries, the world terms of trade must be 1 in this Nash equilibrium and we can now interpret the intersection at B as the Nash equilibrium in tariffs that arise after balanced growth. The last step is to ask how balanced growth has affected the incentives of countries to impose tariffs, and what the relationship is between the Nash equilibrium tariffs at B and at A. To examine this question, calculate the elasticity of Home's and Foreign's offer curves to find that:

$$(dM_t/dX_t)(X_t/M_t) = (y_{it}/y_{2t})(M_t/X_t)(1/S_t)$$
$$(dX_t^*/dM_t^*)(M_t^*/X_t^*) = (y_{it}^*/y_{2t}^*)(X_t^*/M_t^*)(T_t)$$

Because balanced growth leaves the ratio of outputs in each country unaffected, and the world terms-of-trade remains at 1, we know that the tariffs supporting the Nash equilibrium at B are identical to those at A. Balanced growth (via integrated knowledge flows) has left the Nash equilibrium tariff levels constant. The final use of Figure 15.1 is to reinterpret points A, B and C as a sequence of tariff wars. Note that, in each case, the volume of trade is rising but the trade ratio is constant across equilibria. As a result, Devereux finds that, in the case of balanced growth, tariffs remain constant over time and the trade ratio is constant. He then extends this analysis to examine whether trade liberalization over time can be supported by trigger strategies and shows that, while lower tariffs may be sustained, the lowest co-operative tariff that can be supported (by the threat of infinite reversion to autarky) is constant over time. Hence, in this case, ongoing growth does not make it more likely that we should observe tariffs falling over time.

An interesting feature of this balanced growth scenario is the extent to which ongoing growth *does not change* our standard intuition regarding tariff wars. Note that the conclusions reached above are independent of the degree of increasing returns in the learning-by-doing technology, and hence are independent of the rate of growth in either country. What we find is that, when spillovers are perfect, much of the intuition we would draw from dynamic and static tariff analysis holds up in this endogenous growth context.

Unbalanced Growth via Less Than Perfect Spillovers

What if spillovers are not perfect? With imperfect spillovers, each country gains less from the accumulation of production experience in the other country. Growth is now different across the import and export sectors of each economy and hence 'unbalanced'. Each country specializes in its export good to an increasing extent over time. At Home the ratio of good 1 to good 2 production rises over time; and in Foreign, the ratio of good 2 to good 1 production rises over time. Given the symmetry of the situation, it is still true that the world terms of trade remain at 1, with or without a tariff war, but by using the elasticity formula and noting the definition of unbalanced growth, we know that the offer curves (evaluated along the 45° line) are becoming more inelastic over time. The dashed lines in Figure 15.1 are meant to represent partially-drawn offer curves in this unbalanced growth case.

Unbalanced growth and a fall in elasticities has two consequences for trade policy. First, the incentive to impose tariffs gets stronger over time. In fact, in the sequence of one-period tariff wars, Devereux finds that tariffs rise monotonically over time and trade is driven to zero asymptotically. In Figure 15.1, if we move from *A* to *B* and to *C*, the dashed offer curves are becoming less elastic at the terms-of-trade of 1 and hence the corresponding one-period Nash equilibrium tariffs are rising over time. When Devereux considers self-enforcing agreements he finds that because the two countries are becoming increasingly dissimilar over time, the threat of infinite reversion to autarky becomes more potent over time. Therefore, the lowest co-operative tariff that can be supported by a trigger strategy falls over time. Moreover, for some parameter values, free trade will be an endogenous outcome driven entirely by the process of ongoing and endogenous growth. He also finds that the stronger is learning-by-doing and the smaller are spillovers across countries, the faster is growth and the faster tariffs fall over time.

4 CONCLUSIONS AND SUGGESTIONS FOR RESEARCH

This chapter has presented a partial review and synthesis of research linking trade and trade policy to endogenous growth. While the current work has extended our understanding of the links between trade policy and growth, there is still much left to be done. Devereux (1997) is suggestive of the type of work that should be done in examining the links between ongoing endogenous growth and the pattern of protection over time. To my knowledge, there is very little similar work, and given that his model is quite simple and stylized, extensions to allow for ongoing R&D, product cycles in a North–South context, or sector-specific factors, may be relatively easy to examine.

In addition to following up Devereux (1997) I would suggest further work on 'knowledge spillovers'. The most consistent finding of this review must be that our assumptions regarding knowledge spillovers are often critically important for our answers to questions such as: how does trade affect growth, or how does trade policy affect growth? At one level this should be obvious, since intertemporal spillovers are the driving force behind continual innovation and growth in these models, but at another level it is somewhat disturbing that so much appears to hang on so little. In my discussion of integration effects, the impact of goods trade on growth depended on whether or not knowledge flows were integrated. In the allocation section, I showed how the impact of trade policy can rely quite sensitively on whether knowledge diffuses slowly over time or instantaneously. In the spillovers section, the extent of knowledge spillovers was again critical because it could lead to hysteresis. Finally, in my discussion of Devereux's paper the extent of spillovers had a large impact on both the one-period incentive to restrict trade and the viability of self-enforcing trade liberalizations.

When small changes in assumptions yield large changes in a model's predictions, the theoretically inclined typically suggest changes that make endogenous those formally rigid aspects of the model. Here that would mean moving away from assumptions where knowledge is either local or global to models where knowledge flows are endogenously determined within the system. The problem remains, however, as to how this should be done. Should we model the process as being under the direct control of economic agents or not? For the answer to this question we shall need to look to empirical work to give us direction. Recent work by Coe and Helpman (1995) along these lines is a good start, but until we have a good understanding of how knowledge flows across national boundaries the implications of endogenous growth theory for trade policy will remain unclear.

Notes

1. As a result, I will not be reviewing the influential work of Lucas (1988) or Young (1991), but see section 3 for an analysis of trade policy within the learning-by-doing model of Devereux (1997).
2. For some examples and an appreciation of the difficulties involved, see Helpman (1993), Baldwin (1992), and Taylor (1994).
3. For example, Jones (1995) argues quite strongly that scale effects are at odds with the existing empirical evidence on OECD coutries; Young (1995) offers a slightly more favourable view of the evidence.
4. For example, technological progress or an increase in factor endowment that shifts R&D activity to the country with a comparative disadvantage in R&D will almost certainly lower growth, and can even stop it entirely.
5. Devereux notes that his atemporal analysis draws heavily on Kennan and Riezman (1988).

References

Baldwin, R. E. (1992) 'Measurable Dynamic Gains from Trade', *Journal of Political Economy*, vol. 100, no. 1, pp. 162–74.

Devereux, M. (1997) 'Growth, Specialization, and Trade Liberalization', *International Economic Review*, vol. 38, no. 3.

Devereux, M. and B. J. Lapham (1994) 'The Stability of Economic Integration and Endogenous Growth', *Quarterly Journal of Economics*, February, pp. 299–305.

Coe, D. T. and E. Helpman (1996) 'International R&D Spillovers', *European Economic Review*, vol. 39, pp. 859–87.

Feenstra, R. (1990) 'Trade and Uneven Growth', Working Paper no. 3276 (Cambridge, Mass.: (National Bureau of Economic Research).

Grossman, G. and E. Helpman (1990) 'Comparative Advantage and Long Run Growth', *American Economic Review*, vol. 80, pp. 796–815.

Grossman, G. and E. Helpman (1991a) 'Trade, Knowledge Spillovers and Growth', *European Economic Review*, vol. 35, pp. 517–26.

Grossman, G. and E. Helpman (1991b) 'Quality Ladders in the Theory of Growth', *Review of Economic Studies*, vol. 58, pp. 43–61.

Grossman, G. and E. Helpman (1993a) *Innovation and Growth in the Global Economy* (Cambridge, Mass.: MIT Press).

Grossman, G. and E. Helpman (1993b), 'Growth and Welfare in a Small Open Economy', in E. Helpman and A. Razin (eds), *International Trade and Trade Policy* (Cambridge, Mass.: MIT Press), pp. 141–63.

Helpman, E. (1993) 'Innovation, Imitation and Intellectual Property Rights', *Econometrica*, vol. 61, no. 6, pp. 1247–80.

Jones, C. I. (1995) 'R&D-Based Models of Economic Growth', *Journal of Political Economy*, vol. 103, no. 4, pp. 759–84.

Kennan, J. and R. Riezman (1988) 'Do Big Countries Win Tariff Wars', *International Economic Review*, vol. 29, no. 1, pp. 81–91.

Lucas, R. E. Jr (1988) 'On the Mechanics of Economic Development', *Journal of Monetary Economics*, vol. 22, pp. 3–42.

Rivera-Batiz, L. and P. Romer (1991a) 'International Trade with Endogenous Technological Change', *European Economic Review*, vol. 35, pp. 715–21.

Rivera-Batiz, L. and P. Romer (1991b) 'International Integration and Endogenous Growth', *Quarterly Journal of Economics*, vol. 106, pp. 531–56.

Romer, P. (1987) 'Growth Based on Increasing Returns Due to Specialization', *American Economic Review*, vol. 77, no. 2, May, pp. 56–62.

Segerstrom, P. S., T. C. A. Anant and E. Dinopoulos (1990) 'A Schumpetarian Model of the Product Life Cycle', *American Economic Review*, vol. 80, pp. 1077–92.

Taylor, M. S. (1994) 'Once-off and Continuing Gains from Trade', *Review of Economic Studies*, vol. 61, pp. 589–601.

Young, A. (1991) 'Learning by Doing, and the Dynamic Effects of International Trade', *Quarterly Journal of Economics*, vol. 101, pp. 369–405.

Young, A. (1995) 'Growth Without Scale effects', Working paper no. 5211 (Cambridge, Mass.: National Bureau of Economic Research).

Comment

Neil Vousden
AUSTRALIAN NATIONAL UNIVERSITY

Scott Taylor has provided an excellent and lucid survey of the recent literature on trade and growth in the presence of spillovers. The Rivera-Batiz/Romer taxonomy which separates the effects of trade into scale/integration, allocation, spillover and redundancy effects is a helpful way of organizing a large and disparate literature. Of course, as with all such classifications, it admits exceptions, not least the trade version of the Lucas (1988) model with learning-by-doing. In this model, protection of the high-tech sector can increase growth by shifting the mobile factor into the high-tech sector, thus increasing scale and learning-by-doing, a response which some may view as a combined scale/allocation effect or simply a scale effect.[1] Nevertheless, the taxonomy serves this particular survey well and facilitates our understanding of the class of spillover models primarily associated with Grossman and Helpman, and Rivera-Batiz and Romer.

My first set of comments is concerned with the policy implications of the trade and growth literature. The main point here is that while the effects of trade on growth are clearly understood, the role of trade *policy* is sometimes obscured. In this context, two questions that are of particular interest are: (i) Does a particular growth effect of freer trade require a *bilateral* liberalization, or can it be achieved with *unilateral* liberalisation? (ii) Does the size of the effect vary across states of partially restricted trade, or is the move from autarky to free trade the whole story – in other words, do *non-prohibitive* trade restrictions have a role to play? Although the answers to these questions are implicit in all the papers surveyed, the role of both partial and unilateral trade liberalization could perhaps receive more emphasis. For the most part, scale effects associated with integration of goods trade depend on *bilateral* trade liberalisation; they are driven by greater access to the foreign market.

In contrast, allocation effects such as those identified in Rivera-Batiz and Romer (1991a) and the small-country model of Grossman and Helpman (1993b), as well as those in the Lucas (1988) model are achievable via unilateral liberalization. It may be curious to emphasize this distinction in a world where bilateralism seems to be in the ascendancy. However, many trade economists still feel the need to search for gains from unilateral reform. Perhaps this is because much of the rhetoric of protectionist lobbies offers failure of trading partners to liberalize as a reason why their own economy should not liberalize. In this context, arguments for unilateral reform have a particular appeal.

In other cases, it is worth asking whether trade *policy* matters *per se*, or whether a small amount of trade has the same effect on growth as a full movement to free trade. In particular, it would seem that non-prohibitive tariffs have a limited role to play in the case of redundancy effects. In models of redundancy, such as that in Rivera-Batiz and Romer (1991a) so long as no tariffs are prohibitive, the incentive not to replicate foreign designs will be independent of the size of the tariff. On the other hand, this is probably less true for non-prohibitive quotas, since domestic firms facing an inelastic supply of imports may still find it profitable to duplicate foreign designs when quotas are below a certain level. This last observation suggests that there may be some interesting work to be done comparing the effects of different types of trade policy on growth. Grossman and Helpman (1993b) is one of the few papers to compare tariffs and quotas in a growth context and while it may not be one of the big questions, it would certainly be interesting to explore further whether the relatively pernicious effects of quotas in a static economy carry over into a dynamic world.

Taylor has advisedly limited the scope of his survey to the class of spillover models primarily associated with Grossman and Helpman, and Rivera-Batiz and Romer, and it is perhaps unfair for me to take the discussion beyond that important paradigm. However, I think it is worth asking how much we can say about the growth effects of trade in the absence of spillover effects and/or increasing returns. One obvious alternative is to employ the constant-returns framework of Rebelo (1991) and others to explore the effects of trade in the endogenous growth framework which most closely resembles the neoclassical model. Using such a model, it is possible to explore the effects of unilateral changes in tariffs on world savings and hence on real interest rates and growth.

Another, less obvious, alternative is to allow for what might be termed *incentive effects*. This rather loose terminology is intended to describe the effects of changes in productivity associated with such things as improved work practices, increased managerial effort, a lower-cost firm structure and so on. Casual evidence suggests that such changes can be a very important part of the growth process, particularly in economies in transition.[2] Several recent papers have analysed the effects of trade on the productivity of firms in a static context.[3] However, such effects may also have implications for growth. In most endogenous growth models, the long-run growth rate will depend at least on the productivity parameter in the 'growth' sector, be it R&D as in the spillover models, or simply the sector producing the accumulable factor in the constant-returns models of Rebelo (1991) and others. If freer trade leads to increased productivity in such a sector, long-run growth will be increased. Moreover, such effects may tend to offset other effects in spillover models.

For example, in models where protection raises growth by pushing more resources to the R&D sector it may also reduce productivity in that sector via the incentive effect causing growth to fall, the net effect being ambiguous.

Finally, I have some thoughts on section 3 of Taylor's paper, which offers a very neat exposition of the paper by Devereux (1997) on the effects of growth on trade policy. To date, the trade and growth literature has focused almost exclusively on the effects of trade/trade policy on growth and neglected the feedback of growth on policy. However the *endogenous policy* implications of endogenous growth clearly represent an important and fertile area for future research. The Devereux paper sets out to explain why faster growth may induce trade liberalization, and slower growth may lead to higher trade barriers. This outcome is derived as a possible consequence of imperfect spillovers of knowledge across countries, resulting in unbalanced growth, with economies becoming more dissimilar over time. In such a case, there is an equilibrium in which the tariffs emerging from a self-reinforcing agreement fall over time as the costs of reverting to autarky increase, whereas the one-shot Nash equilibrium leads to the opposite result (tariffs rising with growth). This is an elegant model and I find its story appealing. However, other explanations are possible, and some of these may involve tariffs falling with growth even in the simple one-shot Nash equilibrium. In many ways, the central question posed by Devereux harks back to issues raised in political economy models of endogenous policy determination. This literature has devoted some attention to the question how redistributional policies such as tariffs are affected by changes in the 'size of the cake' and it retains an ongoing interest in the similar question of how policy determination is related to the economic cycle. For example, Magee, Brock and Young (1989) have analyzed the response of endogenous tariffs to different patterns of factor growth in a Heckscher–Ohlin–Samuelson economy.[4] Hillman's (1982) model of endogenous protection in declining industries analyzes the response of a country's politically-determined tariff to a terms-of-trade improvement. A possible outcome of this model is that an improvement in terms-of-trade may lead to lower tariffs; thus, as a particular country's 'cake' expands, its politically optimal tariff falls. If the cake is expanding because *all* countries are growing, similar analysis would suggest for the two-country case that each country's tariff reaction curve may shift inwards, implying at least the possibility of lower tariffs over time as growth proceeds. Whether such alternative explanations do provide a more convincing rationale for the observed phenomenon of higher growth leading to freer trade is beside the point. All I wish to convey here is that the endogenous policy literature may provide a fertile source of ideas for those who wish to take up the challenge that Devereux has presented.

Notes

1. The empirical tests in Backus *et al.* (1992) certainly treat learning-by-doing in the Lucas model as an example of a scale effect.
2. See, for example, McMillan *et al.* (1989).
3. See, for example, Vousden and Campbell (1994) and Horn *et al.* (1995).
4. Magee *et al.* analyze the *endowment effect*, their term for the hypothesis that increases in the ratio of capital to labour decreases protection.

References

Backus, D. K., P. J. Kehoe and T. J. Kehoe (1992) 'In Search of Scale Effects in Trade and Growth', *Journal of Economic Theory*, vol. 58, pp. 377–409.

Hillman, A. L. (1982) 'Declining Industries and Political Support Protectionist Motives', *American Economic Review*, vol. 72, pp. 1180–7.

Horn, H., H. Lang and S. Lundgren, (1995) 'Managerial Effort Incentives, X-Inefficiency and International Trade', *European Economic Review*, vol. 39, pp. 117–38.

Lucas, R. E. (1988), 'On the Mechanics of Economic Development', *Journal of Monetary Economics*, vol. 22, pp. 3–42.

McMillan, J., J. Whalley and L. Zhu (1989) 'The Impact of China's Economic Reforms on Agricultural Productivity Growth', *Journal of Political Economy*, vol. 97, pp. 781–807.

Magee, S. P., W. A. Brock and L. Young (1989) *Black Hole Tariffs and Endogenous Policy Theory: Political Economy in General Equilibrium* (New York: Cambridge University Press).

Rebelo, S. (1991) 'Long-Run Policy Analysis and Long-Run Growth', *Journal of Political Economy*, vol. 99, pp. 500–21.

Vousden, N. and N. Campbell (1994) 'The Organizational Cost of Protection', *Journal of International Economics*, vol. 37, pp. 219–38.

16 Emulative Development through Trade Expansion: East Asian Evidence[1]

Pham Hoang Van and Henry Y. Wan, Jr
CORNELL UNIVERSITY

1 INTRODUCTION

This paper distils theory from the facts of development in East Asian countries: the government attracts foreign firms bringing technology. Local agents receive enough of it to achieve fast growth, but not enough to outcompete foreign firms or to deter their entry.

Currently, the East Asian economies have received much attention because of their sustained rapid growth (see World Bank, 1993), in spite of their lack of activity in research and development (R&D). Their mode of 'late industrialization' (Amsden, 1989) is characterized by an 'emulative process'. In this exploratory study, the mechanism of this process is analyzed, for two purposes. First, on the *normative* side, to design a policy regime that facilitates the acquisition of useful information and, second, on the *descriptive* side, to draw implications about the source and future of East Asian growth. Specifically, we consider:

(i)   the role of the state (see Amsden and Singh, 1994; and Bhagwati, 1996);
(ii) the contribution of *trade, technical progress* and *accumulation* to growth (see Young, 1994); and
(iii) the prospect of a Soviet-style collapse (see Krugman, 1994)

In studying the process of emulation, we build upon the literature of 'New Growth Theory', 'New Trade Theory' and economic development. As in the theory of endogenous growth, the rate of technology diffusion is seen to depend on the intention and capability of the agents. It is the equilibrium outcome of an extensive game between the government of the developing country and some interacting agents: firms from the developed economy, who are initially better informed, and individuals in the developing economy, who may gain information by association.

This game-theoretic approach extends the literature on North–South trade (as surveyed by Grossman and Helpman, 1995), for example in several directions. In contrast to the study of Rivera-Batiz and Romer (1992) on the informational interaction of two symmetrically similar economies, we focus on the interaction between a single, small developing economy and various developed countries.

The key is to capture, with a tractable model, additional realism in a complex world where the heterogenous interact strategically under the influence of competition among the similars. It is the South–South competition that keeps the North–South wage gap wide, and the North–North competition that quickens the pace of the product cycle.

Krugman (1979) and Grossman and Helpman (1991) have represented the North–South technology gap with a number of goods initially producible only by the North. At any instant, diffusion transfers the technology of a *constant fraction* of such products to the South. We continue this revealing line of analysis to address two questions which concern the developing countries most: (i) *What* decides that fraction? and (ii) *How* can the rate of diffusion be raised?

Alone, in the literature, Findlay (1978) has identified direct foreign investment as a catalyst for technology diffusion. We seek answers to two follow-up questions: (i) Does direct foreign investment play this role equally well under all policies? (ii) Can other forms of international economic relationships (for example, sub-contracting) serve as a catalyst?

With the exception of Findlay, the analytical literature has abstracted from the specifics of the North–South association, and left no role for trade and foreign investment to play in technology diffusion. It is silent on the reasons why many developing countries offer tax holidays to foreign firms using advanced technology. Nor does it explain why growth has accelerated in Chile and the Peoples' Republic of China (PRC) soon after their outward-oriented reforms. In fact, one cannot find in that literature the defects of inward-looking development, which has been the bane of China, Cuba, India and Egypt for more than 30 years.

To us, the heart of the emulation process is the information asymmetry and its reduction. We try to capture the *details* of real life: *who* learns *what* from *whom* and *how*? It is the details that explain *why* some developing economies outperform others, sometimes overtaking the latter after lagging behind. Such an analysis may also suggest *which* development policies work and *which* do not.

To pursue our specific goals, we draw insights from the literature on economic development and, in particular, studies of Japan, both as a recipient and as a source of technical information; for example, Komiya (1972) and Uchida (1991) on the former, and Kojima (1978) and Ozawa (1979) on the latter.[2]

But to distil insight from experiences in some situations, for other contexts differing in time and place, one needs a theory. Only a formal theory can organize facts to make inferences. This study is undertaken in an attempt to determine endogenously the rate of cross-national technological diffusion and, in particular, the role played by the policy regime of the developing economy. Accordingly, we simplify drastically the dynamics to incorporate the elements of mechanism design, as in Green and Laffont (1979), and the information-theoretic structure of Nermuth (1982). We set up a model more information-theoretic than usual (for example, as surveyed by Grossman and Helpman, 1991.). At that basic level we show that emulation depends on close association with the better-informed. Specifically, this is through the Bayesian updating of prior beliefs.

Ours is part of a broader study, which includes the conceptual frameworks in Wan (1993 and 1996), the empirical discussions in Lau and Wan (1994a) and Lin and Wan (1996), as well as the growth-theoretical inferences in Lau and Wan (1994b). Through a sequence of models like these, one hopes to gain insight into the nature of the catch-up process.

The justification for our unusual approach is its relevance to policy, especially for transitional economies like China, India and Russia, as well as certain African and South-American economies. Catch-up depends on rapid technology transfer; technology transfer requires an outward orientation (encouraging a closer relationship with the outside world). To illustrate this, we present a case related by Wong (1976) and commented on by Watanabe (1980) (from now on referred to as the Wong–Watanabe case).

In the next section, we summarize the Wong–Watanabe case along with six other selected cases related to East Asian growth, and draw from them a theoretical model. Section 3 presents a model where technology is specified as information-dependent, and information is acquired by rational agents in an environment decided by government policy. This exercise sheds light on the questions mentioned above and provides insights for the design of policy. Conclusions follow in the fourth section.

2 SOME SALIENT FACTS

The Wong–Watanabe Case in Brief [1]

An American firm assembled radios in Hong Kong from imported parts. The local supervisors learnt crucial lessons about the recruitment, training and supervision of indigenous labour, quality control, the scheduling of delivery and production layout. They then quit the US firm and started their own businesses assembling digital watches for export.

The above case is not an isolated incident, but a theme with many variations.

The General Instrument Variation [2]

The American firm General Instruments made certain simple products in Taiwan. The indigenous employees became so proficient that later many left to set up eleven new firms supplying similar items (Business Week, 3 March, 1986).

The Taiwanese Footwear Variation [3]

As Japanese wages rose, Mitsubishi, a supplier of plastic shoes to America, shifted its supply base from Kobe, Japan, to its Taiwanese sub-contractors. To reduce cost, it further encouraged Taiwanese skilled workers to spin off and act as new sub-contractors and many small firms arose (Levy, 1990). Then American chain stores came, sub-contracting and helping local firms to make leather shoes for them. Still later, Taiwanese firms, such as the Hongson Company, exported leather shoes to America under their own brand name (Seetoo, 1992).

The Taiwanese Bicycle Variation [4]

In the import substitution phase of policy in Taiwan, four major Taiwanese firms assembled low-grade bicycles from Japanese parts for local use. Many rivals then entered the market with cheaper products at even lower quality, and locally assembled motorcycles also appeared. All the 'big four' failed. After the outward-oriented policy reform in Taiwan, Schwinn, a popular American bicycle firm, contracted Giant, a local sporting-goods supplier, to hire the former employees of the 'big four' and import better Japanese parts to produce bicycles for the American market. Eventually, Taiwan became the world's largest bicycle exporter (by dollar value) with Giant shipping some outputs under its own brand name (Chu and Lee, 1996).

The Mauritian Knitwear Variation [5]

Because of (i) quota restrictions under the Multi-fibre Agreements; (ii) the Lomé Convention which favours former European colonies in the *European Union* (EU) market; and (iii) the presence of a small Chinese community in Mauritius, the Hong Kong Chinese produced knitted woollen gloves for the European market under the institutions of an export zone which had been adapted from Taiwan to Mauritius. Even though there is not a single sheep in Mauritius, business boomed, surplus labour was absorbed and wages rose. Eventually non-Chinese local businesses joined the industry successfully (Findlay and Wellisz, 1993).

The Colombian Apparel Variation [6]

Colombians could export textiles to Venezuela behind the trade barriers of the Andean Plan, but not to the lucrative American market against East Asian competition. The stumbling block was apparently the bureaucratic Colombian trade regime, making it hard to deliver on time – while for the American fashion market punctual delivery is indispensable. Thus cut off from the American market, local firms also saw no need to be reliable in quality or well-informed about the sizes of American clients (Morawetz, 1981).

The Beijing Jeep Variation [7]

The American Motor Corporation (AMC) co-produced jeeps with the PRC in Beijing, aiming for the export market. But it was found that locally-produced parts were not of exportable quality and the cumbersome exchange control system made it impractical to import such inputs. The output was therefore reoriented towards the local market. Conflicts arose between the partners over issues of national prestige (Mann, 1989). In those days, Chinese employees served in a joint venture for only a fixed duration and on leaving foreign joint ventures, they had neither the opportunity to start businesses of their own, nor the chance to work as decision-makers elsewhere.

The seven cases can be summarized in the structured comparison in Table 16.1.

From the comparisons in Table 16.1, we can draw the following conclusions:

(a) Skill acquired may be either product-specific or not product-specific.
(b) The emulation process follows principles applicable in East Asia as well as elsewhere. In particular:

  • goods for high income markets often contain characteristics hard to supply and hence are highly-valued;
  • firms from the developed countries are better informed to supply such characteristics;
  • by close association with those better-informed, individuals from a developing economy can become better-informed themselves; and,
  • competition among the parties, which initially possessed better information, may prevent them from appropriating all the potential gains from the bargain.

(c) Both direct foreign investment and sub-contracting arrangements can facilitate emulation.
(d) Failure in emulation may be caused either by difficulties in importing required inputs or by lack of incentive for local individuals to learn.

Table 16.1   Selected cases related to East Asian growth

Case	Technology transferred	Relationship with foreign firm	The host economy	Remarks
[1]	Not product specific	Employee	East Asia	Temporal pattern: Foreign direct investment, Employment, Local entry
[2]	Product specific	Employee	East Asia	Temporal pattern: Foreign direct investment, Employment, Local entry
[3]	Product specific	Sub-contractor	East Asia	
[4]	Product specific	Employee of sub-contractor	East Asia	
[5]	Product specific	Bystanders	Not East Asia	Temporal–spatial pattern: Foreign direct investment, Local entry
[6]	?	Sub-contractor	Not East Asia	Problem: Input control
[7]	?	Joint venture	East Asia	Problems: Input control; No incentives for Employees

(e)   What is worth noting is not that General Instruments shifted production to Taiwan to cut labour cost (as trade theory predicts), but that many local Taiwanese producers of the same items entered the market after General Instruments, and that these local producers were former employees of General Instruments.

(f)   Again, what is remarkable is not the initial 'quota-jumping' into the EU by the Hong Kong investors but that the subsequent entries came from Mauritian South Asians and not from South Asians from Bombay or Karachi. The opportunity to observe the Hong Kong investors at close range clearly gave the former group an advantage. Thus, the emulation process is alive and well in variations [3] and [5].

3   A THEORETICAL EXAMPLE OF TECHNOLOGY TRANSFER

In a 'stylized fashion', the Wong–Watanabe case is now modelled as a three-period, three-player game: Player 1 represents the government of a developing economy; Player 2 the representative foreign firm in a developing economy; and Player 3 the representative individual in the developing economy in question.

The evolution of the game is described in Table 16.2.

Table 16.2   The evolution of a three-period, three-player game

Period 1	Period 2	Period 3
Government of LDC chooses policy regime.	Representative foreign firm chooses good for production. Representative individual from the LDC chooses learning effort.	Representative individual from the LDC chooses whether to start own business with the information gained in period 2, or to continue working for the foreign firm.

In period 1, the policy regime is chosen by player 1, the government of the less developed country (LDC). This decides the production possibilities of player 2, the representative foreign firm, and the information structures available to player 3, the representative local individual, in subsequent periods. The government maximizes the payoffs of its constituents, as represented by wages earned and the information acquired for future production, perhaps at some cost of effort.

The foreign firm maximizes the present value of its profit stream. At the beginning of period 2, it decides which good to produce in the LDC. Endowed with one unit of entrepreneurial input, the foreign entrepreneur has full information on the possible production of every product. The entrepreneur makes certain key decisions for the firm, to maximize the residual revenue from the enterprise, after all other inputs have been rewarded.

The representative individual in the LDC may work for wages at the foreign firm. Meanwhile, production information may be gained by observing both the (imperfect) signals about the production process and the concurrent actions of the foreign firm. With such acquired information, the local individual may either continue to work for the foreigner in period 3, or start a business of his/her own with the acquired expertise.

The developing economy can produce food, the numeraire, or three different manufactured goods for which it assembles imported inputs. The world prices for goods x (radios for the world market) and z (digital watches for the world market) are given (the developing country is small). Good y is a lower-quality variant of good x and is used only for domestic consumption. For simplicity, good y is assumed to be a perfect substitute for 'food'.

The individuals in the developing economy may gain production information in period 2 that is useful in period 3. In contrast, we assume, for simplicity, that firms from the developed economy face the same opportunities in period 3, regardless of what happens in period 2. In case history [1], this means the demand for high-quality radios is neutral relative to demand for watches; in case history [2], the foreign investor sells at competitive prices in period 3, where the entry of the spin-off firms matters little.

The manufactured goods are made with a Leontief technology, using imported inputs α, local labour β, and entrepreneurial service γ. Imported inputs include materials and tools/equipment. Labour is divided into direct and supervisory types, in fixed proportions. For simplicity, they are assumed to command the same wage. The production condition is random and not perfectly observable. For example, the climate may make the plant 'too hot' or 'too wet', rendering the product quality unacceptable. Based on the available information signal, decisions must be made to apply specific preventive preparations to the material: 'COOLING' when 'hot'; 'DRYING' when 'wet'.[3] Imperfect information may be refined by testing, at some cost.

The interactions between information, decisions and incentives make the development problem non-trivial. The government acts to maximize the payoff of its constituents. Government matters because its constituents cannot select the policy regime; only the government can do this.

We now construct an example to capture the essence of the Wong–Watanabe case. Recall that the condition of production is assumed to be random and not directly observable. It may be represented by any one of the six states in:

$$E = \{1, 2, 3, 4, 5, 6\} \tag{16.1}$$

with equal probability: the probability of e in E is $h(e) = 1/6$ for all e.

What is observed is signal s in some finite signal space S. The probability of observing signal s in state e is:

$$q(s, e) = Pr[s \mid e]; \quad \sum_{s \in S} q(s, e) = 1 \tag{16.2}$$

Information is a stochastic matrix $Q = [q(s, e)]$, and the ordered pair (S, Q) is player-specific, updated by experience.

In the present context, the signal space available depends on the initial knowledge and experience of the individual in question. In particular, we assume the following. Firms from developed countries always have perfect information:

$$S = E, \ q(s, e) = 1, \ \text{if and only if}, \ e = s \tag{16.3}$$

The individuals of the LDC initially have null information:

$$S' = \{0\}, \ q'(0, e) = 1, \ \text{for all } e \in E \tag{16.4}$$

The individuals of the LDC may acquire imperfect information after working with the foreign firm:

$$S'' = \{LOW, HIGH\}, \ LOW = \{1, 2, 3\} \ \text{and} \ HIGH = \{4, 5, 6\} \tag{16.5}$$

under the *assumption* that if the state of the environment e is in a particular subset of E then the individual will receive *with certainty* a signal denoting that subset. Thus,

$$q''(LOW, e) = 1, \text{ if and only if, } e \in LOW$$
$$q''(HIGH, e) = 1, \text{ if and only if, } e \in HIGH \qquad (16.6)$$

The imperfectness of information here is a 'coarsening' of the perfect information case.

Table 16.3 summarizes the signal space and information map for each player, with:

$$Q = \begin{bmatrix} 1 & 0 & 0 & 0 & 0 & 0 \\ 0 & 1 & 0 & 0 & 0 & 0 \\ 0 & 0 & 1 & 0 & 0 & 0 \\ 0 & 0 & 0 & 1 & 0 & 0 \\ 0 & 0 & 0 & 0 & 1 & 0 \\ 0 & 0 & 0 & 0 & 0 & 1 \end{bmatrix}; \ Q' = \begin{bmatrix} 1 \\ 1 \\ 1 \\ 1 \\ 1 \\ 1 \end{bmatrix}; \ Q'' = \begin{bmatrix} 1 & 0 \\ 1 & 0 \\ 1 & 0 \\ 0 & 1 \\ 0 & 1 \\ 0 & 1 \end{bmatrix} \qquad (16.7)$$

Table 16.3   Signal space and information map for each player

	Signal space	Information map
Player 2 (foreign firm)	S	Q
Player 3 (local employee)		
Inexperienced	S'	Q'
Experienced	S''	Q''

Once the production condition signal is received, the firm will select one of the alternatives; 'drying' or 'cooling', for the input. The alternatives are denoted, respectively,

$$a \in A = \{DRYING, COOLING\} \qquad (16.8)$$

The portion of acceptable outputs for production process i is the yield value, $u_i(a, e)$ (for the same (a, e) pair the yield may be product dependent). Writing:

$$ODD = \{1, 3, 5\} \quad \text{and} \quad EVEN = \{2, 4, 6\} \qquad (16.9)$$

where '*ODD*' signals a wet condition and '*EVEN*' signals a hot condition, we assume that for goods x and y (high- and low-quality radios, respectively),

$$u_x(a,e) = u_y(a,e) = 1, \text{ if, } e \in a$$
$$u_x(a,e) = u_y(a,e) = 0, \text{ if } e \notin a \tag{16.10}$$

with

$$x = u_x(a,e) \min[\alpha/a_{\alpha x}, \beta/a_{\beta x}, \gamma/a_{\gamma x}]$$
$$y = u_y(a,e) \min[\alpha/a_{\alpha y}, \beta/a_{\beta y}, \gamma/a_{\gamma y}] \tag{16.11}$$

where a_{ij} is the requirement of input i for one unit of output j.

Good y is produced for the domestic market of the developing economy. By assumption, it is a perfect substitute for food, with a constant relative price in 'food', $p_y < p_x$, the world relative price for x. Moreover, the relative input contents are assumed to be such that:

$$a_{\alpha x}/p_x < a_{\alpha y}/p_y \quad \text{and} \quad a_{\beta x}/p_x < a_{\beta y}/p_y \tag{16.12}$$

implying that such 'localized' products are not very attractive for the foreign producer.

Good z (a digital watch) is a relatively simpler product than x and y, so that:

$$u_z(a,e) = 1, \quad \text{if } e \in a$$
$$u_z(a,e) \in (0,1), \quad \text{if } e \notin a \tag{16.13}$$

The last statement indicates that although the 'actions' taken may not be the best, the output need not be a total loss for the simpler products. For good z, the production function is now

$$z = u_z(a,e) \min[\alpha/a_{\alpha z}, \beta/a_{\beta z}, \gamma/a_{\gamma z}] \tag{16.14}$$

All players share the following information as common knowledge:

- State space: $E \equiv \{1,2,3,4,5,6\}$; ODD $\equiv \{1,3,5\}$; EVEN $\equiv \{2,4,6\}$.
- Prior probability: $h(e) = 1/6, \forall e \in E; h(\text{ODD}) = 1/2 = h(\text{EVEN})$.
- Action space: $A \equiv \{\text{DRYING, COOLING}\}$.
- Yield (reward) index: $u_i(a,e) \in (0,1), u_i(a,e) = 1$ if $e \in a$ for $i = x, y, z$.
- The optimal rule with perfect information, χ:
  'COOLING if e is EVEN; DRYING if e is ODD'.
- Player 2 is perfectly informed.

Player 2 (the foreign entrepreneur) has perfect information (Q), and so will always take the optimal action.

On receiving a signal of LOW or HIGH, the inexperienced player 3 (the local individual) does not know how this signal relates to the true state. Thus receiving a LOW signal does not allow him/her then to assign higher probability to any state than before. Null information (Q') essentially remains, and there is only a 50–50 chance of taking the proper action.

The experience of working inside a foreign firm makes all the difference. During that period the local worker observes both an imperfect signal, and the actions taken by the foreign entrepreneur. Since the foreigner is known always to take the optimal action, it is known that DRYING reflects the ODD signal; and COOLING reflects the EVEN signal:

$$\Pr[s \in \{1,3,5\} \mid a = DRYING] = 1 = \Pr[s \in \{2,4,6\} \mid a = COOLING] \qquad (16.15)$$

Further, by knowing that the foreigner has perfect information (about the state of nature), the worker can then deduce that DRYING action reflects the ODD state:

$$\Pr[e \in \{1,3,5\} \mid a = DRYING] = 1 = \Pr[e \in \{2,4,6\} \mid a = COOLING] \qquad (16.16)$$

By repetitively observing the frequency of the actions of the foreign entrepreneur and their correlation with those signals received by himself:[4]

(i) $h''(ODD) = \Pr[a = DRYING] = 1/2 = \Pr[a = COOLING] = h''(EVEN)$; and

(ii) $\Pr[LOW \mid a = DRYING] = 2/3$; $\Pr[LOW \mid a = COOLING] = 1/3$ $\qquad (16.17)$
$\Pr[HIGH \mid a = DRYING] = 2/3$; $\Pr[HIGH \mid a = COOLING] = 1/3$

With this information, the local employees can spin off and start operating on their own in period 3. By then, without the benefit of observing the actions of the former employer, they must fall back on their own received signals. However, the updated beliefs about the signals promise better actions. Using Bayes' rule and the probabilities in (16.15) to (16.17), the conditional probability of a state belonging to a particular subset, given the local individuals' own imperfect signals, becomes:

$$\Pr[e \in \{1,3,5\} \mid s'' = LOW] = \Pr[a = DRYING \mid s'' = LOW]$$
$$= \frac{\Pr[LOW] \mid [a = DRYING] \times \Pr[ODD]}{\Pr[LOW \mid a = DRYING] \times \Pr[ODD] + \Pr[LOW \mid a = COOLING] \times \Pr[EVEN]}$$
$$= \frac{(2/3)(1/2)}{(2/3)(1/2) + (1/3)(1/2)} = 2/3$$

$$\Pr[e \in \{2,4,6\} \mid s'' = LOW] = \Pr[a = COOLING \mid s'' = LOW] = 1/3$$
$$\Pr[e \in \{1,3,5\} \mid s'' = HIGH] = \Pr[a = DRYING \mid s'' = HIGH] = 1/3 \qquad (16.8)$$
$$\Pr[e \in \{2,4,6\} \mid s'' = HIGH] = \Pr[a = COOLING \mid s'' = HIGH] = 2/3$$

From these, the local entrepreneur can adopt the rule: 'COOLING if the signal is HIGH; DRYING when the signal is LOW'.

The above notation may make this outcome seem trivial, but one should recognize that, without the benefit of observing the foreigner in the previous period, the local entrepreneur would have no way to relate the LOW (or HIGH) signal to the states, and the probability of taking the proper action would have been 1/2. With the benefit of observing the foreigner, the local entrepreneur can now take correct action two-thirds of the time.

To illustrate the outcomes in choosing different policy regimes, we assign numerical values to various parameters. Suppose the three output prices are:

$$p_x = 5; \quad p_y = 1; \quad p_z = 3 \tag{16.19}$$

and the prices of the inputs α and β are,

$$p_\alpha = p_\beta = 1 \tag{16.20}$$

where p_α, the price of imported inputs, is the CIF price (taxes included). The unit input requirements for the three outputs are:

$$
\begin{aligned}
x &: a_{\alpha x} = a_{\beta x} = a_{\gamma x} = 1 \\
y &: a_{\alpha y} = a_{\beta y} = a_{\gamma y} = 2/9 \\
z &: a_{\alpha z} = a_{\beta z} = a_{\gamma z} = 3/4
\end{aligned} \tag{16.21}
$$

Further, assume that the yield for good z is 1/2 if the 'proper' action is not taken:

$$u_z(a,e) = 1/2 \text{ if } e \notin a \tag{16.22}$$

The expected yields of x, y and z for the three information structures are:

$$
x : \begin{cases}
\text{with null information :} & Eu_x(a,e) = (6)(1/6)[(1/2)(0) + (1/2)(1)] = 1/2 \\
\text{with perfect information :} & Eu_x(a,e) = (6)(1/6) = 1 \\
\text{with imperfect information :} & Eu_x(a,e) = (1/6)[1 + 0 + 1] + (1/6)[1 + 0 + 1] = 2/3
\end{cases}
$$

$$
y : \begin{cases}
\text{with null information :} & Eu_y(a,e) = (6)(1/6)[(1/2)(0) + (1/2)(1)] = 1/2 \\
\text{with perfect information :} & Eu_y(a,e) = (6)(1/6) = 1 \\
\text{with imperfect information :} & Eu_y(a,e) = (1/6)[1 + 0 + 1] + (1/6)[1 + 0 + 1] = 2/3
\end{cases}
$$

$$
z : \begin{cases}
\text{with null information :} & Eu_z(a,e) = (6)(1/6)[(1/2)(1/2) + (1/2)(1)] = 3/4 \\
\text{with perfect information :} & Eu_z(a,e) = (6)(1/6) = 1 \\
\text{with imperfect information :} & Eu_z(a,e) = (1/6)[1 + 1/2 + 1] + 1/6[1 + 1/2 + 1] \\
& \qquad\qquad = 5/6
\end{cases}
$$

In period 2, the foreign firm would compute the residual return for each of the three goods. In period 3, the local individual would do the same and

Table 16.4   Reward in the three industries using the optimal rule under different information structures

	I *Null information* *(Local-inexperienced)*	II *Imperfect information* *(Local-experienced)*	III *Perfect information* *(Foreign firm)*
Supervisory return			
Good x	1/2	1/3	$\boxed{3}$
Good y	1/4	1	5/2
Good z	$\boxed{1}$	$\boxed{4/3}$	2
Local worker wage			
	$\boxed{1}$	1	—

Note: Boxed figures denote the maximum reward in each column.

compare them to the opportunity wage of working for the foreign firm. These are shown in Table 16.4.[5]

With the information in Table 16.4, we can determine the equilibrium evolution for our extensive game. To save space, we shall sketch it with the following game tree (the equilibrium choices are marked with thick lines). Player 1 will choose an outward-oriented strategy, g_0 (marked with a thick line in Figure 16.1), rather than other policy options such as g_1, the avoidance of 'export dependence' as practised by the Indian government with respect to the machine tool industry (see Lin and Wan 1996).[6] By column III of Table 16.4, player 2 would produce good x (rather than y, z or ϕ – no entry) and adopt the full information optimum decision rule, χ. By column II in Table 16.4, player 3, who has already been in close association with player 2 in period 2, will acquire imperfect information, and then choose to apply this in the production of good z (rather than x, y or ϕ – continue working for wages) using the imperfect information rule, χ''.

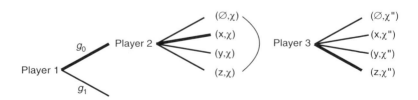

Figure 16.1   Game tree, showing equilibrium choices

Note that the acquisition of information by player 3 in period 2 is itself a purposeful choice. Such an option is preferred when one compares column I to column II. If the institutional environment does not favour certain entrepreneural activities, then any ε cost of information acquisition will deter player 3 from making this choice.[7] Furthermore, the fact that player 3 only acquires imperfect information prevents him/her from competing with player 2 in producing good x during period 3.[8] This assures that those in the position of player 2 will reveal their expertise in period 2.

The above simple example has captured the essence of a plausible scenario. We now summarize some of the lessons gained from the exercise as follows:

Proposition
In the context of the case studied, we found the following:
1. By closely associating with better-informed (foreign) individuals, less-informed persons from a developing economy can:

   (a) improve their own probability estimates about the state, based on imperfect signals (that is, $(S', Q') \to (S'', Q'')$);
   (b) modify their decision rules accordingly (that is, $\chi' \to \chi''$, where χ' is a completely random decision rule); and
   (c) improve their payoff (from 1 to 4/3 in period 3) as a consequence.

2. The technology transfer that favours the developing economy poses no threat to the interests of the initial foreign investors (because x and z are different goods).
3. The operation of an 'export platform'[9] may benefit all parties concerned (see item 1(c) above for the host country, and even without any information about the opportunity cost for the foreign firm, the fact that they come to invest reveals that they benefit).

Remarks
1. To include an import substitution regime, our example must be extended to include a process of producing inputs at home. In real life, one may learn about producing inputs under such a policy. But a foreign firm facing a 'sheltered' home market and not the highly competitive world may reveal less valuable information (see case history [6] on p. 352).
2. In our example, North–South interaction takes the form of direct investment: the foreign firm–local worker nexus conveys production information. In contrast, interaction in the alternative form of sub-contracting may convey market information through the observed pattern of response from the foreign buyers to market signals (see case history [3] on p. 351).
3. Our example may also be modified to study information propagation among persons in the developing economy (see case history [5] on

p. 351), though more periods must be added. Our analysis is equally applicable to technology acquisition between developed economies. With threatened quotas, the US government induced Toyota to co-produce cars in Fremont, California; it was the American car makers' opportunity to observe Japanese managerial expertise.

4 CONCLUSION

We have proposed an approach that is more explicit where information is concerned than the development literature.[10] We specify the content of, and channel for, information transmission in the emulative process. By capturing selected aspects of real life in our example, this study offers an information-theoretic approach for the fine-tuning of policy design.

Specifically, we distinguish 'lacking information' between (i) a coarse partition of information; and (ii) the inability to assess such information. Partitions can be associated with (possibly costly) actions of information-gathering (that is, a 'test'). How costly the test is may again depend upon how well- informed is the agent.

In the above example, to generate $S' = \{\{1, 2, 3\}, \{4, 5, 6\}\}$, one may apply the test:

$$T(S') = e > \#(E)/2?$$

where $\#(E) =$ number of elements in set E. A negative (affirmative) answer corresponds to the set $\{1, 2, 3\}$ ($\{4, 5, 6\}$). The test comes with a cost $C[T(S')]$.

The alternative test:

$$T'' = |e - 7/2| = 5/2?$$

partitions E into $\{\{2, 5\}, \{1, 3, 4, 6\}\}$. The application of both T'' and $T(S')$ generates the four-member partition, $\{\{1, 3\}, \{5\}, \{2\}, \{4, 6\}\}$. By a union operation, we get a 'sufficient' partition: $\{\{1, 3, 5\}, \{2, 4, 6\}\}$, which offers the maximum information value – as high as full information.

In a multi-period context, our approach identifies 'path-dependence'. It shows that it matters whether $T(S')$ or T'' is applied first. When used alone, $T(S')$ improves the value of information, but T'' does not. This cannot be shown with a numerical representation of information. Some industrialization policies (for example, export-led growth) may both acquire useful information and pay their own way. Others (for example, import substitution) may not do so.

Future extensions may elaborate on the fact that technical progress may involve the production of goods with 'more demanding characteristics', which are typically afforded only by the more affluent developed world. Manufacturing export to the North is therefore especially important. This may be studied using insights from Engel's Law, captured, for example, in Basu and Van (1998), with the Geary–Stone preference.

Returning to the descriptive issues mentioned in the Introduction above, the case studies presented and our subsequent analysis suggest certain points.

First, trade is essential in the emulative process because it is trade that induces technology transfer, which may induce another round of trade. However, it should be noted that the initial spark comes from trade and not from technology transfer. The foreign investment that brings technology is attracted to the sites of export platforms. One should also note that, as in the Wong–Watanabe case, the assembly of digital watches may require different equipment from that needed for the assembly of radios. Therefore, in the putty-clay context, gross investment will rise because of trade-induced technology progress.

Second, as wages rise, labour shortage may make the equipment underutilized in industries which arose during an early cheap-labour phase. Therefore, net capital accumulation may be seriously overstated, which could lead to the conclusions drawn by Young (1994) and Kim and Lau (1994).[11]

Third, both *laissez-faire* Hong Kong and state-guided Korea have benefited from similar outward-looking orientation. Hence the difference in the role played by the state may not matter all that much.

Fourth, the investment in all four Asian NIEs is largely market-driven. Unlike the Soviet Union, their consumption forgone has never been directed to outmoded equipment for outdated products. They cannot fail in the Soviet way.

Finally, from Lau and Wan (1994a), the technology transfer from Hong Kong has spurred growth across the border inside the PRC.[12] The phenomenon is clear-cut, since the growth rates are higher in locations closer to Hong Kong. This seems to indicate that Krugman (1994) may be too complacent about the Asian challenge. The slowing down of growth within the four NIEs does not necessarily imply the slowing-down of growth in Asia as a whole. Problems such as trade adjustment, resource shortage and environmental pressure, as discussed in Wan (1996), could become very serious.

Notes

1. We appreciate the helpful comments received when earlier versions of this chapter were presented at Cornell University; the National Chengchi University, Taipei; the Institute of Economics, Academia Sinica, Nankang, Taiwan; and the Hong Kong University of Science and Technology. Special thanks are due

(chronologically) to our discussant Professor Peter Warr, Miss Nita Watts, an anonymous referee, and Professor Alan Woodland. Their advice enabled us to make great improvements. All remaining imperfections are our responsibility.

2. The role of direct foreign investment in technology diffusion is neither new nor an East Asian phenomenon. The English businessman, John Cockerill, was instrumental in spreading the Industrial Revolution to continental Europe via his Belgian investment (Henderson, 1954).

3. To simplify exposition, 'code words' *hot* and *wet* as well as *cooling* and *drying* are used for actual events and corresponding actions in our stylized example. The following quotations on machining and welding are cited to show that our example does capture the essence. On machining: 'Many decisions may be arrived at seemingly by "gut feeling". For instance, a machinist may be able to tell when a cutting tool is dull simply by looking at it...the general shape of wear scars on the top face, corner, and flank face of the tool, and in addition [s/he is able to] relate these features to events in the last machining pass. Changes in chip color, vibrations of the machine tool, and the surface finish obtained on the component are the first signs that the tool is becoming worn and should be checked at the end of the machining pass' (Wright and Bourne, 1988, p. 19); and on welding: 'Of interest are the effects of current, voltage, and travel speed on the quality of the weld. Because of the extremely large number of materials, electrodes, shielding gases, and other variables; an experimental design to determine the interaction effects is prohibitively large...Experienced welding engineers have encountered many of the interaction effects of these variables throughout their careers. They use this knowledge whenever they estimate the values for the welding situation they have not previously encountered. This knowledge, in the form of experience, was coupled with the knowledge of the steps they use to solve the problem' (Tonkay and Knott, 1989, pp. 647–8).

4. The transfer of knowledge by repeated observation is pervasive and manufacturing is no exception. This notion is implied in the following quotation: 'It takes many years for a person to acquire enough information to be called an expert. It usually takes a long time...to get the information out of the expert person... but hopefully not as long as it took the expert to acquire the information in the first place' (Wright and Bourne, 1988, p. 19).

5. The rate of return to supervisory effort, r_i is calculated as follows:

$$r_i = \frac{p_i E u_i(a,e) - a_{\alpha i} p_\alpha - a_{\beta i} p_\beta}{a_{\gamma i}}, \; i = x, y, z$$

6. If this developing economy was intending to consume y it must import α and pay for it with 'food' export.

7. See case study [7].

8. In case history [2] the former employees of General Instruments did establish eleven firms to produce their product, which apparently contradicts the above discussion. In private communication, a former officer of General Instruments informed the second author that spin-off firms only entered when that product no longer commanded any innovators' profits. Thus the delayed competition does not offset the initial gain from wage-saving.

9. That is, an 'offshore' production basis.

10. See Easley and Kiefer (1988) for references on an alternative approach to such problems.

11. For a more detailed argument, see Van and Wan (1997).

12. Hong Kong itself, however, does not exhibit a growth rate higher than its neighbours. That is because the rise of the ability to emulate is more than offset by the exhaustion of available technology that is easy to emulate. This is precisely why Verspagen (1991) derived a hat-shaped growth profile over time (see Lau and Wan, 1994b).

References

Amsden, A. H. (1989) *Asia's Next Giant: South Korea And Late Industrialization* (New York: Oxford University Press).

Amsden, A. H. and A. Singh (1994) 'The Optimal Degree of Competition and Dynamic Efficiency in Japan and Korea', *European Economic Review*, vol. 38, no. 3–4, pp. 941–51.

Basu, K. and P. H. Van (1998) 'The Economics of Child Labor', *American Economic Review* forthcoming.

Bhagwati, J. (1996) 'The "Miracle" that did not happen: Understanding East Asia in Comparative Perspective', in E. Thorbecke and H. Y. Wan (eds), *Government and Market: The Relevance of the Taiwanese Performance 1945–95* (Ithaca, NY: Cornell University Press).

Chu W. W. and J. J. Li (1996) 'Growth and Industrial Organization: A Comparative Study of the Bicycle Industry in Taiwan and Korea', *Journal of Industry Studies*, vol. 3, no. 1, pp. 35–52.

Easley, D. and N. Kiefer (1988) 'Controlling a Stochastic Process with Unknown Parameters', *Econometrica*, vol. 56, no. 5, pp. 1045–64.

Findlay, R. (1978) 'Some Aspects of Technology Transfer and Direct Foreign Investment', *American Economic Review*, vol. 68, no. 2, pp. 275–9.

Findlay, R. and S. Wellisz (1993) (eds), *The Political Economy of Poverty, Equity, and Growth: Five Open Economies* (New York: Oxford University Press).

Green, J. R. and J. J. Laffont (1979) *Incentives in Public Decision-Making* (New York: Elsevier North-Holland).

Grossman, G. M. and E. Helpman (1991) *Innovation and Growth in the Global Economy* (Cambridge, Mass: MIT Press).

Grossman, G. M. and E. Helpman (1995) 'Technology and Trade', in G. M. Grossman and K. Rogoff (eds), *Handbook of International Economics: Volume III* (Amsterdam: Elsevier).

Henderson, W. O. (1954) *Britain and Industrial Europe, 1750–1870: Studies in British Influence on the Industrial Revolution in Western Europe* (Liverpool: Liverpool University Press).

Kim, J.-I. and L. J. Lau (1994) 'The Sources of Economic Growth of East Asian Newly Industrialized Countries', *Journal of the Japanese and International Economies*, vol. 8, no. 3, pp. 235–71.

Komiya, R. (1972) 'Direct Foreign Investment in Post War Japan', in P. Drysdale (ed.), *Foreign Investment in Asia and the Pacific* (Toronto: University of Toronto Press).

Kojima, K. (1978) *Direct Foreign Investment: A Japanese Model, Multinational Business Operations* (London: Croom Helm).

Krugman, P. (1979) 'A Model of Innovation, Technology Transfer, and the World Distribution of Income', *Journal of Political Economy*, vol. 87, no. 2, pp. 253–66.

Krugman, P. (1994) 'The Myth of Asia's Miracle', *Foreign Affairs*, vol. 73, no. 6, pp. 62–78.

Lau M.-L. and H. Y. Wan Jr (1994a) 'The Hong Kong–Guangdong Nexus', mimeo, Cornell University, Ithaca, New York.

Lau M.-L. and H. Y. Wan Jr (1994b) 'On The Mechanism of Catching Up', *European Economic Review*, vol. 38, no. 3–4, pp. 952–63.

Levy, B. (1990) 'Transaction Costs, the Size of Firms and Industrial Policy: Lessons from a Comparative Case Study of the Footwear Industry in Korea and Taiwan', *Journal of Development Economics*, vol. 34, no. 1–2, pp. 151–78.

Lin, Y. and H. Y. Wan Jr (1996) 'Laissez Faire as a Source of Comparative Advantage – Experiences from the Taiwanese Machine Tool Industry', mimeo, Cornell University, Ithaca, New York.

Lucas, R. E. Jr (1988) 'On the Mechanics of Economic Development', *Journal of Monetary Economics*, vol. 22, no. 1, pp. 3–42.

Mann, J. (1989) *Beijing Jeep* (New York: Simon & Schuster).

Morawetz, D. (1981) *Why the Emperor's New Clothes Are Not Made in Colombia: A Case Study in Latin American and East Asian Manufacturing Export* (Oxford: Oxford University Press).

Nermuth, M. (1982) *Information Structures in Economics* (Berlin: Springer-Verlag).

Ozawa, T. (1979) *Multinationalism, Japanese Style: The Political Economy of Outward Dependency* (Princeton, NJ: Princeton University Press), esp. ch. 3.

Rivera-Batiz, L. and P. Romer (1992) 'Economic Integration and Endogenous Growth', in G. M. Grossman (ed.), *Imperfect Competition and International Trade* (Cambridge; Mass.: MIT Press), pp. 347–66.

Seetoo, D. H. (1992) 'Globalisation with Self-Owned Brands: The Case of Hongson', in N. T. Wang (ed.), *Taiwan's Enterprises in Global Perspective* (New York: M. E. Sharpe), pp. 327–41.

Tonkay, G. L. and K. Knott (1989) 'An Expert System for Welding', in S. T. Kumara, R. L. Kashyap and A. L. Soyster (eds), *Artificial Intelligence: Manufacturing Theory and Practice* (USA: The Institute of Industrial Engineers).

Uchida, H. (1991) 'The Transfer of Electrical Technologies from the U.S. and Europe to Japan: 1869–1914', in D. J. Jeremy (ed.), *International Technology Transfer: Europe, Japan and the U.S.A., 1700–1914* (Aldershot: Edward Elgar).

Van, P. H. and H. Y. Wan Jr (1997) 'Interpreting East Asian Growth', in B. S. Jensen and K. Y. Wong (eds), *Dynamics, Economic Growth and International Trade* (Ann Arbor, Mich.: University of Michigan Press).

Verspagen, B. (1991) 'A New Empirical Approach to Catching Up or Falling Behind', *Structural Change and Economic Dynamics*, vol. 2, no. 2, pp. 359–80.

Wan, H. Y. Jr (1993) 'Trade, Development and Inventions', in H. Herberg and N. V. Long (eds), *Current Issues in International Trade Theory* (Ann Arbor, Mich.: University of Michigan Press), pp. 239–54.

Wan, H. Y. Jr (1996) 'Six Challenges Facing the Chinese Economies', in L. F.-Y. Ng, and C. Tuan (eds), *Three Chinese Economies: China, Hong Kong, and Taiwan: Challenges and Opportunities* (Hong Kong: Chinese University Press), pp. 11–27.

Watanabe, S. (1980) 'Multinational Enterprises and Employment Oriented Appropriate Technologies in Developing Countries', *ILO Working Papers* (Multinational Enterprise Programme), no. 14.

Wong, F.-T. (1976) 'Country Paper, Hong Kong' in *Intra-national Transfer of Technology* (Tokyo: Asian Productivity Organization), pp. 2–3.

World Bank (1993) *The East Asian Miracle: Economic Growth and Public Policy* (New York: Oxford University Press).

Wright, P. K. and D. A. Bourne (1988) *Manufacturing Intelligence* (Reading, Mass.: Addison Wesley).

Young, A. (1994) 'Lessons from the East Asian NICS: A Contrarian View', *European Economic Review*, vol. 38, no. 3–4, pp. 964–73.

Comment

Peter G. Warr
AUSTRALIAN NATIONAL UNIVERSITY

The authors have contributed a useful and original chapter on this important subject. I shall organize my comments around four questions. What is the question the chapter addresses? Does it matter? What does this chapter do? And, finally, what doesn't it do?

What is the Question?

The chapter poses two questions: (a) How does technology come to be transferred from foreign firms to the domestic economy? and (b) How does this process depend on government policy? Some answers are attempted to the first of these questions, but the second is not pursued in any depth. Posing question (a) is in itself important conceptually. 'Technology transfer' has all too often been treated as a black box in the trade and development literature. This chapter attempts to look into the box.

Does it Matter?

No, if we believe Paul Krugman's now famous 1994 *Foreign Affairs* article. Krugman cited empirical work conducted by Young and others to suggest that total-factor productivity growth has been unimportant in explaining the growth of the 'big four' newly industrializing economies (NIEs) – Korea, Taiwan, Hong Kong and Singapore. According to Krugman, there is very little 'technology transfer' to be explained.

More recent studies of these countries do not seem to confirm the earlier findings, but studies of the next round of industrializing economies – Thailand, Indonesia, Malaysia, and now the south-eastern provinces of China, suggest that total-factor productivity growth has been high during the economic booms they all experienced from 1988 onwards. It is notable that their booms were all characterized by massive levels of foreign investment. Unlike the (much lower) volumes of foreign investment they experienced previously, the foreign investment of this post-1988 period was characterized by high proportions of foreign investment from Taiwan, Hong Kong and Singapore, the earlier round of NIEs, rather than the traditional sources: Japan, the USA and Europe. While the jury is still out on the sources of growth in the NIEs, I conclude that the central questions of this chapter do, indeed, matter considerably.

What Does the Chapter Do?

The strength of the chapter is that it provides an analytical starting point for answering question (a) above, and then tries to bring this analysis to bear on a practical problem. It does the first more successfully and does so by outlining a game-theoretic/information-theoretic framework, in which information acquisition is the outcome of a rational decision-making process. I found this aspect of the chapter innovative and original. The chapter then illustrates this process by summarizing eight stylized case studies, most of which involve technology transfer via the foreign firm's local employees.

What Doesn't the Chapter Do?

I shall list six issues that the chapter does not discuss, or does not discuss in any depth. I am not necessarily suggesting that any of what I describe here should have been included. My comments should therefore not be read as criticisms of this particular chapter but as an attempt to locate it conceptually and to indicate where future work might proceed.

First, the chapter does not discuss forms of emulative development involving trade but *not* involving foreign investment. In this respect, the title is perhaps misleading. The scope of the chapter is much narrower than the title suggests. Second, there is no discussion of technology transfer through foreign investment which does not involve the firm's local employees. What about suppliers, contractors and so on? In some cases, technology transfer through them might be more important than that operating through local employees. Third, the distinction between 'soft' and 'hard' technology is not made clearly. Both kinds are presumably important for the chapter, but 'soft' technology transfer seems to be more important in the case studies.

My fourth point is that rivalry *among* foreign firms is not recognised in this chapter. I regard this as the most serious omission from the analysis. Firms with valuable technology protect it. Their motive is not primarily to protect their technological assets from being pilfered by local firms. These local firms are, in general, tiny players in the global market environment in which multinational firms operate. The primary goal is to protect this technology from their foreign competitors. The latter are a major threat because they are capable of replicating the technology on a massive scale, globally, and therefore of challenging the market advantage of the firm that currently possesses this information. Of course, the foreign competitors are operating in the local environment as well, and they are keen to acquire their competitors' knowledge. So to protect the firm's technology from foreign competitors is to protect it from everyone, including their local employees. Among firms who do have valuable technology to protect, various devices are used to minimize the amount of valuable information any one local employee can acquire through his or her work in the firm.

Fifth, I do not see why the analysis did not put rational information acquisition into a conventional optimization framework. Imagine the worker maximizing his or her expected future income stream over the available alternatives, with information acquisition from the current employee as a control variable. The firm is doing something different – maximizing expected future profit, taking the rate of obsolescence of the technology and the employees' behaviour into account. What would be wrong with that much simpler approach? The chapter does not tell me why game theory is needed. Someone should attempt to answer this chapter's questions with the simpler analytical approach that would seem to be possible.

Finally, I return to question (b) above: the role of the policy environment. How does it affect the outcome of the information-acquisition process that the authors analyze? What difference does it make to the overall welfare gain from foreign investment? The overall gain includes not only gains from technology transfer, but also net gains from tax revenues minus subsidies, and net gains from employment of domestic factors (especially labour) at returns that exceed their domestic opportunity costs. These sources of social gain from foreign investment may well outweigh any gains from technology transfer, so they cannot be ignored. These issues remain for others to explore.

17 Foreign Direct Investment, International Trade and Transfer of Technology: A Case Study in South-East Asia

Motoshige Itoh
UNIVERSITY OF TOKYO

1 INTRODUCTION

The miraculous economic growth of the South-East Asian economies in the last decade cannot be considered in isolation from the active foreign direct investment (FDI) into this region, and the resulting changes in the pattern of trade. The South-East Asian countries started growing rapidly after they changed their policy stance from protectionist import substitution policies to more liberal attitudes to capital inflow and a policy orientated towards exports. The changes in their trade positions have coincided with very active foreign direct investment from some countries such as Japan.

Many of the factories established by foreign firms in this region are located in so-called free-trade zones, and most of their products are exported to other parts of the world. The export-promoting effect of FDI on the economies of the South-East Asian countries is accentuated by the fact that production by the foreign-owned factories normally constitutes quite a large proportion of the output of the economies where they are established. Furthermore, these factories are involved in active intraregional trade in parts and equipment based on cross-border division of labour. Thus, intra-regional, intra-firm trade in intermediate goods and capital goods has been expanding rapidly in the last decade.

In this chapter, the pattern of trade and technology transfer by multinational companies (MNEs) in the South-East Asian region is illustrated by a case study. I conducted a field study of the Sony Corporation's activities in South-East Asia, visiting eight local subsidiaries of Sony in Singapore, Malaysia and Indonesia in September 1995, and my analysis is based solely on my interviews with managers in these subsidiaries.

370

The importance of the technological factor in international trade and investment, especially for the industries where multinational companies are active, has been pointed out by many people.[1] Technology is transferred from the home country to the host country through such channels as (i) trade in intermediate goods and capital goods containing technological information; and (ii) workers' acquisition of skills in MNEs' factories in the host countries and its spread through turnover of workers. Technological skills and information transmitted through these channels are often so substantial that the growth rates and trade pattern of the entire economy are affected. Literature on trade and growth utilizing the framework of endogenous growth models (for example, Grossman and Helpman, 1991) illustrates theoretically the importance of the technological factor.

The electrical and electronics industry is interesting, for various reasons. First, it accounts for the largest share of FDI in this region; and in Malaysia it has now become the most important export industry as a result of the activities of foreign-owned firms. Second, the technological characteristics of the industry have led to a large volume of trade in intermediate products, resulting from cross-border division of labour. Noting that trade in intermediate goods is an important channel for technology transfer, it is interesting to examine the pattern of intermediate goods trade as well as local procurement. The electrical and electronics industry, where procurement of intermediate goods is an important factor in a firm's competitiveness, is thus an appropriate industry for a case study.

My case study has, of course, many limitations. It is a study of only one company and we must be careful in interpreting the results. The overall picture may be very different from that given by the one case; but while acknowledging its limitations, I still think my case study can yield useful information. It is often difficult to get detailed information on the pattern of intrafirm trade from published data, and impossible to learn from macro data how technology is transferred to the host country. But we can put these questions directly to the people involved in production and trade.

The content of this chapter is as follows. In Section 2 a brief overall picture of FDI into this region is given. The third and fourth sections are based on the case study. In the third section I discuss such issues as the nature of location choice by Sony, intraregional cross-border division of labour inside the multinational company, and the pattern of trade. In Section, 4 I discuss various issues relating to the transfer of technology to the host country through the activities of the multinational company. Concluding remarks follow in Section 5.

2 FOREIGN DIRECT INVESTMENT BY THE ELECTRICAL AND ELECTRONICS INDUSTRIES IN SOUTH EAST ASIA

FDI into South-East Asian countries and exports from these countries have expanded rapidly since the mid-1980s. Various measures to attract such investment, including major changes in trade policy in the latter half of the 1980s, were introduced by the South-East Asian countries and are said to have been very effective.

Table 17.1 shows the flows of FDI into Asian countries during 1987–95. One can note a drastic increase in the inflow into South-East Asian countries up to the early 1990s. FDI into Malaysia, for example, increased about twenty times from 1987 to 1990.

FDI from Japan into some of the South-East Asian countries also increased rapidly in the later 1980s. The yen appreciated, (in terms of its nominal effective exchange rate) by about 64 per cent from 1985 to 1988, and in terms of its real exchange rate by 35 per cent; and this rapid appreciation made it difficult for Japanese export industries to maintain their competitive position, forcing some of them to relocate some of their production sites to low-wage countries in South-East Asia.

Table 17.2 shows the industrial composition of Japan's FDI into some of the South-East Asian countries, and that the electrical and electronics industry constitutes a large share of the total in Thailand, Malaysia and Singapore. This reflects the changing industrial structure in Japan

Table 17.1   Foreign direct investment into Asian countries, US$ 100 billions

Country	1987	1988	1989	1990	1991	1992	1993	1994	1995
China	37.1	53	62.9	69.9	124.2	587.4	1114	814	903
Korea	10.6	12.8	10.9	8	14	8.9	10.4	13.2	9.5
Taiwan	14.2	11.8	24.2	23	17.8	14.6	12.1	16.3	10.1
Singapore	6.9	8.2	8.3	12.2	14.3	16.8	19.7	28.3	15
Asia NIEs	31.7	32.8	43.4	43.2	46.1	40.3	42.2	57.8	34.6
Indonesia	14.6	44.1	47.2	87.5	87.8	103.2	81.4	237.2	321.5
(from Japan)	5.45	5.86	6.31	11.05	11.93	16.76	8.13	17.59	16.47
Thailand	19.3	61.8	80	141.3	49.9	100.2	42.9	58.8	88.8
(from Japan)	2.5	8.59	12.76	11.54	8.07	6.57	5.78	7.19	12.72
Malaysia	3	7.7	31.9	65.2	62	69.7	24.4	42.8	36.5
(from Japan)	1.63	3.87	6.73	7.25	8.8	7.04	8	7.42	5.9
Phillipines	1.7	4.5	8	9.6	7.8	2.8	5.3	23.4	15.9
(from Japan)	0.72	1.34	2.02	2.58	2.03	1.6	2.07	6.68	7.36
ASEAN 4	38.6	118.1	167.1	303.6	207.5	275.9	153.3	362.2	
Vietnam		0.4	0.5	0.6	1.3	1.9	2.8	4	7.7
India	0.8	1.7	2	0.7	2.4	15	29.1	45.2	100
Total FDI from Japan	48.7	55.7	82.4	70.5	59.4	64.2	66.4	97	

Source: Economic Planning Agency, Japan.

Table 17.2 Foreign direct investment by Japan, millions yen

Industry	Indonesia		Malaysia		Thailand		Singapore	
	1995	1987–95	1995	1987–95	1995	1987–95	1995	1987–95
Food	1 598	25 930		10 446	3 423	60 470	617	75 374
Textiles	14 843	201 513	246	40 857	3 317	93 667		23 030
Wood and pulp		60 306	1 897	29 380	610	9 295	203	8 604
Chemicals	17 188	289 648	8 757	106 636	5 308	61 502	7 138	196 866
Steel and other metals	18 504	353 775	4 235	90 614	22 464	104 395	1 245	28 145
Machinery	2 859	19 601	3 447	52 069	6 617	108 263	2 235	101 162
Electrical and electronics	23 584	72 971	17 033	242 890	30 136	207 321	21 239	151 553
Transport equipment	8 760	84 173	2 285	46 347	11 906	65 776		35 039
Other	13 208	91 275	10 192	137 757	12 849	97 001	12 231	94 690
Manufacturing total	100 547	1199 197	48 096	757 000	96 636	807 694	44 911	714 466
Non-manufacturing total	44 592	2218 430	7 360	267 317	16 418	326 918	69 417	891 981
Total	154 812	3429 782	55 456	1027 901	119 562	1173 676	114 329	1631 390

Source: Japanese Ministry of Finance, International Finance Year Book, various years.

Table 17.3   Exports of manufactures from Malaysia, RM millions

Year	Textiles, clothing and footwear	Electrical goods	Other	Total exports
1970	—	—	—	0.6
1975	0.2	0.3	1.5	2.0
1980	0.8	3.0	2.5	6.3
1984	1.1	6.7	4.7	12.5
1985	1.3	6.5	4.7	12.5
1986	1.6	8.5	5.3	15.4
1987	2.0	11.0	7.3	20.3
1988	2.4	15.2	9.2	26.8
1990	4.0	26.5	16.3	46.8
1992*	5	38.6	22.5	66.1

Note:—indicates nil or not known, * Estimates.

Source: Jomo (1994), p. 40.

caused by the appreciation of the yen as well as changing structure in the host countries.

In Malaysia, for example, there was a drastic change to a liberal policy towards inward FDI in the mid-1980s, and the expansion of FDI into Malaysia coincided with this liberalization. Japan was a large contributor and, as mentioned above, investment in the electrical and electronics industry constituted a large share of the Japanese total. The value of Malaysia's exports expanded very rapidly after 1985 and electrical and electronics products increased their share substantially (see Table 17.3). It is thus apparent that the foreign-owned subsidiaries contributed considerably to this changing pattern of trade.

Matsushita's factories in Malaysia provide a useful example of the scale of the activity of Japanese factories in this region. In 1993 there were about 20 000 employees in Matsushita's factories, and the value of their output was about 3 per cent of Malaysia's gross domestic product (GDP). The growth of these subsidiaries has been very fast, from about 4500 workers in 1985, and about 8500 in 1988. Various of their products, such as colour televisions and air conditioners, are exported to the whole world, including Japan. Sony also has a similar level of activity in Malaysia (see below), so that the activities of Japanese firms in this country are very significant.

Expanding trade and inward direct investment have changed the characteristics of international trade in this region:

(i)   The share of intra-industry trade between Japan and East Asian countries has increased. The South-East Asian countries, whose main exports in the past were primary goods, now export a large quantity of industrial products, both finished (assembled) goods, and parts; and they also import a large quantity of high-tech parts and capital goods from Japan.

(ii) Intra-firm trade has become more noticeable in such industries as automobiles, and electrical and electronics goods, with multinationals adopting strategic locations to take advantage of cross-border division of labour.

(iii) Not only trade in finished goods but also, and more importantly, trade in intermediate goods and parts has expanded, reflecting a complicated division of labour across the borders in the region.

(iv) The industrial structure of South-East Asian countries has changed substantially, and factors of production have shifted from agriculture and other primary goods production to manufacturing industry; and FDI into this region has been a very important factor promoting this structural change.

Although (i) to (iv) above represent a general trend in all the countries in South-East Asia, and in most industries in these countries, some differences among industries can be seen in the changing pattern of trade, in corporate strategies in the region, and in the effects of various national policies on the promotion of trade and investment. Comparing three industries: the electrical and electronics industry; the automobile industry; and the textile and apparel industry (the three most important industries in this region promoted by FDI), we can see that the patterns of production and trade by Japanese subsidiaries differ from one to another. We can also see the differences between the subsidiaries in South-East Asia and those in North America (see Table 17.4). The main points revealed by the table are:

(i) Not only domestic sales by the subsidiary and exports to Japan, but also exports to third countries are very significant in the electrical and electronics subsidiaries in Asia, while most of the output of the sub-sidiaries of the Japanese automobile industry in Asia is sold in the host countries. For the textiles and apparel industry, sales in the host country are large, both for subsidiaries in Asia and for those in North America, but exports to Japan are larger for the Asian subsidiaries than for the North American.

(ii) In the electrical and electronics industry the patterns of trade of the Asian subsidiaries and the North American subsidiaries are quite different: sales are evenly spread between the three destinations shown in Table 17.4 in the former case, while local sales predominate in the latter. On the procurement side, North American subsidiaries purchase considerably more from Japan than from the local or other markets, while Asian subsidiaries import quite a large amount (though

Table 17.4   Percentage distribution of trade of subsidiaries of Japanese firms in
North America and Asia

Area and industry	Sales of products			Purchases of parts and equipment		
	Local sales	Exports to Japan	Other exports	Local purchases	Imports from Japan	Other imports
North America						
Textiles and apparel	97.8	2.2	–	72.8	20.4	6.7
Electrical and electronics	92.9	2.4	4.8	25.5	66.6	8.0
Automobiles	96.7	0.7	2.6	56.6	36.5	6.9
Asia						
Textiles and apparel	76.0	8.3	15.7	66.0	16.1	17.9
Electrical and electronics	33.0	33.9	33.1	32.8	48.3	18.9
Automobiles	92.8	1.7	5.5	52.3	43.3	4.3

Source: Ministry of International Trade and Industry (1994) 'Foreign Operations
of Japanese Firms' (Tokyo) (based on a survey in 1992).

still the smallest share) from third countries, probably other Asian
countries.

(iii)   Japanese motor vehicles are normally exported directly from Japan to
markets in North America and Asia, or manufactured (often just finally
assembled) in the consuming market. Third-country trade, which can
be observed in the textiles and apparel industry, and in the electrical
and electronics sector in Asia, is nowhere common in the motor vehicle
industry.

Considering all the differences among industries mentioned above, a comparative study of these industries would be desirable. However, I have so far
been able to study only one case, in the electrical and electronics industry.
Thus, some of the results obtained in my case study may be quite specific to
this industry and not applicable to others.

3   LOCAL PRODUCTION AND INTRAREGIONAL DIVISION OF LABOUR

Local Subsidiaries and the Pattern of Trade

It may be useful to summarize first the nature of the Sony company. The basic
characteristics of Sony and of its multinational activities are as follows:

(i)   Like other electrical and electronics manufacturers in Japan, Sony
manufactures a wide variety of goods, from low-skill, labour-intensive

products to high-skill, capital-intensive ones. Typical examples of the former are audio equipment and colour televisions, while the latter include digital video cameras, automatic insertion machines and lithium batteries. Naturally, the labour-intensive and technologically simple products are those produced in the South-East Asian region. This pattern of locational choice (that is, low-tech goods in South-East Asia and high-tech goods in Japan) implies smooth technology transfer, since the host countries absorb the technology of low-tech goods more easily than that of high-tech goods. Since it does not pay Sony to manufacture these low-tech goods in Japan, the Company shifts most of its production capacity for of these goods to foreign factories, and even also shifts some of its design engineers to them. However, even within this region we can observe some crucial differences in the types of product produced in each country. Moreover, some technologically sophisticated products are also produced in this region, not in the main because of lower production costs, but because of the importance of the local network of division of labour.

(ii) Electrical and electronics products are assembled from a multitude of parts, some produced by Sony itself but many purchased from other firms. Sony's activity in South-East Asia encouraged FDI into this region by the manufacturers of parts, and Sony has also increased procurement from local manufacturers. However, some kinds of parts are imported from Japan, and this is a factor in the increase of exports from Japan to the region.

(iii) Although Sony has operated for a long time in North America and Europe, its activity in Asia is a recent phenomenon, in contrast with some other Japanese manufacturers of electrical goods, such as Matsushita and Sanyo, which have had operations in this region since the 1970s. All the Sony factories I visited were less than seven years old; and it is obvious that the appreciation of the yen since 1985 and rapid industrialization in this region, together with more liberal policies, have promoted Sony's activity here.

Table 17.5 shows the eight subsidiaries visited in this region and basic information about them is provided in the Appendix. From this we can see that, even among the three countries in the region, there are some crucial differences in the way Sony's subsidiaries operate, and these are related to the differences between the labour markets in the three countries.

Roughly speaking, there are two types of worker in the factories: engineers and operatives.[2] Engineers have university degrees or higher qualifications, or have graduated from engineering schools; operatives are manual workers with less educational background. The conditions of supply of engineers and operatives differ among the three countries. There is a good supply of

Table 17.5   Sony's subsidiaries in Singapore, Malaysia and Indonesia

Company	Location	Number of workers (Japanese)	Products	Starting year
SONIS	Singapore	700 (120)	Local headquarters	1988
SDS (Sony Display Devices)	Singapore	900 (30)	TV tubes	1992
SPEC (Sony Precision Engineering Centre)	Singapore	1350 (50)	Engineering support, parts	1987
SVM (Sony Video Malaysia)	Bangi, Malaysia	2714 (n.a.)	VCR, CD-ROM drives	1990
STIM (Sony TV Industry Malaysia)	Bangi, Malaysia	3800 (40)	Colour TVs	1988
SEM (Sony Electronics Malaysia)	Penang, Malaysia	8000 (28)	Audio equipment	1988
SMM (Sony Mechatronic Products Malaysia)	Penang, Malaysia	2700 (16)	Floppy disk drives	1990
SII (Sony Electronics Indonesia)	Indonesia	2800 (25)	Audio equipment	1992

engineers in Singapore, but they are scarcer in Malaysia and Indonesia. Indeed, in Indonesia, engineers are so scarce that there is severe competition for them among foreign firms operating there.

Sony's locational choices reflect these labour market conditions. In the two factories in Singapore, Sony manufactures products based on extremely capital-intensive technologies, and in both factories more than 50 per cent of workers have a high school, or higher, education. But in the factories in Malaysia and Indonesia, more than 90 per cent of workers are operatives (mostly female). In Singapore it is impossible to find low-wage operatives and the factories therefore use foreign workers, since the Singapore government now permits a quota for foreign workers for each factory, under certain conditions.

Although operatives were abundant in Malaysia in the past, it is becoming more difficult to recruit them following the expansion of foreign-owned factories there. In the Sony factories in Penang about 3 per cent of operatives quit their job every month, which implies that a third are replaced every year. Such a high turnover incurs high training costs for the firm. In the case of SEM, where the annual turnover rate is 36 per cent, it takes one week to teach basic skills to new workers. This factory has about 8000 operatives, and newly-hired operatives are trained in a separate room for a week. Thus, every year 2500 worker-weeks of training is provided by the firm. Moreover, it is also becoming more difficult to hire new workers to replace those who leave.

Facing the increasing scarcity of operatives in Malaysia, Sony is gradually shifting labour-intensive operations from Malaysia to Indonesia. Such products as radio-cassette tape-recorders and audio equipment, which were originally produced in Malaysia, are gradually being shifted to Indonesia, and the factories in Malaysia are now changing some of their product lines. CD-ROM production has started in the factory where floppy disks were originally produced, and other higher-grade products are now produced in Malaysia. In Indonesia, however, there is an abundant supply of operatives and, according to a local manager, about 3000 people applied for his 100 jobs. Production in Indonesia is expanding rapidly and replacing some of the production located earlier in Malaysia.

The diversity of labour market conditions among the South-East Asian countries combined with the diversity of Sony's products, from low-tech to high-tech goods, allows Sony optimal choice of location for its operations. If one overlays the map of the USA on the map of the South-East Asian region, one will find that the distances between the latter countries are comparable with those between the states in the USA. However, the diversity of labour market conditions, including wage differences, among the Asian countries is much greater than among the states in the USA. By utilizing this diversity of labour market conditions, multinationals can make strategic locational choices for their production.

There is not a large intraregional trade in assembled goods in South-East Asian. Most products from the subsidiaries are exported to other regions, such as North America and Europe, since there is not yet a large local market for them. It is clear that the incentive for direct investment in this region to produce such products is solely low-cost operation, not local demand; and it was relatively easy to expand these factories rather quickly, since they are specialized in production for the world market (see the role of local headquarters, below).

With large amounts of both parts and finished products moving to and from the local factories, an efficient transportation system is essential for their operation. I was impressed by the volume of products shipped out of these factories. There are about 1500 containers shipped from SONIS each month, and a large proportion of the products from the factories in Indonesia and Penang are transported without going through Singapore. Inventories of products are not held in the factories, products being dispatched as soon as one container is filled. Trucks go from the factory to the port every two to three hours, and it is thus natural that all factories are located near ports. Local governments have made great efforts to improve the transportation infrastructure, involving road construction, expansion of port facilities and so on. Although there is little intraregional trade in finished goods, there is a large trade in parts and equipment, the factories in this region making large shipments world-wide.

The Role of the Local Headquarters

The local headquarters in Singapore plays an important role in the operation of Sony's trade in this region, both co-ordinating intrafirm trade and the related logistic operations, as well as engaging in longer-run activities, such as the training of workers and financial management. One important feature of Sony and, of course, of other large multinationals, is that there are many kinds of close interaction among the local subsidiaries; and the local headquarters is the core of the local network.

Among the various functions of this headquarters, the following are particularly important:

(i) All transactions by the subsidiaries in this region, at least financially, though not necessarily physically, go through this headquarters. Thus the goods produced by the subsidiaries are first sold to the local headquarters, and the headquarters sells them on. Similarly, all purchases of parts are made through the local headquarters. When the local factories import parts, they buy from the local headquarters.[3] The local headquarters buys these parts from other Sony factories, or from independent suppliers in this region, in Japan and in the rest of the world. The decisions regarding from whom to purchase parts are often made by the managers in the user factories, and the order transmitted directly from the local user factories to the suppliers, but the financial transactions still go through the local headquarters.

(ii) All the transactions between a local subsidiary and the headquarters are in the currency of the local subsidiary. For example, when a subsidiary in Malaysia exports its products to the USA, the products are first sold to the local headquarters in Malaysian currency (RM). The products are then sold to Sony's sales company in the USA in US dollars. Thus, neither the factories in Malaysia nor sales companies in importing countries bear the exchange risk, which is covered by the local headquarters.

(iii) Through the transaction outlined above, a large amount of profit accumulates in the local headquarters, and a large portion of this accumulated fund is not returned to Japan, for several reasons. First, the corporate tax rate is much higher in Japan than in Singapore; second, there is a large investment demand in this region, for which funds accumulated in the local headquarters can be used; and third, the very liberal regulation of financial activities and well-developed networks of financial companies make Singapore a good place for the financial operations of multinationals such as Sony.[4]

(iv) Efficient logistical operations are essential for the successful operation of the regional network. There are about 2000 types of product (counting different models of the same product) supplied by the factories in this region, and about 60 000 kinds of major part used.[5] The production and transportation of these products and parts takes time (what the engineers call 'lead time'). The co-ordination role of the local headquarters is thus important if the local factories are to carry minimum inventories of parts without increasing the risk of shortage. The task is not easy, since it involves various levels of co-ordination of planning of production, procurement, distribution and so on.[6] Moreover, as noted above, local factories do not carry any inventory of their products. Once a container-full of products is produced, it is transported to a neighbouring port. In other words, inventories of products produced by a factory are controlled by the local headquarters, and not by the factory itself.

(v) The local headquarters plays many roles when a new factory starts production. The new factories must depend on the local headquarters for the procurement of parts, and the local headquarters offers various forms of technical support as well as assistance with training.

While the local headquarters co-ordinates the operation of subsidiaries in the region and assists in such areas as training, legal matters, information, finance and so on, the subsidiaries also have close relations with each other. A newly-established factory in Indonesia, for example, depends heavily on the skills and know-how of the factories in Malaysia, which started earlier and have produced similar products. The factories in Malaysia and Indonesia depend on SPEC in Singapore for various kinds of technical support. They obtain information from each other on suppliers of parts in the region, as well as from the local headquarters which accumulates information systematically on the network of suppliers.

The rapid expansion of local factories would have been impossible without the support of the local headquarters; but the division of labour between the local headquarters and the local factories is changing with the stage of development of local production. More responsibilities are delegated to the local factories as they accumulate production experience.

Cost Structure and Local Content

For the assembling factories in Malaysia and Indonesia the cost of parts is critical for their efficient operation. The ratio of value-added to the value of final output is less than 10 per cent for assembled goods such as colour televisions and audio equipment, with more than 90 per cent of total cost being parts. This contrasts with products such as TV tubes and mechanical decks (intermediate products), whose value added is 80–90 per cent of total production costs, with cost of parts being less than 20 per cent.

It is important to note that local content ratios are quite high in these factories, despite the fact that all the factories started their production recently. The importance of purchased parts in total production costs forced the factories to use as many locally manufactured parts as possible. In Bangi in Malaysia, where production by SVM started in the early 1990s, the local content ratio already exceeds 86 per cent (in this case including parts purchased in Malaysia and Singapore). Even in the newer factory in Indonesia (SEI), the local content ratio exceeds 55 per cent (in this case not including parts purchased from Singapore and Malaysia, which would make the local content ratio much higher if they were included).

The extra cost the local factory would have to pay for parts from Japan or other distant countries includes not only transportation costs but also costs related to efficient delivery and inventory management. Although it would be possible to carry an ample inventory of parts in local factories, the cost of doing so would raise the local production cost. According to a manager in Penang, an average inventory of parts in Sony's comparable factories in Japan is about 0.2 to 0.3 months' volume, while that in Penang is about 0.65 months' volume.[7]

There are a large number of small and medium-sized Japanese firms in Singapore and Malaysia producing components for televisions and audio equipment and, according to a local Sony manager, investment by large firms such as Sony and Matsushita triggered the investment by these small and medium-sized firms in production of parts for the large multinationals. As a result of these investment flows there is now a well-developed local network of procurement of components in this region. Among the 86 per cent local content of SVM in Malaysia, 83 per cent came from the subsidiaries of Japanese companies and only 3.2 per cent from indigenous local firms. Similarly, in SEI in Indonesia, among the 54 per cent local content, 47.6 per cent came from the subsidiaries of Japanese companies and only 6.7 per cent from indigenous local firms.

According to local managers it is not easy to find indigenous suppliers able to supply good-quality products. SVM purchases from local indigenous firms such parts as boxes, shock-absorbing materials for packaging, and printed materials such as manuals; all electrical and mechanical parts are purchased from local Japanese subsidiaries, or are imported. For other factories, such as those in Singapore and in Penang, the share of local indigenous firms seems to be higher. Although we could not obtain exact data, local managers claim to buy many electrical and mechanical parts from indigenous firms.

It takes some time for the local network of component suppliers to be established. Singapore and Penang have long histories of foreign direct investment. In Singapore, IBM started its production in the 1970s, and Hewlett Packard, Apple and Motorola have had large production facilities there for some time. Because of its long history of FDI from various countries, there already exists a well-developed network of parts suppliers in Singapore, some foreign-owned but also a large number of indigenous firms. Similarly, in Penang, Hitachi, National Semiconductor, Siemens and Bosch have had their factories for some time, and when Sony started operations in Penang there were already quite a large number of sufficiently skilled indigenous firms supplying parts.

An Example of a Japanese Subsidiary Supplying Parts

When a large company such as Sony starts operating in the South-East Asian region, some small and medium-sized suppliers of parts always follow from Japan. I visited one such firm in Indonesia, with a factory located about 10 minutes' car ride from the Sony factory. The firm's operation is a very simple one – jointing small connectors to electric wires – and the factory had started its operation about six months before my visit. There were about 300 local operatives and three Japanese employees (two engineers and one manager). This firm set up its first foreign factory in Taiwan in the late 1980s, as a joint venture with local capital, and opened its Malaysian factory six years ago. Before starting up the factory in Indonesia, about sixty-five operatives had been sent to the Malaysian factory for six months training.

Sony's factory in Indonesia originally purchased parts from this firm's Malaysian factory, but as the operation of Sony's Indonesian factory expanded, the firm started producing parts in Indonesia. Sony started up its Indonesia factory because of increasing difficulty in obtaining operatives in Malaysia, with the factory in Indonesia replacing some of the Malaysian production capacity. The supplier of parts faced the same labour conditions in Malaysia, and the manager commented that his Malaysia factory would now shift to more technologically advanced products, with labour-intensive production being moved to Indonesia.

4 EMPLOYMENT AND TRANSFER OF TECHNOLOGY

On-the-job Training of Engineers and Spillover of Skills

Technology is transferred through workers, and both engineers and operatives accumulate their skills mainly through on-the-job-training (OJT). The acquired skills will then spill over inside the factory through the expansion of the firm's operations, and to other firms through job hopping, and to suppliers of parts though the trading of parts.

Most of the daily operation of the factories is run by local engineers, and they are often also involved in the design process. The nature of technology transfer through OJT differs considerably from one place to another, depending on how deeply local engineers are involved in the factory's operations. Comparing the factories in the three countries reveals some of the differences.

In Indonesia, where there is not an ample supply of high quality engineers, determination of the production process is simple: the factory simply borrows the production system from Japan. Thus, most of the design process is undertaken in Japan, and the Indonesian factory simply imitates the design. However, even in this factory there are many small unexpected changes needed in day to day operations, so that locally employed engineers have opportunities to learn various skills through learning-by-doing.

However, from the viewpoint of Sony, this situation is unsatisfactory. First, given the short cycle of many new models, it is far more desirable to start production from the beginning in the local factories than to wait for the production process to be stabilized in Japan. In the early stage of production of any new model, many unexpected small changes have to be made, and the production process, as well as the specification of parts, may be altered many times. It is the role of designers and engineers to solve these problems on the factory floor, but if there are few good engineers in a local subsidiary, all this stabilizing process must be finished in a factory in Japan. In such a case, know-how and skills are not transferred to the local subsidiary. However, if the local subsidiary has sufficient skilled engineers to deal with the early stage, production can start there immediately after the basic designing of the product.

A second reason for dissatisfaction is related to the fact that a large portion of total cost is cost of parts. As mentioned earlier, it is vital to save costs by buying as many parts as possible in the local market. All managers emphasized that the local factory must have a design section if it is to buy parts from the local market. During the early stage of production there will be a series of interactions between the design change and the purchase of parts. Availability of local parts and their quality can make it necessary for the Sony subsidiary to change the design of products and of the production process, on the one hand, and trial and error in the factory can make it necessary for Sony to ask local manufacturers for different specifications of various components, on the other. One production-process engineer pointed out that designers become busier after production starts than before. The skills of engineers, as well as designers, are crucial for efficient interaction between changes in the factory and in the local parts supplied to it. Therefore, to expand local procurement of parts, it is necessary for the local subsidiary to have adequate engineering expertise.

Comparison of SEM in Penang and SEI in Indonesia is useful in this context. Both factories manufacture similar products. However, SEM has a much larger design and engineering capacity than SEI. Thus, SEM can become the mother factory for SEI, but the reverse is not possible.

Spillover of Skills into the Economy

As already mentioned, there are three main routes for the spread of technology: the first is through the expansion of local factories; the second through the trade in parts; and the third via job-hopping by engineers. The first route is obvious. If the local subsidiaries expand their capacity, they will employ more engineers, and these newly-employed engineers have opportunities to learn skills, both from Japanese engineers and from local engineers who have had experience of working in the factory for some time. The second route is through the interactions between assemblers and their components producers, already discussed above. In my interviews I heard of various cases in which Sony is teaching skills to indigenous, as well as foreign, producers of parts for its factories; a higher level of skills in the firms producing parts is certainly beneficial to Sony.

The most controversial route for the spillover of skills is through job-hopping by engineers. In Malaysia and Indonesia, where engineers are very scarce, there are many opportunities for this. This is especially so for Sony's engineers, who are viewed in the labour market as being well trained. The turnover rate is, in fact, quite high. In SVM in Malaysia about 10 per cent of engineers go to other companies every year, and a manager in SEI in Indonesia told me that all local engineers in SEI had received letters with job offers from a Korean company.

The fact that there is much job hopping and many job offers implies that skills which local engineers obtain in Sony factories are valuable for other companies; and that job-hopping is a crucial route for the transfer of technology from Sony to other companies. The availability of these engineers is an important reason for other companies to invest in this region.

The higher the rate of turnover of engineers, the more intense the spillover of skills will be. However, if the turnover rate is very high, a company like Sony will be discouraged from transferring skills and technology to local workers, since they will be used to the advantage of other companies. But a modest rate of turnover of engineers may increase the degree of technology transfer. When skilled workers quit, Sony must employ new ones and give them training. The more engineers they employ, the more training they must give. Thus a modest rate of job-hopping by engineers may result in both a valuable cycle of skill acquisitions by Sony's employees and also in a spillover of their skills into the rest of the economy. The situation is very similar to the standard economic model of innovation activities and technology spillover under a patent system. A stronger patent right gives stronger incentives for innovation activities, but a smaller amount of technology spillover, while a weaker patent right discourages innovation.

Comparison of the three countries makes it clear that availability of well-educated engineers is a crucial factor in the transfer of technology. In all the factories I visited, daily operations were mainly controlled by local staff; it simply cost too much to bring engineers from Japan for that purpose, as the cost of one Japanese engineer is almost equivalent to hiring five local engineers with college degrees, or fifty local operatives, in Indonesia. It is almost impossible to localize factories engaged in advanced levels of production where there are no good local engineers; and one Japanese manager in Indonesia complained that the scarcity of good engineers in Indonesia made it difficult for local factories to move on from simple assembling to having a design process inside the factory. Moreover, as mentioned earlier, good quality design staff inside the factory is essential if a firm is to expand local procurement of parts and thus to enhance technology transfer.

Cross-border Transfer of Technology

In the factories we visited, we observed phenomena that we have called cross-border and intra-regional transfer of technology:

(i)   In SDS in Singapore, there were about 153 operatives from China who, according to a manager, will later become technicians in China, their experience in Singapore being used in Sony's operations in China.

(ii) The small-parts producer in Indonesia which is a sub-contracting company for Sony sent sixty-five operatives (out of 300) to its factory in Malaysia for six months, both for training, as mentioned above, as well as to have low-cost workers for its factory in Malaysia.

(iii) Some engineers in this region are sent to Sony's factory in Japan for a year or so to acquire skills through on-the-job training and the Japanese government provides financial support for this.[8]

There are a variety of interactions among local factories in this region, and there is a technological hierarchy among the Sony factories. Factories in Singapore are more technologically advanced than those in Malaysia or in China, and skills in Singapore are transferred to Malaysia and China. Similarly, the factory in Indonesia learns a lot from the experiences of those in Malaysia, even some Japanese managers being transferred from the factories in Malaysia to Indonesia.

For some kinds of technology and skills, intraregional transfer is more effective and costs less than transfer from the home country of the firm, in this case Japan. Economic and cultural backgrounds are similar among the countries of the region; the technological gap is less between the factories in the region than between them and Japan, and the smaller gap helps the smooth transfer of some kinds of skill. It costs a lot to send engineers to Japan or to bring Japanese engineers to local factories, partly because of the higher cost of living in Japan than in these countries.

5 CONCLUDING REMARKS

The case study of the Sony Corporation in the South-East-Asian region suggests various interesting issues that are worth further theoretical and empirical research:

(i) A wide diversity of labour market conditions, including wage differences, allows a firm to utilize the differences to its advantage. For an industry such as the electrical and electronics industry, where a wide variety of products is made, this diversity has promoted foreign direct investment into the region.

(ii) The local headquarters plays an important role in co-ordinating local operations in this region. All transactions go through the local headquarters, and various financial aspects of local factories' operations are delegated to the local headquarters. The factories are specialized in their production activities and are dependent on the local headquarters for various forms of support.

(iii) Huge amounts of freight come into and out of the factories, and efficient logistics are essential for efficient production. All factories are located near ports, and possibilities of sea transportation are fully utilized.

(iv) Job-hopping is one crucial route for technological spillover from the subsidiaries to the rest of the local economy. The more job-hopping the more technology transfer, subject to the caveat that too much job-hopping may reduce incentives for the multinational to transfer technology.

(v) The local availability of good engineers is an important factor in technology transfer. This is not only because abundant engineers allows active absorption of foreign technology but also, and perhaps more importantly, because local availability of engineers allows foreign firms to deepen the level of technology transfer by increasingly localizing their production.

(vi) For the factories manufacturing assembled goods, the share of parts in total costs is quite high, which makes it necessary for the local factories to procure as many parts as possible from domestic suppliers. This is an important driving force for technology transfer and for additional FDI from abroad.

Although the above findings are based on one sample study, they have various connections with theoretical and empirical research on multinationals and the transfer of technology. Let me note the implication of our analysis for the literature on the pattern of trade in intermediate goods. As analyzed by monopolistic competition models with intermediate goods (Ethier, 1982; and Grossman and Helpman, 1991), division of labour in the production of intermediate goods and the resulting international trade in these intermediate goods enhance production opportunities for the developing countries. The large share of costs of intermediate goods in the electrical and electronics industry confirm the importance of this mechanism.

However, as seen in our case, the relationship between intermediate goods trade and technology transfer is not restricted only to the division of labour in the production of intermediate goods. As noted above, the location of the production of intermediate goods has a crucial effect on how the multinationals affect local factories. The larger the local content ratio, the more commitment is made to technology transfer to the local subsidiaries. Noting the political importance of local-content issues, further research into this relationship should be conducted.

My conclusions on the relationship between labour market conditions and the pattern of technology spillover also need further theoretical and empirical research. In many studies, spillover of technology from the multinationals to the rest of the economy is given by an exogenously-determined mechanism. However, as our case study illustrates, labour market conditions, such as the job-hopping rate and availability of engineers, affect the way the multinationals train their workers. Just as in the literature on research and development (for example, Tirole, 1988, ch. 10), which considers investment in technology as an endogenous variable depending on such factors as legal protection of patent, rivals' behaviour and market conditions, the pace of technology transfer from multinationals to the host country should be analyzed as an endogenous variable depending on similar factors.

Appendix: Brief Description of the Subsidiaries

SONIS (the Local Headquarters): Singapore

The regional headquarters for the South-East Asian countries; its main function being to control and co-ordinate the activities of local subsidiaries. There are about 700 employees, including 120 from Japan. The company started as a regional distribution centre for parts and became the local headquarters in 1988, when the rapid expansion of Sony's operations in the region began.

Sony Precision Engineering Centre (SPEC) and Sony Display Devices (SDS): Singapore

These two subsidiaries (factories) share many of the features typical of operation in a high-wage country such as Singapore. SPEC originated as an engineering support centre for this region, but then started production of such parts as optical devices, drum heads for video cassette recorders (VCRs), mechanical decks, and electric guns for colour TV tubes. The are 1300 local staff and fifty people from Japan. More than 50 per cent of the local employees have a high-school or higher education. Thirteen per cent of the products of this factory are sold to Japan, 10 per cent to Europe and North America, and the remaining 77 per cent within the region. The share of value-added in the total value of output is more than 90 per cent, which contrasts with the assembling factories in Indonesia and Malaysia.

SDS started its operation, producing TV tubes, in 1992. There are 900 employees, including thirty from Japan. The factory has very capital-intensive production lines, almost all of them automated. Among the employees are 101 engineers (with university-graduate or higher qualifications); 357 technician/mechanics, and forty-nine supervisors (high school or engineering school graduates); and 290 operatives. There are about 153 operatives from China in the factory, who will become technicians when they return to China. The Singapore government recently deregulated the entry of foreign workers, which has benefited foreign factories experiencing the scarcity of operatives in Singapore, and there are also about 300 workers from Malaysia, mostly operatives. This factory purchases electric guns (the most important parts for TV tubes) from SPEC, nearby, and the tubes produced are transported by truck to Malaysia and by sea to other countries (there is a large TV factory in Thailand). There are about 1300 containers (each 130 feet in length) leaving this factory every month. For 14-inch TV tubes, about 80 per cent of the parts are produced in South-East Asia.

Sony Video Malaysia (SVM) and Sony TV Industries Malaysia (STIM): Bangi, Malaysia

STIM started its operation in 1988 for the assembling of colour TVs, and SVM was established in 1989 and started producing VCDs in 1990. It also started producing CD-ROMs in 1994. These two factories are located in the same area. My information relates mainly to SVM, but the two factories are similar in many respects.

There are 2714 workers in SVM, of which 25.4 per cent are male and 74.6 per cent female; and SVM ships out 200 containers (each 40 feet in length) every month. The destination of the products is: North America, 42 per cent; Middle and South America, 12 per cent; Middle East, 12 per cent; Pan-Asia, 14 per cent; Europe, 6 per cent; and Japan, 1 per cent. Value-added is only 10 per cent of the total value of the products. The local content of all parts bought in is 83 per cent from local Japanese subsidiaries and 3.2 per cent from domestic indigenous firms, with the remaining local supply coming from other South-East Asian countries. The turnover rate per year (the share of workers moving to other firms) is 10 per cent for engineers and 30 per cent for operatives.

Sony Electronics Malaysia (SEM) and Sony Mechatronics Products Malaysia (SMM): Penang, Malaysia

There are 8000 workers in SEM (18 Japanese), and 2700 in SMM (16 Japanese). SEM manufactures audio equipment, and SMM floppy disks. SEM started its operation in

1988, and SMM in 1990. SEM has experienced a very rapid increase in its sales (units are one billion RM, will 2.5 RM being about one yen): 253 in 1988; 1354 in 1991; 1791 in 1994; and 3300 in 1995.

There were already various foreign firms in this area (Penang island), including Hitachi, National Semiconductors, Siemens and Bosch. There are now about seventy Japanese companies in the city, and 35 000 workers in these companies. Sony's share is about a third (12 000 workers including Toyo audio, Sony's subsidiary). The output of Sony's subsidiaries in Malaysia represents about 6.6 per cent of Malaysian GDP. Wage cost accounts for about 5 per cent of the sales value, and thus constitutes about 0.3 per cent of Malaysia's GDP.

Fifty-one per cent of the products of SEM are exported to North America; 25 per cent to Europe; and 3 per cent to Japan. Products are transported by medium-sized boats to Kaohsiung (Taiwan), Yokohama (Japan) and Singapore, where they are trans-shipped to larger container ships.

About 25 per cent of operatives are from Penang island; about 60 per cent from neighbouring areas; and about 15 per cent from the east coast of Malaysia. Workers from the east coast live in dormitories. About 90 per cent of total cost is the cost of parts, among which two motors, two semiconductors and one magnetic head constitute 75 per cent. These major components, except for integrated cricuits, come from Japanese subsidiaries in Malaysia.

Sony Electronics Indonesia (SEI): Indonesia

This factory started production in 1992. Its main products are audio equipment and radio-cassette tape-recorders and it ships out about 700 containers a month. More than 60 per cent of the products are exported to North America, with exports to Japan being very small.

Indonesia has a large population and the Indonesian government allows foreign subsidiaries in the free trade zones to sell up to 30 per cent of their products to the domestic market. Although the tariff on radio-cassette tape-recorders imported from abroad is 30 per cent, the rate for the products from this factory is 9 per cent, which is a good incentive for Sony to go to Indonesia.

There is an ample supply of operatives, but engineers and technicians are very scarce, and foreign firms compete for engineers. According to a local manager, there are eighty-two Indonesian managers, who will become the core of the factory after the training given to them by Japanese staff.

Suppliers of parts here are not so well qualified as those in Malaysia, and the firm therefore chose about ten major suppliers and offers various kinds of technical assistance to them in order to nurture them as main subcontractors.

Notes

1. See Caves (1982) and Dunning (1993) for comprehensive surveys of the literature on MNE and the technology factor in international trade.
2. There are of course, other types of worker, such as office workers. But since the situation of these other workers is not important in our discussion, I have ignored them.

3. When they buy parts from the domestic market, then the local headquarters is not involved.

4. Obviously, this type of behaviour annoys the Japanese tax authorities, who have expressed increasing concern about transfer pricing by Japanese multinationals. The issue is also relevant to other Asian countries: the lower the export price from Malaysia to Singapore, the lower will be the profit left in Malaysia.

5. These data are based on my interview.

6. Take the following example. Suppose that there are some orders for VCRs. The request for production is transferred through SONIS, the local headquarters, to the factory in Malaysia. The factory in Malaysia then sets up a production plan and orders parts directly, or through SONIS from various companies. For example, the order for the mechanical deck, a crucial part of a VCR, is given either to SPEC (Sony's subsidiary in Singapore which produces this product) or to the Sony factory in Japan. These factories make their production plan for mechanical decks and order the parts necessary for their production, and so on. As there are about 2000 models of VCRs, with frequent introduction of new models, more than twenty factories in this region, and a very complicated pattern of division of labour in parts production, co-ordination by the local headquarters is essential.

7. Even shipment of parts from Malaysia to Indonesia incurs some additional cost. According to a local manager in Indonesia, the cost of insurance, freight and packaging is about 5–6 per cent of the cost; the part that costs US$50 in Malaysia costs US$53 after shipment to Indonesia.

8. The Japanese government subsidizes the wages paid to foreign workers working in factories in Japan for a year or so, the purpose of this programme being to promote technology transfer from Japan to host countries. Many firms, large multinationals as well as small and medium-sized firms, utilize this scheme.

References

Caves, R. E. (1982) *Multinational Enterprise and Economic Analysis* (Cambridge: Cambridge University Press).

Dunning, J. H., (1993) *Multinational Enterprises and the Global Economy* (Wokingham: Addison-Wesley).

Ethier, W. J. (1982) 'National and International Returns to Scale in the Modern Theory of International Trade', *American Economic Review*, vol. 72, pp. 389–405.

Grossman, G. M. and E. Helpman (1991) *Innovation and Growth in the Global Economy* (Cambridge, Mass.: MIT Press).

Jomo, K. S. (ed.) (1994) *Malaysia's Economy in the Nineties* (Kuala Lumpur: Pelanduk Publications).

Tirole, J. (1988) *The Theory of Industrial Organization* (Cambridge, Mass.: MIT Press).

Comment

Wilfred J. Ethier
UNIVERSITY OF PENNSYLVANIA

Good case studies generate many interesting hypotheses, and this is a good case study. Brevity precludes an attempt to catalogue all the hypotheses; instead I choose just one and discuss it in some detail. Consider the following:

> There is a class of goods whose multi-stage production process is such that firms producing them are tempted to undertake direct investment in regions characterized by:
>
> (i) large *differences* in relative factor endowments within the region; and
> (ii) low economic *distances* between points in the region.

Sufficient barriers to intra-regional migration and a sufficient number of goods that do not enter into intra-regional trade would allow differences in relative factor endowments across a region to persist and to generate intra-regional disparities in factor rewards. Compact geography, an abundance of waterways, and extensive transportation infrastructure would keep economic distances low within a region.

The above hypothesis has an immediate implication for reform-minded LDCs anxious to attract FDI as a fast track to modernization, technology transfer, and economic development. To the extent that goods satisfying the hypothesis are potentially relevant to such countries, they should wish to establish regional arrangements with other countries that are:

(i) close, in terms of economic distance; and
(ii) different from themselves, in terms of relative factor endowments.

Existing regional arrangements do not, on the whole, appear to display these characteristics strongly, though Mexico in NAFTA perhaps fits the bill. But the potential seems strong for APEC, in which the diversity of its members is a dominant characteristic.

I cannot resist the temptation to digress with a speculation concerning possible implications for my own Chapter 6 in this volume. The relevance is most direct to the road to regionalism that I call 'reform facilitation'. Replace the assumption that all LDCs are identical with one that they differ in the two

392

dimensions discussed above. Suppose that each differentiated commodity x is produced with many stages, not just two. Then one would expect regional equilibria to be characterized by clusters of disparate LDCs linking together with a single developed country. The ability of regional arrangements to ensure successful reform should be widened – that is, the sufficient conditions for the outcome that any LDC that would wish to reform were its success certain can, in fact, enter into a regional arrangement, should become weaker.

But the greatest potential interest would attach to a possible dynamic extension. The case study suggests strongly that the ratio of human capital to labour is the factor endowment ratio that matters most, and this is endogenous in a proper dynamic framework. This, in turn, suggests that successful reform efforts would cause the membership of regional clusters to evolve over time. Such a process could provide the basis for a regional dynamics quite different from the two common alternatives: a process of bloc enlargement and consolidation leading to free multilateral trade, or, alternatively, to a small number of hostile blocs.

I thank Professor Itoh for an informative and stimulating chapter.

Part V
Conference Summaries

18 Summing-up I

Elhanan Helpman
TEL AVIV UNIVERSITY

The IEA Conference on International Trade Policy and the Pacific Rim brought together a diverse group of experts who were able to engage productively in a discussion of important policy issues. Professional and public debates concerning desirable modifications to the world's trading system have existed for a long time, but a new sense of urgency has developed in recent years with the conclusion of the Uruguay Round and the proliferation of regional free-trade agreements. Unlike some other economic problems, this one in particular calls for a multi-faceted approach. To deal with it adequately, we need to frame it in a suitable theoretical framework, to develop a good understanding of the facts and the institutional constraints, and to account for the political forces that operate in each country and in the international arena. For these reason a multi-faceted approach that tackles the problem from all these angles simultaneously is most desirable. Indeed, the organizers of this conference recognized the need for such a broad approach, which was well reflected during deliberations in various sessions.

Being especially concerned with the Pacific Rim, a significant effort was made in the conference to discuss APEC. APEC is interesting in many ways. Clearly, it is an important regional institution that may have major effects on its member countries. But beyond such local concerns it is interesting as an innovative institution that experiments with modes of operation that differ substantially from other regional arrangements. Despite the fact that it was formed in 1989 in response to fears about the Uruguay Round, and therefore commenced with a defensive posture, it later proceeded to push for regional liberalization. Importantly, it has emphasized not only trade but also investment measures. In addition it has developed some unique characteristics. Reforms in APEC are unilateral and voluntary. It is not a free-trade area in the usual sense, because its trade liberalization is carried out on an MFN basis. APEC has an evolving structure and a well-defined timetable. It represents a unique experiment in international economic organization from which there is much to be learned.

During the conference, the discussion of APEC was put in a broader context of unilateralism, multilateralism and regionalism. The extent to which these alternative routes to liberalization of the world trading system are substitutes and the extent to which they are complements was (as usual) hotly debated. But this was an informative debate that drew on the rich experience of many of the conference's participants in both academic research and policy making. We saw how imaginative theorizing can enlighten this sort of debate, how factual insights can play a role, how useful can be an understanding of the policy process, and how important are political considerations. Unfortunately, in all these dimensions our understanding is still very incomplete and one senses that disagreements in the debate often resulted from implicit different assessments of the missing components.

To begin with, we do not have a good theory for assessing alternative routes of trade liberalization. As a result, it is not entirely clear what needs to be measured in order to sum up the relevant quantitative effects. But the fact of the matter is that even in cases in which some components of the quantitative analysis have been clearly identified (such as the importance of trade diversion), good estimates of these effects are rarely available. Such difficulties exist when we think about these problems in static terms, and they become even more pronounced when we expand existing lines of reasoning to dynamic environments. There is some evidence that trade agreements affect not only the static efficiency of economies, but also rates of growth of output. If this is true, then dynamic effects may swamp the static effects. At the same time, we know little about the dynamic effects, certainly in quantitative terms.

To these difficulties we may add the lack of a clear standard of comparison. For example, what is the alternative to a regional free-trade agreement? Is it the current situation? Or perhaps a bilateral agreement with a large country? The choice of a standard of comparison is not trivial, because it requires a judgement of how a system will evolve if a particular arrangement is not adopted. Moreover, in evaluating a specific arrangement it has to be judged against other *feasible* alternatives only, not against some abstract set of alternatives. The emphasis on feasible alternatives is important. Nevertheless, the identification of such alternatives is not simple. In order to assess which alternatives *are* feasible it is necessary to add political considerations, because an economic reform never really takes off unless it is able to amass enough political support.

In short, a systematic evaluation of alternative regimes of international trade and investment requires:

(i)   A suitable theoretical framework that can identify what needs to be measured empirically.
(ii) A framework which has to embody political-economy considerations as well as economic and political dynamics; these dynamics being needed in order to evaluate alternative trajectories of change.
(iii) Quantitative estimates of the most important elements that need to be measured, as suggested by the theoretical framework.

My outline of a desired approach is, of course, quite idealistic; it is hard to think about a major problem for which information of this sort has been provided. Nevertheless, I believe that we should strive to approximate this goal as much as we can. In the meantime, while public and professional debates cannot be avoided, they can be improved. Participants in these debates should recognize that opinions about the desirability of various alternatives are based only partly on available information and partly (or even to a large extent) on subjective evaluations of key elements of the problem. As a result, it would be helpful if these subjective evaluations were stated clearly at the outset, and thereby used to separate disagreements about subjective evaluations from logical reasoning based on a set of premises. Many discussions of the international trading system lack clarity of this type and can therefore be greatly improved. Good examples of how this can be done were provided during the conference.

19 Summing-up II

L. Alan Winters
THE WORLD BANK

A good three-day conference generates a huge volume of information, not only from the papers and formal discussions, but also from participants' comments and informal interaction. I do not want to summarize it all – indeed, I could not – but rather try to use this brief summary to make links between sessions and draw some conclusions. In doing so I shall try to identify both common themes and unresolved disputes. I shall not be designing a future research programme, but I hope that some of my points will be taken on to someone's agenda. My comments are divided into five parts, in more-or-less random order.

1 EAST ASIA'S GROWTH

It is impossible to discuss the Asia-Pacific region without wondering what lies behind the prodigious growth rates recorded by many countries of the region. Conference participants seem predominantly to believe that something needs to be explained, that East Asian success was a result of more than just accumulation.[1] There is widespread agreement that sound macroeconomic policies, openness and efficient administration lie behind them, but through what mechanism? Eu Chye Tan has considered one popular causal variable – export growth – and finds it wanting. While one might explain his failure to find exports and income cointegrated in terms of his short sample, disequilibria phenomena and the composition of exports, his results are a challenge. Exports are sometimes held to be the proximate cause of growth and these results make it more difficult to maintain such a position.

Henry Wan – and, implicitly, Motoshige Itoh – suggest a quite different route – technology spillovers from foreign-owned firms. This view is plausible and is receiving an increasing degree of empirical support. It seems to me, however, premature to believe that this is the key. Given its relatively low volume and its narrow geographical and sectoral distribution, foreign direct investment (FDI) is not self-evidently sufficient to explain East Asian economic performance. Thus, while this seems to me to be a very important factor, I should like to see much more work devoted to quantifying its effects using case studies, and micro and macro analyses. I also believe that we still need further work to separate the contributions to economic growth of accumulation and total factor productivity (TFP) changes, as well as to identify the various forces acting on TFP growth. This will be empirical rather than theoretical work, and will thus be slow and expensive. None the less, I think it is warranted.

2 TRADE POLICY

I detect two common themes on trade policy. First, and very strongly, unilateralism is the key dimension in East Asia and Oceania. It is worth observing that these are not the only continents to discover the virtues of unilateralism – consider, for example, Latin America or Eastern Europe – but it does seem that unilateralism is more firmly ingrained here than elsewhere. One question is: why? Do East Asia and Oceania have better economists? Peter Lloyd does not quite say this, but he does argue that the intellectual climate was a fundamental component of the Australian and New Zealand decisions to reform. Maybe the World Bank has helped in this regard in East Asia, certainly among the countries that have taken off more recently.

Two other dimensions of the unilateralism question seem worth remarking upon. First, the importance of exploring the dynamic aspects of unilateralism in models of growth. As Neil Vousden observes, most growth analysis looks at simultaneous, symmetric, global liberalization, whereas policy-makers typically have to advise on unilateral alternatives in real time. Second, Peter Lloyd hints at the relationship between bilateralism and unilateralism – that the bilateral CER Agreement smoothed the path of Australia's and New Zealand's unilateral reforms. This is a subplot of the 'regionalism versus multilateralism' debate, but an important and fascinating one.

The second aspect of trade policy that I want to note is the possible role of export promotion. This has been a feature of several East Asian countries' policies and is frequently asserted to have been important. Richard Harris and Nicolas Schmitt do not deny this, but rather offer an antidote to the seductive notion that you can avoid the harm of protection by promoting exports. They examine two neat models which refute this proposition and, while taking nothing away from their efforts, I would reiterate the importance of the more traditional, but theoretically less elegant, refutations deriving from rent-seeking and administrative constraints.

3 FOREIGN DIRECT INVESTMENT

FDI lies at the heart of several chapters in this volume, as well as at the heart of APEC. It is a more prominent issue in the Asia-Pacific region than elsewhere in the world, and is clearly among the most important, both practically and analytically. *Prima facie*, FDI appears to be complementary to trade in this region: big traders are big recipients of FDI, and many multinationals are quite obviously heavily engaged in exporting. But, to policy-makers, a substitution relationship sometimes looks attractive. The Uruguay Round's General Agreement on Trade in Services (GATS) allowed discrimination between different modes of delivering a given service, and governments have frequently taken advantage of this to discriminate against trade but in favour of FDI (for example, by restricting trade but confirming the right of foreign firms to establish bases in their countries).

This brings me to an important implication of the current fashionability of FDI in development debates. Is the right policy prescription 'FDI at any cost'? Since the benefits of FDI to a host economy rely quite heavily on externalities (spillovers) should we be recommending subsidies?[2] If we are to promote the virtues of FDI as a route to modernization and growth, we have to cope with this question, and, until we have quantitative evidence on the extent of spillovers, we cannot. The evidence, while suggestive, is not yet unambiguous that there are in fact spillovers from foreign to domestic firms, and even where there are, we have very little idea of their magnitude. Thus I carry away from this conference a strong message that work on spillovers – and other externalities – deriving from FDI is a very high priority.

I should also voice a concern about our current knowledge on the link between FDI and growth. The correlation of FDI and growth does not necessarily entail the causation implied in the previous paragraph. Growth could generate FDI, but more importantly, both could stem from the same exogenous cause – good policy. I have already noted the links running from sound macro economic policy and openness on the one hand to growth on the other, and there is plenty of evidence that similar links run to FDI. In other words, FDI may just be an indicator of good policy rather than a link in the causal chain. This leads me to re-emphasize the importance of empirical work on FDI, and growth based on well-specified structural models.

4 DOMESTIC POLICY

The previous section has already identified an important aspect of domestic policy, namely macroeconomic policy. In this section I want to explore another aspect.

Discussions of trade policy, and even more of regional economic arrangements, frequently assert that the distinction between trade and domestic policy can no longer be maintained. Thus, for example, the Uruguay Round agreements on agriculture, services and TRIPs all refer to domestic as well as trade policies. The new agenda, with its environmental and competition policy concerns, threatens to weaken the distinction further. There is a major danger here. GATT was pretty successful in achieving a limited objective – moving towards freer trade – and there is a danger that by increasing its scope and ambition we not only fail on the new issues but undermine progress on the old. While I would not wish to advocate ignoring the domestic policy concerns that are manifest today, I would urge great caution. First, we need to be clear that the instruments of trade negotiation will be effective against domestic policies, and that there are genuinely no better alternative routes towards achieving these ends. Second, we need to devise means of insulating the old agenda from the new. Even if failure on the new issues would not reverse the advances on the old (which is not guaranteed), it is not clear that we should wait for progress on the new before locking deals on the old. There is a broad consensus that trade liberalization is desirable. There is no such consensus on the correct role or form of competition policy.

I have no suggestions at present about how to preserve the old while advancing the new, but I do believe that solving this dilemma should be a high priority for policy analysts.

5   ASIA-PACIFIC ECONOMIC CO-OPERATION FORUM (APEC)

APEC hovers beneath the surface of any contemporary discussion about the Asia-Pacific region. The conference's symposium session on APEC, and the frequent allusions to it in other sessions, helped me to clarify in my mind what it is: it is both a forum and an arrangement to pursue trade and FDI liberalization on a concerted but voluntary basis until, in the year 2010 for developed countries and 2020 for developing countries, free trade will have been achieved. Many contributors stressed the complete commitment of most APEC member governments to avoid creating a discriminatory trading bloc.

I find this picture of APEC very attractive and hope earnestly that it comes about. I hope it is not discouraging – and it is certainly not intended to be denigrating – for me to observe, however, that such an outcome is not yet assured. Particularly given APEC's lack of institutional development (not necessarily a bad thing – indeed, probably a good one) and the huge diversity of its membership, there are still many possible paths along which it could develop. I wholly endorse Elhanan Helpman's view that APEC's evolution will offer a nice experiment for students of institutional development, and that we should watch it carefully. However, my interest is not just scientific: I believe that academics and policy analysts have a role to play in influencing that development for the better.

Of the huge number of questions that spring to mind about APEC, let me isolate five. First, what will be the United States' role? Even without going as far as Ryutaro Komiya and seeing APEC as merely an extension of US unilateralism, one can question whether the USA could live with the unreciprocated trade liberalization foreseen by other members. Maybe it could, but that would represent a big break with the past. Maybe diplomatic relations and relative levels of influence in the region will change so much over the next fifteen years that, as several participants felt, the USA will feel unable to resist the other members. But the issue is 'What if it does resist?' Will the Asian and Oceanian members feel able to proceed without the USA and, probably, Canada and Mexico? Most conference participants felt that they would. Interesting times, indeed!

One slightly alarming feature of the APEC 'conversation' so far is that, while members have agreed to aim for free trade by 2020, they have not agreed on what free trade is! Indeed, some politicians have declared that it is nothing so old-fashioned as zero tariffs and the absence of non-tariff barriers. Here is an important role for academics – as guardians of terminological precision. Practical politics requires compromises and, frequently, constructive ambiguity; but it would be a huge setback if, in an effort to show that APEC had succeeded, we surrendered the definition of free trade. Let APEC compromise, but let it at least recognize that it has done so. Thus, commentators and politicians should do everything they can to avoid the sort of polarization that characterized the US debate on NAFTA. We should maintain sufficient distance from APEC – and a sufficiency of language to describe it – that we can recognize both pluses and minuses, and allow that APEC could advance the cause of free trade and efficiency without being synonymous with it.

A second interesting aspect of APEC is whether it advances multilateralism or not. On the optimistic scenario above, it clearly does. More interesting, intellectually, is the case of preferential trading blocs. Two chapters in this volume deal directly with this question – Wilfred Ethier's, and Kyle Bagwell and Rod Staiger's. The former's benign view of regionalism sees no conflict, while the latter answers, very sensibly, 'that depends on how well multilateralism is doing in the first place'. It seems to me that this is an important question and one that requires more work. The existing literature is completely divided on the issue (see Winters, 1996).

A much less interesting question is whether APEC is a 'natural' trading bloc. Putting aside the view that it is not, and could not become, a bloc, the term 'natural' has so many definitions that it clouds rather than clarifies debate.

The CER between Australia and New Zealand has fostered deep integration between the partners, and APEC aspires to deep integration in several ways, as Mari Pangestu points out. It might be thought that the former would be a role model for the latter, but while the CER might be an inspiration I do not think it would be a practical guide for APEC, for it is smaller and much more homogeneous than APEC.

Finally, reverting in a sense to my first APEC question, it is important to ask 'What are the alternatives?' APEC is clearly hugely important but it is not the only possible route for the Asia-Pacific region, nor are intraregional affairs the only ones that matter. It is important that the APEC process does not displace thought of all other processes. For example, traditional (unconcerted) unilateralism still has a role, as do discussions with Europe, South Asia and Africa. It is not necessary to press all trade policy action into a single (APEC) mould.

As I hope this Summary has demonstrated, the meeting leading to the production of this volume was a rich and fine one. I congratulate both the organisers and the participants.

Notes

1. This view does not necessarily conflict with Young's (1995) conclusions, for he adjusts his input data extensively for quality and these quality adjustments need to be explained.
2. Of course, there are already plenty of explicit or implicit subsidies, and the dangers of subsidy competitions between potential hosts are well known.

References

Winters, L. A. (1996) 'Regionalism versus Multilateralism', Policy Research Working Paper, no. 1687, The World Bank.
Young, A. (1995) 'Tyranny of Numbers: Confronting the Statistical Realities of the East Asian Growth Experience', *Quarterly Journal of Economics*, vol. 110, pp. 641–80.

Index of Names

Subject Index